Fodor's 2008

D1487863

MAUI

WITH MOLOKA'I AND LĀNA'I

Where to Stay and Eat
for All Budgets

Must-See Sights
and Local Secrets

Ratings You Can Trust

Portions of this book appear in Fodor's Hawai'i 2008
Fodor's Travel Publications   New York, Toronto, London, Sydney, Auckland
www.fodors.com

FODOR'S MAUI 2008

Editors: Amanda Theunissen and Linda Cabasin

Editorial Production: Evangelos Vasilakis
Editorial Contributors: Wanda Adams, Cathy Sharpe, Joana Varawa, Amy Westervelt, Shannon Wianecki
Maps & Illustrations: Henry Columb and Mark Stroud; David Lindroth, Inc.; William Wu; Bob Blake and Rebecca Baer, *map editors*
Design: Fabrizio La Rocca, creative director; Siobhan O'Hare, Chie Ushio, Tina Malaney, Brian Panto, Moon Sun Kim
Photography: Melanie Marin, senior picture editor
Cover Photo: (green sea turtle with snorkeler): Michael S. Nolan/age fotostock
Production/Manufacturing: Angela L. McLean

ISBN 978-1-4000-1791-1

ISSN 1559-0798

SPECIAL SALES

This book is available at special discounts for bulk purchases for sales promotions or premiums. Special editions, including personalized covers, excerpts of existing books, and corporate imprints, can be created in large quantities for special needs. For more information, write to Special Markets/Premium Sales, 1745 Broadway, MD 6-2, New York, New York 10019, or e-mail specialmarkets@randomhouse.com.

AN IMPORTANT TIP & AN INVITATION

Although all prices, opening times, and other details in this book are based on information supplied to us at press time, changes occur all the time in the travel world, and Fodor's cannot accept responsibility for facts that become outdated or for inadvertent errors or omissions. So always confirm information when it matters, especially if you're making a detour to visit a specific place. Your experiences—positive and negative—matter to us. If we have missed or misstated something, please write to us. We follow up on all suggestions. Contact the Maui editor at editors@fodors.com or c/o Fodor's at 1745 Broadway, New York, NY 10019.

PRINTED IN THE UNITED STATES OF AMERICA
10 9 8 7 6 5 4 3 2 1

Be a Fodor's Correspondent

Your opinion matters. It matters to us. It matters to your fellow Fodor's travelers, too. And we'd like to hear it. In fact, we need to hear it.

When you share your experiences and opinions, you become an active member of the Fodor's community. That means we'll not only use your feedback to make our books better, but we'll publish your names and comments whenever possible. Throughout our guides, look for "Word of Mouth," excerpts of your unvarnished feedback.

Here's how you can help improve Fodor's for all of us.

Tell us when we're right. We rely on local writers to give you an insider's perspective. But our writers and staff editors—who are the best in the business—depend on you. Your positive feedback is a vote to renew our recommendations for the next edition.

Tell us when we're wrong. We're proud that we update most of our guides every year. But we're not perfect. Things change. Hotels cut services. Museums change hours. Charming cafés lose charm. If our writer didn't quite capture the essence of a place, tell us how you'd do it differently. If any of our descriptions are inaccurate or inadequate, we'll incorporate your changes in the next edition and will correct factual errors at fodors.com immediately.

Tell us what to include. You probably have had fantastic travel experiences that aren't yet in Fodor's. Why not share them with a community of like-minded travelers? Maybe you chanced upon a beach or bistro or B&B that you don't want to keep to yourself. Tell us why we should include it. And share your discoveries and experiences with everyone directly at fodors.com. Your input may lead us to add a new listing or highlight a place we cover with a "Highly Recommended" star or with our highest rating, "Fodor's Choice."

Give us your opinion instantly at our feedback center at www.fodors.com/feedback. You may also e-mail editors@fodors.com with the subject line "Maui Editor." Or send your nominations, comments, and complaints by mail to Maui Editor, Fodor's, 1745 Broadway, New York, NY 10019.

You and travelers like you are the heart of the Fodor's community. Make our community richer by sharing your experiences. Be a Fodor's correspondent.

Aloha!

Tim Jarrell, Publisher

CONTENTS

MAUI IN FOCUS

ABOUT THIS BOOK

Our Ratings

Sometimes you find terrific travel experiences and sometimes they just find you. But usually the burden is on you to select. That's where our ratings come in.

As travelers we've all discovered a place so wonderful that its worthiness is obvious. And sometimes that place is so unique that superlatives don't do it justice. These sights, properties, and experiences get our highest rating, Fodor's Choice ★, indicated by orange stars throughout this book. Black stars highlight sights and properties we deem **Highly Recommended** ★, places that our writers, editors, and readers praise for consistency and excellence.

By default, there's another category: any place we include in this book is by definition worth your time, unless we say otherwise. And we will.

Disagree with any of our choices? Care to nominate a place or suggest that we rate one more highly? Visit our feedback center at www.fodors.com/feedback.

Budget Well

Hotel and restaurant price categories from ¢ to $$$$ are defined in the opening pages of each chapter. For attractions, we always give standard adult admission fees; reductions are usually available for children, students, and senior citizens. Want to pay with plastic? **AE, D, DC, MC, V** following restaurant and hotel listings indicate whether American Express, Discover, Diners Club, MasterCard, and Visa are accepted.

Restaurants

Unless we state otherwise, restaurants are open for lunch and dinner daily. We mention dress only when there's a specific requirement and reservations only when they're essential or not accepted—it's always best to book ahead.

Hotels

Hotels have private bath, phone, TV, and air-conditioning and operate on the European Plan, meaning without meals, unless we specify that they use the Continental Plan (CP, with a continental breakfast), Breakfast Plan (BP, with a full breakfast), or Modified American Plan (MAP, with breakfast and dinner), or are all-inclusive (AI, including all meals and most activities). We always list facilities but not whether you'll be charged an extra fee to use them, so when pricing accommodations, find out what's included.

Many Listings

★	Fodor's Choice
★	Highly recommended
✉	Physical address
✛	Directions
⌂	Mailing address
☎	Telephone
🖷	Fax
⊕	On the Web
✑	E-mail
🎫	Admission fee
☉	Open/closed times
Ⓜ	Metro stations
▭	Credit cards

Hotels & Restaurants

🏨	Hotel
🛏	Number of rooms
♨	Facilities
🍴	Meal plans
✕	Restaurant
🖉	Reservations
⤡	Smoking
BYOB	BYOB
✕🏨	Hotel with restaurant that warrants a visit

Outdoors

🏌	Golf
⛺	Camping

Other

☺	Family-friendly
⇒	See also
✉	Branch address
☞	Take note

Experience Maui

WORD OF MOUTH

"My top 'To Do' on Maui is watch the sunrise from the top of Hale-akala!"

—pijeta

"My favorite Maui memory—being in a 28-foot boat and having a 45-foot-long humpback whale surface three feet from our side of the boat, exhale, and create a rainbow in her spray."

—ms_go

WELCOME TO MAUI

Getting Oriented

Any description of Maui's beauty is a cliché by now—we've all seen the postcards and the movies and heard stories from friends. Still, when you experience Maui firsthand, it's hard not to gush about the long perfect beaches, dramatic cliffs, greener-than-green rainforests, and that unbelievable plumeria perfume that hangs over it all. Add to that the fresh pineapple, the amazing marine life, the fascinating culture and history of the Hawaiian people, and the location (at nearly 1,900 mi from the next continent, the Hawaiian islands are the most isolated in the world—talk about getting away from it all), and it's easy to see why it has been such a popular destination for so long.

■ **TIP→** Directions on the island are often given as *mauka* (toward the mountains) and *makai* (toward the ocean).

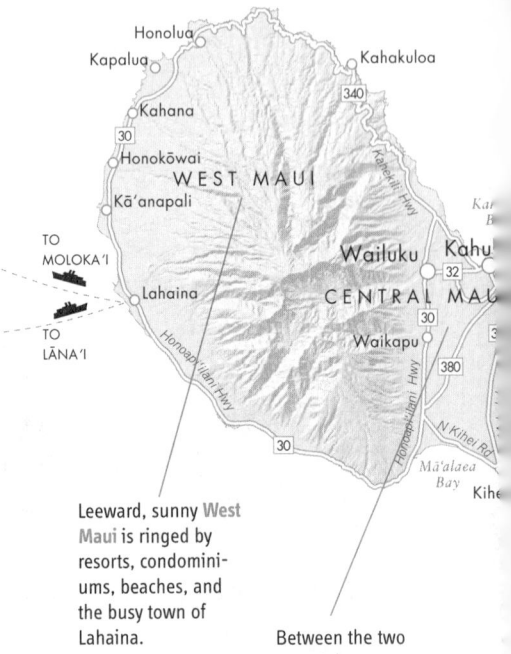

Leeward, sunny **West Maui** is ringed by resorts, condominiums, beaches, and the busy town of Lahaina.

Between the two mountain areas is **Central Maui**, the location of the county seat of Wailuku. Kahului Airport is also here.

The island's northeastern, windward side is largely one great rain forest, traversed by the **Road to Hāna**.

Island residents affectionately call the regions climbing up the slope of Haleakalā crater **Upcountry**.

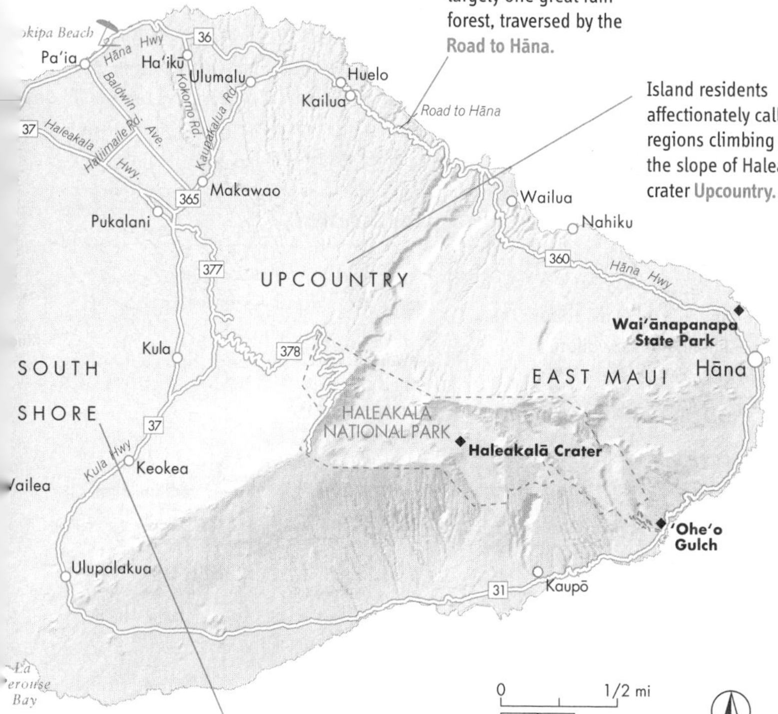

okipa Beach
Pa'ia — Hāna Hwy — Ha'ikū — 36
Baldwin Rd. — Ulumalu — Huelo
Kokomo Rd. — Kailua
Kaupakalua Rd. — *Road to Hāna*
37 — Haleakala — Haleakala Hwy. — Hauimaile Hwy.
Ave. — Makawao
365 — Wailua
Pukalani — Nahiku
377 — 360 — Hāna Hwy
UPCOUNTRY

Wai'ānapanapa State Park

SOUTH — Kula — 378
SHORE — **EAST MAUI** — **Hāna**
37 — HALEAKALĀ NATIONAL PARK
Vailea — Kula Hwy — Keokea — ◆ **Haleakalā Crater**
◆ **'Ohe'o Gulch**
Ulupalakua
31 — Kaupō
La erouse Bay

0 ——— 1/2 mi
0 ——— 1/2 km

The leeward side of Maui's eastern half is what most people mean when they say **South Shore**. This popular area is sunny and warm year-round and is home to the beautiful resort area, Wailea.

MAUI PLANNER

When You Arrive

Most visitors arrive at Kahului Airport. The best way to get from the airport to your destination is in your own rental car. The major car-rental companies have desks at the airport and can provide a map and directions to your hotel. ■ TIP→ Arriving flights in Maui tend to land around the same time. This can lead to extremely long lines at the car rental windows. If possible, send one member of your group to pick up the car while the others wait for the baggage.

Getting Around

If you need to ask for directions, try your best to pronounce the multi-vowel road names. Locals don't use (or know) highway route numbers and will respond with looks as lost as yours.

Tips for High Season Travelers

If you're coming during the peak season, be sure to book hotels and car rentals ahead of time. Advance booking of activities is also a good idea. This will ensure you get to do the activity you want and can often save you 10% or more if you book on individual outfitters' Web sites.

Traffic tends to overwhelm the island's simple infrastructure during these busy times. Try to avoid driving during typical commuter hours, and always allow extra travel time to reach your destination.

Where to Stay

Deciding where to stay is difficult, especially if you're a first-time visitor. To help narrow your choices, consider what type of property you'd like to stay at (big, flashy resort or private vacation rental) and what type of island climate you're looking for (beachfront strand or remote rain forest). If you're staying for more than a week, we recommend breaking your trip into two or even three parts. Moving around may sound daunting, and will rule out longer-stay discounts, but remember: each area of the island offers tons to do. If you stay in one spot, chances are you'll spend a lot of time driving to the sites and activities elsewhere.

Car Rentals

A rental car is a must on Maui. It's also one of the biggest expenses of your trip, especially when you add in the price of gasoline—higher on Maui than on O'ahu or the mainland.

TIPS→
■ Soft-top jeeps are a popular option, but they don't have much space for baggage and it's impossible to lock anything into them. Four-wheel-drive vehicles are the most expensive options and not really necessary.

■ Don't be surprised if there is an additional fee for parking at your hotel or resort; parking is not always included in your room rate or resort fee.

■ Booking a car-hotel or airfare package can save you money. Even some B&Bs offer packages—it never hurts to ask.

Island Hopping

If you have a week or more on Maui you may want to set aside a day or two for a trip to Moloka'i or Lāna'i. Tour operators such as Trilogy offer day-trip packages to Lāna'i which include snorkeling and a van tour of the island. Ferries are available to both islands. (The Moloka'i channel can be rough, so avoid ferry travel on a blustery day.)

If you prefer to travel to Moloka'i or Lāna'i by air, and you're not averse to flying on 4- to 12-seaters, your best bet is a small air taxi. Book with Pacific Wings (see Transportation in Maui Essentials) for flights to small airports such as Hāna, Maui or Kalaupapa, Moloka'i, as well as the main airports.

If you're planning a longer trip and are considering a visit to Kaua'i, Oahu, or the Big Island, see Maui Essentials for your travel options. This section also discusses the new Hawai'i Superferry service, which at this writing was scheduled to start in summer 2007. These high-speed ferries provide an alternative to air travel between Maui and Oahu and Maui and Kaua'i.

Timing Is Everything

Each season brings its own highlights to Maui. The humpback whales start arriving in November, are in full force by February, and are gone by April. The biggest North Shore waves also show up in winter, whereas kite boarders and windsurfers enjoy the windy, late summer months. Jacarandas shower Upcountry roads in lilac-color blossoms in spring, and the truly astounding silverswords burst forth their blooms in summer. Fall is the quietest time on the island, a good time for a getaway. And, of course, there's what's known as high season—June through August, Christmas, and spring break—when the island is jam-packed with visitors.

Guided Activities

In winter, Maui is *the* spot for whale-watching. Sure, you can see whales on other islands, but they're just passing through to get to their real hang-out. The same could be said for windsurfers and kite boarders: Maui's North Shore is their mecca. This chart lists rough prices for Maui's most popular guided activities.

ACTIVITY	COST
Deep Sea Fishing	$80–$180
Golf	$50–$300
Helicopter Tours	$125–$350
Lū'au	$50–$95
Parasailing	$48–$55
Kayaking Tours	$65–$140
Snorkel Cruises	$80–$180
Surfing Lessons	$55–$325
Windsurfing	$80–$120
Whale-Watching	$20–$40

Will It Rain?

Typically the weather on Maui is drier in summer (more guaranteed beach days) and rainier in winter (greener foliage, better waterfalls). Throughout the year, West Maui and the South Shore (the Leeward areas) are the driest, sunniest areas on the island—hence all the resorts here. East Maui and Hāna (the Windward areas) get the most rain, are densely forested, and abound with waterfalls and rainbows.

TOP MAUI EXPERIENCES

Hike Haleakalā

(A) Be humbled as you trek down into Haleakalā National Park's massive bowl and see proof of how very powerful the earth's exhalations can be. You won't see landscape like this anywhere, outside of visiting the moon. The barren terrain is deceptive, however—many of the world's rarest plants, birds, and insects live here. *See page 43.*

Kick back in Hāna

(B) "Kicking back," or relaxing, is an art perfected by Hāna residents. Try it: around town, wave to pedestrians, and "talk story" with locals in line at Hasegawa store. Watch offshore rainstorms roll in and turn to mist when they hit Hāna mountain. It's easy to forget what day it is while exploring the multicolored beaches, waterfalls, and taro patches. *See page 51.*

Finding Nemo

(C) Snorkeling is a must. Wherever you duck under, you'll be inducted into a mesmerizing world underwater. Slow down and keep your eyes open: even fish dressed in camouflage can be spotted when they snatch at food passing by. *See page 84.*

WORD OF MOUTH

"I would say that Haleakalā IS Maui's claim to fame. . . . Many people take the day to drive aaalll the way up to the crater rim, climb out of the car, and stand at the rim only long enough to take some photos and get cold. I'd recommend a day hike inside the crater. The cinder cones have beautiful swirls of purples, oranges, and greens. At different times of the day, different colors sparkle in the sunshine."

—outtabed

Mākena (Big Beach)
(D) This is the sand dreams are made of: deep, golden, and pillowy. Don't be discouraged by the crammed parking lots; there's more than enough room. Big Beach is still wild. There are no hotels, minimarts, or even public restrooms nearby—instead there's crystal-clear water, the occasional pod of dolphins, and drop-dead gorgeous scenery (including the other sunbathers). See page 68.

Tropical fruit at a roadside stand
(E) Your first taste of ripe guava or mango is something to remember. Delicious lychees, mangos, star fruit, bananas, passion fruit, and papaya can be bought on the side of the road with the change in your pocket. Go on, let the juice run down your chin. No one's looking!

Resorts, resorts, resorts
(F) Indulge your inner rock star at the posh resorts and spas around the island.

Sip a "Tommy Girl" in the hot tub at the Four Seasons or get massaged poolside at the Grand Wailea. Even if you don't stay the night, you can enjoy the opulent gardens, restaurants, art collections, and perfectly cordial staff.

Escape to a bed-and-breakfast
(G) Being a shut-in isn't so bad at a secluded B&B. It's a sure way to get a taste of what it's really like to live in Paradise: ripe fruit trees outside your door, late-night tropical rainstorms, a wild chicken or two. Rather than blasting the air-conditioning in a stuffy hotel room, relax with the windows open in a historic plantation house designed to capture sea breezes.

Whale-watch
(H) Maui is the cradle for hundreds of humpback whales that return every year to frolic in the warm waters and give birth. Watch a mama whale teach her

one-ton calf how to tail-wave. You can eavesdrop on them, too: book a tour boat with a hydrophone or just plunk your head underwater to hear the strange squeaks, groans, and chortles of the cetaceans. *See page 94.*

Listen to Hawaiian music

(I) Before his untimely death in 1997, Israel Kamakawiwoʻole or "IZ" woke the world to the sound of modern Hawaiian music. Don't leave without hearing it live. The Ritz-Carlton's Slack Key Guitar Festival features guest performers who play Hawaiʻi's signature style. The "Wailea Nights" show at Mulligan's might be the best—great dinner with unforgettable music by Hapa.

Surfing on West Maui

(J) The first thing your friends at home will ask is: did you learn to surf? Don't disappoint them. Feel the thrill of a wave rushing beneath your feet at any one of the beginner's breaks along Honoapiʻilani Highway. You can bring surf wax home as a souvenir. *See page 89.*

Old Lahaina Lūʻau

(K) The Old Lahaina Lūʻau performers won the hearts of TV viewers when they danced hula at the Macy's Thanksgiving Day parade. This lūʻau has a warm heart—and seriously good *poke* (chopped, raw tuna tossed with herbs and other seasonings). Tuck a flower behind your ear, mix a dab of *poi* (paste made from pounded taro root) with your *lomilomi* salmon (rubbed with onions and herbs), and you'll be living like a local. *See page 137.*

Kayaking on the South Shore

(L) Kayaking alone can be an unintended study in survival, but with a good tour company kayaking is just about the best introduction to Maui's marine world. *See page 77.*

1

Tour the Upcountry

(M) Die-hard beach lovers might need some arm-twisting to head up the mountain for a day, but the 360-degree views are ample reward. On the roads winding through ranchlands, crisp, high-altitude air is scented with eucalyptus and lavender. *See page 41.*

'Ono Kine Grinds

(N) "'Ono kine grinds" is local slang for delicious food you'll find at a dozen restaurants island-wide. Maui chefs take their work seriously, and they have good material to start with: sun-ripened produce and seafood caught the very same morning. Sample as many types of fish as you can and don't be shy: try it raw.

Windsurfing at Kanaha or Ho'okipa

(O) You might not be a water-sports legend, but that doesn't mean you can't get out on the water and give it a try. In the early morning, some of windsurfing's

big-wave spots are safe for beginners. Don't settle for the pond in front of your hotel—book a lesson on the North Shore and impress yourself by hanging tough where the action is. *See page 96.*

WHEN TO GO

Long days of sunshine and fairly mild year-round temperatures make Hawai'i an all-season destination. Most resort areas are at sea level, with average afternoon temperatures of 75°F to 80°F during the coldest months of December and January; during the hottest months of August and September the temperature often reaches 90°F. Higher "Upcountry" elevations typically have cooler and often misty conditions. Only at mountain summits does it reach freezing.

Moist trade winds drop their precipitation on the north and east sides of the Islands, creating tropical climates, whereas the south and west sides remain hot and dry with desertlike conditions. Rainfall can be high in winter, particularly on those north and east shores.

Most travelers head to the Islands in winter, specifically during Christmas and spring break. This high season means that fewer travel bargains are available; room rates average 10% to 15% higher during this season than the rest of the year.

Climate
The following are average maximum and minimum temperatures for Lahaina; the temperatures throughout the Hawaiian Islands are similar.

Forecasts Weather Channel Connection (⊕ www.weather.com).

Only in Hawai'i Holidays
Hawaiians appreciate any occasion to celebrate; not only are indigenous Hawaiian holidays honored, so are those of the state's early immigrant cultures. If you happen to be in the Islands on March 26 or June 11, you'll notice light traffic and busy beaches—these are state holidays not celebrated anywhere else. March 26

recognizes the birthday of Prince Jonah Kūhio Kalaniana'ole, a member of the royal line who served as a delegate to Congress and spearheaded the effort to set aside homelands for Hawaiian people. June 11 honors the first island-wide monarch, Kamehameha I; locals drape his statues with lei and stage elaborate parades. May 1 isn't an official holiday, but it's the day when schools and civic groups celebrate the quintessential Island gift, the flower lei, with lei-making contests and pageants. Statehood Day is celebrated on the third Friday in August (Admission Day was August 21, 1959). Most Japanese and Chinese holidays are widely observed. On Chinese New Year, homes and businesses sprout bright red good-luck mottoes, lions dance in the streets, and everybody eats *gau* (steamed pudding) and *jai* (vegetarian stew). Good Friday is a state holiday in spring, a favorite for family picnics.

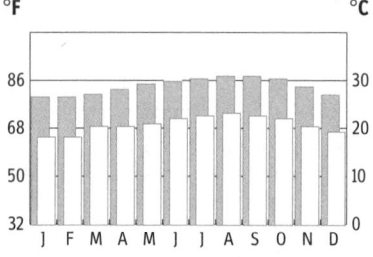

GREAT ITINERARIES

Maui's landscape is incredibly diverse, offering everything from underwater encounters with eagle rays to treks across moonlike terrain. Although daydreaming at the pool or on the beach may fulfill your initial island fantasy, Maui has much more to offer. The following one-day itineraries will take you to our favorite spots on the island.

Beach Day in West Maui

West Maui has some of the island's most beautiful beaches, though many of them are hidden by megaresorts. If you get an early start, you can begin your day snorkeling at Slaughterhouse Beach (in winter, D. T. Fleming Beach is a better option as it's less rough). Then spend the day beach-hopping through Kapalua, Nāpili, and Kāʻanapali as you make your way south. You'll want to get to Lahaina before dark so you can spend some time exploring the historic whaling town before choosing a restaurant for a sunset dinner.

Focus on Marine Life on the South Shore

Start your South Shore trip early in the morning, and head out past Mākena into the rough lava fields of rugged La Pérouse Bay. At the road's end, the ʻĀhihi-Kīnaʻu Marine Preserve has no beach, but it's a rich spot for snorkeling and getting to know Maui's spectacular underwater world. Head to Kīhei for lunch, then enjoy the afternoon learning more about Maui's marine life at the Maui Ocean Center at Māʻalaea.

Haleakalā National Park, Upcountry & the North Shore

If you don't plan to spend an entire day hiking in the crater at Haleakalā National Park, this itinerary will at least allow you to take a peek at it. Get up early and head straight for the summit of Haleakalā (if you're jet-lagged and waking up in the middle of the night, you may want to get there in time for sunrise). Bring water, sunscreen, and warm clothing; it's freezing at sunrise. Plan to spend a couple of hours exploring the various lookout points in the park. On your way down the mountain, turn right on Makawao Avenue, and head into the little town of Makawao. You can have lunch here, or make a left on Baldwin Avenue and head downhill to the town of Pāʻia where there are a number of great lunch spots and shops to explore. Spend the rest of your afternoon at Pāʻia's main strip of sand, Hoʻokipa Beach.

The Road to Hāna

This cliff-side driving tour through rainforest canopy reveals Maui's most lush and tropical terrain. It will take a full day, especially if you plan to make it all the way to ʻOheo Gulch. You'll pass through communities where old Hawaiʻi still thrives, and where the forest runs unchecked from the sea to the summit. You'll want to make frequent exploratory stops. To really soak in the magic of this place, consider staying overnight in Hāna town. That way you can spend a full day winding toward Hāna, hiking and exploring along the way, and the next day traveling leisurely back to civilization.

For more details on any of the destinations mentioned in these *itineraries, see* chapter 2, *Exploring Maui.*

WEDDINGS & HONEYMOONS

There's no question that Hawai'i is one of the country's foremost honeymoon destinations. Romance is in the air here, and the white, sandy beaches, turquoise water, swaying palm trees, balmy tropical breezes, and perpetual summer sunshine put people in the mood for love. It's easy to understand why Hawai'i is fast becoming a popular wedding destination as well, especially as the cost of airfare has gone down, and new resorts and hotels entice visitors. You can plan a traditional ceremony in a place of worship followed by a reception at an elegant resort, or you can go barefoot on the beach and celebrate at a lū'au. There are almost as many wedding planners in the Islands as real-estate agents, which makes it oh-so-easy to wed in paradise, and then, once the knot is tied, stay and honeymoon as well.

The Big Day

Choosing the perfect place. When choosing a location, remember that you really have two choices to make: the ceremony location and where to have the reception. For the former, there are beaches, bluffs overlooking beaches, gardens, private residences, resort lawns, and, of course, places of worship. As for the reception, you have these same choices, as well as restaurants and even lū'au. If you decide to go outdoors, remember the seasons—yes, Hawai'i has seasons. If you're planning a winter wedding outdoors, be sure you have a back-up plan (such as a tent), in case it rains. Also, if you're planning an outdoor wedding at sunset—which is very popular—be sure you match the time of your ceremony to the time the sun sets at that time of year. If you choose indoors, be sure to ask for pictures of the environs when you're planning. You don't want to plan a pink wedding, say, and wind up in a room that's predominantly red. Or maybe you do. The point is, it should be your choice.

Now, as for the exact location—we recommend you discuss this at length with your wedding officiant or wedding planner, which brings us to our next point.

Finding a wedding planner. If you're planning to invite more than a minister and your loved one to your wedding ceremony, seriously consider an on-island wedding planner who can help select a location, design the floral scheme, recommend a florist as well as a photographer, help plan the menu and choose a restaurant, caterer, or resort, and suggest any special Hawaiian traditions to incorporate into your ceremony. And more: Will you need tents? Of course, a cake. Music. Maybe transportation. Lodging. Many planners have relationships with vendors, providing packages—which mean savings.

If you're planning a resort wedding, most have on-site wedding coordinators; however, there are many independents around the island and even those who specialize in certain types of ceremonies—by locale, size, religious affiliation, and so on. A simple "Maui weddings" Google search will reveal dozens. What's important is that you feel comfortable with your coordinator. Ask for references—and call them. Share your budget. Get a proposal—in writing. Ask how long they've been in business, how they charge, how often you'll meet with them, and how they select vendors. Request a detailed list of the exact services they'll provide. If you can afford it, you might want to consider meeting the planner in person.

Getting your license. The good news about marrying in Hawai'i is that no waiting period, no residency or citizenship, and no blood tests or shots are required. However, both the bride and groom must appear together in person before a marriage-license agent to apply for a marriage license. You'll need proof of age—the legal age to marry is 18. Upon approval, a marriage license is immediately issued and costs $60, cash only. Your officiant will want to see the license, because it authorizes a marriage to take place. After the ceremony, your officiant will mail the marriage license to the state. Approximately 120 days later, you will receive a copy in the mail. (For $10 extra, you can expedite this process. Ask your marriage license agent when you apply for your license.) For more detailed information, visit ⊕ www.hawaii.gov or call ☎ 808/241–3498.

The person performing your wedding must be licensed by the Hawai'i Department of Health, even if he or she is a licensed minister. Ask! First things first: make an appointment with a marriage license agent by calling the Department of Health at ☎ 808/241–3495.

Wedding attire. In Hawai'i, basically anything goes, from long, formal dresses with trains to white bikinis. Floral sundresses are fine, too. For the men, tuxedos are not the norm; a pair of solid-colored slacks with a nice aloha shirt is. In fact, tradition in Hawai'i for the groom is a plain white aloha shirt (they do exist) with slacks or long shorts and a colored sash around the waist. If you're planning a wedding on the beach, go barefoot.

If you decide to marry in a formal dress and tuxedo, you probably should make

your selections on the mainland and hand-carry them aboard the plane. (Formal wear is available on Maui but the selection is limited.) Yes, it can be a pain, but ask your wedding-gown retailer to provide a special carrying bag. After all, you don't want to chance losing your wedding dress in a wayward piece of luggage. Fittings are something you'll want to take care of before you arrive on Maui.

Local customs. The most obvious tradition is the lei exchange in which the bride and groom take turns placing a lei around the neck of the other—with a kiss. Bridal lei are usually floral, whereas the groom's is typically made of maile, a green leafy garland. Brides often also wear a haku lei—a circular floral headpiece. Other Hawaiian customs include the blowing of the conch shell, hula, chanting, and Hawaiian music.

The Honeymoon

Do you want champagne and strawberries delivered to your room each morning? A maze of a swimming pool in which to float? Then a resort is the way to go. If, however, you prefer the comforts of a home, try a B&B. A B&B is also good if you're on a tight budget or don't plan to spend much time in your room. On the other hand, maybe you want your own private home in which to unwind. In that case, a private vacation rental home or maybe a condominium resort is the answer. That's another beautiful thing about Hawai'i: the lodging accommodations are almost as plentiful as the beaches, and there's one to match your tastes and budget.

CRUISING THE HAWAIIAN ISLANDS

Cruising has become extremely popular in Hawai'i. For first-time visitors, it's an excellent way to get a taste of all the Islands; and if you fall in love with one or even two, you know how to plan your next trip. It's also a comparatively inexpensive way to see Hawai'i. The limited amount of time in each port can be an argument against cruising—there's enough to do on any island to keep you busy for a week, so some folks feel short-changed by cruise itineraries.

Cruising to Hawai'i

Until 2001 it was illegal for any cruise ships to stop in Hawai'i unless they originated from a foreign port, or were including a foreign port in their itinerary. The law has changed, but most cruises still include a stop in the Fanning Islands, Ensenada, or Vancouver. Gambling is legal on the open seas, and your winnings are tax-free; most cruise ships offer designated smoking areas and now enforce the U.S. legal drinking age (21) on Hawai'i itineraries.

Carnival Cruises. They call them "fun ships" for a reason—Carnival is all about keeping you busy and showing you a good time, both onboard and onshore. Great for families, Carnival always plans plenty of kid-friendly activities, and their children's program rates high with the little critics. Carnival offers itineraries starting in Ensenada, Vancouver, and Honolulu. Their ships stop on Maui (Kahului and Lahaina), the Big Island (Kailua-Kona and Hilo), O'ahu, and Kaua'i. ☎888/227–6482 ⊕ www.carnival.com.

Celebrity Cruises. Celebrity's focus is on service, and it shows. From their wait-staff to their activity directors to their fantastic Hawaiian cultural experts, every aspect of your trip has been well thought out. They cater more to adults than children, so this may not be the best line for families. Celebrity's Hawai'i cruises depart from Los Angeles and stop in Maui (Lahaina), O'ahu, the Big Island (Hilo and Kailua-Kona), and Kaua'i. ☎800/647–2251 ⊕ www.celebrity.com.

Holland America. The grande dame of cruise lines, Holland America has a reputation for service and elegance. Holland America's Hawai'i cruises leave and return to San Diego, CA, and stop on Maui (Lahaina), the Big Island (Kailua-Kona and Hilo), O'ahu, and for half a day on Kaua'i. ☎877/724–5425 ⊕ www.hollandamerica.com.

Norwegian Cruise Lines. Norwegian has traditionally been one of the more casual cruise lines and offers a variety of service, activity, and excursion options. Their boats maintain a family-friendly focus (there are no casinos). The only line with ships not required to stop in foreign ports, NCL has itineraries that originate either in Vancouver or Honolulu and include stops on Maui (Kahului and Lahaina), O'ahu, the Big Island (Hilo and Kona), and Kaua'i (Nawiliwili). ☎800/327–7030 ⊕ www.ncl.com.

Princess Cruises. Princess strives to offer affordable luxury. Their prices start out a little higher, but you get more bells and whistles (more affordable balcony rooms, nice decor, more restaurants to choose from, personalized service). They're not fantastic for kids, but they do a great job of keeping teenagers occupied. Princess's Hawaiian cruise is 15 days, round-trip from Los Angeles, with a service call in Ensenada. The *Island Princess* stops

in Maui (Lahaina), the Big Island (Hilo and Kailua-Kona), O'ahu, and Kaua'i. ☎ 800/774–6237 ⊕ www.princess.com.

Royal Caribbean. Royal Caribbean's cruises originate in Los Angeles only, and stop in Maui (Lahaina), Kaua'i, O'ahu and the Big Island (both Hilo and Kailua-Kona). Royal Caribbean offers a huge variety of activities and services onboard and more excursions on land than any other cruise line. ☎ 800/521–8611 ⊕ www.royalcaribbean.com.

Cruising within Hawai'i

If you'd like to cruise from island to island, Norwegian is the only major cruise-line option. For a different experience, Hawai'i Nautical offers cruises on smaller boats.

Norwegian Cruise Lines. Norwegian is the only major operator to offer interisland cruises in Hawai'i. Several of their ships cruise the islands—the main ones are *Pride of Aloha* (older, Hawaiian-themed, priced lowest), *Pride of Hawai'i* (suites available, Hawaiian themed, slightly pricier; it will not cruise Hawai'i after February 2008), and *Pride of America* (Vintage Americana theme, big family focus with lots of connecting staterooms and suites). All three offer seven-day itineraries within the Islands, stopping on Maui, O'ahu, the Big Island, and overnighting in Kaua'i. ☎ 800/327–7030 ⊕ www.ncl.com.

Hawai'i Nautical. Offering a completely different sort of experience, Hawai'i Nautical provides private multiple-day interisland cruises on their catamarans, yachts, and sailboats. Prices are higher, but service is completely personal, right down to the itinerary. ☎ 808/234–7245 ⊕ www.hawaiinautical.com.

TIPS

■ On all but the cruises operated by Norwegian Cruise Lines, you must bring a passport, as you will be entering foreign ports of call.

■ Think about booking your own excursions directly (except on Maui). You'll often pay less for greater value.

■ Tendering in Maui can be a tedious process—if you want to avoid a little bit of the headache (and hours waiting in the sun), be sure to book an excursion there through the ship and you'll have smooth sailing.

■ Most U.S. mainland cell phones will work without a hitch on board between the Islands and at all Hawaiian ports of call.

Exploring Maui

WORD OF MOUTH

"There is no question in my mind—the Road to Hāna is a fantastic trip. We have taken the trip four times and loved it every time. Our best two trips were the ones where we spent the night."

—LGay

"Mākena State Park's cliffs were nice to photograph, and, if you're looking for rainbows, seems there is always one behind Lahaina in a light rain. (Just like in the postcards)."

—Peterman

Updated
by Shannon
Wianecki

MAUI IS MORE THAN A sandy beach with palm trees. The natural bounty of this place is impressive. Pu'u Kukui, the 5,788-foot interior of the West Maui Mountains, is one of the earth's wettest spots—annual rainfall of 400 inches has sculpted the land into impassable gorges and razor-sharp ridges. On the opposite side of the island, the blistering lava fields at 'Āhihi-Kīna'u receive scant rain. And just above this desert, *paniolo,* Hawaiian cowboys, herd cattle on rolling, fertile ranchlands reminiscent of northern California.

But nature isn't all Maui has to offer—it's also home to a rich and vivid culture. In small towns like Pā'ia and Hāna you can see remnants of the past mingling with modern-day life. Ancient *heiau* (Hawaiian stone platforms once used as places of worship) line busy roadways. Old coral and brick missionary homes now house broadcasting networks. The antique smokestacks of sugar mills tower above communities where the children blend English, Hawaiian, Japanese, Chinese, Portuguese, Filipino, and more into one colorful language. Hawai'i is a melting pot like no other. Visiting an eclectic mom-and-pop shop (like Komoda Store & Bakery) can feel like stepping into another country, or back in time. The more you look here, the more you will find.

WEST MAUI

Separated from the remainder of the island by steep *pali* (cliffs), West Maui has a reputation for attitude and action. Once upon a time, this was the haunt of whalers, missionaries, and the kings and queens of Hawai'i. Today, crowds stroll Front Street in Lahaina, beating the heat with ice cream or shave ice, while pleasure-seekers indulge in golf, shopping, and white-sand beaches in the Kā'anapali and Kapalua resort areas.

LAHAINA

Lahaina has been welcoming visitors for more than 200 years. In 1798, after waging a terrible war to unite the Hawaiian Islands, Kamehameha the Great chose Lahaina, then called *Lele,* as the seat of his monarchy. Warriors from Kamehameha's 800 war canoes that were stretched along the coast from Olowalu to Honokōwai, turned to the land and filled the lush valleys with networks of stream-fed *loi* or taro patches. For nearly 50 years, Lahaina remained the capital of the Hawaiian Kingdom. During this period, the scent of Hawaiian sandalwood brought Chinese traders to these waters. European whaling ships followed close behind, chasing the sperm whale from Japan to the Arctic. Lahaina became known around the world for its rough-and-tumble ways. Despite the efforts of several determined missionaries, smallpox and venereal disease took a terrible toll on the native population.

Then, almost as quickly as it had come, the tide of foreign trade receded. The Hawaiian capital was moved to Honolulu in 1845 and by 1860, the sandalwood forests were empty and sperm whales nearly extinct. Luckily, Lahaina had already grown into an international, sophisticated (if sometimes rowdy) town, laying claim to the first printing press and high school west of the Rockies. Sugar interests kept the town afloat until tourism stepped in. Keeping pace with the times, today's entrepreneurs lure visitors from around the world to Lahaina with interesting restaurants, shops, and galleries. Tourists can board sunset cruises or hum along to "Cheeseburger in Paradise" steps away from the battleground of ancient kings.

> **SNACK TIME**
>
> The sandwiches have real Gruyère and Emmentaler cheese at **Maui Swiss Cafe** (✉ *640 Front St.*)—expensive ingredients with affordable results. The friendly owner scoops the best and cheapest locally made ice cream in Lahaina. Daily lunch specials are less than $6.

■TIP→ **IF YOU ARRANGE TO spend a Friday afternoon exploring Front Street, you can dine in town and hang around for Art Night, when the galleries stay open into the evening and entertainment fills the streets.**

MAIN ATTRACTIONS

★ **Baldwin Home.** In 1836, missionary and doctor Dwight Baldwin moved his family into this attractive house of coral and stone. The home has been carefully restored to reflect the period; many of the original furnishings remain. You can view the family's grand piano, the carved four-poster bed, and most interestingly, Dr. Baldwin's dispensary. During a brief tour conducted by Lahaina Restoration Foundation volunteers, you'll be shown the "thunderpot" and told how the doctor single-handedly inoculated 10,000 Maui residents for smallpox. ✉ *696 Front St., Lahaina* ☎ *808/661–3262* ⊕ *www.lahainarestoration. org* ⊒ *$3* ⊙ *Daily 10–4.*

Banyan Tree. This massive tree was planted in 1873. It's the largest of its kind in the state and provides a welcome retreat for the weary that come to sit under its awesome branches. ■TIP→**The Banyan Tree is a popular and hard-to-miss meeting place if your party splits up for independent exploring.** It's also a terrific spot to be when the sun sets—mynah birds settle in here for a screeching symphony, which can be an event in itself. ✉ *Front St., between Hotel and Canal Sts., Lahaina.*

Hale Pa'ahao (Old Prison). Lahaina's jailhouse dates to rowdy whaling days. Its name literally means "stuck-in-irons house," referring to the wall shackles and ball-and-chain restraints. The compound was built in the 1850s by convict laborers out of blocks of coral that had been salvaged from the demolished waterfront Fort. Most prisoners were sent here for desertion, drunkenness, or reckless horse riding. Today, a wax figure representing an imprisoned old sailor tells his recorded tale of woe. ✉ *Waine'e and Prison Sts., Lahaina* ⊒ *Free* ⊙ *Daily 8–5.*

Holy Innocents' Episcopal Church. Built in 1908, this beautiful open-air church is decorated with paintings depicting Hawaiian versions of Christian symbols, including a Hawaiian Madonna and child, rare or extinct birds, and native plants. The congregation is beautiful, typically dressed in traditional clothing from Samoa and Tonga. Anyone

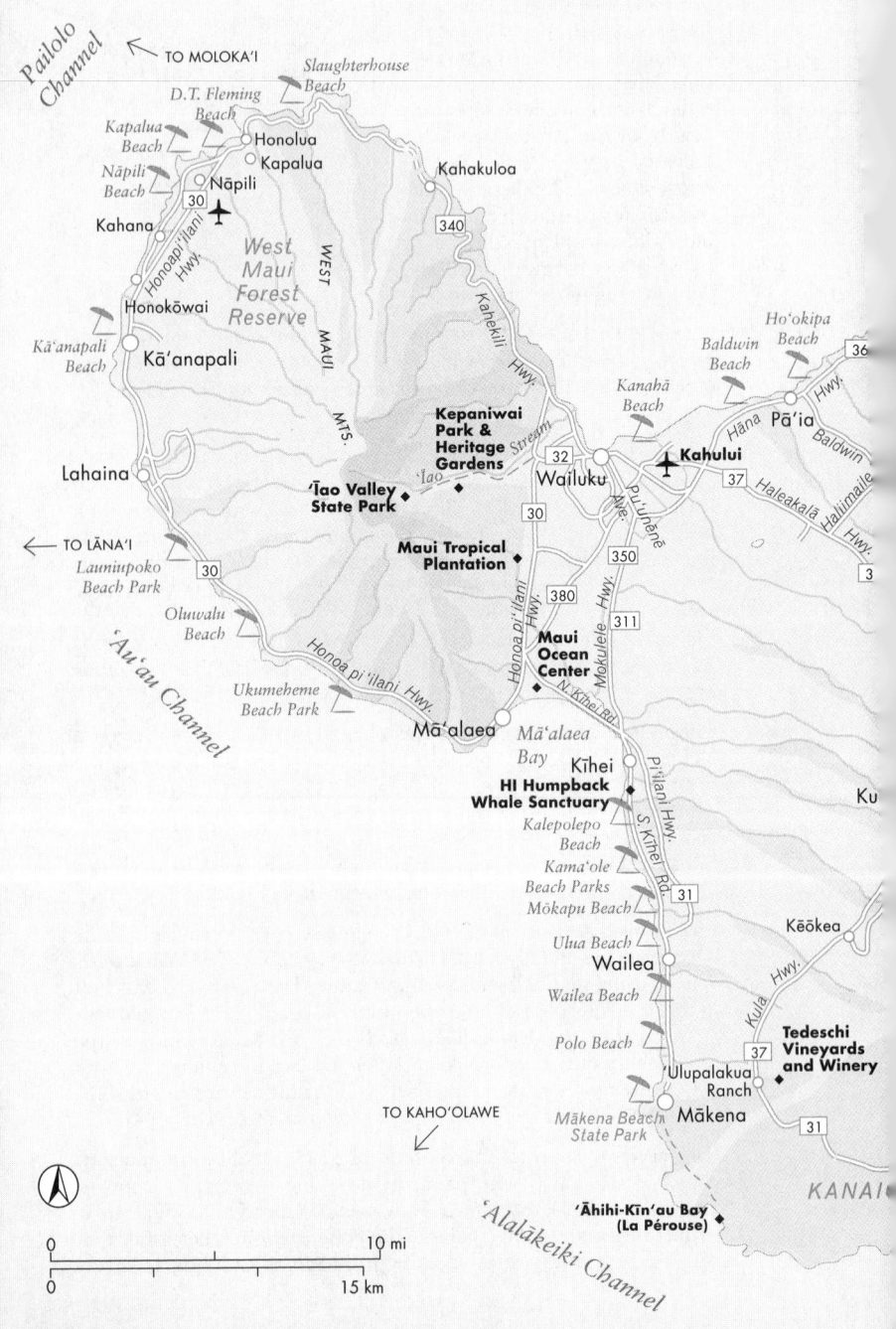

Maui

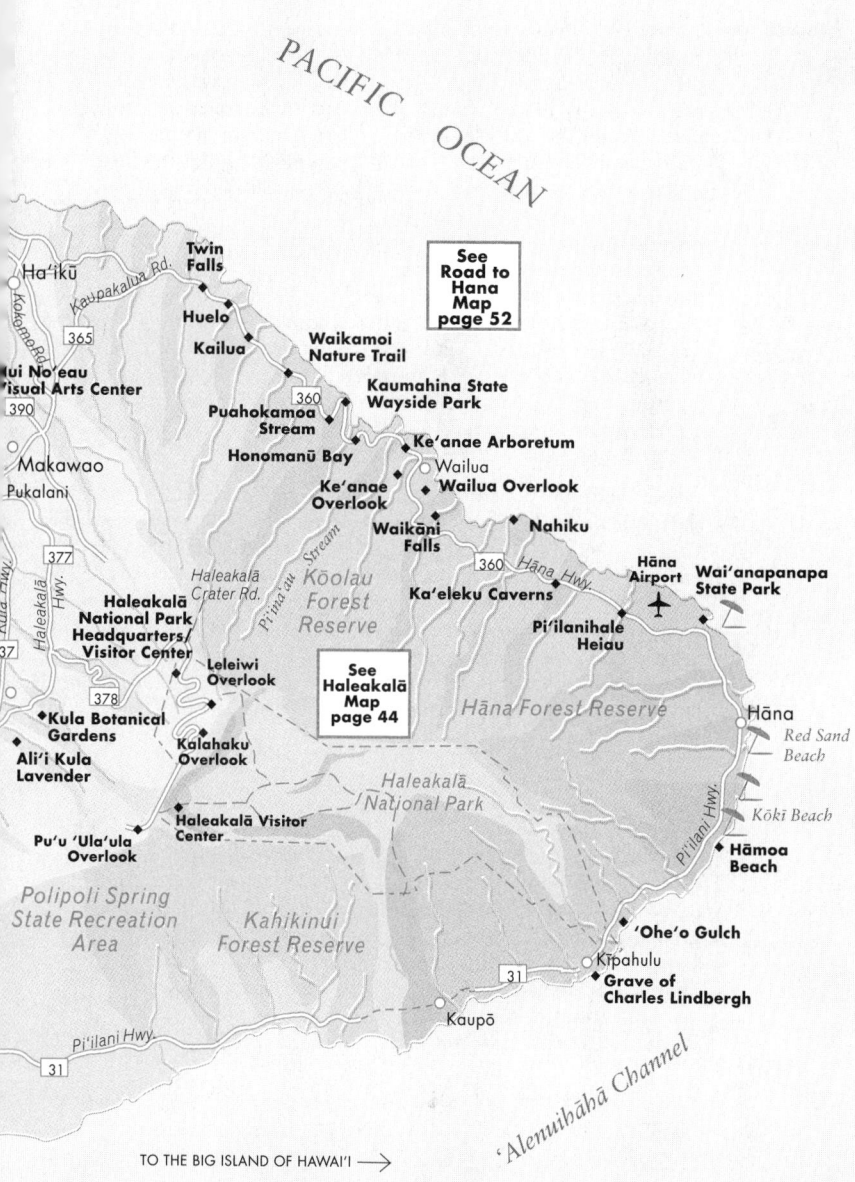

PACIFIC OCEAN

Ha'ikū

365

Maui No'eau
Visual Arts Center

390

Makawao

Pukalani

377

Haleakalā National Park Headquarters/ Visitor Center

37

378

Kula Botanical Gardens

Ali'i Kula Lavender

Pu'u 'Ula'ula Overlook

Polipoli Spring State Recreation Area

31

Pi'ilani Hwy

Twin Falls

Huelo

Kailua

Kaupakalua Rd.

Aokoamoa Rd

Kula Hwy

Haleakalā Hwy

Haleakalā Crater Rd.

Waikamoi Nature Trail

360

Puahokamoa Stream

Honomanū Bay

Kaumahina State Wayside Park

Ke'anae Arboretum

Wailua

Ke'anae Overlook

Wailua Overlook

Waikāni Falls

Nahiku

360

Hāna Hwy

Ka'eleku Caverns

Pi'ilanihale Heiau

Hāna Airport

Wai'anapanapa State Park

See Road to Hana Map page 52

See Haleakalā Map page 44

Leleiwi Overlook

Kalahaku Overlook

Haleakalā Visitor Center

Kōolau Forest Reserve

Pi'ina'au Stream

Haleakalā National Park

Hāna Forest Reserve

Kahikinui Forest Reserve

Hāna

Red Sand Beach

Kōkī Beach

Pi'ilani Hwy

Hāmoa Beach

'Ohe'o Gulch

Kīpahulu

Grave of Charles Lindbergh

31

Kaupō

'Alenuihāhā Channel

TO THE BIG ISLAND OF HAWAI'I →

is welcome to slip into one of the pews, carved from native woods. Queen Liliuokalani, Hawai'i's last reigning monarch, lived in a large grass house on this site as a child. ⊠ *South end of Front St. near Mokuhina St., Lahaina.*

Fodor'sChoice **Lahaina Court House.** The Lahaina Restoration Foundation occu-
★ pies this charming old government building in the center of town. Pump the knowledgeable staff for interesting trivia and ask for their walking-tour brochure, a comprehensive map to historic Lahaina sites. Erected in 1859 and restored in 1999, the

> ### WALKING TOURS
>
> Lahaina's fascinating side streets are best explored on foot. Both the Baldwin Home and the Lahaina Court House offer free self-guided walking tour brochures and maps. The Court House booklet is often recommended and includes more than 50 sites. The Baldwin Home brochure is less well-known but, in our opinion, easier to follow. It details a short but enjoyable loop tour of the town.

building has served as a customs and court house, governor's office, post office, vault and collector's office, and police court. On August 12, 1898, its postmaster witnessed the lowering of the Hawaiian flag when Hawai'i became a U.S. territory. The flag now hangs above the stairway. You'll find terrific museum displays, the active Lahaina Arts Society, and an art gallery. ■TIP➔**There's also a public restroom.** ⊠ *649 Wharf St., Lahaina* ☎ *808/661–0111* ☐*Free* ⊙ *Daily 9–5.*

Waiola Church and Cemetery. The Waiola Cemetery is actually older than the neighboring church; it dates back to the death of Kamehameha the Great's sacred wife, Queen Keōpūolani. She was one of the first Hawaiian monarchs to convert to Christianity and was buried here in 1823. The church was erected in 1832 by Hawaiian chiefs and was originally named Ebenezer by the queen's second husband and widower, Governor Hoapili. Aptly immortalized in James Michener's *Hawai'i* as the church that wouldn't stand, it was burned down twice and demolished in two windstorms. The present structure was put up in 1953 and named Waiola (water of life). ⊠ *535 Waine'e St., Lahaina* ☎ *808/661–4349.*

★ **Wo Hing Museum.** Smack-dab in the center of Front Street, this eye-catching Chinese temple reflects the importance of early Chinese immigrants to Lahaina. Built by the Wo Hing Society in 1912, the museum now contains beautiful artifacts, historic photos of old Lahaina, and a Taoist altar. Bon dances and moon festivals are held annually on the grounds. Don't miss the films playing in the rustic theater next door—some of Thomas Edison's first films, shot in Hawai'i circa 1898, show Hawaiian wranglers herding steer onto ships. Ask the docent for some star fruit from the tree outside, for the altar or for yourself. ⊠ *858 Front St., Lahaina* ☎ *808/661–5553* ☐*$1* ⊙ *Daily 10–4.*

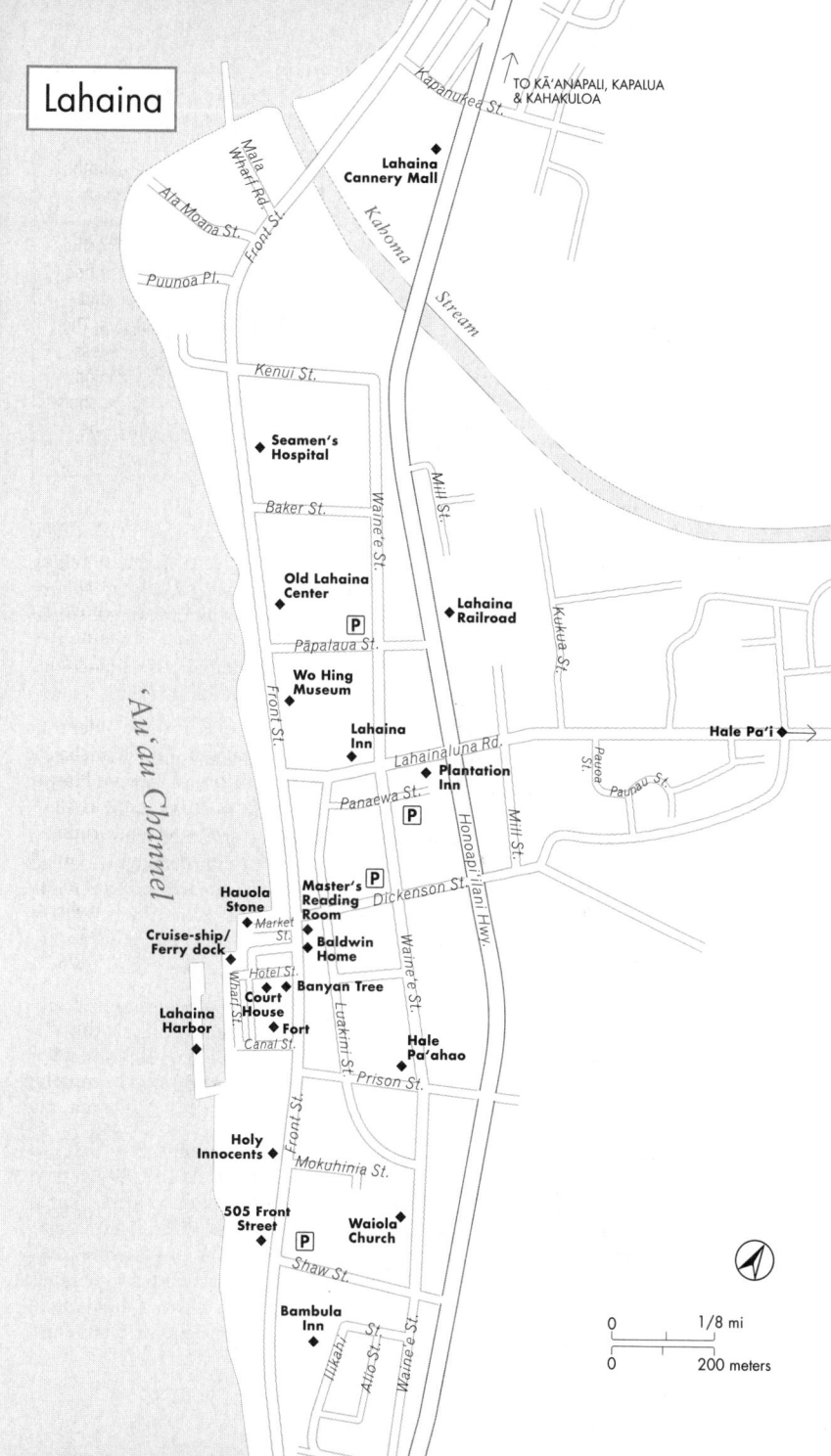

Lahaina

TO KĀʻANAPALI, KAPALUA & KAHAKULOA

Kapanukea St.

Kahoma Stream

Mala Wharf Rd.

Ala Moana St.

Front St.

Puunoa Pl.

Lahaina Cannery Mall

Kenui St.

Seamen's Hospital

Baker St.

Waineʻe St.

Mill St.

Old Lahaina Center

Lahaina Railroad

Kukua St.

Pāpalaua St.

Wo Hing Museum

Front St.

Lahaina Inn

Lahainaluna Rd.

Hale Paʻi

Pauoa St.

Paupau St.

Plantation Inn

Panaewa St.

Honoapiʻilani Hwy.

Mill St.

ʻAuʻau Channel

Master's Reading Room

Dickenson St.

Hauola Stone

Market St.

Baldwin Home

Cruise-ship/ Ferry dock

Hotel St.

Banyan Tree

Waineʻe St.

Lahaina Harbor

Court House

Wharf St.

Fort

Luakini St.

Hale Paʻahao

Canal St.

Prison St.

Front St.

Holy Innocents

Mokuhinia St.

505 Front Street

Waiola Church

Shaw St.

Bambula Inn

Iliahi St.

Ailo St.

Waineʻe St.

0   1/8 mi

0   200 meters

ALSO WORTH SEEING

505 Front Street. The quaint, New England–style mall on this quiet stretch of Front Street has many treasures, notably a resident endangered sea turtle. Year after year, turtle 5690 awes researchers and tourists alike by laying a record eight nests in the sand just steps from the mall. Catching sight of a nestling is rare, but 505's superb restaurants, galleries, surf shack, day spa, and local designer's boutique are accessible any day of the week. ⊠*South end of Front St. near Shaw St., Lahaina.*

FUN THINGS TO DO IN WEST MAUI

■ Get into the Hawaiian swing of things at the Old Lahaina Lū'au.

■ Grab a bite to eat beside real boat captains at Lahaina Coolers.

■ Make an offering at the Taoist altar in the Wo Hing Museum.

■ Sail into the sunset from Lahaina Harbor.

■ Attend the mynah birds' symphony beneath the Banyan Tree.

Fort. Used mostly as a prison, this fortress was positioned so that it could police the whaling ships that crowded the harbor. It was built from 1831 to 1832 after sailors, angered by a law forbidding local women from swimming out to ships, lobbed cannonballs at the town. Cannons raised from the wreck of a warship in Honolulu Harbor were brought to Lahaina and placed in front of the fort, where they still sit today. The building itself is an eloquent ruin. ⊠*Canal and Wharf Sts., Lahaina.*

Hale Pa'i. Protestant missionaries established Lahainaluna Seminary as a center of learning and enlightenment in 1831. Six years later, they built this printing shop. Here at the press, they and their young Hawaiian scholars created a written Hawaiian language and used it to produce a Bible, history texts, and a newspaper. An exhibit displays a replica of the original Rampage press and facsimiles of early printing. The oldest U.S. educational institution west of the Rockies, the seminary now serves as Lahaina's public high school. ⊠*980 Lahainaluna Rd., Lahaina* ☎*808/661–3262* ✉*Donations accepted* ☉ *Weekdays 10–4.*

Hauola Stone. Just visible above the tide is a gigantic stone perfectly molded into the shape of a low-backed chair. Used by ancient Hawaiians as a birthing stone, it sits in the harbor at the intersection of salt and fresh water and was believed to promote health. ⊠*In water behind public library on Front St., Lahaina* ✉*Free.*

Lahaina Harbor. For centuries, Lahaina has drawn ships of all sizes to its calm harbor. King Kamehameha's conquering fleet of 800 carved *koa* canoes gave way to Chinese trading ships, Boston whalers, United States Navy frigates, and finally, a slew of cruise ships, catamarans, and deep-sea fishing operators. During World War II, "a white tide" of navy seamen flooded the town. Stroll past the various tour boats to see who's had the best luck fishing. If they're filleting their catch, you might glimpse eagle rays underwater snapping up the trimmings. ⊠*Wharf St., Lahaina* ✉*Free.*

🚂 **Lahaina–Kā'anapali & Pacific Railroad.** Affectionately called the Sugarcane Train, this is Maui's only passenger train. It's an 1890s-vintage railway that once shuttled sugar but now moves sightseers between Kā'anapali and Lahaina. This quaint little attraction with its singing conductor is a big deal for Hawai'i but probably not much of a thrill for those more accustomed to trains (though children like it no matter where they grew up). A barbecue dinner with entertainment is offered on Thursday at 5 PM. ⌧ *1½ blocks north of Lahainaluna Rd. stoplight, at Hinau St., on Honoapi'ilani Hwy., Lahaina* ☎ *808/661–0080* 🎫 *Round-trip $15.75, one-way $11.50, dinner train $65* ⏲ *Daily 10:15–4.*

WHILE YOU'RE HERE

You may want to combine sightseeing in Central Maui with some shopping. There are three large shopping centers—Ka'ahumanu Center, Maui Mall, and Maui Marketplace *(see chapter 6, Shops & Spas).* This is also one of the best areas on the island to stock up on groceries and basic supplies, thanks to major retailers including Wal-Mart, Kmart, Costco, and Home Depot. Grocery prices, particularly for packaged goods, on Maui are much higher than on the mainland. *See page 36.*

Master's Reading Room. This could be Maui's oldest residential building, constructed in 1834. In those days the ground floor was a mission's storeroom, and the reading room upstairs was for sailors. Today it houses local art and crafts for sale. ⌧ *Front and Dickenson Sts., Lahaina* ☎ *808/661–3262.*

NORTH OF LAHAINA

As you drive north from Lahaina, the first resort community you come to is Kā'anapali, a cluster of high-rise hotels framing a beautiful white-sand beach. A little farther up the road lie the condo-filled beach towns of Honokōwai, Kahana, and Nāpili, followed by the stunning resort area, Kapalua. At the very end of the Honoapi'ilani Highway you'll find the remote village of Kahakuloa.

KĀ'ANAPALI

In ancient times, this area was known for its bountiful fishing (especially lobster) and its seaside cliffs. Pu'u Keka'a, known today as "Black Rock," was the site of many a heroic warrior's leap. But times changed and the sleepy fishing village was washed away by the wave of Hawai'i's new economy: tourism. Clever marketers built this sunny shoreline into a playground for the world's vacationers. The theatrical look of Hawai'i tourism—planned resort communities where luxury homes mix with high-rise hotels, fantasy swimming pools, and a theme-park landscape—all began right here in the 1960s. Three miles of uninterrupted white beach and placid water form the front yard for this artificial utopia, with its 40 tennis courts and 2 championship golf courses. The six major hotels here are all worth visiting just for a look around, especially the Hyatt Regency Maui, which has a multi-million-dollar art collection and South African penguins in the lobby.

Whalers Village. While the kids hit Honolua Surf Company, mom can peruse Versace, Prada, Coach, and several fine jewelry stores at this casual, classy mall fronting Kāʻanapali Beach. Pizza and Hāagen-Dazs ice cream are available in the center courtyard. At the beach entrance, you'll find several good restaurants, including Leilani's and Hula Grill. ⊠ *2435 Kāʻanapali Pkwy.* ☎ *808/661–4567* ⊕ *www.whalersvillage.com.*

Whalers Village Museum. A giant bony whale greets shoppers to Whalers Village. The massive skeleton is the herald of a small museum where you'll hear stories of the 19th-century *Moby-Dick* era. Baleen, ambergris, and other mysterious artifacts are on display. A short film features Hawaiian turtles and the folklore surrounding them. ⊠ *2435 Kāʻanapali Pkwy., Suite H16* ☎ *808/661–5992* ▨ *Free* ⊙ *Daily 9 AM–10 PM.*

KAPALUA

Beautiful and secluded, Kapalua is West Maui's northernmost resort community. The area got its first big boost in 1978, when the Maui Land & Pineapple Company (ML&P) built the luxurious Kapalua Bay Hotel. ML&P owns the entire area known as "Kapalua Resort," which includes the Ritz-Carlton, three golf courses, and the surrounding fields of Maui Gold pineapple. The quaint Kapalua Bay Hotel has been replaced by an innovative coastal wellness retreat. The area's shopping and freestanding restaurants cater to dedicated golfers, celebrities who want to be left alone, and some of the world's richest folks. Mists regularly envelop Kapalua, which is cooler and quieter than its southern neighbors. The landscape of tall Cook pines and rolling fairways is reminiscent of Lānaʻi, and the beaches and dining are among Maui's finest.

KAHAKULOA

This is the wild side of West Maui. Untouched by progress, this tiny village at the north end of Honoapiʻilani Highway is a relic of pre–jet travel Maui. Remote villages similar to Kahakuloa were once tucked away in several valleys of this area. Many residents still grow taro and live in the old Hawaiian way. The unimproved road weaves along coastal cliffs. Watch out for stray cattle, roosters, and falling rocks. True adventurers will find terrific snorkeling and swimming along this drive, as well as some good hiking trails. *See* chapters 4 and 5, *Water Sports & Tours and Golf, Hiking & Outdoor Activities.*

Waterfall on the Road to Hāna.

Windsurfer at Hoʻokipa Beach. (*opposite page, top*) Dancers at the Old Lahaina Lūʻau. (*opposite page, bottom*) Haleakalā National Park.

(*top*) Watching the sunrise at Haleakalā. (*bottom*) Green Sea Turtle. (*opposite*) Mākena Beach (popularly known as Big Beach).

(*top*) Humpback whale calf breaching. (*bottom left*) Fire knife dancer. (*bottom right*) Fruit stand.

(*top*) Kahakuloa, West Maui. (*bottom*) Horses on Maui's North Shore.

Wai'ānapanapa State Park on the Road to Hāna.

THE SOUTH SHORE

■ Swim with green sea turtles at Ulua beach.

■ Spike a volleyball at Kalama Park.

■ Witness the hammerheads feeding at the Maui Ocean Center.

■ Follow the Hoapili Trail through an ancient Hawaiian village.

■ Sink into Mākena's (Big Beach's) endlessly soft sand.

■ Decipher whale song at the HI Humpback Whale Sanctuary.

Blessed by more than its fair share of sun, the southern shore of Haleakalā was an undeveloped wilderness until the 1970s. Then the sun-worshippers found it; now restaurants, condos, and luxury resorts line the coast from the world-class aquarium at Māʻalaea Harbor, through working-class Kīhei, to lovely Wailea, a resort community rivaling those on West Maui. Farther south, the road disappears and unspoiled wilderness still has its way.

Because the South Shore includes so many fine beach choices, a trip here (if you're staying elsewhere on the island) is an all-day excursion—especially if you include a visit to the aquarium. Get active in the morning with exploring and snorkeling, then shower in a beach park, dress up a little, and enjoy the cool luxury of the Wailea resorts. At sunset, settle in for dinner at one of the area's many fine restaurants.

MĀʻALAEA

Māʻalaea, pronounced Mah-*ah*-lye-*ah*, is not much more than a few condos, an aquarium, and a wind-blasted harbor—but that's more than enough for some visitors. Humpback whales seem to think Māʻalaea is tops for meeting mates. Green sea turtles treat it like their own personal spa, regularly seeking appointments with cleaner wrasses in the harbor. Surfers revere this spot for "freight train," reportedly the world's fastest wave.

A small Shinto shrine stands at the shore here, dedicated to the fishing god Ebisu Sama. Across the street, a giant hook often swings heavy with the sea's bounty, proving the worth of the shrine. Down Hauʻoli Street (Hawaiian for *happy*) the Waterfront restaurant has benefited from its close proximity to the harbor. At the end of Hauʻoli Street (the town's single road), a small community garden is sometimes privy to traditional Hawaiian ceremonies. That's all; there's not much else. But the few residents here like it that way.

Māʻalaea Small Boat Harbor. With only 89 slips and so many good reasons to take people out on the water, this active little harbor needs to be expanded. The Army Corps of Engineers has a plan to do so, but harbor users are fighting it—particularly the surfers, who say the plan would destroy their surf breaks. In fact, the surf here is world-renowned. The elusive spot to the left of the harbor called "freight train" rarely breaks, but when it does, it's said to be the fastest anywhere. ⊠ *Off Honoapiʻilani Hwy., Rte. 30.*

☺ **Maui Ocean Center.** You'll feel as though you're walking from the sea-
Fodor'sChoice   shore down to the bottom of the reef, and then through an acrylic
★ tunnel in the middle of the sea at this aquarium, which focuses on Hawaiʻi and the Pacific. Special tanks get you up close with turtles, rays, sharks, and the unusual creatures of the tide pools. The center is part of a growing complex of retail shops and restaurants overlooking the harbor. ⊠ *Enter from Honoapiʻilani Hwy., Rte. 30, as it curves past Māʻalaea Harbor, Māʻalaea* ☎ *808/270–7000* ⊕ *www.mauiocean-center.com* ⊡ *$23* ⊙ *Daily 9–5.*

KĪHEI

Twenty-five years ago a scant few adventurers lived in Kīhei. Now about one third of the Maui population lives here in one of the fastest-growing towns in America. Development is still under way: a greenway for bikers and pedestrians is under construction, as is a multitude of new homes and properties.

Traffic lights and minimalls may not fit your notion of paradise, but Kīhei offers dependably warm sun, excellent beaches, and a front-row seat to marine life of all sorts. The county beach parks such as Kamaʻole I, II, and III have lawns, showers, and picnic tables. ■TIP➡**Remember: beach park or no beach park, the public has a right to the entire coastal strand.** Besides all the sun and sand, the town's relatively inexpensive condos and excellent restaurants make this a home base for many Maui visitors.

★ ☺ **HI Humpback Whale Sanctuary.** The Sanctuary Education Center is beside a restored ancient Hawaiian fishpond, in prime humpback-viewing territory. Whether the whales are here or not, the center is a great stop for youngsters curious to know how things work underwater. Interactive displays and informative naturalists will explain it all. Throughout the year, the center hosts intriguing activities, ranging from moonlight tidal-pool explorations to "Two Ton Talks." ⊠ *726 S. Kīhei Rd., Kīhei* ☎ *808/879–2818 or 800/831–4888* ⊕ *www.hawaiihumpback-whale.noaa.gov* ⊡ *Free* ⊙ *Daily 10–3.*

★ ☺ **Kealia Pond National Wildlife Reserve.** Long-legged stilts casually dip their beaks in the shallow waters of this Wildlife Reserve as traffic shuttles by. If you take time to read the interpretive signs on the new boardwalk, you'll learn that endangered hawksbill turtles return to the sandy dunes here year after year. Sharp-eyed birders may catch sight of occasional migratory visitors, such as a falcon or osprey. ⊠ *N. Kīhei Rd., Kīhei* ⊡ *Free.*

WAILEA & FARTHER SOUTH

Wailea, the South Shore's resort community, is slightly quieter and drier than its West Side sister, Kā'anapali. Most visitors cannot pick a favorite, and stay at both. The first two resorts were built here in the late 1970s. Soon a cluster of upscale properties sprung up, including the Four Seasons and the Fairmont Kea Lani. Check out the Grand Wailea Resort's chapel, which tells a Hawaiian love story in stained glass. The luxury of the resorts (edging on overindulgence) and the simple grandeur of the coastal views make the otherwise stark landscape an outstanding destination. A handful of perfect little beaches, all with public access, front the resorts.

★ **Coastal Nature Trail.** A paved beach walk allows you to stroll among Wailea's prettiest properties, restaurants, and rocky coves. The trail teems with joggers in the morning hours. The *makai*, or ocean, side is landscaped with exceptionally rare native plants. Look for the silvery *hinahina*, named after the Hawaiian moon goddess because of its color. In winter this is a great place to watch whales. ⊠ *Accessible from Polo or Wailea Beach parks.*

The Shops at Wailea. Louis Vuitton, Tiffany & Co., and the sumptuous Cos Bar lure shoppers to this elegant mall. Honolulu Coffee brews perfect shots of espresso to fuel those "shop-'til-you-drop" types. The kids can buy logo shirts in Pacific Sun while mom and dad ponder vacation ownership upstairs. Tommy Bahama's, Ruth's Chris, and Longhi's are all good dining options. ⊠ *3750 Wailea Alanui Dr.* ☏ *808/891–6770* ⊕ *www.shopsatwailea.com.*

Fodor'sChoice **Mākena Beach State Park.** "Big Beach" they call it—a huge stretch of
★ heavenly golden sand without a house or hotel in sight. More than a decade ago, Maui citizens campaigned successfully to preserve this beloved beach from development. It's still wild, lacking in modern amenities (such as plumbing) but frequented by dolphins, turtles, and glorious sunsets. At the far left end of the beach, skimboarders catch air. On the right rises the beautiful hill called Pu'u Ōla'i, a perfect cinder cone. A climb over the steep rocks at this end leads to "Little Beach," where the (technically illegal) clothing-optional attitude prevails. On Sunday, Little Beach is a mecca for drummers and island gypsies. On any day of the week watch out for the mean shore break—those crisp, aquamarine waves are responsible for more than one broken arm.

'Āhihi-Kīna'u (La Pérouse Bay). Beyond Mākena Beach, the road fades away into a vast territory of black-lava flows, the result of Haleakalā's last eruption. Also known as La Pérouse Bay, this is where Maui received its first official visit by a European explorer—the French admiral Jean-François de Galaup, Comte de La Pérouse, in 1786. Before it ends, the road passes through the 'Āhihi-Kīna'u Marine Preserve, an excellent place for morning snorkel adventures *(see chapter 4, Water Sports & Tours).* This is also the start of the Hoapili Trail, or "the King's Trail," where you can hike through the remains of one of Maui's ancient villages. Bring water and a hat, as there is little shade and no public facilities.

CENTRAL MAUI

Kahului, where you most likely landed when you arrived on Maui, is the industrial and commercial center of the island. The area was developed in the early 1950s to meet the housing needs of the large sugarcane interests here, specifically those of Alexander & Baldwin. The company was tired of playing landlord to its many plantation workers and sold land to a developer who promised to create affordable housing. The scheme worked, and "Dream City," the first planned city in Hawaiʻi, was born.

West of Kahului, Wailuku, the county seat since 1950, is the most charming town in Central Maui—though it wasn't always so. Its name means "Water of Destruction," after the fateful battle in ʻIao Valley that pitted King Kamehameha I against Maui warriors. Wailuku was a politically important town until the sugar industry began to decline in the 1960s and tourism took hold. Businesses left the cradle of the West Maui Mountains and followed the new market to the shore, where tourists arrived by the boatload. Wailuku still houses the county government, but has the feel of a town that's been asleep for several decades. The interesting shops and offices now inhabiting Main Street's plantation-style buildings serve as reminders of a bygone era.

TIMING

You can explore Central Maui comfortably in little more than a half day. These are good sights to squeeze in on the way to the airport, or if you want to combine sightseeing with shopping. Hikers may want to expand their outing to a full day to explore ʻIao Valley State Park.

KAHULUI & WAILUKU

MAIN ATTRACTIONS

★ **Bailey House.** This was the home of Edward and Caroline Bailey, two prominent missionaries who came to Wailuku to run the first Hawaiian girls' school on the island, the Wailuku Female Seminary. The school's main function was to train girls in the "feminine arts." It once stood next door to the Baileys' home, which they called Halehōʻikeʻike (House of Display), but locals always called it the Bailey House, and the sign painters eventually gave in. Construction of the house, between 1833 and 1850, was supervised by Edward Bailey himself. The Maui Historical Society runs a museum in the plastered stone house with a small collection of artifacts from before and after the missionaries'

2

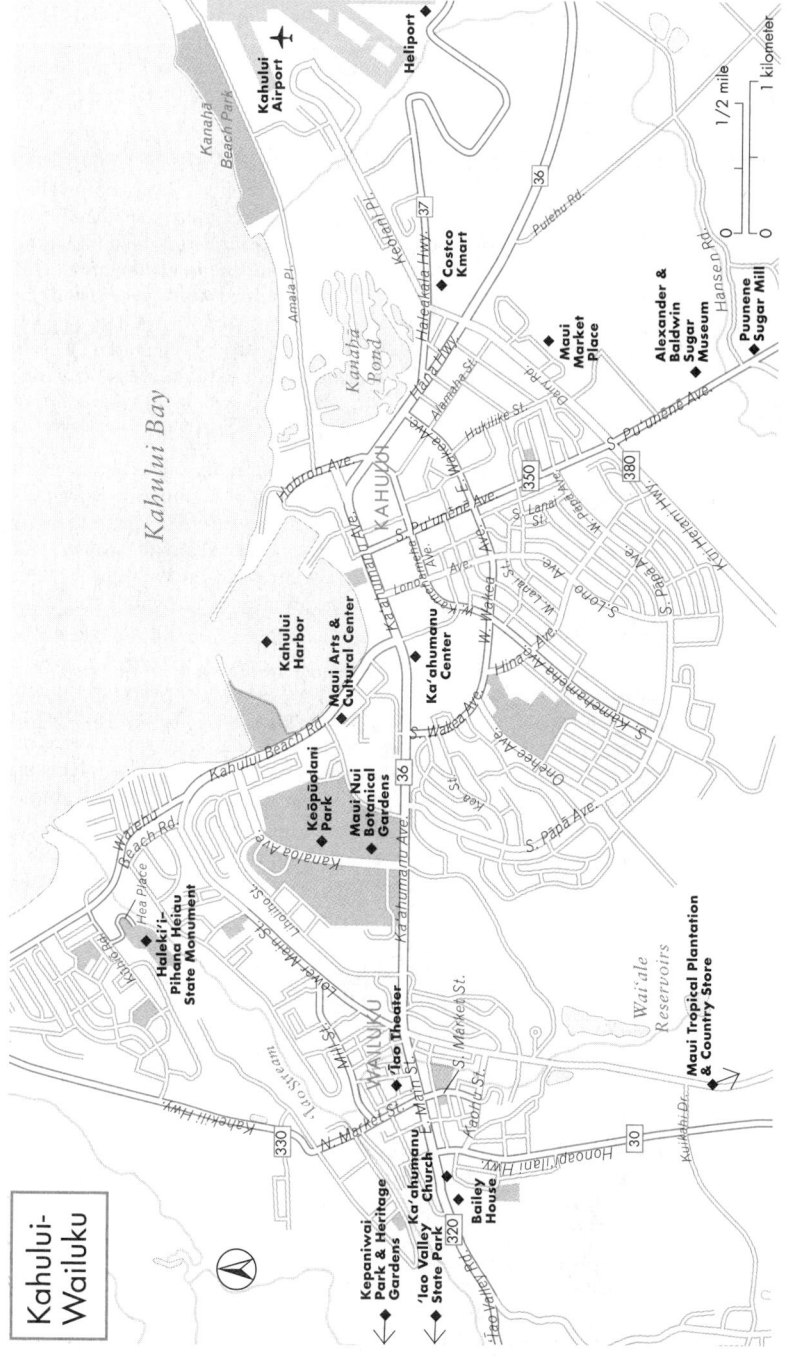

Kahului-Wailuku

Kahului Airport

Heliport

Kanahā Beach Park

Kahului Bay

Kanahā Pond

Costco
Kmart

Maui
Market
Place

Alexander &
Baldwin
Sugar
Museum

Puunene
Sugar Mill

36

37

Pulehu Rd.

Hansen Rd.

S. Puʻunene Ave.

Keolani Pl.

Haleakala Hwy.

Hāna Hwy.

ʻAmala Pl.

Hobron Ave.

Alamaha St.

Hukilike St.

Mahalani St.

350

380

S. Wakea Ave.

S. Lono Ave.

KAHULUI

Puʻunene Ave.

S. Lanai St.

W. Papa Ave.

S. Papa Ave.

Kahului Harbor

Maui Arts &
Cultural Center

Kaʻahumanu
Center

Kaʻahumanu Ave.

Lono Ave.

S. Market Ave.

W. Kaahumanu Ave.

W. Lani St.

Onehee Ave.

S. Kamehameha Ave.

Hinano Ave.

Kahului Beach Rd.

Keōpūolani
Park

Maui Nui
Botanical
Gardens

36

Kanaloa Ave.

Kaʻahumanu Ave.

Kea St.

Waiale
Reservoirs

Waiehu
Beach Rd.

Halekiʻi-
Pihana Heiau
State Monument

Hea Place

Lower Main St.

Limaha St.

Mill St.

Iao Theater

WAILUKU

Iao Stream

N. Market St.

S. Market St.

Vineyard St.

Maui Tropical Plantation
& Country Store

Honoapiilani Hwy.

30

Kulahi Dr.

330

Kahekili Hwy.

Kepaniwai
Park & Heritage
Gardens

ʻIao Valley
State Park

Kaʻahumanu
Church

320

Bailey
House

Iao Valley Rd.

N

0   1/2 mile   1 kilometer

arrival and with Mr. Bailey's paintings of Wailuku. Some rooms have missionary-period furniture. The Hawaiian Room has exhibits on the making of tapa cloth, as well as samples of pre–Captain Cook weaponry. ⊠ *2375A Main St., Wailuku* ☎ *808/244–3326* ⊕ *www.mauimuseum.org* ✉ *$5* ⊘ *Mon.–Sat. 10–4.*

FodorśChoice
★
ʻIao Valley State Park. When Mark Twain saw this park, he dubbed it the Yosemite of the Pacific. Yosemite it's not, but it's a lovely deep valley with the curious ʻIao Needle, a spire that rises more than 2,000 feet from the valley floor. You can take one of several easy hikes from the parking lot across ʻIao Stream and explore the junglelike area. This park has a beautiful network of well-maintained walks, where you can stop and meditate by the edge of a stream or marvel at the native plants and flowers (*see chapter 5, Golf, Hiking & Outdoor Activities*). Locals come to jump from the rocks or bridge into the stream. Mist occasionally rises if there has been a rain, which makes being here even more magical. ⊠ *Western end of Rte. 32* ✉ *Free* ⊘ *Daily 7–7.*

☺ **Kepaniwai Park & Heritage Gardens.** This county park is a memorial to Maui's cultural roots, with picnic facilities and ethnic displays dotting the landscape. Among the displays are an early-Hawaiian shack, a New England–style saltbox, a Portuguese-style villa with gardens, and dwellings from such other cultures as China and the Philippines. Next door, the Hawaiʻi Nature Center has an interactive exhibit and hikes good for children.

The peacefulness here belies the history of the area. During his quest for domination, King Kamehameha I brought his troops from the Big Island of Hawaiʻi to the Valley Isle in 1790 and waged a successful and particularly bloody battle against the son of Maui's chief, Kahekili, near Kepaniwai Park. An earlier battle at the site had pitted Kahekili himself against an older Big Island chief, Kalaniʻōpuʻu. Kahekili prevailed, but the carnage was so great that the nearby stream became known as Wailuku (water of destruction) and the place where fallen warriors choked the stream's flow was called Kepaniwai (the water dam). ⊠ *ʻIao Valley Rd., Wailuku* ✉ *Free* ⊘ *Daily 7–7.*

Market Street. An idiosyncratic assortment of shops makes Wailuku's Market Street a delightful place for a stroll. The Good Fortune Trading Company and Brown-Kobayashi carry interesting antiques and furnishings, whereas Gallerie Ha and the Sig Zane are sophisticated studio gift shops. Cafe Marc Aurel brews excellent espresso, which you can enjoy while sampling the selection of new and used CDs at the corner music shop. ⊠ *Wailuku.*

ALSO WORTH SEEING

★ **Alexander & Baldwin Sugar Museum.** "A&B," Maui's largest landowner, was one of the "Big Five" companies that spearheaded the planting, harvesting, and processing of sugarcane. Although Hawaiian cane sugar is now being supplanted by cheaper foreign versions—as well as by sugar derived from inexpensive sugar beets—the crop was for many years the mainstay of the Hawaiian economy. You can find the museum in a small, restored plantation manager's house next to the post office

MAUI SIGHTSEEING TOURS

This is a big island to see in one day, so tour companies tend to offer specialized tours, visiting either Haleakalā or Hāna and its environs. A tour of Haleakalā and Upcountry is usually a half-day excursion and is offered in several versions by different companies for about $60 and up. The trip often includes stops at a protea farm and at Tedeschi Vineyards, Maui's only winery.

A Haleakalā sunrise tour starts before dawn so that you can get to the top of the dormant volcano before the sun peeks over the horizon. Because they offer island-wide hotel pickup, many sunrise trips leave around 2:30 AM.

A tour of Hāna is almost always done in a van, since the winding road to Hāna just isn't built for bigger buses. Of late, Hāna has so many of these one-day tours that it seems as if there are more vans than cars on the road. Still, to many it's a more relaxing way to do the drive than behind the wheel of a car. Guides decide where you stop for photos. Tours run from $80 to $120.

When booking a tour, remember that some tour companies use air-conditioned buses, whereas others prefer small vans. Then you've got your minivans, your microbuses, and your minicoaches.

The key is to ask how many stops you get and how many other passengers will be on board—otherwise you could end up on a packed bus, sightseeing through a window.

Most of the tour guides have been in the business for years. Some were born in the Islands and have taken special classes to learn more about their culture and lore. They expect a tip ($1 per person at least), but they're just as cordial without one.

Maui Pineapple Plantation Tour. Explore one of Maui's pineapple plantations on this tour that takes you right into the fields in a company van. The 2½-hour, $26 trip gives you first-hand experience of the operation and its history, some incredible views of the island, and the chance to pick a fresh pineapple for yourself.

Tours depart weekday mornings and afternoons from the Kapalua Logo Shop. ⊠ *Kapalua Resort Activity Desk, 500 Office Rd., Kapalua* ☎ *808/669–8088.*

Polynesian Adventure Tours. This company uses large buses with floor-to-ceiling windows. The drivers are fun and really know the island. ☎ *808/877–4242 or 800/622–3011* ⊕ *www.polyad.com.*

Roberts Hawai'i Tours. This is one of the state's largest tour companies, and its staff can arrange tours with bilingual guides if asked ahead of time. Eleven-hour trips venture out to Kaupo, the wild area past Hāna. ☎ *808/871–6226 or 800/767–7551* ⊕ *www.robertshawaii.com.*

Temptation Tours. Temptation Tours has targeted members of the affluent older crowd (though almost anyone would enjoy these tours) who don't want to be herded onto a crowded bus. Tours in plush six-passenger limovans explore Haleakalā and Hāna, and range from $110 to $249 per person. The "Hāna Sky-Trek" includes a return trip via helicopter—perfect for those leery of spending the entire day in a van. ☎ *808/877–8888 or 800/817–1234* ⊕ *www.temptationtours.com.*

and the still-operating sugar refinery (black smoke billows up when cane is burning). Historic photos, artifacts, and documents explain the introduction of sugarcane to Hawai'i and how plantation managers brought in laborers from other countries, thereby changing the Islands' ethnic mix. Exhibits also describe the sugar-making process. ⊠ *3957 Hansen Rd., Pu'unēnē* ☎ *808/871–8058* ⊒ *$5* ⊘ *Mon.–Sat. 9:30–4:30; last admission at 4.*

Haleki'i-Pihana Heiau State Monument. Stand here at either of the two *heiau* (ancient Hawaiian stone platforms once used as places of worship) and imagine the king of Maui surveying his domain. That's what Kahekili, Maui's last fierce king, did, and so did Kamehameha the Great after he defeated Kahekili's soldiers. Today the view is most instructive. Below, the once-powerful 'Iao Stream has been sucked dry and boxed in by concrete. Before you is the urban heart of the island. The suburban community behind you is all Hawaiian Homelands—property owned solely by native Hawaiians. ⊠ *End of Hea Pl., off Kuhio Pl. from Waiehu Beach Rd., Rte. 340, Kahului* ⊒ *Free* ⊘ *Daily 7–7.*

🔆 **Keōpūolani Park.** Covering 101 acres in Central Maui, this park reflects island residents' traditional love of sports. It was originally named "Maui Central Park," but school children argued before the County Council that it be named for Hawai'i's most sacred queen, who was born near here and was later forced to flee across the mountains when Kamehameha the Great's army arrived. The park includes seven playing fields, a running path, skate ramp, and grass amphitheater. ⊠ *Kanaloa Ave. next to YMCA.*

★ **Maui Arts & Cultural Center.** An epic fund drive by the citizens of Maui led to the creation of this $32 million facility. The top-of-the-line Castle Theater seats 1,200 people on orchestra, mezzanine, and balcony levels; rock stars play the A&B Amphitheater. The MACC (as it's called) also includes a small black-box theater, an art gallery with interesting exhibits, and classrooms. The building itself is worth a visit: it incorporates work by Maui artists, and its signature lava-rock wall pays tribute to the skills of the Hawaiians. But the real draw is the Schaeffer International Gallery, which houses superb rotating exhibits. ⊠ *Above harbor on Kahului Beach Rd.* ☎ *808/242–2787, 808/242–7469 box office* ⊕ *www.mauiarts.org* ⊘ *Weekdays 9–5.*

★ 🔆 **Maui Nui Botanical Gardens.** The fascinating plants grown here are representative of pre-contact Hawai'i. Both native and Polynesian-introduced species are cultivated—including ice-cream bananas, varieties of sweet potatoes and sugarcane, native poppies, hibiscus, and *anapanapa*, a plant that makes a natural shampoo when rubbed between your hands. Ethnobotany tours and presentations are offered on occasion. ⊠ *150 Kanaloa Ave.* ☎ *808/249–2798* ⊘ *Mon.–Sat. 8–4.*

🔆 **Maui Tropical Plantation & Country Store.** When Maui's once-paramount crop declined in importance, a group of visionaries decided to open an agricultural theme park on the site of this former sugarcane field. The 60-acre preserve, on Route 30 just outside Wailuku, offers a 30-minute tram ride through its fields with an informative narration covering growing processes and plant types. Children will probably enjoy the historical-characters exhibit as well as fruit-tasting, coconut-husking, and lei-making demonstrations, not to mention some entertaining spider monkeys. There's a restaurant on the property and a "country store" specializing in "Made in Maui" products. ⊠*Honoapi'ilani Hwy., Rte. 30, Waikapu* ☎*808/244–7643* 🖃*Free; tram ride with narrated tour $9.50* ⊙ *Daily 9–5.*

> FUN THINGS TO
> DO UPCOUNTRY
>
> ■ Swig a cup of joe with a Hawaiian *paniolo* (Hawaiian cowboy) at Grandma's Coffee Shop in Kēōkea.
>
> ■ Nibble lavender scones with a view of the Valley Isle at Ali'i Kula Lavender farm.
>
> ■ Gawk at the scenery along Kula Highway.
>
> ■ Taste pineapple wine at Tedeschi Vineyards and Winery.
>
> ■ Stumble across a plein-air painter at the Hui.

UPCOUNTRY MAUI

The west-facing upper slopes of Haleakalā are locally called "Upcountry." This region is responsible for much of Hawai'i's produce—lettuce, tomatoes, strawberries, and sweet Maui onions for starters. You'll notice cactus thickets mingled with purple jacaranda, wild hibiscus, and towering eucalyptus trees. Upcountry is also fertile ranch land; cowboys still work the fields of the historic 20,000-acre 'Ulupalakua Ranch and the 32,000-acre Haleakalā Ranch. Keep an eye out for *pueo*, Hawai'i's native owl, which hunts these fields during daylight hours.

TIMING

A drive to Upcountry Maui from Wailea or Kā'anapali can be an all-day outing if you take the time to visit Tedeschi Vineyards and the tiny town of Makawao. You may want to cut these sidetrips short and combine your Upcountry tour with a visit to Haleakalā National Park (⇨ *Haleakalā National Park feature in this chapter*). If you leave early enough to catch the sunrise from the summit, you'll have plenty of time to explore the mountain, have lunch in Kula or at 'Ulupalakua Ranch, and end your day with dinner in Makawao.

THE KULA HIGHWAY

Kula … most Mauians say it with a hint of a sigh. Why? It's just that much closer to heaven. On the broad shoulder of Haleakalā, this is blessed country. From the Kula Highway most of Central Maui is visible—from the lava-scarred plains of Kenaio to the cruise-ship-lit waters of Kahului Harbor. Beyond the central valley's sugarcane fields, the plunging profile of the West Maui Mountains can be seen in its entirety, wreathed in ethereal mist. If this sounds too prosaic a description, you haven't been here yet. These views, coveted by many, continue to drive real-estate prices further skyward. Luckily, you can still have them for free—just pull over on the roadside and drink them in.

★ **Aliʻi Kula Lavender.** Reserve a spot for tea or lunch at this lavender farm with a falcon's view. It's *the* relaxing remedy for those suffering from too much sun, shopping, or golf. Owners Aliʻi and Lani lead tours through winding paths of therapeutic lavender varieties, proteas, succulents, and rare Maui wormwood. Their logo, a larger-than-life dragonfly, darts above chefs who are cooking up lavender-infused shrimp appetizers out on the lānai. The gift shop abounds with the farm's own innovative lavender products. ⊠*1100 Waipoli Rd., Kula* ☎*808/878–3004* ⊕*www.mauikulalavender.com* ☜*$10 walking tours, $35 tea tours, $70 lunch and wreath-making* ⚊*Reservations essential* ⊙*Daily 10–4, walking tours at noon and 2:30.*

Kēōkea. More of a friendly gesture than a town, this tiny outpost is the last bit of civilization before Kula Highway becomes the winding backside road, heading east around to Hāna. A coffee tree pushes through the sunny deck at Grandma's Coffee Shop, the morning watering hole for Maui's cowboys who work at ʻUlupalakua or Kaupō ranch. Kēōkea Gallery next door sells some of the most original artwork on the island. ■TIP→**The only restroom for miles is across the street at the public park, and the view makes stretching your legs worth it.**

Kula Botanical Gardens. This well-kept garden has assimilated itself naturally into its craggy 6-acre habitat. There are beautiful trees here, including native koa (prized by woodworkers) and *kukui* (the state tree, a symbol of enlightenment). There's also a good selection of proteas, the flowering shrubs that have become a signature flower crop of Upcountry Maui. A natural stream feeds into a koi pond, which is also home to a pair of African cranes. ⊠*638 Kekaulike Hwy., Kula* ☎*808/878–1715* ☜*$5* ⊙*Daily 9–4.*

Tedeschi Vineyards and Winery. You can tour the winery and its historic grounds, the former Rose Ranch, and sample the island's only wines: a pleasant Maui Blush, Maui Champagne, and Tedeschi's annual Maui Nouveau. The top-seller, naturally, is the pineapple wine. The tasting room is a cottage built in the late 1800s for the frequent visits of King Kalākaua. The cottage also contains the ʻ**Ulupalakua Ranch History Room,** which tells colorful stories of the ranch's owners, the *paniolo* (Hawaiian cowboy) tradition that developed here, and Maui's polo teams. The old General Store may look like a museum, but in fact it's an excellent pit stop. ⊠*Kula Hwy., ʻUlupalakua Ranch* ☎*808/878–6058* ⊕*www.mauiwine.com* ☜*Free* ⊙*Daily 9–5, tours at 10:30 and 1:30.*

MAKAWAO

This once-tiny town, at the intersection of Baldwin and Makawao avenues, has managed to hang on to its country charm (and eccentricity) as it has grown in popularity. The district was originally settled by Portuguese and Japanese immigrants who came to Maui to work the sugar plantations and then moved Upcountry to establish small farms, ranches, and stores. Descendants now work the neighboring Haleakalā and ʻUlupalakua ranches. Every July 4 the *paniolo* (Hawaiian cowboy)

Continued on page 49

HALEAKALĀ NATIONAL PARK

HALEAKALA CRATER

From the Tropics to the Moon! Two hours, 38 mi, 10,023 feet—those are the unlikely numbers involved in reaching Maui's highest point, the summit of Haleakalā. Nowhere else on earth can you drive from sea level (Kahului) to 10,023 feet (the summit) in only 38 mi. And what's more shocking—in that short vertical ascent, you'll journey from lush, tropical-island landscape to the stark, moonlike basin of the volcano's enormous, otherworldly crater.

Established in 1916, Haleakalā National Park covers an astonishing 27,284 acres. Haleakalā Crater is the centerpiece of the park though it's not actually a crater. Technically, it's an erosional valley, flushed out by water pouring from the summit through two enormous gaps. The mountain has terrific camping and hiking, including a trail that loops through the crater, but the chance to witness this unearthly landscape is reason enough for a visit.

THE CLIMB TO THE SUMMIT

To reach Haleakalā National Park and the mountain's breathtaking summit, take Route 36 east of Kahului to the Haleakalā Highway (Route 37). Head east, up the mountain to the unlikely intersection of Haleakalā Highway and Haleakalā Highway. If you continue straight the road's name changes to Kula Highway (still Route 37). Instead, turn left onto Haleakalā Highway—this is now Route 377. After about 6 mi, make a left onto

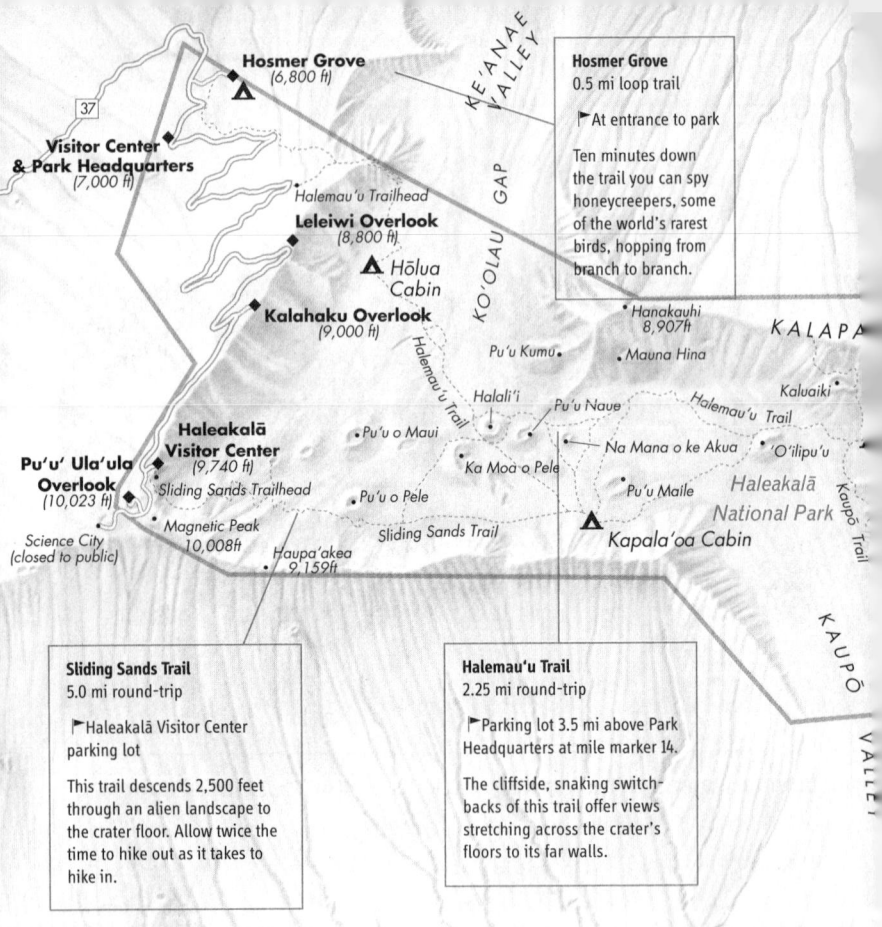

Hosmer Grove (6,800 ft)

Visitor Center & Park Headquarters (7,000 ft)

37

KE'ANAE VALLEY

Hosmer Grove
0.5 mi loop trail

► At entrance to park

Ten minutes down the trail you can spy honeycreepers, some of the world's rarest birds, hopping from branch to branch.

Halemau'u Trailhead

Leleiwi Overlook (8,800 ft)

Hōlua Cabin

Kalahaku Overlook (9,000 ft)

KO'OLAU GAP

Hanakauhi 8,907ft

KALAPA

Pu'u Kumu

Mauna Hina

Halemau'u Trail

Halali'i

Pu'u Nave

Kaluaiki

Halemau'u Trail

Haleakalā Visitor Center (9,740 ft)

Pu'u o Maui

Na Mana o ke Akua

O'ilipu'u

Pu'u' Ula'ula Overlook (10,023 ft)

Ka Moa o Pele

Sliding Sands Trailhead

Pu'u o Pele

Pu'u Maile

Haleakalā National Park

Kaupō Trail

Science City (closed to public)

Magnetic Peak 10,008ft

Sliding Sands Trail

Haupa'akea 9,159ft

Kapala'oa Cabin

KAUPŌ VALLEY

Sliding Sands Trail
5.0 mi round-trip

► Haleakalā Visitor Center parking lot

This trail descends 2,500 feet through an alien landscape to the crater floor. Allow twice the time to hike out as it takes to hike in.

Halemau'u Trail
2.25 mi round-trip

► Parking lot 3.5 mi above Park Headquarters at mile marker 14.

The cliffside, snaking switchbacks of this trail offer views stretching across the crater's floors to its far walls.

Crater Road (Route 378). After several long switchbacks (look out for downhill bikers!) you'll come to the park entrance.

■ **TIP→** Before you head up Haleakalā, call for the latest **park weather conditions** (☎ 808/877–5111). Extreme gusty winds, heavy rain, and even snow in winter are not uncommon. Because of the high altitude, the mountaintop temperature is often as much as 30 degrees cooler than that at sea level. Be sure to bring a jacket. Also make sure you have a full tank of gas. No service stations exist beyond Kula.■

There's a $10 parking fee to enter the park; but it's good for one week and can

be used at 'Ohe'o Gulch (Seven Sacred Pools), so save your receipt.

6,800 feet, Hosmer Grove. Just as you enter the park, Hosmer Grove has campsites and interpretive trails (*see* Hiking & Camping *on the following pages*). Park rangers maintain a changing schedule of talks and hikes both here and at the top of the mountain. Call the park for current schedules.

7,000 feet, Park Headquarters/Visitor Center. Not far from Hosmer Grove, the Park Headquarters/Visitor Center (open daily from 8 to 4) has trail maps

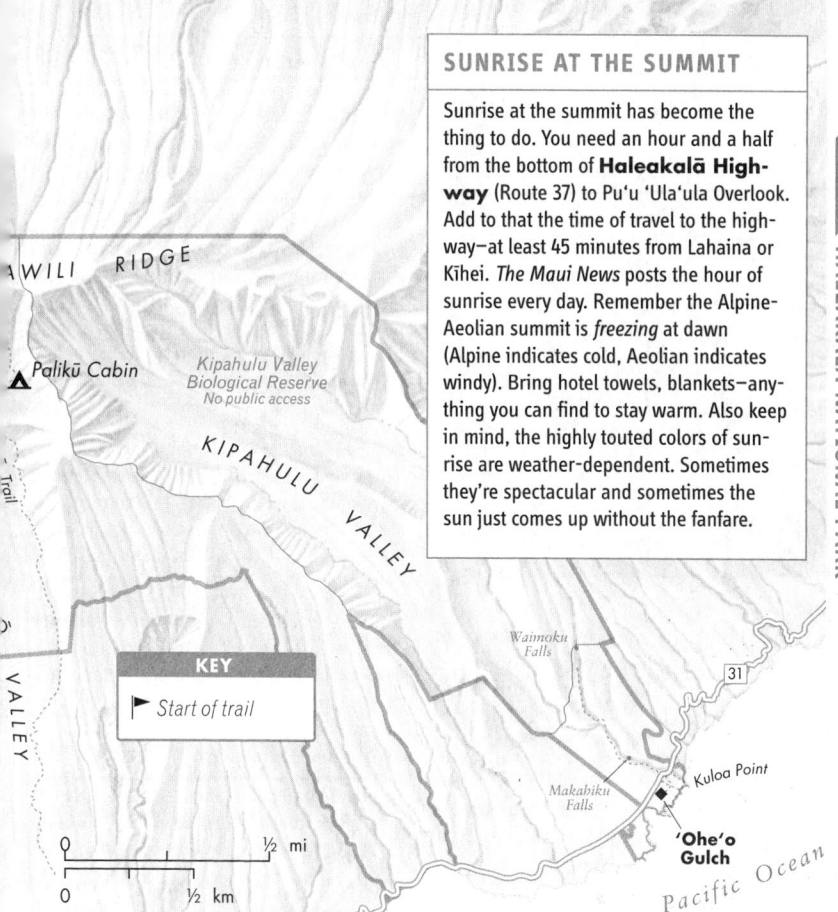

AWILI RIDGE

Palikū Cabin

Kipahulu Valley
Biological Reserve
No public access

KIPAHULU VALLEY

Trail

VALLEY

Waimoku
Falls

31

KEY

► Start of trail

Kuloa Point

Makahiku
Falls

'Ohe'o
Gulch

Pacific Ocean

0   ½ mi

0   ½ km

SUNRISE AT THE SUMMIT

Sunrise at the summit has become the thing to do. You need an hour and a half from the bottom of **Haleakalā Highway** (Route 37) to Pu'u 'Ula'ula Overlook. Add to that the time of travel to the highway—at least 45 minutes from Lahaina or Kīhei. *The Maui News* posts the hour of sunrise every day. Remember the Alpine-Aeolian summit is *freezing* at dawn (Alpine indicates cold, Aeolian indicates windy). Bring hotel towels, blankets—anything you can find to stay warm. Also keep in mind, the highly touted colors of sunrise are weather-dependent. Sometimes they're spectacular and sometimes the sun just comes up without the fanfare.

and displays about the volcano's origins and eruption history. Hikers and campers should check-in here before heading up the mountain. Maps, posters, and other memorabilia are available at the gift shop.

8,800 feet, Leleiwi Overlook. Continuing up the mountain, you come to Leleiwi Overlook. A short walk to the end of the parking lot reveals your first awe-inspiring view of the crater. The small hills in the basin are volcanic cinder cones (called *pu'u* in Hawaiian), each with a small crater at its top, and each the site of a former eruption.

WHERE TO EAT

KULA LODGE (✉ Haleakalā Hwy., Kula ☎ 808/878-2517) serves hearty breakfasts from 7 to 11 AM, a favorite with hikers coming down from a sunrise visit to Haleakalā's summit, as well as those on their way up for a late-morning tramp in the crater. Spectacular ocean views fill the windows of this mountainside lodge.

If you're here in the late afternoon, it's possible you'll experience a phenomenon called the Brocken Specter. Named after a similar occurrence in East Germany's

Silversword

10,023 feet, Pu'u 'Ula'ula Overlook.
The highest point on Maui is the Pu'u
'Ula'ula Overlook, at the 10,023-foot
summit. Here you find a glass-enclosed
lookout with a 360-degree view. The
building is open 24 hours a day, and this
is where visitors gather for the best sunrise view. Dawn begins between 5:45 and
7, depending on the time of year. On a
clear day you can see the islands of
Moloka'i, Lāna'i, Kaho'olawe, and
Hawai'i (the Big Island). On a *really* clear
day you can even spot O'ahu glimmering
in the distance.

■ **TIP→** The air is very thin at 10,000 feet. Don't
be surprised if you feel a little breathless while walking around the summit. Take it easy and drink lots
of water. Anyone who has been scuba diving within
the last 24 hours should not make the trip up
Haleakalā.

On a small hill nearby, you can see **Science
City**, an off-limits research and communications center straight out of an espi-
onage thriller. The University of Hawai'i
maintains an observatory here, and the
Department of Defense tracks satellites.

For more information about Haleakalā National Park, contact the **National Park Service**
(☎ 808/572-4400, ⊕ www.nps.gov/hale).

Harz Mountains, the specter allows you
to see yourself reflected on the clouds and
encircled by a rainbow. Don't wait all day
for this because it's not a daily occurrence.

9,000 feet, Kalahaku Overlook. The
next stopping point is Kalahaku Overlook. The view here offers a different perspective of the crater and at this elevation,
the famous silversword plant grows amid
the cinders. This odd, endangered beauty
grows only here, and at the same elevation
on the Big Island's two peaks. It begins life
as a silver, spiny-leaf rosette and is the
sole home of a variety of native insects (it's
the only shelter around). The silversword
reaches maturity between 7 and 17 years,
when it sends forth a 3- to 8-foot-tall stalk
with several hundred tiny sunflowers. It
blooms once, then dies.

9,740 feet, Haleakalā Visitor Center.
Another mile up is the Haleakalā Visitor
Center (open daily from sunrise to 3 PM).
There are exhibits inside, and a trail from
here leads to White Hill—a short easy
walk that will give you an even better view
of the valley.

HIKING & CAMPING

Exploring Haleakalā Crater is one of the
best hiking experiences on Maui. The volcanic terrain offers an impressive diversity
of colors, textures, and shapes—almost
as if the lava has been artfully sculpted. The
barren landscape is home to many plants,
insects, and birds that exist nowhere else
on earth and have developed intriguing survival mechanisms, such as the sun-re-
flecting, hairy leaves of the silversword,
which allow it to survive the intense climate.

Stop at park headquarters to register
and pick up trail maps on your way into
the park.

1-Hour Hike. Just as you enter Haleakalā National Park, **Hosmer Grove** offers a short 10-minute hike, and an hour-long, $^{1}/_{2}$-mi loop trail into the Waikamoi Cloud Forest that will give you insight into Hawai'i's fragile ecology. Anyone can go on the short hike, whereas the longer trail through the cloud forest is accessible only with park ranger–guided hikes. Call park headquarters for the schedule. Facilities here include six campsites (no permit needed, available on a first-come, first-served basis), pit toilets, drinking water, and cooking shelters.

4-Hour Hikes. Two half-day hikes involve descending into the crater and returning the way you came. The first, **Halemau'u Trail** (trailhead is between mile markers 14 and 15), is 2.25 mi round-trip. The cliffside, snaking switchbacks of this trail offer views stretching across the crater's pu'u-speckled floor to its far walls. On clear days you can peer through the Ko'olau Gap to Hāna. Native flowers and shrubs grow along the trail, which is typically misty and cool (though still exposed to the sun). When you reach the gate at the bottom, head back up.

The other hike, which is 5 mi round-trip, descends down **Sliding Sands Trail** (trailhead is at the Haleakalā Visitor Center) into an alien landscape of reddish black cinders, lava bombs, and silverswords. It's easy to imagine life before humans in the solitude and silence of this place. Turn back when you hit the crater floor.

■ **TIP →** Bring water, sunscreen, and a reliable jacket. These can be demanding hikes if you're unused to the altitude. Take it slowly to acclimate, and give yourself additional time for the uphill return trip.

8-Hour Hike. The recommended way to explore the crater in a single, but full day is to go in two cars and ferry yourselves back and forth between the head of **Halemau'u Trail** and the summit. This way, you can hike from the summit down **Sliding Sands Trail**, cross the crater's floor, investigate the **Bottomless Pit** and **Pele's Paint Pot**, then climb out on the switchback trail (**Halemau'u**). When you emerge, the shelter of your waiting car will be very welcome (this is an 11.2-mi hike). If you don't have two cars, hitching a ride from Halemau'u back to the summit should be relatively safe and easy.

■ **TIP→** Take a backpack with lunch, water, sunscreen, and a reliable jacket for the beginning and end of the 8-hour hike. This is a demanding trip, but you will never regret or forget it.

Overnight Hike. Staying overnight in one of Haleakalā's three cabins or two wilderness campgrounds is an experience like no other. You'll feel like the only person on earth when you wake up inside this enchanted, strange landscape. Nēnē and ʻuʻau (endangered storm petrels) make charming neighbors. The cabins, each tucked in a different corner of the crater's floor, are equipped with 12 bunk beds, wood-burning stoves, fake logs, and kitchen gear.

Hōlua cabin is the shortest hike, less than 4 hours (3.7 mi) from Halemauʻu Trail. **Kapalaʻoa** is about 5 hours (5.5 mi) down Sliding Sands Trail. The most cherished cabin is **Palikū,** a solid eight-hour (9.3-mi) hike starting from either trail. It's nestled against the rain-forested cliffs above the Kaupō Gap. To reserve a cabin you have to apply to the National Park Service at least 90 days in advance and hope the lottery system is kind to you. Tent campsites at Hōlua and Palikū are free and easy to reserve on a first-come, first-served basis.

■ **TIP→** Toilets and nonpotable water are available—bring iodine tablets to purify the water. Open fires are not allowed and packing out your trash is mandatory.

For more information on hiking or camping, or to reserve a cabin, contact the National Park Service (⊠ Box 369, Makawao 96768 ☏ 808/572-9306 ⊕ www.nps.gov/hale).

OPTIONS FOR EXPLORING

If you're short on time you can drive to the summit, take a peek inside, and drive back down. But the "House of the Sun" is really worth a day, whether you explore by foot, bicycle, horseback, or helicopter.

Note: At this writing the road between ʻOheʻo Gulch and Kaupō was closed due to earthquake damage. Check with the park for updates.

BIKING
You can cruise the 38 mi from the summit down the outside of the mountain all the way to Pāʻia at sea level. The views are exquisite, but dodging traffic can be a headache. If you rent bikes on your own, you'll need someone to ferry you up. Tours provide shuttle service and equipment.

HELICOPTER TOURS
Viewing Haleakalā from above can be a mind-altering experience, if you don't mind dropping $200 per person for a few blissful moments above the crater. Most tours buzz Haleakalā, where airspace is regulated, then head over to Hanā in search of waterfalls.

HORSEBACK RIDING
Several companies offer half-day, full-day, and even overnight rides into the crater. Advanced or at least confident riders can travel up the stunning Kaupō Gap with Charley's Trail Rides and stay overnight at Palikū.

For complete information on any of these activities, see chapter 5, Golf, Hiking & Outdoor Activities.

set comes out in force for the Makawao Rodeo. The crossroads of town—lined with chic shops and down-home eateries—reflects a growing population of people who came here just because they liked it. For those seeking lush greenery rather than beachside accommodations, there are great, secluded little bed-and-breakfasts in and around the town.

Hui No'eau Visual Arts Center. The main house of this nonprofit cultural center on the old Baldwin estate, just outside the town of Makawao, is an elegant two-story Mediterranean-style villa designed in the 1920s by the defining Hawai'i architect C. W. Dickey. "The Hui" is the grande dame of Maui's well-known arts scene. The exhibits are always satisfying, and the grounds might as well be a botanical garden. The Hui also offers classes and maintains artists' studios. ⊠ *2841 Baldwin Ave., Makawao* ☎ *808/572–6560* ⊒ *Free* ⏰ *Daily 10–4.*

> **CREAM PUFFS, YUM!**
>
> One of Makawao's most famous landmarks is **Komoda Store & Bakery** (⊠ *3674 Baldwin Ave.* ☎ *808/572–7261*), a classic mom-and-pop store that has changed little in three-quarters of a century, where you can get a delicious cream puff if you arrive early enough. They make hundreds but sell out each day.

THE NORTH SHORE

Blasted by winter swells and wind, Maui's North Shore draws watersports thrill-seekers from around the world. But there's much more to this area of Maui than coastline. Inland, a lush, waterfall-fed garden of Eden beckons. In forested pockets, wealthy hermits have carved out a little piece of paradise for themselves. A few of them are even willing to invite you in, as guests at their vacation rentals.

North Shore action centers around the colorful town of Pā'ia and the windsurfing mecca, Ho'okipa Beach.

PĀ'IA

★ This little town on Maui's north shore (at the intersection of Hāna Highway [Highway 36] and Baldwin Avenue) was once a sugarcane enclave, with a mill, plantation camps, and shops. The town boomed during World War II when the marines set up camp in nearby Ha'ikū. The old HC&S sugar mill finally closed and no sign of the military remains, but the town continues to thrive. In the 1970s, Pā'ia became a hippie town as dropouts headed for Maui to open boutiques, galleries, and unusual eateries. In the 1980s windsurfers discovered nearby Ho'okipa Beach and brought an international flavor to Pā'ia.

At the intersection of Hāna Highway and Baldwin Avenue, eclectic boutiques supply everything from high fashion to hemp-oil candles. Some of Maui's best shops for surf trunks, Brazilian bikinis, and other beachware are here. The restaurants provide excellent people-watching and an array of dining options. A French-Caribbean bistro with a sushi bar in back, a French-Indian creperie, a neo-Mexican gourmet restaurant, and a fish market all compete for your patronage. This abundance is helpful because Pā'ia is the last place to snack before the pilgrimage to Hāna and the first stop for the famished on the return trip.

★ **Ho'okipa Beach.** There's no better place on this or any other island to watch the world's finest windsurfers in action. The surfers know the five different surf breaks here by name. Unless it's a rare day without wind or waves, you're sure to get a show.

■ TIP➔It's not safe to park on the shoulder. Use the ample parking lot at the county park entrance. ⊠*2 mi past Pā'ia on Rte. 36.*

> **FUN THINGS TO DO ON THE NORTH SHORE**
>
> ■ Buy a teeny-weenie Maui Girl bikini.
>
> ■ Watch windsurfers somersault over waves at Ho'okipa.
>
> ■ Get lost and find yourself in the Ha'ikū forest.
>
> ■ Rub elbows with yogis and tow-in surfers at Anthony's Coffee Shop.
>
> ■ Dig into a fish sandwich and fries at the Pā'ia Fishmarket.

NEED A BREAK?

Anthony's Coffee (⊠*90 Hāna Hwy.* ☎*808/579–8340*) roasts its own beans, sells ice cream and picnic lunches, and is a great place to eavesdrop on the windsurfing crowd. **Charley's Restaurant** (⊠*Hāna Hwy.* ☎*808/579–9453*), is an easygoing saloon-type hangout with pool tables. **Mana Foods** (⊠*49 Baldwin Ave.* ☎*808/579–8078*), the North Shore's natural-foods store, has an inspired deli with wholesome hot and cold items. The long line at **Pā'ia Fishmarket Restaurant** (⊠*2A Baldwin Ave.* ☎*808/579–8030*) attests to the popularity of the tasty mahi sandwiches. Pā'ia has an excellent wine store, the **Wine Corner** (⊠*149 Hāna Hwy.* ☎*808/579–8904*), helpful because two good eateries nearby are BYOB.

HA'IKŪ

At one time this area vibrated around a couple of enormous pineapple canneries. Both have been transformed into rustic warehouse malls. Because of the post office next door, Old Ha'ikū Cannery earned the title of town center. Here you can snack on pizza at Colleen's or get massaged by the students at Spa Luna. Follow windy Ha'ikū Road to Pauwela Cannery, the other defunct factory-turned-hangout. Don't fret if you get lost. This jungle hillside is a maze of flower-decked roads that seem to double back upon themselves. Up Kokomo Road is a large pu'u capped with a grove of columnar pines, and the **4th Marine Division Memorial Park.** During World War II, American GIs trained here for battles on Iwo Jima and Saipan. Locals nicknamed the cinder cone Giggle Hill because it was a popular hangout for Maui women and their favorite servicemen.

ROAD TO HĀNA

As you round the impossibly tight turn, a one-lane bridge comes into view. Beneath its worn surface, a lush forested gulch plummets toward the coast. The sound of rushing water fills the air, compelling you to search the overgrown hillside for waterfalls. This is the Road to Hāna, a 55-mi journey into the unspoiled heart of Maui. Tracing a centuries-old path, the road begins as a well-paved highway in Kahului and ends in the tiny town of Hāna on the island's rain-gouged windward side.

★ Fodor's Choice — Despite the twists and turns, the road to Hāna is not as frightening as it may sound. You're bound to be a little nervous approaching it the first time; but afterwards you'll wonder if somebody out there is making it sound tough just to keep out the hordes. The challenging part of the road takes only an hour and a half, but you'll want to stop often and let the driver enjoy the view, too. Don't expect a booming city when you get to Hāna. Its lure is its quiet timelessness. Like the adage says, the journey *is* the destination.

During high season, the road to Hāna tends to clog—well, not clog exactly, but develop little choo-choo trains of cars, with everyone in a line of six or a dozen driving as slowly as the first car. The solution: leave early (dawn) and return late (dusk). And if you find yourself playing the role of locomotive, pull over and let the other drivers pass. You can also let someone else take the turns for you—several companies offer van tours, which make stops all along the way (*see* Maui Sightseeing Tours *box in this chapter*).

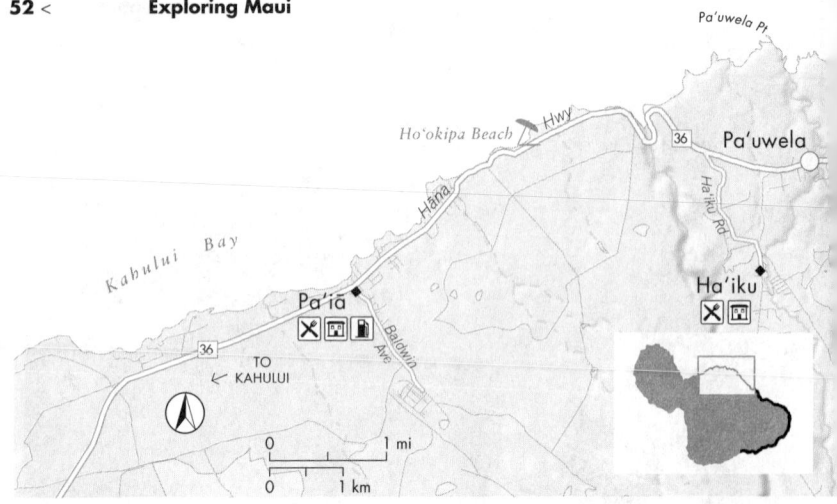

DRIVING THE ROAD TO HĀNA

Begin your journey in Pā'ia, the little town on Maui's North Shore. Be sure to fill up your gas tank here. There are no gas stations along Hāna Highway, and the station in Hāna closes by 6 PM. You should also pick up a picnic lunch. Lunch and snack choices along the way are limited to rustic fruit stands.

About 10 mi past Pā'ia, at the bottom of Kaupakalua Road, the roadside mileposts begin measuring the 36 mi to Hāna town. The road's trademark noodling starts about 3 mi after that. Once the road gets twisty, remember that many residents make this trip frequently. You'll recognize them because they're the ones zipping around every curve. They've seen this so many times before they don't care to linger. Pull over to let them pass.

All along this stretch of road, waterfalls are abundant. Roll down your windows. Breathe in the scent of guava and ginger. You can almost hear the bamboo growing. There are plenty of places to pull completely off the road and park safely. Do this often, since the road's curves make driving without a break difficult.

1 Twin Falls. Keep an eye out for the fruit stand just after mile marker 2. Stop here

and treat yourself to some fresh sugarcane juice. If you're feeling adventurous, follow the path beyond the stand to the paradisiacal waterfalls known as Twin Falls. Once a rough trail plastered with no trespassing signs, this treasured spot is now easily accessible. In fact, there's usually a mass of cars surrounding the fruit stand at the trail head. Several deep, emerald pools sparkle beneath waterfalls and offer excellent swimming and photo opportunities.

While it's still private property, the no trespassing signs have been replaced by colorfully painted arrows pointing away from residences and toward the falls. ■ TIP→ Bring water shoes for crossing streams along the way. Swim at your own risk and beware: flash floods here and in all East Maui stream areas can be sudden and deadly. Check the weather before you go.

2 Huelo & Kailua. Dry off and drive on past the sleepy country villages of Huelo (near mile marker 5) and Kailua (near mile marker 6). The little farm town of Huelo has two quaint churches and several lovely B&Bs. It's a good place to stay if you value privacy, but it also provides an opportunity to meet local residents and learn about a rural lifestyle you might not expect to find on the Islands. The same can

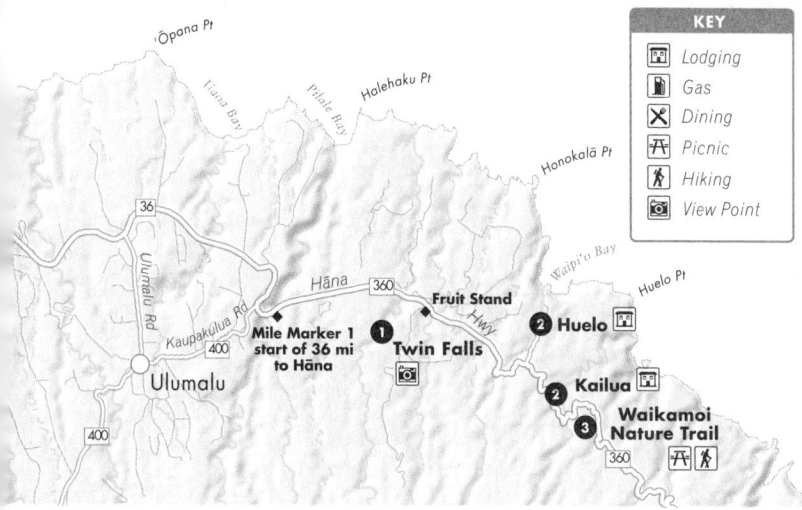

KEY

🏨 Lodging
⛽ Gas
✗ Dining
🎪 Picnic
🧍 Hiking
📷 View Point

be said for nearby Kailua, home to Alexander & Baldwin's irrigation employees.

❸ Waikamoi Nature Trail. Between mile markers 9 and 10, the Waikamoi Nature Trail sign beckons you to stretch your car-weary limbs. A short (if muddy) trail leads through tall eucalyptus trees to a coastal vantage point with a picnic table and barbecue. Signage reminds visitors QUIET, TREES AT WORK and BAMBOO PICKING PERMIT REQUIRED. Awapuhi, or Hawaiian shampoo ginger, sends up fragrant shoots along the trail.

❹ Puahokamoa Stream. About a mile farther, near mile marker 11, you can stop at the bridge over Puahokamoa Stream. This is one of many bridges you cross en route from Pā'ia to Hāna. It spans pools and waterfalls. Picnic tables are available, but there are no restrooms.

❺ Kaumahina State Wayside Park. If you'd rather stretch your legs and use a flush toilet, continue another mile to Kaumahina State Wayside Park (at mile marker 12). The park has a picnic area, restrooms, and a lovely overlook to the Ke'anae Peninsula. Hardier souls can camp here, with a permit. The park is open from 8 AM to 4 PM and admission is free. ☎ 808/984–8109

⏱ | **TIMING TIPS**

With short stops, the drive from Pā'ia to Hāna should take you between two and three hours one-way. Lunching in Hāna, hiking, and swimming can easily turn the round-trip into a full-day outing. Since there's so much scenery to take in, we recommend staying overnight in Hāna. It's worth taking time to enjoy the waterfalls and beaches without being in a hurry. Try to plan your trip for a day that promises fair, sunny weather—though the drive can be even more beautiful when it's raining. ■ TIP→ If you decide to spend a night or two in Hāna, you may want to check any valuable luggage with the valet at your previous hotel. That way, you won't have to leave it in your car unattended when you stop to see the sights on your way to Hāna.

Ke'anae Peninsula

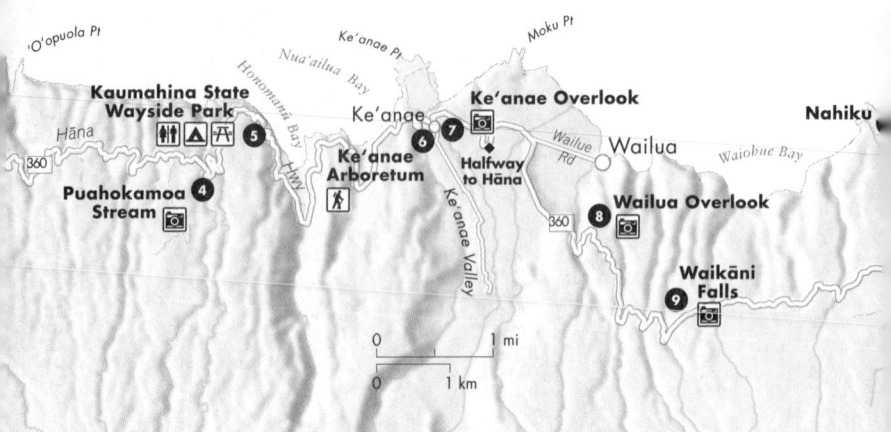

Near mile marker 14, before Ke'anae, you find yourself driving along a cliff side down into deep, lush Honomanū Bay, an enormous valley, with a rocky black-sand beach.

The Honomanū Valley was carved by erosion during Haleakalā's first dormant period. At the canyon's head there are 3,000-foot cliffs and a 1,000-foot waterfall, but don't try to reach them. There's not much of a trail, and what does exist is practically impassable.

❻ Ke'anae Arboretum. Another 4 mi brings you to mile marker 17 and the Ke'anae Arboretum where you can add to your botanical education or enjoy a challenging hike into a forest. Signs help you learn the names of the many plants and trees now considered native to Hawai'i. The meandering Pi'ina'au Stream adds a graceful touch to the arboretum and provides a swimming pond.

You can take a fairly rigorous hike from the arboretum if you can find the trail at one side of the large taro patch. Be careful not to lose the trail once you're on it. A lovely forest waits at the end of the 25-minute hike. Access to the arboretum is free.

❼ Ke'anae Overlook. A half mile farther down Hāna Highway you can stop at the Ke'anae Overlook. From this obser-

vation point, you can take in the patch-work-quilt effect the taro farms create below. The people of Ke'anae are working hard to revive this Hawaiian agricultural art and the traditional cultural values that the crop represents. The ocean provides a dramatic backdrop for the farms. In the other direction there are awesome views of Haleakalā through the foliage. This is a great spot for photos.

■ **TIP→ Coming up is the halfway mark to Hāna. If you've had enough scenery, this is as good a time as any to turn around and head back to civilization.**

❽ Wailua Overlook. Between mile markers 20 and 21 you find Wailua Overlook. From the parking lot you can see Wailua Canyon, but you have to walk up steps to get a view

Taro Farm viewed from Hāna Highway

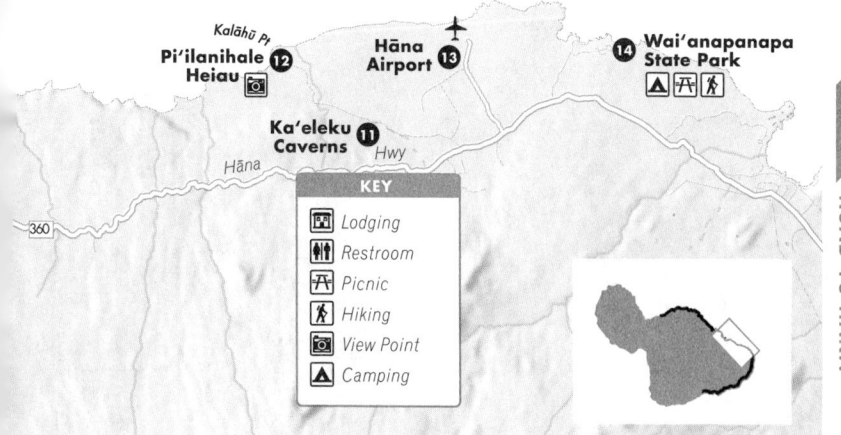

of Wailua Village. The landmark in Wailua Village is a church made of coral, built in 1860. Once called St. Gabriel's Catholic Church, the current Our Lady of Fatima Shrine has an interesting legend surrounding it. As the story goes, a storm washed enough coral up onto shore to build the church and then took any extra coral back to sea.

9 Waikāni Falls. After another $\frac{1}{2}$ mi, past mile marker 21, you hit the best falls on the entire drive to Hāna, Waikāni Falls. Though not necessarily bigger or taller than the other falls, these are the most dramatic falls you'll find in East Maui. That's partly because the water is not diverted for sugar irrigation; the taro farmers in Wailua need all the runoff. This is a particularly good spot for photos.

10 Nahiku. At about mile marker 25 you see a road that heads down toward the ocean and the village of Nahiku. In ancient times this was a busy settlement with hundreds of residents. Now only about 80 people live in Nahiku, mostly native Hawaiians and some back-to-the-land types. A rubber grower planted trees here in the early 1900s, but the experiment didn't work out, and Nahiku was essentially abandoned. The road ends at the sea in a pretty landing. This is the rainiest, densest part of the East Maui rain forest.

Coffee Break. Back on the Hāna Highway, about 10 minutes before Hāna town, you can stop for—of all things—espresso. The tiny, colorful **Nahiku Ti Gallery and Coffee Shop** (between mile markers 27 and 28) sells local coffee, dried fruits and candies, and delicious (if pricey) banana bread. Sometimes the barbecue is fired up and you can try fish skewers or baked breadfruit (an island favorite nearly impossible to find elsewhere). The Ti Gallery sells Hawaiian crafts.

11 Ka'eleku Caverns. If you're interested in exploring underground, turn left onto 'Ula'ino Road, just after mile marker 31, and follow the signs to Ka'eleku Caverns. **Maui Cave Adventures** leads amateur spelunkers into a system of gigantic lava tubes, accentuated by colorful underworld formations.

Monday through Thursday, from 10:30 to 3:30, you can take a self-guided, 30- to 45-minute tour for $11.95 per person. Friday and Saturday, choose either the 75-minute walking tour (at 11:15 AM; $29 per person) or the two-and-a-half-hour adventure tour (at 1:15 PM; $79 per person). Gear—gloves, flashlight, and hard hat—is provided, and visitors must be at least six years of age (15 years of age for the adventure tour). Call ahead to reserve a spot on the guided tours. ☎ 808/248–7308 ⊕ *www.mauicave.com*

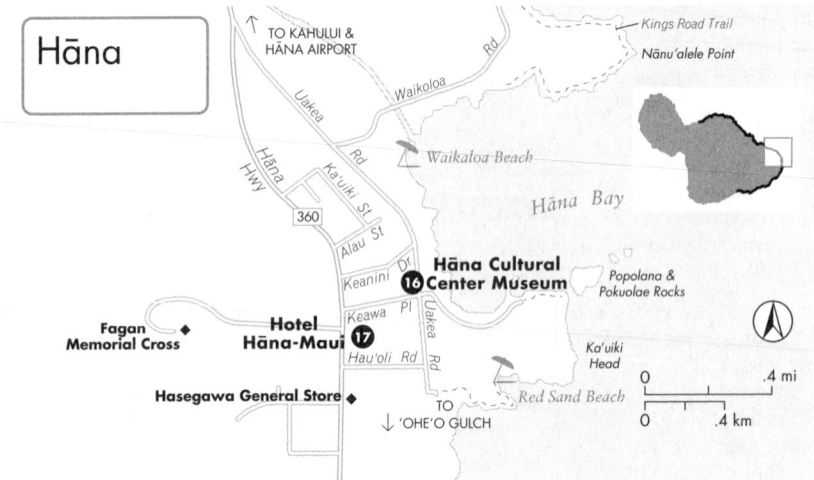

★ **⑫ Pi'ilanihale Heiau.** Continue on 'Ula'ino Road, which doubles back for a mile, loses its pavement, and even crosses a stream before reaching Kahanu Garden and Pi'ilanihale Heiau, the largest prehistoric monument in Hawai'i. This temple platform was built for a great 16th-century Maui king named Pi'ilani and his heirs. This king also supervised the construction of a 10-foot-wide road that completely encircled the island. (That's why his name is part of most of Maui's highway titles.)

Hawaiian families continue to maintain and protect this sacred site as they have for centuries, and they have not been eager to turn it into a tourist attraction. However, they now offer a brochure so you can tour the property yourself for $5 per person. Parties of four or more can reserve a guided tour, for $10 per person, by calling 48 hours in advance. Tours include the 122-acre **Kahanu Garden**, a federally funded research center focusing on the ethno-botany of the Pacific. The heiau and garden are open weekdays from 10 AM to 2 PM. ☎ *808/248–8912*

⑬ Hāna Airport. Back on the Hāna Highway, and less than ¹/₂ mi farther, is the turnoff for the Hāna Airport. Think of Amelia Earhart. Think of Waldo Pepper. If these picket-fence runways don't turn your thoughts to the derring-do of barnstorming pilots, you haven't seen enough old movies. Only the smallest planes can land and depart here, and when none of them happens to be around, the lonely wind sock is the only evidence that this is a working airfield. ☎ *808/248–8208*

★ **⑭ Wai'anapanapa State Park.** Just beyond mile marker 32 you reach Wai'anapanapa State Park, home to one of Maui's only volcanic-sand beaches and some freshwater caves for adventurous swimmers to explore. The park is right on the ocean, and it's a lovely spot to picnic, camp, hike, or swim. To the left you'll find the black-sand beach, picnic tables, and cave pools. To the right you'll find cabins and an ancient trail which snakes along the ocean past blowholes, sea arches, and archaeological sites.

The tide pools here turn red several times a year. Scientists say it's explained by the arrival of small shrimp, but legend claims the color represents the blood of Popoalaea, a princess said to have been murdered in one of the caves by her husband, Chief Kaakea. Whichever you choose to believe, the drama of the landscape itself—black sand, green beach vines, azure water—is bound to leave a lasting impression.

With a permit you can stay in state-run cabins here for less than $45 a night—the price varies depending on the number of people—but reserve early. They often book up a year in advance. ☎ *808/984–8109*

⓯ **Hāna.** By now the relaxed pace of life that Hāna residents enjoy should have you in its grasp, so you won't be discouraged to learn that "town" is little more than a gas station, a post office, and a ramshackle grocery.

Hāna, in many ways, is the heart of Maui. It's one of the few places where the slow pulse of island life is still strong. The town centers on its lovely circular bay, dominated on the right-hand shore by a pu'u called Ka'uiki. A short trail here leads to a cave, the birthplace of Queen Kā'ahumanu. This area is rich in Hawaiian history and legend. Two miles beyond town another pu'u presides over a loop road that passes two of Hāna's best beaches—Koki and Hāmoa. The hill is called Ka Iwi O Pele (Pele's Bone). Offshore here, at tiny 'Ālau Island, the demigod Maui supposedly fished up the Hawaiian islands.

Sugar was once the mainstay of Hāna's economy; the last plantation shut down in the '40s. In 1946 rancher Paul Fagan built the **Hotel Hāna-Maui** and stocked the surrounding pastureland with cattle. The cross you see on the hill above the hotel was put there in memory of Fagan. Now it's the ranch and hotel that put food on most tables, though many families still farm, fish, and hunt as in the old days. Houses around town are decorated with glass balls and nets, which indicate a fisherman's lodging.

⓰ **Hāna Cultural Center Museum.** If you're determined to spend some time and money in Hāna after the long drive, a single turn off the highway onto Ukea Street, in the center of town, will take you to the Hāna Cultural Center Museum. Besides operating a well-stocked gift shop, it displays artifacts, quilts, a replica of an authentic *kauhale* (an ancient Hawaiian living complex, with thatch huts and food gardens), and other Hawaiiana. The knowledgeable staff can explain it all to you. ☎ *808/248–8622*

⓱ **Hotel Hāna-Maui.** With its surrounding ranch, the upscale hotel is the mainstay of Hāna's economy. It's pleasant to stroll around this beautifully rustic property. The library houses interesting, authentic Hawaiian artifacts. In the evening, while local musicians play in the casual lobby bar, their friends jump up to dance hula. The Sea Ranch cottages across the road, built to look like authentic plantation housing from the outside, are also part of the hotel. *See* Where to Stay *for more information.*

Hala Trees, Wai'anapanapa State Park

Hāna

Don't be suprised if the mile markers suddenly start descending as you head past Hāna. Technically, Hāna Highway (Route 360) ends at the Hāna Bay. The road that continues south is Piʻilani Highway (Route 31)—though everyone still refers to it as the Hāna Highway.

⑱ Hāmoa Beach. Just outside Hāna, take a left on Haneoʻo Loop to explore lovely Hāmoa. Indulge in swimming or bodysurfing at this beautiful salt-and-pepper beach. Picnic tables, restrooms, and showers beneath the idyllic shade of coconut trees offer a more than comfortable rest stop.

The road leading to Hāmoa also takes you to **Kōkī Beach**, where you can watch the Hāna surfers mastering the swells and strong currents, and the seabirds darting over **Ālau**, the palm-fringed islet off the coast. The swimming is safer at Hāmoa.

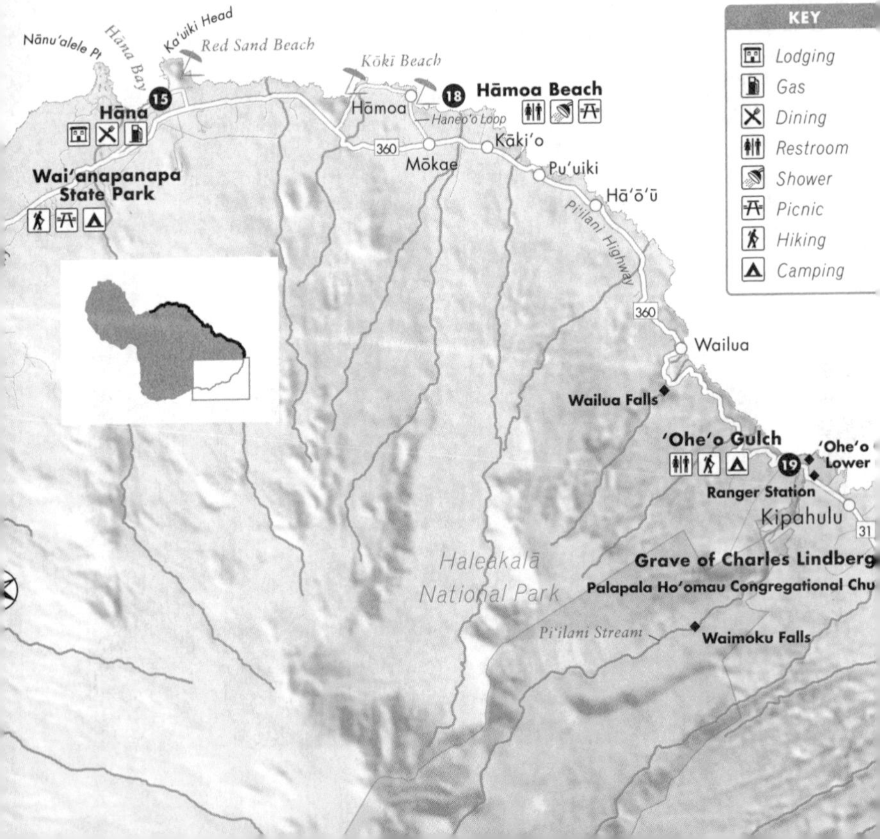

Nānuʻalele Pt

Hāna Bay

Kaʻuiki Head

Red Sand Beach

Kōkī Beach

Hāna ⑮

Hāmoa Beach ⑱

Hāmoa

Haneoʻo Loop

Waiʻanapanapa State Park

360

Mōkae

Kākiʻo

Puʻuiki

Hāʻōʻū

Piʻilani Highway

360

Wailua

Wailua Falls

ʻOheʻo Gulch

⑲

ʻOheʻo Lower

Ranger Station

Kipahulu

31

Haleakalā National Park

Grave of Charles Lindberg

Palapala Hoʻomau Congregational Chu

Piʻilani Stream

Waimoku Falls

KEY	
Lodging	
Gas	
Dining	
Restroom	
Shower	
Picnic	
Hiking	
Camping	

★ ⓳ 'Ohe'o Gulch. Ten miles past town, at mile marker 42, you'll find the pools at 'Ohe'o Gulch. One branch of Haleakalā National Park runs down the mountain from the crater and reaches the sea here, where a basalt-lined stream cascades from one pool to the next. Some tour guides still call this area Seven Sacred Pools, but in truth there are more than seven, and they've never been considered sacred. You can park here—for a $10 fee—and walk to the lowest pools for a cool swim. The place gets crowded, since most people who drive the Hāna Highway make this their last stop.

If you enjoy hiking, go up the stream on the 2-mi hike to **Waimoku Falls**. The trail crosses a spectacular gorge, then turns into a boardwalk that takes you through an amazing bamboo forest. You can pitch a tent in the grassy campground down by the sea. *See* Hiking *in* Golf, Hiking & Outdoor Activities.

⓴ **Grave of Charles Lindbergh.** Many people travel the mile past 'Ohe'o Gulch to see the Grave of Charles Lindbergh. You see a ruined sugar mill with a big chimney on the right side of the road and then, on the left, a rutted track leading to Palapala Ho'omau Congregational Church. The simple one-room church sits on a bluff over the sea, with the small graveyard on the ocean side. The world-renowned aviator chose to be buried here because he and his wife, writer Anne Morrow Lindbergh, spent a lot of time living in the area. He was buried here in 1974. Since this is a churchyard, be considerate and leave everything exactly as you found it. Next to the churchyard on the ocean side is a small county park, good for a picnic.

Kaupō Road. The road to Hāna continues all the way around Haleakalā's "back side" through 'Ulupalakua Ranch and into Kula. The desertlike area, with its grand vistas, is unlike anything else on the island, but the road itself is bad, sometimes impassable in winter. Car-rental agencies call it off-limits to their passenger cars and there is no emergency assis-

The drive to Hāna wouldn't be as enchanting without a stop or two at one of the countless fruit and flower stands alongside the highway. Every 1/2 mi or so a thatched hut tempts passersby with apple bananas, liliko'i (passion fruit), avocados, or starfruit just plucked from the tree. Leave 50¢ or $1 in the can for the folks who live off the land. Huge bouquets of tropical flowers are available for a handful of change, and some farms will ship.

tance available. The danger and dust from increasing numbers of speeding jeep drivers are making life tough for the residents, especially in Kaupō, with its 4 mi of unpaved road. The small communities around East Maui cling tenuously to the old ways. Please keep them in mind if you do pass this way. If you can't resist the adventure, try to make the drive just before sunset. The light slanting across the mountain is incredible. At night, giant potholes, owls, and loose cattle can make for some difficult driving.

Important note: The road beyond 'Ohe'o Gulch to Kaupō was closed at this writing because of a 2006 earthquake that caused some instability and falling rocks. Check with officials at Haleakalā National Park (☎ 808/572–4400; dial 0 during the recorded message to speak to a representative during office hours) before traveling beyond 'Ohe'o Gulch.

Beaches

WORD OF MOUTH

"[Ho'okipa Beach is] world famous for wind surfing. This is where the Big Dogs go. Unless you are an expert, just go and watch. It's unbelievable . . . and free!"

—issy

"We drove ourselves to Hamoa beach, what a spectacular beach this was. The sand is gray; I had never seen sand like that—it was baby soft."

—lasjas

Updated
by Amy
Westervelt

OF ALL THE HAWAIIAN ISLANDS, Maui's beaches are some of the most diverse. You'll find the pristine, palm-lined shores you expect with waters as clear and inviting as sea-green glass, but you'll also discover rich red-and black-sand beaches, craggy cliffs with surging whitecaps, and year-round sunsets that quiet the soul. As on the other isles, all Maui's beaches are public—but that doesn't mean it's not possible to find a secluded cove where you can truly get away from the world.

The island's leeward shores (the South Shore and West Maui) have the calmest, sunniest beaches. Hit the beach early, when the aquamarine waters are as accommodating as bathwater. In summer, afternoon winds can be a sandblasting force, which can chase even the most dedicated sun worshippers away. From November through May, the South and West beaches are also great spots to watch the parade of whales that spend the winter and early spring in Maui's waters.

Windward shores (the North Shore and East Maui) offer more adventurous beach-going. Beaches face the open ocean (rather than other islands) and tend to be rockier and more prone to powerful swells. This is particularly true in winter, when the North Shore becomes a playground for experienced big-wave riders and windsurfers. Don't let this keep you away completely, however; some of the island's best beaches are those remote slivers of volcanic sand found on the wild windward shore.

WEST MAUI

West Maui beaches are legendary for their glittering aquamarine waters banked by long stretches of golden sand. Reef fronts much of the western shore, making the underwater panorama something to behold. The beaches listed here start in the north at Kapalua and head south past Kā'anapali and Lahaina. Note that there are a dozen roadside beaches to choose from on Route 30; those listed here are the ones we like best.

"Slaughterhouse" (Mokuleia) Beach. The island's northernmost beach is part of the Honolua-Mokuleia Marine Life Conservation District. "Slaughterhouse" is the surfers' nickname for what is officially Mokuleia. When the weather permits, this is a great place for bodysurfing and sunbathing. Concrete steps and a green railing help you get down the sheer cliff to the sand. The next bay over, Honolua, has no beach but offers one of the best surf breaks in Hawai'i. Often you can see competitions happening there; look for cars pulled off the road and parked in the pineapple field. ⊠ *Mile marker 32 on Rte. 30 past Kapalua* ⚭ *No facilities.*

D. T. Fleming Beach. Because the current can be quite strong, this charming, mile-long sandy cove is better for sunbathing than for swimming or water sports. Still, it's one of the island's most popular beaches. Part of the beach runs along the front of the Ritz-Carlton's Beachhouse Bar & Grill—a good place to grab a cocktail and enjoy the view. ⊠ *Rte.*

30, 1 mi north of Kapalua ⚐*Toilets, showers, picnic tables, grills/firepits, parking lot.*

Kapalua Bay Beach. Kapalua was once named the "world's nicest beach" by *Sunset* magazine. Walk through the tunnel at the end of Kapalua Place and you'll see why—the beach fronts a pristine bay good for snorkeling, swimming, and general lazing. Located just north of Nāpili Bay, this lovely, sheltered shore often remains calm late into the afternoon, although there may be strong currents offshore. This area is quite popular and is bordered by the Kapalua Resort so don't expect to have the beach to yourself. ⊠*From Rte. 30, turn onto Kapalua Pl., walk through tunnel* ⚐*Toilets, showers, parking lot.*

☺ **Nāpili Beach.** Surrounded by sleepy condos, this round bay is a turtle-
Fodor'sChoice filled pool lined with a sparkling white crescent of sand. Sunbathers
★ love this beach. The shore break is steep but gentle and it's easy to keep an eye on kids here as the entire bay is visible from any point in the water. The beach is right outside the Nāpili Kai Beach Club, a popular little resort for honeymooners, only a few miles south of Kapalua. It's also a terrific sunset spot. ⊠*5900 Lower Honoapi'ilani Hwy., look for Nāpili Pl. or Hui Dr.* ⚐*Showers, parking lot.*

☺ ★ **Kā'anapali Beach.** Stretching from the Sheraton Maui at its northern-most end to the Hyatt Regency Maui at its southern tip, Kā'anapali Beach is lined with resorts, condominiums, restaurants, and shops. If you're looking for quiet and seclusion, this is not the beach for you. But if you want lots of action, lay out your towel here. Also called "Dig Me Beach," this is one of Maui's best people-watching spots: catamarans, windsurfers, and parasailers head out from here while the beautiful people take in the scenery. A cement pathway weaves along the length of this 3-mi-long beach, leading from one astounding resort to the next.

The drop-off from Kā'anapali's soft, sugary sand is steep, but waves hit the shore with barely a rippling slap. The area at the northernmost end (in front of the Sheraton Maui), known as Black Rock, has prime snorkeling. The fish and eels here are tame from hand-feeding, but be aware—they can still bite! ⊠*Follow any of 3 Kā'anapali exits from Honoapi'ilani Hwy. and park at any hotel* ⚐*Toilets, showers, parking lot.*

BEACHES KEY

🚻	Restroom
🚿	Showers
🏄	Surfing
🤿	Snorkel/Scuba
🚼	Good for kids
P	Parking

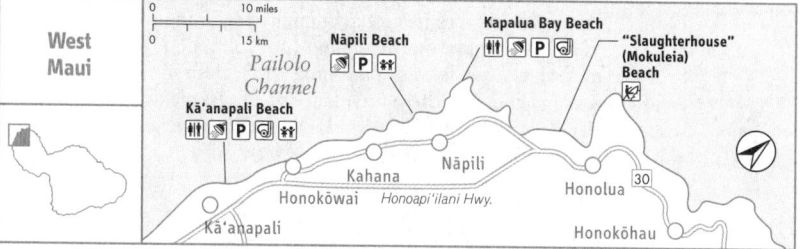

Puamana Beach Park. Puamana is both a friendly beach park and a surf spot for mellow, longboard rides. With a narrow, sandy beach and grassy area providing plenty of shade, Puamana offers mostly calm swimming conditions and a good view of neighboring Lāna'i. Smaller than Launiupoko, this beach park tends to attract locals looking to surf and BBQ. ⊠ *On Rte. 30, ¼ mi south of Lahaina* ⛳ *Toilets, showers, picnic tables, grills/firepits.*

DON'T FORGET

All of the island's beaches are free and open to the public—even those that grace the front yards of fancy hotels—so you can make yourself at home on any one of them. Some of the prettiest beaches are often hidden by buildings; look for the blue BEACH ACCESS signs that indicate rights-of-way through condominiums, resorts, and other private properties.

Launiupoko State Wayside Park. Launiupoko is the beach park of all beach parks. Both a surf break and a beach, it offers a little something for everyone with its inviting stretch of lawn, soft white sand, and gentle waves. The shoreline reef creates a protected wading pool, perfect for small children. Outside the reef, beginner surfers will find good longboard rides. From the long sliver of beach (good for walking), you'll enjoy superb views of neighbor islands, and landside, of deep valleys jetting through the West Maui Mountains. Because of its endless sunshine and serenity—not to mention its many amenities—Launiupoko draws a crowd on the weekends, but there's space for everyone (and overflow parking across the street). ⊠ *On Rte. 30, just south of Lahaina at mile marker 18* ⛳ *Toilets, showers, picnic tables, grills/firepits.*

Olowalu. Olowalu is more an offshore snorkel spot than a beach, but it's a great place to watch for turtles and whales in-season. The beach is literally a pullover from the road, which can make for some unwelcome noise if you're looking for quiet. The entrance can be rocky (reef shoes help) but if you've got your snorkel gear, it's just a swim away to an extensive and diverse reef (200 yards). Shoreline visibility can vary depending on the swell and time of day (late morning is best). Except for during a south swell, the waters are usually calm. A half mile north of mile marker 14 you'll find the rocky surf break, also called Olowalu, which is a local (and at times, unfriendly) hangout, so it's better to stick to the beach. ⊠ *South of Olowalu General Store, on Rte. 30 at mile marker 14* ⛳ *No facilities.*

Ukumeheme Beach Park. This popular park is also known as "Thousand Peaks," because the waves just keep coming. Beginning to intermediate wave riders will enjoy this as a good spot to longboard or boogie board. The beach itself leaves something to be desired, as it's more dead grass than sand, but there are plenty of BBQs, picnic tables, and some shade. Portable toilets are available. ⊠ *On Rte. 30, near mile marker 12* ⛳ *Toilets, picnic tables, grills/firepits.*

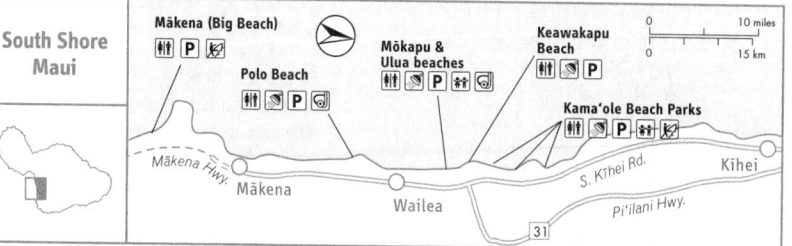

South Shore Maui

THE SOUTH SHORE

Sandy beach fronts nearly the entire southern coastline of Maui, from Kīhei at the northern end to Mākena at the southern tip. The farther south you go, the better the beaches get. Kīhei has excellent beach parks right in town, with white sand, showers, restrooms, picnic tables, and BBQs. Good snorkeling can be found along the beaches' rocky borders. As good as Kīhei is, Wailea is even better. Wailea's beaches are cleaner, facilities tidier, and views even more impressive. ⚠ **Note that break-ins have been reported at many of these beach parking lots.** As you head out to Mākena, the terrain gets wilder. Bring lunch, water, and sunscreen with you. The following South Shore beaches are listed from north Kīhei southeast to Mākena.

Kalepolepo Beach Park. This tiny spit of beach and rock is the site of the ancient Kalepolepo Village, a large settlement and the prized property of Maui's King Kamehameha in the 1850s. Here the *maka 'ānana* (commoners) tended the man-made pond, farmed, fished, and raised taro. Today the park has lots of shady trees and stays pretty quiet, making it a good getaway from the crowd and sun. However, the beach (if you can call it that) is only a small sprinkling of sand, and swimming in the often-murky waters isn't recommended. Toilets are portable. ✉ *726 S. Kīhei Rd., just south of Hawaiian Islands Humpback Whale National Marine Sanctuary* ♿ *Toilets, picnic tables, grills/firepits, parking lot.*

Waipuliani Park. Fronting the Maui Sunset Resort, Waipuliani Park is a spectacular place to lay out or picnic on golf-course-quality grass. A small beach hides behind the dunes, although it's usually speckled with seaweed and shells; swimming isn't recommended as the park is not far from a water-treatment plant. This park often hosts local activities, such as volleyball and croquet, and it attracts many dog lovers. Although it has a resort feel and can be crowded, it's still a perfect place to watch the sunset. ✉ *From S. Kīhei Rd., turn at Star Market onto W. Waipuliani Rd.* ♿ *Toilets, grills/firepits.*

Kalama Park. This 36-acre beach park is great for families and sports-lovers. With its extensive lawns and sports fields, the park has volleyball, baseball, tennis, and even a skateboard park. Stocked with grills, picnic pavilions, and plenty of shade, it's a recreational mecca. The beach itself is all but nonexistent, but swimming is fair—though you must brave the rocky steps down to the water. If you aren't completely comfortable with the rocky entrance, you're better off sticking to the burgers and Bocce Ball than venturing into the ocean. ✉ *On S. Kīhei Rd. across from Kīhei Kalama Village* ♿ *Toilets, showers, picnic tables, grills/firepits, playground.*

The Cove Beach Park. Go to the Cove if you want to learn to surf. All of the surf schools are here in the morning, pushing longboard beginners onto the bunny-slope waves. For spectators there's a grassy area with some shade, and a tiny blink of a beach. If you aren't here to learn to surf, don't bother swimming. The water is sketchy at best, and there are plenty of better beaches. ✉ *On S. Kīhei Rd., turn onto 'Ili 'Ili Rd.* ♿ *No facilities.*

Charley Young Beach. This secluded 3-acre park sits off the main drag in a residential area. The sand is soft and smooth, with a gentle slope into the ocean. A cloister of lava rocks shelters the beach from heavy afternoon winds, making this a mellow spot to laze around. The usually gentle waves make for good swimming, and you'll find good snorkeling along the rocks on the north end. Portable toilets are on-site. ✉ *From S. Kīhei Rd., turn onto Kaiau' St., just north of Kama'ole I* ♿ *Toilets, shower.*

🕐 **Kama'ole I, II, and III.** Three steps from South Kīhei Road, you can find three golden stretches of sand separated by outcroppings of dark, jagged lava rocks. You can walk the length of all three beaches if you're willing to get your feet wet. The northernmost of the trio, Kama'ole I (across from the ABC Store, in case you forgot your sunscreen), offers perfect swimming with a sandy bottom a long way out and an active volleyball court. If you're one of those people that like your beach sans sand, there's also a great lawn for you to spread out on at the south end of the beach. Kama'ole II is nearly identical minus the lawn. The last beach, the one with all the people on it, is Kama'ole III, perfect for throwing disk or throwing down a blanket. This is a great family beach, complete with a playground, volleyball net, BBQs, kite flying, and frequently, rented inflatable castles—a birthday-party must for every cool kid living on the island.

Locally known as "Kam" I, II, and III, all three beaches have great swimming and lifeguards. In the morning the water can be as still as a lap pool. Kam III offers terrific breaks for beginning bodysurfers. ■ TIP➔ The public restrooms have seen better days; decent facilities are found at convenience stores and eateries across the street. ✉ *S. Kīhei Rd.,*

BEACH SAFETY

The ocean is an amazing but formidable playground. Conditions can change quickly throughout the day. **Pay attention to any signs or flags** warning of high surf, rough currents, or jellyfish.

It's best to watch the surf for a while before entering. Notice where other people are swimming and how often swells come in. Swells arrive in sets of five or six. If you should get caught in a largish swell, **don't panic.** Take a deep breath and dive beneath each oncoming wave. When you feel comfortable, you can swim back to shore with the swell.

Remember the ocean is also home to an array of fragile marine life. **Never stand on or touch coral reefs.** Hefty fines apply to anyone who chases or grabs at turtles, dolphins, and other federally protected animals. It's wise to avoid swimming at dawn, dusk, or in murky waters.

Some general rules of thumb when beach-going:

■ Check with lifeguards on beach and surf conditions.

■ Always swim or snorkel with a buddy.

■ Never turn your back on the ocean.

■ Don't swim in murky water.

■ If the big lava-rock boulders you're about to go exploring are wet, that means a wave may wash in and knock you down.

■ When in doubt, don't go out.

between Ke Ali'i Alanui Rd. and Keonekai Rd. ⚐ *Lifeguard, toilets, showers, picnic tables, grills/firepits, playground, parking lot.*

Keawakapu Beach. Who wouldn't love Keawakapu with its long stretch of golden sand, near-perfect swimming, and stunning views of the crater? It's great fun to walk or jog this beach south into Wailea (you can go all the way to the Renaissance), as the path is lined with remarkable residences—can you guess which one belongs to Stephen King? The winds pick up in the afternoon, so beware of irritating sand storms. Keawakapu has two entrances: one at the Mana Kai Maui Resort (look for the blue SHORELINE ACCESS sign and the parking at Kilohana Street), and the second at the dead end of Kīhei Road. Toilets are portable. ⊠ *S. Kīhei Rd. at Kilohana St.* ⚐ *Toilets, showers, parking lot.*

☾ **Mōkapu & Ulua.** Look for a little road and public parking lot wedged between the first two big Wailea resorts—the Renaissance and the Marriott. This gets you to Mōkapu and Ulua beaches. Though there are no lifeguards, families love this place. Reef formations create tons of tide pools for kids to explore and the beaches are protected from major swells. Snorkeling is excellent at Ulua, the beach to the left of the entrance. Mōkapu, to the right, tends to be less crowded. ⊠ *Wailea Alanui Dr., south of Renaissance resort entrance* ⚐ *Toilets, showers, parking lot.*

Wailea Beach. A road just after the Grand Wailea Resort takes you to Wailea Beach, a wide, sandy stretch with snorkeling, swimming, and, if you're a guest of the Four Seasons Resort, Evian spritzes! If you're not a guest at the Grand Wailea or Four Seasons, the private cabanas and chaise longues can be a little annoying, but any complaint is more than made up for by the calm, unclouded waters and soft, white sand. ✉ *Wailea Alanui Dr., south of Grand Wailea Resort entrance* 👍 *Toilets, showers, parking lot.*

Polo Beach. From Wailea Beach you can walk to this small, uncrowded crescent fronting the Fairmont Kea Lani resort. Swimming and snorkeling are great here and it's a good place to whale-watch. As at Wailea Beach, private cabanas occupy prime sandy real estate, but there's plenty of room for you and your towel, and even a nice grass picnic area. The pathway connecting the two beaches is a great spot to jog or leisurely take in awesome views of nearby Molokini and Kaho'olawe. Rare native plants grow along the ocean, or *makai,* side of the path; the honey-sweet-smelling one is *naio,* or false sandalwood. ✉ *Wailea Alanui Dr., south of Fairmont Kea Lani resort entrance* ☞ *Toilets, showers, picnic tables, grills/firepits, parking lot.*

Fodor's Choice ★ **Mākena (Big Beach).** Locals successfully fought to give Mākena—one of Hawai'i's most breathtaking beaches—state-park protection. Also known as "Big Beach," this stretch of deep-golden sand abutting sparkling aqua water is 3,000-feet-long and 100-feet-wide. It's never crowded, no matter how many cars cram into the lots. The water is fine for swimming, but use caution. ⚠ **The shore drop-off is steep and swells can get deceptively big.** Despite the infamous "Mākena cloud," a blanket that rolls in during the early afternoon and obscures the sun, it rarely rains here. For a dramatic view of Big Beach, climb Pu'u Ōla'i, the steep cinder cone near the first entrance. Continue over the cinder cone's side to discover "Little Beach"—clothing-optional by popular practice. (Officially, nude sunbathing is illegal in Hawai'i.) On Sunday, free spirits of all kinds crowd Little Beach's tiny shoreline for a drumming circle and bonfire. Little Beach has the island's best bodysurfing (no pun intended). Skimboarders catch air at Big Beach's third entrance. Each of the three paved entrances has portable toilets. ✉ *Off Wailea Alanui Dr.* 👍 *Toilets, parking lot.*

THE NORTH SHORE

Many of the folks you see jaywalking in Pā'ia sold everything they owned to come to Maui and live a beach-bum's life. Beach culture abounds on the North Shore. But these folks aren't sunbathers; they're big-wave riders, windsurfers, or kiteboarders. The North Shore is their challenging sports arena. Beaches here face the open ocean and tend to be rougher and windier than beaches elsewhere on Maui—but don't let that scare you off. On calm days, the reef-speckled waters are truly beautiful and offer a quieter and less commercial beach-going experience than the leeward shore. Beaches below are listed from Kahului (near the airport) eastward to Ho'okipa.

Kanahā Beach. Windsurfers, kiteboarders, joggers, and picnicking families like this long, golden strip of sand bordered by a wide grassy area

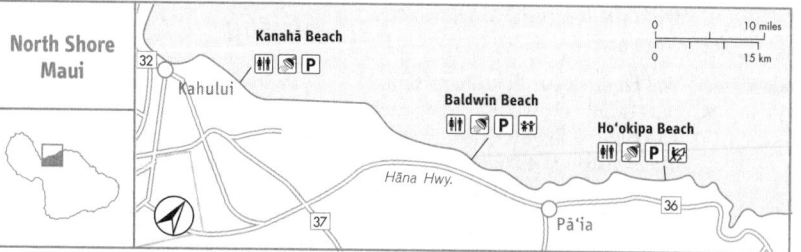

with lots of shade. The winds pick up in the early afternoon, making for the best kiteboarding and windsurfing conditions—if you know what you're doing, that is. The best spot for watching kiteboarders is at the far left end of the beach. ⊠*Drive through airport and make right onto car-rental road (Koeheke); turn right onto Amala Pl. and take any left (there are 3 entrances) into Kanahā* ♿*Toilets, showers, picnic tables, grills/firepits, parking lot.*

☾ ★ **Baldwin Beach.** A local favorite, just west of Pāʻia town, Baldwin Beach is a big stretch of comfortable white sand. This is a good place to lie out, jog, or swim, though the waves can sometimes be choppy and the undertow strong. Don't be afraid of those big brown blobs floating beneath the surface; they're just pieces of seaweed awash in the surf. You can find shade along the beach beneath the ironwood trees, or in the large pavilion, a spot regularly overtaken by local parties and community events.

The long, shallow pool at the Kahului end of the beach is known as "Baby Beach." Separated from the surf by a flat reef wall, this is where ocean-loving families bring their kids (and sometimes puppies) to practice a few laps. The view of the West Maui Mountains is hauntingly beautiful from here. ⊠*Hāna Hwy., 1 mi west of Baldwin Ave.* ♿*Lifeguard, toilets, showers, picnic tables, grills/firepits, parking lot.*

★ **Hoʻokipa Beach.** If you want to see some of the world's finest windsurfers in action, hit this beach along the Hāna Highway. The sport was largely developed right at Hoʻokipa and has become an art and a career to some. This beach is also one of Maui's hottest surfing spots, with waves as high as 20 feet. This is not a good swimming beach, nor the place to learn windsurfing, but plenty of picnic tables and BBQs are available for hanging out and watching the pros. Bust out your telephoto lens at the cliffside lookout. ⊠*2 mi past Pāʻia on Rte. 36* ♿*Toilets, showers, picnic tables, grills/firepits, parking lot.*

EAST MAUI

Hāna's beaches will literally stop you in your tracks, they're that beautiful. Black-and-red sands stand out against pewter skies and lush tropical foliage creating picture-perfect scenes, which seem too breathtaking to be real. Rough conditions often preclude swimming, but that doesn't mean you can't explore the shoreline. Beaches below are listed in order from the west end of Hāna town eastward.

Fodor's Choice
★ **Waiʻānapanapa State Park.** Small but rarely crowded, this beach will remain in your memory long after visiting. Fingers of white foam rush onto a black volcanic-pebble beach fringed with green beach vines and palms. Swimming here is both relaxing and invigorating: strong currents bump smooth stones up against your ankles while seabirds flit above a black, jagged sea arch draped with vines. At the edge of the parking lot, a sign tells you the sad story of a doomed Hawaiian

> ### THE SUN
>
> By far the biggest danger on the island is **sunburn.** The tropical sun is strong. Even at 9 AM, high SPF sunscreen—30 SPF or higher—is a must. Rash guards, those clingy-looking Lycra swim shirts, offer the best protection. Before seeking shade under a coconut palm, be aware that winds can be strong enough to knock fruit off the trees and onto your head (go ahead and giggle but this really can and does happen).

princess. Stairs lead through a tunnel of interlocking Polynesian *hau* branches to an icy cave pool—the secret hiding place of the ancient princess. ⚠ **You can swim in this pool, but be wary of mosquitoes!** In the other direction, a 3-mi, dramatic coastal path continues beyond the campground, past sea arches, blowholes, and cultural sites all the way to Hāna town. Grassy tent sites and rustic cabins that accommodate up to six people are available by reservation only; call ahead for information. ⊠ *Hāna Hwy. near mile marker 32* ☎ *808/984–8109* ⚐ *Toilets, showers, picnic tables, grills/firepits, parking lot.*

★ **Red Sand Beach (Kaihalulu Beach).** Kaihalulu Beach, better known as Red Sand Beach, is unmatched in its raw and remote beauty. It's not simple to find but when you round the last corner of the trail and are confronted with the sight of it, your jaw is bound to drop. Earthy red cliffs tower above the deep maroon–sand beach and swimmers bob about in a turquoise blue lagoon formed by volcanic boulders just offshore (it's like floating around in a giant natural bath tub). It's worth spending a night in Hāna just to make sure you can get here early and have some time to enjoy it before anyone else shows up.

Keep in mind that getting here is not easy and you have to pass through private property along the way—do so at your own risk. You need to tread carefully up and around Kaʻuiki (the red-cinder hill); the cliffside cinder path is slippery and constantly eroding. Hiking is not rec-

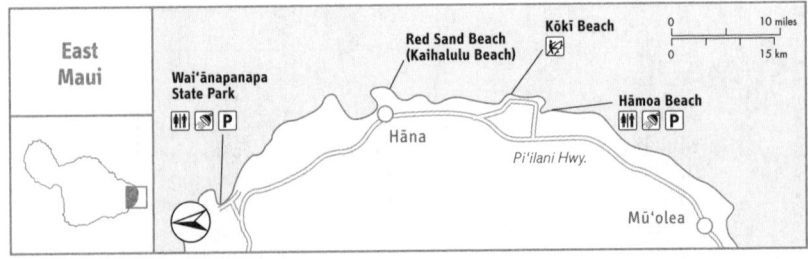

ommended in shoes without traction, or in bad weather. By popular practice, clothing on the beach is optional. ☒ *At end of Uákea Rd. past baseball field. Park near community center, walk through grass lot to trail below cemetery ⬭ No facilities.*

Kōkī Beach. You can tell from the trucks parked every which way alongside the road that this is a favorite local surf spot. ■ **TIP→Watch conditions before swimming or bodysurfing, because the riptides here can be mean.** Look for awesome views of the rugged coastline and a sea arch on the left end. *Iwa,* or white-throated frigate birds, dart like pterodactyls over 'Alau islet offshore. ☒ *Haneo'o Loop Rd., 2 mi east of Hāna town ⬭ No facilities.*

Hāmoa Beach. Why did James Michener describe this stretch of salt-and-pepper sand as the most "South Pacific" beach he'd come across, even though it's located in the North Pacific? Maybe it was the perfect half-moon shape, speckled with the shade of palm trees. Perhaps he was intrigued by the jutting black coastline, often outlined by rain showers out at sea, or the pervasive lack of hurry he felt once settled in here. Whatever it was, many still feel the lure. The beach can be crowded but nonetheless relaxing. Expect to see a few chaise longues and a guest-only picnic area set up by the Hotel Hāna-Maui. At times, the churning surf might intimidate beginning swimmers, but bodysurfing can be great here. ☒ *½ mi past Kōkī Beach on Haneo'o Loop Rd., 2 mi east of Hāna town ⬭ Toilets, showers, picnic tables, parking lot.*

Water Sports & Tours

WORD OF MOUTH

"Have some kids teach you how to really catch the waves on a boogie board . . . we had so much fun, and it was even more fun surrounded by little kids who got a kick out of us."

—turn_it_on

"Molokini snorkeling can be wonderful (though the scuba diving is even better) and what's the worst that happens if it isn't? Several hours on a catamaran enjoying beautiful views . . . what's wrong with that?" —bobludlow

Updated
by Amy
Westervelt

GETTING INTO (OR ONTO) THE water will be the highlight of your Maui trip. At Lahaina and Māʻalaea harbors you can board boats for snorkeling, scuba diving, deep-sea fishing, whale-watching, parasailing, and sunset cocktail adventures. You can learn to surf, catch a ferry to Lānaʻi, or grab a seat on a fast inflatable. Along the leeward coastline, from Kāʻanapali on the West Shore all the way down to the tip of ʻĀhihi-Kīnaʻu on the South Shore, you can discover great snorkeling and swimming. If you're a thrill-seeker, head out to the North Shore and Hoʻokipa, where surfers, kiteboarders, and windsurfers catch big waves and big air.

BOOGIE BOARDING & BODYSURFING

Bodysurfing and "sponging" (as boogie boarding is called by the regulars) are great ways to catch some waves without having to master surfing—and there's no balance or coordination required. A boogie board (or "sponge") is softer than a hard, fiberglass surfboard, which means you can ride safely in the rough-and-tumble surf zone. If you get tossed around (which is half the fun), you don't have a heavy surfboard nearby to bang your head on, but you do have something to hang onto. Serious spongers invest in a single short-clipped fin to help propel them into the wave.

HOW TO CATCH A WAVE

The technique for catching waves is the same with or without a board. Swim out to where the swell is just beginning to break, and position yourself toward shore. When the next wave comes, lie on your board (if you have one), kick like crazy, and catch it! You'll feel the push of the wave as you glide in front of the gurgling, foamy surf. When bodysurfing, put your arms over your head, bring your index fingers together (so you look like the letter 'A'), and stiffen your body like a board to achieve the same effect. If you don't like to swim too far out, stick with boogie boarding and bodysurfing close to shore. Shorebreak (if it isn't too steep) can be exhilarating to ride. You'll know it's too steep if you hear the sound of slapping when the waves hit the sand. You're looking for waves that curl over and break farther out, then roll, not slap onto the sand. Always watch first to make sure the conditions aren't too strong.

BEST SPOTS

If you don't mind nudity (officially illegal, but practiced nonetheless), **Little Beach** (⌧ *On Mākena Rd., first entrance to Mākena State Beach Park; climb rock wall at north end of beach*) is the best break on the island for boogie boarding and bodysurfing. The shape of the sandy shoreline creates waves that break a ways out and tumble on into shore. Because it's sandy, you only risk stubbing a toe on the few submerged rocks, not a reef floor. Don't even think about boogie boarding at neighboring Big Beach—you'll be slapped like a flapjack onto the steep shore.

Kama'ole III (⊠ *S. Kīhei Rd.*) is another good spot for bodysurfing and boogie boarding. It has a sandy floor, with 1- to 3-foot waves breaking not too far out. It's often crowded late into the day, especially on weekends when local kids are out of school. Don't let that chase you away; the waves are wide enough for everyone.

On the North Shore, **Pā'ia Bay** (⊠ *Just before Pā'ia town, beyond large community building and grass field*) has waves suitable for spongers and bodysurfers. ■ TIP➡Park in the public lot across the street and leave your valuables at home, as this beach is known for break-ins.

EQUIPMENT RENTAL

Most condos and hotels have boogie boards available to guests—some in better condition than others (but beat-up boogies work just as well for beginners). You can also pick up a boogie board from any discount shop, such as Kmart or Long's Drugs, for upward of $30.

Auntie Snorkel. You can rent decent boogie boards here for $5 a day, or $15 a week. ⊠ *2439 S. Kīhei Rd., Kīhei* ☎ 808/879–6263.

Honolua Surf. "Waverider" boogie boards with smooth undersides (better than the bumpy kind) can be rented from this surf shop for $8 a day, or $35 a week (with a $100 deposit). ⊠ *2411 S. Kīhei Rd., Kīhei* ☎ 808/874–0999 ⊠ *845 Front St., Lahaina* ☎ 808/661–8848.

DEEP-SEA FISHING

If fishing is your sport, Maui is your island. In these waters you'll find 'ahi, *aku* (skipjack tuna), barracuda, bonefish, *kawakawa* (bonito), mahimahi, Pacific blue marlin, ono, and *ulua* (jack crevalle). You can fish year-round and you don't need a license. ■ TIP➡Because boats fill up fast during busy seasons (Christmas, spring break, tournament weeks), consider making reservations before coming to Maui.

Plenty of fishing boats run out of Lahaina and Mā'alaea harbors. If you charter a private boat, expect to spend in the neighborhood of $600 to $800 for a thrilling half-day in the swivel seat. You can share a boat for much less if you don't mind close quarters with a stranger who may get seasick, drunk, or worse . . . lucky! Before you sign up, you should know that some boats keep the catch. They will, however, fillet a nice piece for you to take home. And if you catch a real beauty, you might even be able to have it professionally mounted.

■ TIP➡Don't go out with a boater who charges for the fish you catch— that's harbor robbery. You're expected to bring your own lunch and nonglass beverages. (Shop the night before; it's hard to find snacks at 6 AM.) Boats supply coolers, ice, and bait. A 10% to 20% tip is suggested.

BOATS & CHARTERS

★ **Finest Kind Inc.** A record 1,118-pound Blue Marlin was reeled in by the crew aboard *Finest Kind*, a lovely 37-foot Merritt kept so clean you'd never guess the action it's seen. Ask Captain Dave about his pet frigate bird—he's been around these waters long enough to befriend other expert fishers.

> **TAKE NOTE**
>
> The 'Āhihi-Kīna'u Natural Area Reserve at the southernmost point of South Maui is closed to commercial traffic and you may not take rented kayaks into the reserve.

This family-run company operates four boats and specializes in live bait. ⊠*Lahaina Harbor, Slip 7* ☎*808/661–0338.*

Hinatea Sportfishing. The active crew aboard this first-class, 41-foot Hatteras has the motto, "No boat rides here—we go to catch fish!" For those conservation-minded folks, Hinatea has tagged and released more marlin than any charter boat on Maui. ⊠*Lahaina Harbor, Slip 27* ☎*808/667–7548* ⊕*www.fishmaui.com/hinatea.*

Iwa Lele Extreme Sportfishing. If you're serious about catching fish, and don't mind the 4:30 AM check-in time, this trip's for you. On a 39-foot custom Force, Captain Fuzzy will get you to the best fishing spots before the masses. You'll troll with lures and live bait—and hopefully, catch the big one. Check out their Web site for good fishing FAQs. ⊠*Lahaina Harbor* ☎*808/661–1118* ⊕*www.fishmaui.com.*

Start Me Up Sportfishing. These 42-foot Bertram Sportfishers will give you one of the most comfortable fishing trips around. With 20 years in business, Start Me Up has a fleet of five boats, all relatively new, complete with all the amenities: air-conditioning, TV, VCR, refrigerator, microwave, and ice chest. They provide the tackle and equipment. Six-person max. ⊠*Lahaina Harbor, Slip 12* ☎*808/667–7879* ⊕*www.startmeupsportfishing.com.*

Strike Zone. This is one of the few charters to offer morning bottom-fishing trips (for smaller fish such as snapper), as well as deep-sea trips (for the big ones—ono, 'ahi, mahimahi, and marlin). *Strike Zone* is a 43-foot Delta that offers plenty of room (16-person max). Lunch and soft drinks are included, and on bottom-fishing you can keep your catch. The cost is $168 per adult and $148 per child for a pole; spectators can ride for $78, plus 7% tax. There is also an afternoon bottom-fishing trip available on *Strike Zone,* which lasts four hours and costs $128 plus tax per person. The six- and four-hour bottom-fishing trips run Monday, Wednesday, Friday, and Saturday; the six-hour deep-sea trips run Tuesday, Thursday, and Sunday. All trips leave at 6:30 AM. ⊠*Mā'alaea Harbor, Slip 64, Mā'alaea* ☎*808/879–4485.*

KAYAKING

Kayaking is a fantastic way to experience Maui's coast up close. Floating aboard a "plastic popsicle stick" is easier than you might think, and allows you to cruise out to vibrant, living coral reefs and waters where dolphins and even whales roam. Kayaking can be a leisurely paddle or a challenge of heroic proportions, depending on your ability, the location, and the weather. ■TIP➔**Though you can rent kayaks independently, we recommend taking a guide.** An apparently calm surface can hide extremely strong ocean currents—and you don't *really* want to take an unplanned trip to Tahiti! Most guides are naturalists who will steer you away from surging surf, lead you to pristine reefs, and point out camouflaged fish, like the stalking hawkfish. Not having to schlep your gear on top of your rental car is a bonus. A half-day tour runs around $75. Custom tours can be arranged.

CANOE RACES

Polynesians first traveled to Hawai'i by outrigger canoe, and racing the traditional craft is a favorite pastime on the Islands. Canoes were revered in old Hawai'i, and no voyage began without a blessing, ceremonial chanting, and a hula performance to ensure a safe journey. In Lahaina in mid-May, the two-week **Festival of Canoes** (☎ *808/667–9193* ⊕ *www.visitlahaina.com*) includes a torch-lighting ceremony, arts-and-crafts demonstrations, a chance for canoe enthusiasts to observe how Polynesian vessels are rigged, and the launching of a "Parade of Canoes."

If you decide to strike out on your own, tour companies will rent kayaks for the day with paddles, life vests, and roof racks, and many will meet you near your chosen location. Ask for a map of good entries and plan to avoid paddling back to shore against the wind (schedule extra time for the return trip regardless). When you're ready to snorkel, secure your belongings in a dry pack onboard and drag your boat by its bowline behind you. (This isn't as bad as it sounds.)

BEST SPOTS

In West Maui, past the steep cliffs on the Honoapi'ilani Highway and before you hit Lahaina, there's a long stretch of inviting coastline, including **Ukumehame** (⊠ *Between mile markers 12 and 14 on Rte. 30*) and **Olowalu** beaches. This is a good spot for beginners; entry is easy and there's much to see in every direction. If you want to snorkel, the best visibility is farther out at Olowalu, at about 25 feet depth. ⚠ **Watch for sharp** *kiawe* **thorns buried in the sand on the way into the water.**

Mākena Landing (⊠ *Off Mākena Rd.*) is an excellent taking-off point for a South Maui adventure. Enter from the paved parking lot or the small sandy beach a little south. The bay itself is virtually empty, but the right edge is flanked with brilliant coral heads and juvenile turtles. If you round the point on the right, you come across **Five Caves,** a system of enticing underwater arches. In the morning you may see dolphins, and the arches are havens for lobsters, eels, and spectacularly hued butterfly fish. Check out the million-dollar mansions lining the shoreline and guess which celebrity lives where.

EQUIPMENT RENTAL & TOURS

Maui Sea Kayaking. Since 1988, this company has been guiding small groups (four-person trips) to secret spots along Maui's coast. They take great care in customizing their outings. For example, the guides accommodate kayakers with disabilities as well as senior kayakers, and they offer kid-size gear. For paddlers looking to try something new, they also offer kayak surfing. Trips leave from various locations, depending upon the weather. ☎ *808/572-6299 ⊕ www.maui.net/~kayaking.*

Fodor's Choice **South Pacific Kayaks.** These guys pioneered recreational kayaking on
★ Maui—they know their stuff. Guides are friendly, informative, and eager to help you get the most out of your experience; we're talking true, fun-loving, kayak geeks. Some activity companies show a strange lack of care for the marine environment; South Pacific stands out as adventurous *and* responsible. They offer a variety of trips leaving from both West Maui and South Shore locations, including an advanced four-hour "Molokini Challenge." ☎ *800/776-2326 or 808/875-4848 ⊕ www.southpacifickayaks.com.*

> ### ON THE SIDELINES
>
> If you're not inclined to take to the air yourself, live vicariously by attending **Red Bull's King of the Air** (⊠ *Ho'okipa Beach Park* ☎ *808/573-3222 ⊕ www.red-bullkingoftheair.com*) showcase contest each fall. Contenders travel from as far as Poland and Norway to compete in this world-class big air and freestyle kiteboarding contest.

KITEBOARDING

Catapulting up to 40 feet in the air above the breaking surf, kiteboarders hardly seem of this world. Silken kites hold the athletes aloft for precious seconds—long enough for the execution of mind-boggling tricks—then deposit them back in the sea. This new sport is not for the weak-kneed. No matter what people might tell you, it's harder to learn than windsurfing. The unskilled (or unlucky) can be caught in an upwind and carried far out in the ocean, or worse—dropped smack on the shore. Because of insurance (or the lack thereof), companies are not allowed to rent equipment. Beginners must take lessons, and then purchase their own gear. Devotees swear that after your first few lessons, committing to buying your kite is easy.

EQUIPMENT RENTAL & LESSONS

Aqua Sports Maui. "To air is human," or so they say at Aqua Sports, which calls itself the local favorite of kiteboarding schools. They've got a great location right near Kite Beach, at the west (left) end of Kanahā Beach, and offer basic through advanced kiteboarding lessons. Rates start at $210 for a three-hour basics course taught by certified instructors. ⊠*90 Amala Pl., near Kite Beach, Kahului* ☎*808/242–8015* ⊕*www.mauikiteboardinglessons.com.*

Hawaiian Sailboarding Techniques. Pro kiteboarder and legendary windsurfer Alan Cadiz will have you safely ripping in no time at lower Kanahā Beach Park. A "Learn to Kitesurf" package starts at $225 for a three-hour private lesson, which includes all equipment. HST is in the highly regarded Hi Tech Surf & Sports store, located in the Triangle Square shopping center. ⊠*425 Koloa St., Kahului* ☎*808/871–5423 or 800/968–5423* ⊕*www.hstwindsurfing.com.*

Kiteboarding School Maui. Call KSM, one of the first kiteboarding schools in the United States and the first on Maui, for one-on-one "flight lessons." Pro kiteboarders will induct you at Kite Beach, at the west (left) end of Kanahā Beach, providing instruction, equipment, snacks, and FAA guidelines. (Seriously, there are rules about avoiding airplanes at nearby Kahului Airport.) Rates start at $290 for four hours or $490 for two-day private lessons. KSM is the only school that offers retail gear as well as instruction. ⊠*22 Hāna Hwy., Kahului* ☎*808/873–0015* ⊕*www.ksmaui.com.*

PARASAILING

Parasailing is an easy, exhilarating way to earn your wings: just strap on a harness attached to a parachute, and a powerboat pulls you up and over the ocean from a launching dock or a boat's platform. ■ TIP→ Keep in mind, parasailing is limited to West Maui, and "thrill craft"—including parasails—are prohibited in Maui waters during humpback whale–calving season, December 15 to April 15.

LESSONS

West Maui Parasail. Launch 400 feet above the ocean for a bird's-eye view of Lahaina, or be daring at 800 feet for smoother rides and better views. The captain will be glad to let you experience a "toe dip" or "freefall" if you request it. For safety reasons, passengers weighing less than 100 pounds must be strapped together in tandem. Hour-long trips departing from Lahaina Harbor, Slip #15, include 8- to 10-minute flights and run from $60 for the 400-foot ride to $68 for the 800-foot ride. Observers must pay $30 each. ☎*808/661–4060* ⊕*www.westmauiparasail.com.*

UFO Parasail. UFO is the only parasail company allowed to take off from Kā'anapali Beach. They offer the standard 7-minute ride at 400 feet ($60), or 10-minute ride at 800 feet ($70). Observers are welcome aboard. Be prepared for lots of jokes about alien abduction. ☎*808/661–7836* ⊕*www.ufoparasailing.com.*

RAFTING

The high-speed, inflatable rafts you find on Maui are nothing like the raft that Huck Finn used to drift down the Mississippi. While passengers grip straps, these rafts fly, skimming and bouncing across the sea. Because they're so maneuverable, they go where the big boats can't—secret coves, sea caves, and remote beaches. Two-hour trips run around $50, half-day trips upward of $100. ■TIP➜**Although safe, these trips are not for the faint of heart. If you have back or neck problems or are pregnant, you should reconsider this activity.**

TOURS

Blue Water Rafting. One of the only ways to get to the stunning Kanaio Coast (the roadless southern coastline beyond ʻĀhihi-Kīnaʻu), this rafting tour begins trips conveniently at the Kīhei boat ramp. Dolphins, turtles, and other marine life are the highlight of this adventure, along with sea caves, lava arches, and views of Haleakalā. Two-hour trips start at $45 plus tax; longer trips cost $90 to $115 and include a deli lunch. ✉*7777 South Kīhei Rd., Kīhei* ☎*808/879–7238* ⊕*www.bluewaterrafting.com.*

Ocean Riders. This West Maui tour crosses the ʻAuʻAu channel to Lānaʻi's Shipwreck Beach, then circles the island for 70 minutes of remote coast. For snorkeling, the "back side" of Lānaʻi is one of Hawaiʻi's unsung marvels. Tours—$115 plus tax per person—depart from Mala Wharf, at the northern end of Front Street and include snorkel gear, a fruit breakfast, and a deli lunch. ✉*Lahaina* ☎*808/661–3586* ⊕*www.mauioceanriders.com.*

SAILING

With the islands of Molokaʻi, Lānaʻi, Kahoʻolawe, and Molokini a stone's throw away, Maui waters offer visually arresting backdrops for sailing adventures. Sailing conditions can be fickle, so some operations throw in snorkeling or whale-watching, and others offer sunset cruises. Winds are consistent in summer, but variable in winter, and afternoons are generally windier all throughout the year. Prices range from around $40 for two-hour trips to $80 for half-day excursions. ■TIP➜**You won't be sheltered from the elements on the trim racing boats, so be sure to bring a hat (one that won't blow away), a light jacket or cover-up, sunglasses, and extra sunscreen.**

BOATS & CHARTERS

America II. This one-time America's Cup contender offers an exciting, intimate alternative to crowded catamarans. For fast action, try a morning trade-wind sail. Sunset sails are generally calmer—a good choice if you don't want to spend two hours fully exposed to the sun. Plan to bring a change of clothes, because you will get wet. ✉*Harbor Slip #6, Lahaina* ☎*808/667–2195* ⊕*www.sailingonmaui.com.*

Paragon. If you want to snorkel and sail, this is your boat. Many snorkel cruises claim to sail but actually motor most of the way; Paragon is an exception. Both Paragon vessels (one catamaran in Lahaina, the other in Māʻalaea) are ship-shape, and crews are competent and friendly. Their mooring in Molokini Crater is particularly good, and they often stay after the masses have left. The Lānaʻi trip includes a picnic lunch on the beach, snorkeling, and an afternoon blue water swim. Extras on their trips to Lānaʻi include mai tais and sodas, hot and cold *pūpū* (Hawaiian tapas), and champagne. ⊠ *Lahaina and Māʻalaea Harbors* ☎ *808/244–2087 or 800/441–2087* ⊕ *www.sailmaui.com.*

Scotch Mist Charters. Follow the wind aboard this 50-foot Santa Cruz sailing yacht. Three-hour snorkeling, sunset, or

> **PRIVATE CHARTERS**
>
> Hiring a private charter will cost you more, but it's one way to avoid crowds. Although almost all sailing vessels (including those in this section) offer private charters, a few cater to them specifically. Among the top three: *Shangri-La* (☎ *888/855–9977* ⊕ *www.sailingmaui.com*) is the largest and most luxurious 65-foot catamaran. *Island Star* (☎ *888/677–7238* ⊕ *www.islandstarsailing.com*) is a 57-foot Columbia offering customized trips out of Lahaina. *Cinderella* (☎ *808/244–0009* ⊕ *www.maui.net/~sailmaui*) is a swift and elegant 50-foot Columbia.

whale-watching trips focus on the sail, and usually carry less than 25 passengers. ⊠ *Lahaina Harbor Slip #2* ☎ *808/661–0386* ⊕ *www.scotchmistsailingcharters.com.*

SCUBA DIVING

Maui is just as scenic underwater as it is on dry land. In fact, Maui has been rated one of the top 10 dive spots in North America. A big advantage on Maui is that divers see more large animals than they would in areas such as the Caribbean. It's common on any dive to see huge sea turtles, eagle rays, and small reef sharks, not to mention many varieties of angelfish, parrotfish, eels, and octopi. Unlike other popular dive destinations, most of the species are unique to this area. For example, of Maui's 450 species of reef fish, 25% are endemic to the island. In addition, the terrain itself is different from other dive spots. Here you'll find ancient and intricate lava flows full of nooks where marine life hide and breed. Although the water tends to be a bit rougher—not to mention colder—here, divers are given a great thrill during humpback-whale season, when you can actually hear whales singing underwater.

Some of the finest diving spots in all of Hawaiʻi lie along the Valley Isle's western and southwestern shores. Dives are best in the morning, when visibility can hold a steady 100 feet. If you're a certified diver, you can rent gear at any Maui dive shop simply by showing your PADI or NAUI card. Unless you're familiar with the area, however, it's probably best to hook up with a dive shop for an underwater tour. Tours include tanks and weights and start around $130. Wetsuits and BCs are rented separately, for an additional $15 to $30. Shops also

DIVING 101

If you've always wanted gills, Hawai'i is a good place to get them. Although the bulky, heavy equipment seems freakish on shore, underwater it allows you to move about freely, almost weightlessly. As you descend into another world, you slowly grow used to the sound of your own breathing and the strangeness of being able to do so 30-plus feet down.

Most resorts offer introductory dive lessons in their pools, which allow you to acclimate to the awkward breathing apparatus before venturing out into the great blue. If you aren't starting from a resort pool, no worries. Most intro dives take off from calm, sandy beaches, such as Ulua or Kā'anapali. If you're bitten by the deep-sea bug and want to continue diving, you should get certified. Only

certified divers can rent equipment or go on more adventurous dives, such as night dives, open-ocean dives, and cave dives.

There are several certification companies, including PADI, NAUI, and SSI. PADI, the largest, is the most comprehensive. Once you begin your certification process, stick with the same company. The dives you log will not apply to another company's certification. (Dives with a PADI instructor, for instance, will not count toward SSI certification.) Remember that you will not be able to fly or go to the airy summit of Haleakalā within 24 hours of diving. Open-water certification will take three to four days and cost around $350. From that point on, the sky . . . or rather, the sea's the limit!

offer introductory dives ($100 to $160) for those who aren't certified.
■ TIP→Before signing on with any of these outfitters, it's a good idea to ask a few pointed questions about your guide's experience, the weather outlook, and the condition of the equipment.

Before you head out on your dive, be sure to check conditions. If you have access to the Internet, check the Glenn James weather site, ⊕*www.hawaiiweathertoday.com*, for a breakdown on the weather, wind, and visibility conditions.

BEST SPOTS

Honolua Bay (⊠*Between mile markers 32 and 33 on Rte. 30, look for narrow dirt road to left*) has beach entry. This West Maui marine preserve is alive with many varieties of coral and tame tropical fish, including large *ulua*, *kāhala*, barracuda, and manta rays. With depths of 20 to 50 feet, this is a popular summer dive spot, good for all levels.
■ TIP→High surf often prohibits winter dives.

Only 3 mi offshore, **Molokini Crater** is world renowned for its deep, crystal-clear, fish-filled waters. A crescent-shape islet formed by the eroding top of a volcano, the crater is a marine preserve ranging 10 to 80 feet in depth. The numerous tame fish and brilliant coral dwelling within the crater make it a popular introductory dive site. On calm days, the back side of Molokini (called Back Wall) can be a dramatic sight for advanced divers—giving them visibility of up to 150 feet. The enormous dropoff into the 'Alalākeiki Channel (to 350 feet) offers awesome seascapes, black coral, and chance sightings of larger pelagic fish and sharks.

On the South Shore, a popular dive spot is **Mākena Landing,** also called **Five Graves** or **Five Caves.** About 1/5 mi down Mākena Road, you'll feast on underwater delights—caves, ledges, coral heads, and an outer reef home to a large green-sea-turtle colony (called "Turtle Town"). ⚠ **Entry is rocky lava, so be careful where you step.** This area is for the more experienced diver. Rookies can enter farther down Mākena Road at Mākena Landing, and dive to the right.

South of Mākena Landing, the best diving by far is at 'Āhihi Bay and La Pérouse Bay, both South Maui marine preserves. In **'Āhihi Bay,** you'll find an area the locals call **Fishbowl,** which is a small cove right beside the road, next to a hexagon-shape house. Here you'll find excellent underwater scenery, with many types of fish and coral. ⚠ **Be careful of the rocky bottom entry (wear reef shoes if you have them).** This area can get crowded, especially in high season. If you want to steer clear of the crowds, look for a second entry ½ mi farther down the road—a gravel parking lot at the surf spot called **Dumps.** Entry into the Bay here is more tricky, as the coastline is all lava.

La Pérouse Bay, formed from the last lava flow 20 years ago, brings you the best variety of fish—more than any other site. The lava rock provides a protective habitat, and all four types of Hawai'i's angelfish can be found here. To dive the spot called **Pinnacles,** enter anywhere along the shore, just past the private entrance to the beach. Again, wear your reef shoes, as entry is sharp. To the right, you'll be in the marine reserve; to the left, you're outside. Look for the white, sandy bottom with massive coral heads. Pinnacles is for experienced divers only.

EQUIPMENT RENTAL & DIVE TOURS

★ **Ed Robinson's Diving Adventures.** Ed wrote the book, literally, on Molokini. Because he knows so much, he includes a "Biology 101" talk with every dive. An expert marine photographer, he offers diving instruction and boat charters to South Maui, the backside of Molokini, and Lāna'i. Weekly night dives are available, and there's a 10% discount if you book three or more days. Check out the Web site for good info and links on scuba sites, weather, and sea conditions. ✉ *50 Koki St., Kīhei* ☎ *808/879–3584 or 800/635–1273* ⊕ *www.mauiscuba.com.*

Lahaina Divers. With more than 25 years of diving experience, this West Maui shop offers tours of Maui, Molokini, and Lāna'i. Big charter boats (which can be crowded, with up to 30 passengers per boat) leave daily for Molokini crater, Back Wall, Lāna'i, Turtle Reef, and more. A continental breakfast and deli lunch are included. Rates range from $109 to $189. For less experienced divers, they offer a "Discover Scuba" lesson daily. ✉ *143 Dickenson St., Lahaina* ☎ *808/667–7496 or 800/998–3483* ⊕ *www.lahainadivers.com.*

Maui Dive Shop. With six locations island-wide, Maui Dive Shop offers scuba charters, diving instruction, and equipment rental. Excursions, offering awe-inspiring beach and boat dives, go to Molokini Back

Wall (most advanced dive), Shipwreck Beach on Lānaʻi, and more. Night dives and customized trips are available, as are full SSI and PADI certificate programs. ✉ *1455 S. Kīhei Rd., Kīhei* ☎ *808/879–3388 or 800/542–3483* ⊕ *www.mauidiveshop.com.*

Mike Severns Diving. Mike takes small groups of certified divers to both popular and off-the-beaten-path dive sites. Boat trips leave from Kīhei Boat Ramp, and go wherever conditions are best: the Marine Life Conservation District, Molokini's Backwall, St. Anthony shipwreck, Mākena, La Pérouse, or the Kanaio Coast. You're free to have a guide during your dive, or go into the depths alone. ✉ *Box 627, Kīhei* ☎ *808/879–6596* ⊕ *www.mikesevernsdiving.com.*

Shaka Divers. Shaka provides personalized dives including a great four-hour intro dive ($89), a refresher course ($79), scuba certification ($375), and shore dives ($59) to Mākena, Ulua, Five Graves (at Mākena Landing), Turtle Town, Bubble Cave, Black Sand Beach, and more. Typical dives last about an hour, with 30 to 45 feet visibility. Dives can be booked on short notice, with afternoon tours available (hard to find on Maui). Shaka also offers night dives, torpedo scooter dives, and "bug hunt" expeditions (lobster hunts). Look for the Scuba Bus, blowing bubbles as it drives down the road. ✉ *24 Hakoi Pl., Kīhei* ☎ *808/250–1234* ⊕ *www.shakadivers.com.*

SNORKELING

No one should leave Maui without ducking underwater to meet a sea turtle, moray eel, or Humuhumunukunukuāpuaʻa—the state fish. Visibility is best in the morning, before the wind picks up.

There are two ways to approach snorkeling—by land or by sea. Daily around 7 AM, a parade of boats heads out to Lānaʻi or Molokini Crater, that ancient cone of volcanic cinder off the coast of Wailea. Boat trips offer some advantages—deeper water, seasonal whale-watching, crew assistance, lunch, and gear. But you don't need a boat; much of Maui's best snorkeling is found just steps from the road. Nearly the entire leeward coastline from Kapalua south to ʻĀhihi-Kīnaʻu offers prime opportunities to ogle fish and turtles. If you're patient and sharp-eyed, you may glimpse eels, octopi, lobsters, eagle rays, and even a rare shark or monk seal.

BEST SPOTS

Snorkel sites here are listed from north to south, starting at the northwest corner of the island.

On the west side of the island, just north of Kapalua, **Honolua Bay** (✉ *Between mile markers 32 and 33 on Rte. 30, dirt road to left*) Marine Life Conservation District has a superb reef for snorkeling. When conditions are calm, it's one of the island's best spots with tons of fish and colorful corals to observe. ■TIP→**Make sure to bring a fish key with you, as you're sure to see many species of triggerfish, filefish, and wrasses.** The coral formations on the right side of the bay are particularly dramatic and feature pink, aqua, and orange varieties. Take care entering the water; there's no beach and the rocks and concrete ramp can be slippery.

The northeast corner of this windward-facing bay periodically gets hammered by big waves in winter, and high-profile surf contests are held here. Avoid the bay then, and after a heavy rain (you'll know because Honolua stream will be running across the access path).

> ### OCEAN ETIQUETTE
>
> "Look, don't touch," is a good motto in the ocean where many creatures don't mind company, but may reveal hidden stingers if threatened. One more warning: Never stand or bump against coral. Touching it—even briefly—can kill the delicate creatures residing within the hard shell.

4

Just minutes south of Honolua, dependable **Kapalua Bay** (⊠ *From Rte. 30, turn onto Kapalua Pl., and walk through tunnel*) beckons. As beautiful above the water as it is below, Kapalua is exceptionally calm, even when other spots get testy. Needle and butterfly fish dart just past the sandy beach, which is why it's sometimes crowded. ⚠ **Sand can be particularly hot here; watch your toes!**

Fodor'sChoice We think **Black Rock** (⊠ *In front of Kā'anapali Sheraton Maui,*
★ *Kā'anapali Pkwy.*), at the northernmost tip of Kā'anapali Beach, is tops for snorkelers of any skill level. The entry couldn't be easier—dump your towel on the sand in front of the Sheraton Maui resort and in you go. Beginners can stick close to shore and still see lots of action. Advanced snorkelers can swim beyond the sand to the tip of Black Rock, or Keka'a Point, to see larger fish and eagle rays. One of the underwater residents, a turtle named "Volkswagen" for its hefty size, can be found here. He sits very still; you must look closely. Equipment can be rented on-site. Parking, in a small lot adjoining the hotel, is the only hassle.

Along Honoapi'ilani Highway (Route 30) there are several favorite snorkel sites including the area just out from the cemetery at **Hanakao'o Beach Park** (⊠ *Near mile marker 23 on Rte. 30*). At depths of 5 and 10 feet, you can see a variety of corals, especially as you head south toward **Waihikuli Wayside Park.** Farther down the highway, the shallow coral reef at **Olowalu** (⊠ *South of Olowalu General Store on Rte. 30, at mile marker 14*) is good for a quick underwater tour, though the best spot is a ways out, at depths of 25 feet or more. Closer to shore, the visibility can be hit or miss, but if you're willing to venture out about 50 yards, you'll have easy access to an expansive coral reef with abundant fish life—no boat required. Swim offshore toward the pole sticking out of the reef. Except for during a south swell, this area is calm and good for families with small children; turtles are plentiful. Boats sometimes stop nearby (they refer to this site as "Coral Gardens") on their return trip from Molokini.

Excellent snorkeling is found down the coastline between Kīhei and Mākena. The best spots are along the rocky fringes of Wailea's beaches,

TIPS ON SAFE SNORKELING

■ Snorkel with a buddy and stay together.

■ Choose a location where lifeguards are present.

■ Ask the lifeguard about conditions, especially currents, before getting in the water.

■ Plan your entry and exit points prior to getting in the water.

■ Swim into the current on entering and then ride the current back to your exit point.

■ Pop your head above the water periodically to ensure you aren't drifting too far out, or too close to rocks.

■ Think of the ocean as someone else's home—don't take anything that doesn't belong to you, or leave any trash behind.

■ Wear a rash guard; it will keep you from being fried by the sun.

■ When in doubt, don't go without a snorkeling professional; try a guided tour.

Mōkapu, Ulua, Wailea, and **Polo,** off Wailea Alanui Drive. Find one of the public parking lots sandwiched between Wailea's luxury resorts, and enjoy these beaches' sandy entries, calm waters with relatively good visibility, and variety of fish species. Of the four beaches, Ulua has the best reef. You can glimpse a box-shape puffer fish here, and listen to snapping shrimp and parrot fish nibbling on coral.

At the very southernmost tip of paved road in South Maui lies **'Āhihi-Kīna'u** (⊠ *Just before end of Mākena Alanui Rd., follow marked trails through trees*) Natural Area Reserve, also referred to as La Pérouse Bay. Despite its barren, lava-scorched landscape, the area recently gained such popularity with adventurers and activity purveyors that it had to be closed to commercial traffic. A ranger is stationed at the parking lot to assist visitors. It's difficult terrain and sometimes crowded, but if you make use of the rangers' suggestions (stay on marked paths, wear sturdy shoes to hike in and out), you can experience some of the reserve's outstanding treasures, such as the sheltered cove known as the "Fish Bowl." ■ TIP➔ Be sure to bring water: this is a hot and unforgiving wilderness.

SNORKEL TOURS

The same boats that offer whale-watching, sailing, and diving also offer snorkeling excursions. Trips usually include visits to two locales, lunch, gear, instruction, and possible whale or dolphin sightings. Some captains troll for fish along the way, and, if they're lucky, will occasionally catch big game fish such as a marlin or mahimahi.

Molokini Crater, a moon-shape crescent about 3 mi off the shore of Wailea, is the most popular snorkel cruise destination. You can spend half a day floating above the fish-filled crater for about $80. Some say it's not as good as it's made out to be, and that it's too crowded, but others consider it to be one of the best spots in Hawai'i. Visibility is generally outstanding and fish are incredibly tame. Your second stop will be somewhere along the leeward coast, either "Turtle Town" near

Mākena or "Coral Gardens" toward Lahaina. ■TIP→Be aware that on blustery mornings, there's a good chance the waters will be too rough to moor in Molokini and you'll end up snorkeling some place off the shore, which you could have driven to for free. For the safety of everyone on the boat, it's the captain's prerogative to choose the best spot for the day.

If you've tried snorkeling and are tentatively thinking about scuba, you may want to try *snuba*, a cross between the two. With snuba, you dive down 20 feet below the surface, only you're attached to an air hose from the boat. Many of the boats now offer snuba as well as snorkeling; expect to pay between $45 and $65 in addition to the regular cost of a snorkel cruise.

Snorkel cruises vary slightly—some serve mai tais and steaks whereas others offer beer and cold cuts. You might prefer a large ferry boat to a smaller sailboat, or vice versa. Whatever trip you choose, be sure you know where to go to board your vessel; getting lost in the harbor at 6 AM is a lousy start to a good day. ■TIP→Bring sunscreen, an underwater camera (they're double the price on board), a towel, and a cover-up for the windy return trip. Even tropical waters get chilly after hours of swimming, so consider wearing a rash guard. Wetsuits can usually be rented for a fee. Hats without straps will blow away, and valuables should be left at home.

★ **Ann Fielding's Snorkel Maui.** For a personal introduction to Maui's undersea universe, this guided tour is the undisputable authority. A marine biologist, Fielding—formerly with the University of Hawai'i, Waikīkī Aquarium, and the Bishop Museum, and the author of several guides to island sea life—is the Carl Sagan of Hawai'i's reef cosmos. She'll not only show you fish, but she'll also introduce you to *individual* fish. This is a good first experience for dry-behind-the-ears types. Snorkel trips include a snack and equipment. Groups travel to snorkel sites by car, not boat. ☎808/572–8437⊕*www.maui.net/~annf.*

Mahana Na'ia. This comfortable catamaran offers a value snorkel trip to Molokini ($85/adult, $60/child). Although marketed as a sailboat, it rarely hoists its sails. The crew works hard to make up for a lackluster boat, providing good service and food on the cruise. Coffee and continental breakfast greet you at the dock, and beer and wine are served with rotisserie chicken and salad for lunch. ⊠*Mā'alaea Harbor Slip* #47☎866/871–6284⊕*www.maui-snorkeling-adventures.com.*

Maui Classic Charters. This company offers two top-rate snorkel trips at a good value. Hop aboard the *Four Winds II,* a 55-foot, glass-bottom catamaran, for one of the most dependable snorkel trips around. You'll spend more time than the other charter boats do at Molokini and enjoy turtle-watching on the way home. The trip includes optional snuba ($49 extra), continental breakfast, and a deluxe barbecue lunch, beer, wine, and soda. For a faster ride, try the *Maui Magic,* Mā'alaea's fastest power cat. This boat takes fewer people (45 max) than some of the larger vessels, and as an added bonus, they offer snuba and play Hawaiian music on the ride. This one's good for kids. Book online at least 7 days in advance for a 15% discount. ⊠*Mā'alaea Harbor Slips*

#55 and #80 ☎808/879–8188 or 800/736–5740 ⊕www.mauicharters. com.

Maui–Moloka'i Sea Cruises. If you're a landlubber who'd still like to see the sea, book a passage on the 92-foot *Prince Kuhio,* one of the largest air-conditioned cruise vessels in Maui waters. In addition to a deli-style lunch and open bar, they offer snuba, snorkeling, and complimentary transportation to the harbor, which relieves you from parking and searching for the boat's slip at 7 AM. ⊠ *Ma'alaea Harbor ☎808/242–8777 or 800/468–1287 ⊕www.mvprince.com.*

☺ ★ **Pacific Whale Foundation.** The knowledgeable folks here will treat you to a Molokini adventure like the others, only with a more ecological bent. Accordingly, they serve Gardenburgers alongside the requisite barbecue chicken, and their fleet runs on bona-fide biodiesel. This is an A-plus trip for kids: the crew assists with an onboard junior naturalist program and throws in a free wildlife guide and poster. The multi-hulled boats are smooth and some have swim on–off platforms. Best of all, a portion of the profits goes to protecting the very treasures you're paying to enjoy. ⊠ *At Ma'alaea Harbor, check-in at Pacific Whale Foundation shop in the Harbor Shops at Ma'alaea; at Lahaina Harbor, check-in at Pacific Whale Foundation shop at 612 Front St. ☎800/942–5311 or 808/249–8811 ⊕www.pacificwhale.org.*

Paragon. With this company, you get to snorkel and sail—they have some of the fastest vessels in the state. As long as conditions are good, you'll hit prime snorkel spots in Molokini, Lāna'i, and occasionally, Coral Gardens. The Lāna'i trip includes a continental breakfast, a picnic lunch on the beach, snacks, open bar, a snorkel lesson, and plenty of time in the water. The friendly crew takes good care of you, making sure you get the most value and enjoyment from your trip. ⊠ *Ma'alaea Harbor Slip #72, or Lahaina Harbor ☎808/244–2087 ⊕www.sail-maui.com.*

Trilogy Excursions. The longest-running operation on Maui is the Coon family's Trilogy Excursions. In terms of comprehensive offerings, this company's got it: they have six beautiful multi-hulled sailing vessels (though they usually only sail for a brief portion of the trip) at three departure sites. All excursions are manned by energetic crews who will keep you entertained with stories of the islands and plenty of corny jokes. A full-day catamaran cruise to Lāna'i includes continental breakfast and a deli lunch on board, a guided van tour of the island, a "Snorkeling 101" class, and time to snorkel in the waters of Lāna'i's Hulopo'e Marine Preserve (Trilogy has exclusive commercial access). There is a barbecue dinner on Lāna'i and an optional dolphin safari. The company also offers a Molokini and Honolua Bay snorkel cruise. Many people consider a Trilogy excursion the highlight of their trip—but if you're not a good "group activity" person, or if you are looking to really sail, there may be better options for you. ⊠ *Ma'alaea Harbor Slip #99, or Lahaina Harbor ☎808/661–4743 or 888/225–6284 ⊕www.sailtrilogy.com.*

EQUIPMENT RENTAL

Most hotels and vacation rentals offer free use of snorkel gear. Beach-side stands fronting the major resort areas rent equipment by the hour or day. ■TIP➔**Don't shy away from asking for instructions; a snug fit makes all the difference in the world. A mask fits if it sticks to your face when you inhale deeply through your nose. Fins should cover your entire foot (unlike diving fins, which strap around your heel).** If you're squeamish about using someone else's gear (or need a prescription lens), pick up your own at any discount shop. Costco and Long's Drugs have better prices than ABC stores; dive shops have superior equipment.

Maui Dive Shop. You can rent pro gear (including optical masks, boo-gie boards, and wet suits) from six locations island-wide. Pump these guys for weather info before heading out—they'll know better than last night's news forecaster, and they'll give you the real deal on condi-tions. ⊠*1455 S. Kīhei Rd., Kīhei* ☎*808/873–3388* ⊕*www.mauidive-shop.com.*

Snorkel Bob's. If you need gear, Snorkel Bob's will rent you a mask, fins, and a snorkel, and throw in a carrying bag, map, and snorkel tips for as little as $9 per week. Avoid the circle masks and go for the split-level ($22 per week); it's worth the extra cash. ⊠*Nāpili Village Hotel, 5425 Lower Honoapi'ilani Hwy., Nāpili* ☎*808/669–9603* ⊠*Dicken-son Square, Dickenson St., Lahaina* ☎*808/662–0104* ⊠*1279 S. Kīhei Rd., #310, Kīhei* ☎*808/875–6188* ⊠*Kamaole Beach Center, 2411 S. Kīhei Rd., Kīhei* ☎*808/879–7449* ⊕*www.snorkelbob.com.*

SURFING

Maui's diverse coastline has surf for every level of waterman or woman. Waves on leeward-facing shores (West and South Maui) tend to break in gentle sets all summer long. Surf instructors in Kīhei and Lahaina can rent you boards, give you onshore instruction, and then lead you out through the channel, where it's safe to enter the surf. They'll shout encouragement while you paddle like mad for the thrill of standing on water—some will even give you a helpful shove. These areas are great for beginners, the only danger is whacking a stranger with your board or stubbing your toe against the reef.

The North Shore is another story. Winter waves pound the windward coast, attracting water champions from every corner of the world. Adrenaline addicts are towed in by Jet Ski to a legendary, deep-sea break called *Jaws.* Waves here periodically tower upward of 40 feet, dwarfing the helicopters seeking to capture unbelievable photos. The only spot for viewing this phenomenon (which happens just a few times a year) is on private property. So, if you hear the surfers next to you crowing about Jaws "going off," cozy up and get them to take you with them.

Whatever your skill, there's a board, a break, and even a surf guru to accommodate you. A two-hour lesson is a good intro to surf culture. Surf camps are becoming increasingly popular, especially with women.

SNORKELING IN HAWAI'I

The waters surrounding the Hawaiian Islands are filled with life—from giant manta rays cruising off the Big Island's Kona Coast to humpback whales giving birth in Maui's Māʻalaea Bay. Dip your head beneath the surface to experience a spectacularly colorful world: pairs of milletseed butterflyfish dart back and forth, red-lipped parrotfish snack on coral algae, and spotted eagle rays flap past like silent spaceships. Sea turtles bask at the surface while tiny wrasses give them the equivalent of a shave and a haircut. The water quality is typically outstanding; many sites afford 30-foot-plus visibility. On snorkel cruises, you can often stare from the boat rail right down to the bottom.

Certainly few destinations are as accommodating to every level of snorkeler as Hawaiʻi. Beginners can tromp in from sandy beaches while more advanced divers descend to shipwrecks, reefs, craters, and sea arches just offshore. Because of Hawaiʻi's extreme isolation, the island chain has fewer fish species than Fiji or the Caribbean—but many of the fish that are here exist nowhere else. The Hawaiian waters are home to the highest percentage of endemic fish in the world.

The key to enjoying the underwater world is slowing down. Look carefully. Listen. You might hear the strange crackling sound of shrimp tunneling through coral, or you may hear whales singing to one another during winter. A shy octopus may drift along the ocean's floor beneath you. If you're hooked, pick up a waterproof fishkey from Long's Drugs. You can brag later that you've looked the Hawaiian turkeyfish in the eye.

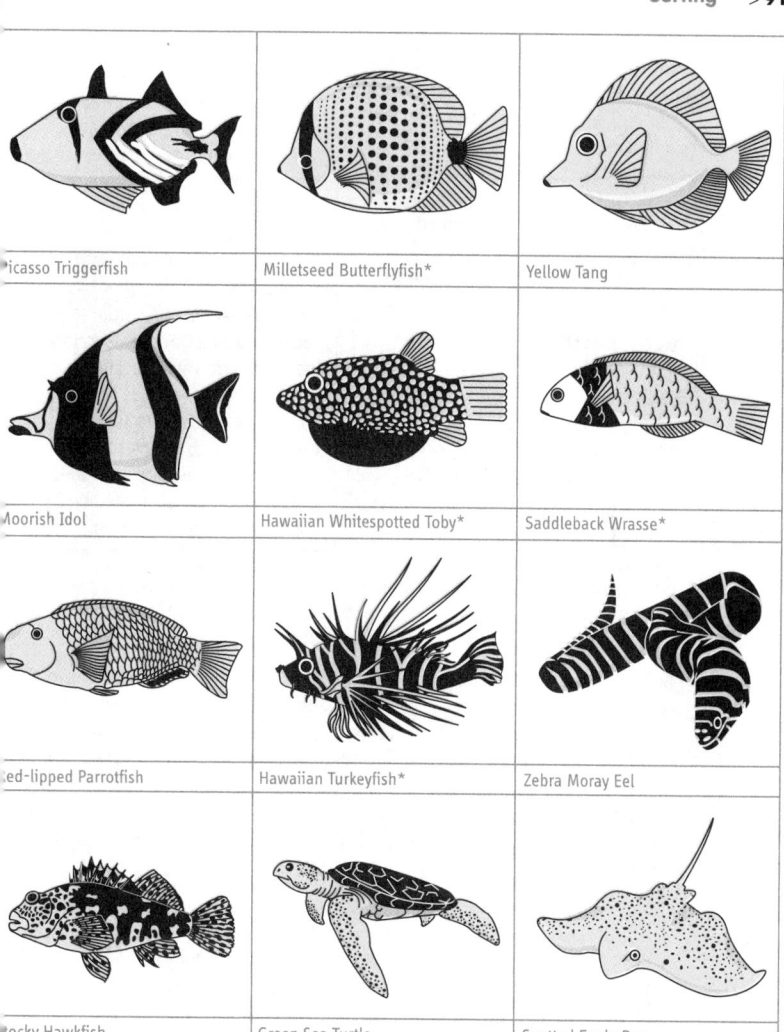

Picasso Triggerfish	Milletseed Butterflyfish*	Yellow Tang
Moorish Idol	Hawaiian Whitespotted Toby*	Saddleback Wrasse*
Red-lipped Parrotfish	Hawaiian Turkeyfish*	Zebra Moray Eel
Rocky Hawkfish	Green Sea Turtle	Spotted Eagle Ray

*endemic to Hawai'i

POLYNESIA'S FIRST CELESTIAL NAVIGATORS: HONU

Honu is the Hawaiian name for two native sea turtles, the hawksbill and the green sea turtle. Little is known about these dinosaur-age marine reptiles, though snorkelers regularly see them foraging for *limu* (seaweed) and the occasional jellyfish in Hawaiian waters. Most female honu nest in the uninhabited Northwestern Hawaiian Islands, but a few sociable ladies nest on Maui beaches. Scientists suspect that they navigate the seas via magnetism—sensing the earth's poles. Amazingly, they will journey up to 800 miles to nest—it's believed that they return to their own birth sites. After about 60 days of incubation, nestlings emerge from the sand at night and find their way back to the sea by the light of the stars.

4

SNORKELING IN HAWAI'I

One- or two-week camps offer a terrific way to build muscle and self-esteem simultaneously. **Maui Surfer Girls** (⊕*www.mauisurfergirls.com*) immerses adventurous young ladies in wave-riding wisdom during overnight, one- and two-week camps. Coed camps are sponsored by **Action Sports Maui** (⊕*www.actionsportsmaui.com*).

BEST SPOTS

Beginners can hang 10 at Kīhei's **Cove Park** (⊠*S. Kīhei Rd., Kīhei*), a sometimes crowded but reliable 1- to 2-foot break. Boards can easily be rented across the street, or in neighboring Kalama Park parking lot. The only bummer is having to balance the 9-plus-foot board on your head while crossing busy South Kīhei Road. But hey, that wouldn't stop world-famous longboarder Eddie Aikau, now would it?

> **HOW BIG IS BIG?**
>
> Before heading out for any water activity, be sure to get a weather and wave report, and make sure the surf report you get is the *full face value* of the wave. "Hawaiian style" cuts the wave size in half. For instance, a Hawaiian might say a wave is 5 feet high, which means 10 feet if you're from New Jersey or Florida. For years, scientists and surfers were using different measurements, as Hawai'i locals measured waves from median sea level to the crest. These days, most surf reports are careful to distinguish between the two—but it can still get confusing.

Long- or shortboarders can paddle out anywhere along Lahaina's coastline. One option is at **Launiupoko State Wayside** (⊠*Honoapi'ilani Hwy. near mile marker 18*). The east end of the park has an easy break, good for beginners. Even better is **Ukumehame** (⊠*Honoapi'ilani Hwy. near mile marker 12*), also called "Thousand Peaks." You'll soon see how the spot got its name—the waves here break again and again in wide and consistent rows, giving lots of room for beginning and intermediate surfers.

Other good surf spots in West Maui include "Grandma's" at **Papalaua Park,** just after the *pali* (cliff)—where waves are so easy a grandma could ride 'em; **Puamana Beach Park** for a mellow longboard day; and **Lahaina Harbor,** which offers an excellent inside wave for beginners (called "Breakwall"), as well as the more advanced outside (a great left if there's a big south swell).

For advanced wave riders, **Ho'okipa Beach Park** (⊠*2 mi past Pā'ia on Ha'na Hwy.*) boasts several well-loved breaks, including "Pavilions," "Lanes," "the Point," and "Middles." Surfers have priority until 11 AM, when windsurfers move in on the action. ■**TIP→Competition is stiff here, and the attitudes can be "agro." If you don't know what you're doing, consider watching from the shore.**

You can get the wave report each day by checking page 2 of the *Maui News,* logging onto the Glenn James weather site at ⊕*www.hawaiiweathertoday.com*, or calling ☎808/871–5054 (for the weather forecast) or ☎808/877–3611 (for the surf report).

SURF SHOPS, EQUIPMENT RENTAL & LESSONS

Big Kahuna. Rent surfboards (soft-top longboards) here for $15 for two hours, or $20 for the day. The shop also offers surf lessons, and rents kayaks and snorkel gear. Located across from Cove Park. ⊠ *Island Surf Bldg., 1993 S. Kīhei Rd. #2, Kīhei* ☎ *808/875–6395* ⊕ *www.big-kahunaadventures.com.*

★ **Goofy Foot.** Surfing "goofy foot" means putting your right foot forward. They might be goofy, but we like the right-footed gurus here. Their safari shop is just plain cool and only steps away from "Breakwall," a great beginner's spot in Lahaina. Two-hour classes with five or fewer students are $55, and six-hour classes with lunch and an ocean-safety course are $250. They promise you'll be standing within a two-hour lesson—or it's free. ⊠ *505 Front St., Lahaina* ☎ *808/244–9283* ⊕ *www.goofyfootsurfschool.com.*

Hāna Highway Surf. If you're heading out to the North Shore surf, you can pick up boards ranging from beginner's soft-tops to high-performance shortboards here for $20 per day. ⊠ *120 Hāna Hwy., Pā'ia* ☎ *808/579–8999.*

Hi Tech Maui. Locals hold Hi Tech in the highest regard. They have some of the best boards, advice, and attitudes around. Rent surfboards for $20 per day (or soft boards for $14); $112 for the week. They rent even their best models—choose from longboards, shortboards, and hybrids. All rentals come with board bags, roof racks, and oh yeah, wax. ⊠ *425 Koloa St., Kahului* ☎ *808/877–2111* ⊕ *www.htmaui.com.*

Nancy Emerson School of Surfing. Nancy's motto is "If my dog can surf, so can you." Instructors here will get even the most shaky novice riding with their "Learn to Surf in One Lesson" program. A two-hour group lesson (six students max) is $75. A private lesson with Nancy herself—a pro surf champion and occasional Hollywood stunt double—costs $215 for one hour or $325 for two; lessons with her equally qualified instructors are $100 for one hour and $165 for two. They provide the boards and rash guards. ⊠ *505 Front St., Ste. 224B, Lahaina* ☎ *808/244–7873* ⊕ *www.mauisurfclinics.com.*

Second Wind. Surfboard rentals at this centrally located shop are a deal—good boards go for $20 per day or $110 per week. They also rent and sell their own *Elua Makani* boards (which means second wind in Hawaiian). Although they don't offer les-

> ### ON THE SIDELINES
>
> Even if you aren't a surfer, watching is just as fun (well, almost). **Ho'okipa Beach Park** (⊠ *2 mi past Pā'ia on Hāna Hwy.*) gives you the perfect grassy overlook to see all the action—pro surf, windsurf, and kiters abound. Near-perfect waves can be seen at **Honolua Bay,** on the northern tip of West Maui. To get there, continue 2 mi north of D.T. Fleming Park on Route 30 and take a left onto the dirt road next to a pineapple field; a path leads down the cliff to the beach. In December, the **Billabong Pro** invites female wave riders to compete at Honolua Bay.

sons themselves, they will book you with the best surfing, windsurfing, and kiteboarding lessons on the island. ⊠ *111 Hāna Hwy., Kahului* ☎*808/877–7467 or 800/936–7787* ⊕*www.secondwindmaui.com.*

WHALE-WATCHING

From November through April, whale-watching becomes one of the most popular activities on Maui. Boats leave the wharves at Lahaina and Māʻalaea in search of humpbacks, allowing you to enjoy the awe-inspiring size of these creatures in closer proximity. As it's almost impossible *not* to see whales in winter on Maui, you'll want to prioritize: is adventure or comfort your aim? If close encounters with the giants of the deep are your desire, pick a smaller boat that promises sightings. If an impromptu marine-biology lesson sounds fun, go with the Pacific Whale Foundation. Two-hour forays into the whales' world start at $20. For those wanting to sip mai tais as whales cruise calmly by, stick with a sunset cruise on a boat with an open bar and *pūpū* ($40 and up). ■TIP→**Afternoon trips are generally rougher because the wind picks up, but some say this is when the most surface action occurs.**

Every captain aims to please during whale season, getting as close as legally possible (100 yards). Crew members know when a whale is about to dive (after several waves of its heart-shape tail) but rarely can predict breaches (when the whale hurls itself up and almost entirely out of the water). Prime-viewing space (on the upper and lower decks, around the railings) is limited, so boats can feel crowded even when half full. If you don't want to squeeze in beside strangers, opt for a smaller boat with fewer bookings. Don't forget to bring sunscreen, sunglasses, light long sleeves, and a hat you can secure. Winter weather is less predictable, and at times can be extreme, especially as the wind picks up. Arrive early to find parking.

BEST SPOTS

From December 15 to May 1 the Pacific Whale Foundation has naturalists stationed in two places—on the rooftop of their headquarters and at the scenic viewpoint at **McGregor Point Lookout** (⊠*Between mile markers 7 and 8 on Honoapiʻilani Hwy., Rte. 30*). Just like the commuting traffic, whales cruise along the *pali*, or cliff-side, of West Maui's Honoapiʻilani highway all day long. ⚠**Make sure to park safely before craning your neck out to see them.**

The northern end of **Keawakapu Beach** (⊠*S. Kīhei Rd. near Kilohana Dr.*) seems to be a whale magnet. Situate yourself on the sand or at the nearby restaurant, and you're bound to see a mama whale patiently teaching her calf the exact technique of flipper-waving.

BOATS & CHARTERS

America II. Want to see sails with your whales? In season, this America's Cup contender offers early-morning whale-watching. Make no mistake: these trips are for sailing die-hards. Don't expect many frills; this one's all about the ride. ⊠*Harbor Slip #6, Lahaina* ☎*808/667–2195* ⊕*www.sailingonmaui.com.*

CLOSE UP
The Humpback's Winter Home

The humpback whales' attraction to Maui is legendary. More than half the Pacific's humpback population winters in Hawai'i, especially in the waters around the Valley Isle, where mothers can be seen just a few hundred feet offshore training their young calves in the fine points of whale etiquette. Watching from shore it's easy to catch sight of whales spouting, or even breaching—when they leap almost entirely out of the sea, slapping back onto the water with a huge splash.

At one time there were thousands of the huge mammals, but a history of overhunting and marine pollution dwindled the world population to about 1,500. In 1966 humpbacks were put on the endangered species list. Hunting or harassing whales is illegal in the waters of most nations, and in the United States, boats and airplanes are restricted from getting too close. The word is still out, however, on the effects military sonar testing has on the marine mammals.

Marine biologists believe the humpbacks (much like the humans) keep returning to Hawai'i because of its warmth. Having fattened themselves in subarctic waters all summer, the whales migrate south in the winter to breed, and a rebounding population of thousands cruise Maui waters. Winter is calving time, and the young whales, born with little blubber, probably couldn't survive in the frigid Alaskan waters. No one has ever seen a whale give birth here, but experts know that calving is their main winter activity, since the 1- and 2-ton youngsters suddenly appear while the whales are in residence.

The first sighting of a humpback whale spout each season is exciting and reassuring for locals on Maui. A collective sigh of relief can be heard, "Ah, they've returned." In the not-so-far distance, flukes and flippers can be seen rising above the ocean's surface. It's hard not to anthropomorphize the tail-waving, it looks like such an amiable, human gesture. Each fluke is uniquely patterned, like a human's fingerprint, and used to identify the giants as they travel halfway around the globe and back.

Kiele V. The Hyatt Regency Maui's *Kiele V,* a 55-foot luxury catamaran, does seasonal whale-watching excursions as well as daily snorkel trips and afternoon cocktail sails. A comfortable ride, the cat leaves from Kāʻanapali Beach, which is more fun than the harbor. The trip costs $60 per adult and includes *pūpū* and an open bar. ✉*200 Nohea Kai Dr., Lahaina* ☎*808/667–4727.*

☾ ★ **Pacific Whale Foundation.** This nonprofit organization pioneered whale-watching back in 1979 and now runs four boats, with 15 trips daily. As the most recognizable name in whale-watching, the crew (with a certified marine biologist on board) offers insights into whale behavior (do they *really* know what those tail flicks mean?) and suggests ways for you to help save marine life worldwide. The best part about these trips is the underwater hydrophone that allows you to actually listen to the whales sing. Trips meet at the Foundation's store, where you can buy whale paraphernalia, snacks, and coffee—a real bonus for

8 AM trips. Passengers are then herded much like migrating whales down to the harbor. These trips are more affordable than others, but you'll be sharing the boat with about 100 people in stadium seating. Once you catch sight of the wildlife up-close, however, you can't help but be thrilled. ⊠ *Mā'alaea and Lahaina harbors* ☎ *800/942–5311 or 808/249–8811* ⊕ *www.pacificwhale.org.*

Pride Charters. Two-hour cruises narrated by a naturalist are offered aboard *Leilani,* a small, maneuverable boat with good viewing opportunities (39 passengers max). There's a main cabin, upper sundeck, and swim platform—and you can listen to the whales sing. Trips start at $26 per adult, and include *pūpū* and an open bar. ⊠ *Mā'alaea Harbor, Slip #70, Mā'alaea* ☎ *877/867–7433 or 808/242–0955* ⊕ *www.prideof-maui.com.*

WINDSURFING

Something about Maui's wind and water stirs the spirit of innovation. Windsurfing, invented in the 1950s, found its true home at Ho'okipa in 1980. Seemingly overnight, windsurfing pros from around the world flooded Maui's North Shore. Equipment evolved, amazing film footage was captured, and a new sport was born.

If you're new to the action, you can get lessons from the experts island-wide. For a beginner, the best thing about windsurfing is (unlike surfing) you don't have to paddle. Instead, you have to hold on like heck to a flapping sail, as it whisks you into the wind. Needless to say, you're going to need a little coordination and balance to pull this off. Instructors start you out on a beach at Kanahā, where the big boys go. Lessons range from two-hour introductory classes to five-day advanced "flight school." If you're an old salt, pick up tips and equipment from the companies below.

BEST SPOTS

After **Ho'okipa Bay** (⊠ *2 mi past Pā'ia on Hāna Hwy.*) was discovered by windsurfers three decades ago, this windy beach 10 mi east of Kahului gained an international reputation. The spot is blessed with optimal wave-sailing wind and sea conditions, and can offer the ultimate aerial experience.

In summer the windsurfing crowd heads south to **Kalepolepo Beach** (⊠ *S. Kīhei Rd. near Ohukai St.*). Trade winds build in strength and by afternoon a swarm of dragon-

PADDLE SURFING

Stand-up paddle surfing, where you stand on a longboard and paddle out with a canoe oar, is the new "comeback kid" of surf sports. Traced back to some of the first surfers on Waikīkī, paddle surfing made its revival in recent years thanks to feats by Archie Kalepa, who crossed between Moloka'i and O'ahu; and Laird Hamilton, who conquered Jaws on a stand-up paddleboard. Paddle-boarding requires even more balance and coordination than regular surfing. But these days you can almost always see at least one lone paddler amid the pack—watch for them.

flysails can be seen skimming the whitecaps, with the West Maui Mountains as a backdrop.

A great site for speed, **Kanahā Beach Park** (⊠*Behind Kahului Airport*) is dedicated to beginners in the morning hours, before the waves and wind really get roaring. After 11 AM, the professionals choose from their quiver of sails the size and shape best suited for the day's demands. This beach tends to have smaller waves and forceful winds—sometimes sending sailors flying at 40 knots. ■TIP➔**If you aren't ready to go pro, this is a great place for a picnic while you watch from the beach.**

EQUIPMENT RENTAL & LESSONS

Action Sports Maui. The quirky, friendly professionals here will meet you at Kanahā, outfit you with your sail and board, and guide you through your first "jibe" or turn. They promise your learning time will be cut in half. Don't be afraid to ask lots of questions. Lessons are held at 9 AM every morning except Sunday at Kanahā, and start at $79 for a 2½-hour class. ⊠*6 E. Waipuilani Rd., Kīhei* ☎*808/871–5857* ⊕*www. actionsportsmaui.com.*

Hi Tech Maui. Known locally as Maui's finest windsurfing school, Hawaiian Sailboarding Techniques (HST, located in Hi Tech) brings you quality instruction by skilled sailors. Founded by Alan Cadiz, an accomplished World Cup Pro, the school sets high standards for a safe, quality windsurfing experience. Hi Tech itself offers excellent equipment rentals; $50 gets you a board, two sails, a mast, and roof racks for 24 hours. ⊠*425 Koloa St., Kahului* ☎*808/877–2111* ⊕*www. htmaui.com.*

Second Wind. Located in Kahului, this company rents boards with two sails for $44 per day. Boards with three sails go for $49 per day. ⊠*11 Hāna Hwy., Kahului* ☎*808/877–7467.*

Golf, Hiking & Outdoor Activities

5

WORD OF MOUTH

"Hike in the 'Iao Valley. It's quiet, green, lush and a totally different experience than the west side of Maui."

—Erin74

"Kapalua Plantation is the one course to play when you can only play one. It's a pretty special place; it's so unique. Where else could I have reached a 585-yard hold (#18) with a driver and a 3-iron? (The trades were sure blowing that day.)"

—kanunu

Updated
by Amy
Westervelt

YOU MAY COME TO MAUI to sprawl out on the sand, but it won't take long before you realize there's much more to Maui than the beach. The island's interior is vast and varied—a mecca of rain forest, valley, waterfalls, and mountains that provide a whirlwind of options for action and adventure. Whether you're riding horseback or backroading it on an ATV, there's plenty to keep you busy. This chapter will get your toes out of the sand, and into your hiking boots or golf shoes. For easy reference, activities are listed in alphabetical order.

ATV TOURS

Haleakalā ATV Tours. Haleakalā ATV Tours explore the mountainside in their own way: propelled through the forest on 350 cc, four-wheel-drive, Honda Rancher all-terrain vehicles. The adventures begin at Haleakalā Ranch and rev right up to the pristine Waikamoi rain-forest preserve. Kids under 15 ride alongside in the exciting Argo Conquest, an eight-wheel amphibious vehicle. Two-hour trips go for $90, and 3½-hour trips are $135. Haleakalā ATV Tours is now offering combination ATV and Zipline tours with Skyline Eco Adventures on Sunday for $177. ☎808/661–0288 or 877/661–0288 ⊕www.atvmaui.com.

BICYCLING

Maui County biking is safer and more convenient than in the past, but long distances and mountainous terrain keep it from being a practical mode of travel. Still, painted bike lanes enable cyclists to travel all the way from Mākena to Kapalua, and you'll see hardy souls battling the trade winds under the hot Maui sun.

Several companies offer guided downhill bike tours from the top of Haleakalā all the way to the coast. From peak to sea level it's 38 mi total with only about 400 yards of actual pedaling required. This activity is a great way to see the summit of the world's largest dormant volcano and enjoy an easy, gravity-induced bike ride, but isn't for those not confident in their ability to handle a bike. The ride is inherently dangerous due to the slope, sharp turns, and the fact that you're riding down an actual road with cars on it. That said, the guided bike companies do take every safety precaution. A few companies are now offering unguided (or as they like to say "self-guided") tours where they provide you with the bike and transportation to the top and then you're free to descend at your own pace. Sunrise is downright brisk at the summit, so dress in layers.

BEST SPOTS

Though it's changing, at present there are few truly good spots to ride on Maui. Street bikers will want to head out to scenic **Thompson Road** (⊠*Off Rte. 37, Kula Hwy., Keokea*). It's quiet, gently curvy, and flanked by gorgeous views on both sides. Plus, because it's at a higher elevation, the air temperature is cooler and the wind lighter. The coast back down toward Kahului is worth the ride up. Mountain bikers have favored the remote **Polipoli Forest** (⊠*Off Rte. 377, end of Waipoli Rd.*) for its bumpy trail through an unlikely forest of conifers. However, a fire in early 2007 caused the closure of the park until summer; call the Maui Visitor Bureau at ☎800/525–6284 for updates before you go.

EQUIPMENT RENTALS & TOURS

HALEAKALĀ BIKE COMPANY. IF YOU'RE thinking about an unguided Haleakalā bike trip, consider one of the trips offered by this company. Meet at the Old Ha'ikū Cannery and take their van shuttle to the top. Along the way you'll learn about the history of the island, the volcano, and other Hawaiiana. Unlike the guided trips, food is not included although there are several spots along the way down to stop, rest, and eat. The simple, mostly downhill route takes you right back to the cannery where you started. HBC offers bike sales, rentals, and services. ⊠*810 Ha'ikū Rd., Suite 120, Ha'ikū* ☎*808/575–9575 or 888/922–2453* ⊕*www.bikemaui.com.*

Island Biker. This is the premiere bike shop on Maui when it comes to rental, sales, and service. They offer 2005 Specialized standard front-shock bikes, road bikes, and full-suspension mountain bikes. Daily or weekly rates range $40 to $150, and include a helmet, pump, water bottle, and flat-repair kit. They can suggest various routes appropriate for mountain or road biking, or you can join them in a bi-weekly group ride. ⊠*415 Dairy Rd., Kahului* ☎*808/877–7744* ⊕*www.island-bikermaui.com.*

Maui Downhill. If biking down the side of Haleakalā sounds like fun, several companies are ready to book you a tour. Maui Downhill vans will pick you up at your resort, shuttle you to the mountaintop, help you onto a bike, and follow you as you coast down through clouds and gorgeous scenery into the town of Pā'ia. Haleakalā summit trips are available for sunrise or midday; sunset half trips from the crater to Kula are also offered. Lunch or breakfast is included, depending on your trip's start time; treks cost $125 to $185, discounts available for Internet bookings. ⊠*199 Dairy Rd., Kahului* ☎*808/871–2155 or 800/535–2453* ⊕*www.mauidownhill.net.*

Maui Mountain Cruisers. Guided sunrise and midday bike trips "cruise" down Haleakalā for $150 to $185 (discounts available if booked in advance). Nonbikers can ride down in a van for $55. ⌂*Box 1356, Makawao* ☎*808/871–6014 or 800/232–6284* ⊕*www.mauimountain-cruisers.com.*

West Maui Cycles. Servicing the west side of the island, WMC offers an assortment of cycles including front-suspension Giant bikes for $40 per day ($160 per week) and Cannondale road bikes for $50 per day ($200 per week). Sales and service are available. ⊠*1087 Limahana St., Lahaina* ☎*808/661–9005* ⊕*www.westmauicycles.com.*

GOLF

Maui's natural beauty and surroundings offer some of the most jaw-dropping vistas imaginable on a golf course. Holes run across small bays, past craggy lava outcrops, and up into cool, forested mountains. Most courses feature mesmerizing ocean views, some close enough to feel the salt in the air. And although many of the courses are affiliated with resorts (and therefore a little pricier), the general-public courses are no less impressive. You might even consider a ferry ride to the neighbor island of Lānaʻi for a round on either of its two championship courses *(F see chapter 11, Lānaʻi).*

Green Fees: Green fees listed here are the highest course rates per round on weekdays and weekends for U.S. residents. (Some courses charge non–U.S. residents higher prices.) Discounts are often available for resort guests and for those who book tee times on the Web. Rental clubs may or may not be included with green fees. Twilight fees are usually offered; call individual courses for information.

WEST MAUI

★ **Kāʻanapali Golf Resort.** The Royal Kāʻanapali (North) Course (1962) is one of three in Hawaiʻi designed by Robert Trent Jones Sr., the godfather of modern golf architecture. The greens average a whopping 10,000 square feet, necessary because of the often-severe undulation. The par-4 18th hole (into the prevailing trade breezes, with out-of-bounds on the left, and a lake on the right) is notoriously tough. The Kāʻanapali Kai (South) Course (Arthur Jack Snyder, 1976) shares similar seaside-into-the-hills terrain, but is rated a couple of strokes easier, mostly because putts are less treacherous. ⊠*2290 Kāʻanapali Pkwy., Lahaina* ☎*808/661–3691* ⊕*www.kaanapali-golf.com* ⚑*. North Course: 18 holes. 6,500 yds. Par 71. Slope 126. Green Fee: $160. South Course: 18 holes. 6,400 yds. Par 70. Slope 124. Green Fee: $175* ⚐ *Facilities: Driving range, putting green, rental clubs, golf carts, lessons, restaurant, bar.*

Fodor'sChoice **Kapalua Resort.** Perhaps Hawaiʻi's best-known golf resort and the
★ crown jewel of golf on Maui, Kapalua hosts the PGA Tour's first event each January: the Mercedes Championships at the Plantation Course at Kapalua. Ben Crenshaw and Bill Coore (1991) tried to incorporate traditional shot values in a very nontraditional site, taking into account slope, gravity, and the prevailing trade winds. The par-5 18th, for instance, plays 663 yards from the back tees (600 yards from the resort tees). The hole drops 170 feet in elevation, narrowing as it goes to a partially guarded green, and plays downwind and down-grain. Despite the longer-than-usual distance, the slope is great enough and the wind at your back usually brisk enough to reach the green with two well-struck shots—a truly unbelievable finish to a course that will challenge, frustrate, and reward the patient golfer.

The Bay Course (Arnold Palmer and Francis Duane, 1975) is the most traditional of Kapalua's triad, with gentle rolling fairways and generous

BEFORE YOU HIT THE 1ST TEE . . .

Golf is golf, and Hawai'i is part of the United States, but Island golf nevertheless has its own quirks. Here are a few tips to make your golf experience in the Islands more pleasant.

■ Sunscreen. Buy it, apply it (minimum 30 SPF). The subtropical rays of the sun are intense, even in December. Good advice is to apply sunscreen, at a minimum, on the 1st and 10th tees.

■ Stay hydrated. Spending four-plus hours in the sun and heat means you'll perspire away considerable fluids and energy.

■ All resort courses and many daily fee courses provide rental clubs. In many cases, they're the latest lines from top manufacturers. This is true for both men and women, as well as lefthanders, which means you don't have to schlepp clubs across the Pacific.

■ Pro shops at most courses are well-stocked with balls, tees, and other accoutrements, so even if you bring your own bag, it needn't weigh a ton.

■ Come spikeless—very few Hawai'i courses still permit metal spikes. And most of the resort courses require a collared shirt.

■ Maui is notorious for its trade winds. Consider playing early if you want to avoid the wind, and remember that while it'll frustrate you at times and make club selection difficult, you may very well see some of your longest drives ever.

■ In theory you can play golf in Hawai'i 365 days a year, but there's a reason the Hawaiian Islands are so green. An umbrella and light jacket can come in handy.

■ Unless you play a muni or certain daily fee courses, plan on taking a cart. Riding carts are mandatory at most courses and are included in the green fees.

greens. The most memorable hole is the par-3 fifth, with a tee shot that must carry a turquoise finger of Onelua Bay. The Kapalua Golf Academy (⊠1000 Office Rd. ☎808/669–6500) offers 23 acres of practice turf and 11 teeing areas, a special golf fitness gym, and an instructional bay with video analysis. Each of the three courses has a separate clubhouse. The Bay Course: ⊠300 Kapalua Dr., Kapalua ☎808/669–8820 ⊕www.kapaluamaui.com/golf ⅃18 holes. 6,600 yds. Par 72. Slope 133. Green Fee: $215 ☞Facilities: Driving range, putting green, rental clubs, pro shop, lessons, restaurant, bar. The Plantation Course: ⊠2000 Plantation Club Dr., Kapalua ☎808/669–8877 ⊕www.kapaluamaui.com/golf ⅃18 holes. 7,411 yds. Par 73. Slope 135. Green Fee: $295 ☞Facilities: Driving range, putting green, golf carts, pull carts, rental clubs, pro shop, golf academy/lessons, restaurant, bar.

THE SOUTH SHORE

elleair Maui Golf Club. Formerly known as Silversword (1987), elleair is an exacting test. Fairways tend to be narrow, especially in landing areas, and can be quite a challenge when the trade winds come up in the afternoon. The course is lined with enough coconut trees to make them a collective hazard, not just a nutty nuisance. ✉ *1345 Pi'ilani Hwy., Kīhei* ☎ *808/874–0777* ⊕ *http://elleairmauigolfclub.com* ⚐ *18 holes. 6,404 yds. Par 71. Slope 117. Green Fee: $120* ⚑ *Facilities: Driving range, putting green, rental clubs, golf carts, lessons, pro shop.*

Fodor'sChoice
★ **Mākena Resort.** Robert Trent Jones Jr. and Don Knotts (not the Barney Fife actor) built the first course at Mākena in 1981. A decade later Jones was asked to create 18 totally new holes and blend them with the existing course to form the North and South courses, which opened in 1994. Both courses—sculpted from the lava flows on the western flank of Haleakalā—offer quick greens with lots of breaks, and plenty of scenic distractions. On the North Course, the fourth is one of the most picturesque inland par 3s in Hawai'i, with the green guarded on the right by a pond. The sixth is an excellent example of option golf: the fairway is sliced up the middle by a gaping ravine, which must sooner or later be crossed to reach the green. Although trees frame most holes on the North Course, the South Course is more open. This means it plays somewhat easier off the tee, but the greens are trickier. The view from the elevated tee of the par-5 10th is lovely with the lake in the foreground mirroring the ocean in the distance. The par-4 16th is another sight to see, with the Pacific running along the left side. ✉ *5415 Mākena Alanui, Mākena* ☎ *808/879–3344* ⊕ *www.princeresortshawaii.com/maui-golf.php* ⚐ *North Course: 18 holes. 6,567 yds. Par 72. Slope 135. Green Fee: $190. South Course: 18 holes. 6,630 yds. Par 72. Slope 133. Green Fee: $190* ⚑ *Facilities: Driving range, putting green, golf carts, rental clubs, pro shop, golf academy/lessons, restaurant, bar.*

Fodor'sChoice
★ **Wailea.** Wailea is one of just two Hawai'i resorts to offer three different courses: Gold, Emerald, and Old Blue. Designed by Robert Trent Jones Jr., these courses share similar terrain, carved into the leeward slopes of Haleakalā. Although the ocean does not come into play, its beauty is visible on almost every hole. ■ **TIP→Remember, putts break dramatically toward the ocean.**

Jones refers to the Gold Course at Wailea (1993) as the "masculine" course. Host to the Championship Senior Skins Game in February, it's all trees and lava and regarded as the hardest of the three courses. The trick here is to note even subtle changes in elevation. The par-3 eighth, for example, plays from an elevated tee across a lava ravine to a large, well-bunkered green framed by palm trees, the blue sea, and tiny Molokini. The course has been labeled a "thinking player's" course because it demands strategy and careful club selection. The Emerald Course at Wailea (1994) is the "feminine" layout with lots of flowers and bunkering away from greens. This by no means suggests that it plays easy. Although this may seem to render the bunker benign, the opposite is

ON THE SIDELINES

Maui has a number of golf tournaments, most of which are of professional caliber and worth watching. Many are also televised nationally. One attention-getter is the **Mercedes-Benz Championship** (☎ *808/669–2440*) held in January. This is the first official PGA tour event, held on Kapalua's Plantation Course. The Aloha Section of the Professional Golfers Association of America hosts the **Hawaiian Tel-Com Hall of Fame Pro-Am & Championship** (☎ *808/669–8877*) tournament at the Plantation Course in May. A clambake feast on the beach tops off the **Kapalua Clam-**

bake Pro-Am (☎ *808/669–8812*) in June.

Over in Wailea, in June, on the longest day of the year, self-proclaimed "lunatic" golfers start out at first light to play 100 holes of golf in the annual **Ka Lima O Maui Celebrity 100** (☎ *808/875–5111*), a fund-raiser for local charity Ka Lima O Maui. The nationally televised **Wendy's Championship Senior Skins** (☎ *808/875–5111*) tournament, held on Wailea's Gold Course in January, pits four of the most respected Senior PGA players against one another.

true. A bunker well in front of a green disguises the distance to the hole. Likewise, the Emerald's extensive flower beds are designed to be dangerous distractions because of their beauty. The Gold and Emerald share a clubhouse, practice facility, and 19th hole. Judging elevation change is also key at Wailea's first course, the Old Blue Course (Arthur Jack Snyder, 1971). Fairways and greens tend to be wider and more forgiving than on the Gold or Emerald, and run through colorful flora that includes hibiscus, wiliwili, bougainvillea, and plumeria. Old Blue Course: ✉ *120 Kaukahi St., Wailea* ☎ *808/875–5155 or 888/328–6284* ⊕ *www.waileagolf.com* ⅃. *18 holes. 6,765 yds. Par 72. Slope 129. Green Fee: $185* ☞ *Facilities: Driving range, putting green, golf carts, rental clubs, pro shop, golf academy/lessons, restaurant, bar*. Gold and Emerald Courses: ✉ *100 Wailea Golf Club Dr., Wailea* ☎ *808/875–7450 or 888/328–6284* ⊕ *www.waileagolf.com* ⅃. *Gold Course: 18 holes. 6,653 yds. Par 72. Slope 132. Green Fee: $200. Emerald Course: 18 holes. 6,407 yds. Par 72. Slope 130. Green Fee: $200* ☞ *Facilities: Driving range, putting green, golf carts, rental clubs, pro shop, golf academy/lessons, restaurant, bar*.

CENTRAL MAUI

Fodor'sChoice ★ **The Dunes at Maui Lani.** This is Robin Nelson (1999) at his minimalist best, a bit of British links in the middle of the Pacific. Holes run through ancient, lightly wooded sand dunes, 5 mi inland from Kahului Harbor. Thanks to the natural humps and slopes of the dunes, Nelson had to move very little dirt and created a natural beauty. During the design phase he visited Ireland, and not so coincidentally the par-3 third looks a lot like the Dell at Lahinch: a white dune on the right sloping down into a deep bunker and partially obscuring the right side of the green—just one of several blind to semi-blind shots here. Popular with residents, this course has won several awards including "Best 35 New Courses in America" by *Golf Magazine* and "Five Best Kept Secret Golf Courses in America" by *Golf Digest.* ⊠*1333 Maui Lani Pkwy., Kahului* ☎*808/873–0422* ⊕*www.dunesatmauilani. com* ⚑*. 18 holes. 6,841 yds. Par 72. Slope 136. Green Fee: $125* ⚐*Facilities: Driving range, putting green, golf carts, rental clubs, pro shop, golf academy/lessons, restaurant, bar.*

> **TIP!**
>
> Resort courses, in particular, offer more than the usual three sets of tees, sometimes four or five. So bite off as much or little challenge as you like. Tee it up from the tips and you'll end up playing a few 600-yard par 5s and see a few 250-yard forced carries.

Kahili Golf Course. The former Sandalwood Course (Robin Nelson, 1991) is back as the Kahili Golf Course. After four years of lying fallow due to financial problems, Kahili was completely redone in 2005 by Nelson himself and is now one of two 18-hole courses—one private (King Kamehameha) and one public (Kahili)—that make up the King Kamehameha Golf Club. Course holes run along the slopes of the West Maui Mountains, overlooking Maui's central plain, and feature panoramic ocean views of both the north and south shores. Consistent winds negate the course's shorter length. ⊠*2500 Honoapi'ilani Hwy., Wailuku* ☎*808/242–4653* ⊕*www.kahiligolf.com* ⚑*. 18 holes. 6,570 yds. Par 72. Slope 124. Green Fee: $110* ⚐*Facilities: Driving range, putting green, rental clubs, golf carts, pro shop, lessons, restaurant, bar.*

Waiehu Golf Course. Maui's lone municipal course, Waiehu is really two courses in one. The front nine opened in 1930 and features authentic seaside links that run along Kahului Bay. The back nine, which climbs up into the lower reaches of the West Maui Mountains through macadamia orchards, opened in 1963 (Arthur Jack Snyder). ⊠*200A Halewaiu Rd., Wailuku* ☎*808/270–7400* ⊕*www.mauicounty.gov/ parks/maui/central/WaiehuGolfCourse.htm* ⚑*. 18 holes. 6,330 yds. Par 72. Slope 120. Green Fee: $45, plus $16 per cart* ⚐*Facilities: Driving range, putting green, golf carts, pull carts, rental clubs, pro shop, restaurant, bar.*

UPCOUNTRY

Pukalani Golf Course. Located 1,110 feet above sea level, Pukalani (Bob E. and Robert L. Baldock, 1970) provides one of the finest vistas in all Hawai'i. Holes run up, down, and across the slopes of Haleakalā. The trade wind tends to come up in the late morning and afternoon. This—combined with frequent elevation change—makes club selection a test. The fairways tend to be wide, but greens are undulating and quick. ⊠*360 Pukalani St., Pukalani* ☎*808/572–1314* ⊕*www.puka-lanigolf.com* ⚑*. 18 holes. 6,962 yds. Par 72. Slope 127. Green Fee: $68* ⚐*Facilities: Driving range, putting green, rental clubs, golf carts, pro shop, restaurant, bar.*

SAVING THE BEST FOR LAST

Among golf's great traditions is the 19th Hole. No matter how the first 18 go, the 19th is sure to offer comfort and cheer, not to mention a chilled beverage. Here's a look at some of the best.

Kapalua boasts three 19th holes with great fare and views—the **Plantation House** has a commanding view of the Plantation Course's 18th hole, the Pailolo Channel, and the island of Moloka'i beyond; the **Pineapple Grill** overlooks the Bay Course's 18th; and **Vino Italian Tapas & Wine Bar** is the Village Course's popular watering-hole restaurant with a spectacular wine selection.

At Wailea's Gold and Emerald Courses, the **Sea Watch** restaurant overlooks the sea in a garden setting and serves excellent food, with a choice selection of single malt scotches and cigars.

The **Kahili Restaurant**, a plantation-style clubhouse at the King Kamehameha Golf Club's Kahili Course, offers commanding views of the ocean on both sides of the island and of 10,000-foot Haleakalā. And though not affiliated with elleair, golfers from this course frequent **Lulu's** and **Henry's** in the heart of Kīhei.

LĀNA'I

The Island of Lāna'i features two championship-caliber golf courses—the Challenge at Manele and the Experience at Ko'ele—that are rarely crowded due to the exclusivity of the island. Both courses require a ferry ride from Lahaina or Mā'alaea harbors on Maui. Transportation–golf packages are available through **Expeditions Ferry** (☎808/661–3756 ⊕www.go-lanai.com).For reviews of the two courses, see chapter 11, Lāna'i.

HANG GLIDING & PARAGLIDING

Hang Gliding Maui. Armin Engert will take you on an instructional powered hang-gliding trip out of Hāna Airport in East Maui. With more than 7,500 hours in flight and a perfect safety record, Armin flies you 1,000 feet over Maui's most beautiful coast. A 30-minute flight lesson costs $130, and a 60-minute lesson is $220. This is easily one of the coolest things you can do in Hāna. Snapshots of your flight from a wing-mounted camera cost an additional $30, and a 34-minute DVD of the flight is available for $70. ✉Hāna Airport, Hāna ☎808/572–6557 ⊕www.hanaglidingmaui.com.

Maluhialani. The name means "beautiful serenity" in Hawaiian, which is appropriate for an airborne trip taking off from Kula, and soaring as far as the West Maui Mountains. Dwight Mounts, your pilot, built a grass runway on his scenic Upcountry property that serves as homebase for his powered hang-gliding trips. ☎808/280–3307 ⊕www.maluhialani.com.

Proflyght Paragliding. Proflyght is the only paragliding outfit on Maui to offer solo, tandem, and instruction at Polipoli State Park. The leeward slope of Haleakalā lends itself perfectly to paragliding with breathtaking scenery and upcountry air currents that increase and rise throughout the day. Polipoli creates tremendous thermals that allow one to peacefully descend 3,000 feet to the landing zone. Owner–pilot Dexter Clearwater boasts a perfect safety record with tandems and student pilots since taking over the company in 2002. Ask and Dexter will bring along his flying duck Chuckie or his paragliding puppy Daisy. Prices start at $175, with full certification available. At this writing, the company was using only its lower launch site, following an early 2007 fire in the park that resulted in the closure of the road to its higher site. ⊠*Polipoli State Park, Kula* ☎*808/874–5433* ⊕*www.paraglidehawaii. com.*

HELICOPTER TOURS

Helicopter flight-seeing excursions can take you over the West Maui Mountains, Hāna, Haleakalā Crater, even the Big Island lava flow, or Molokaʻi. This is a beautiful, exciting way to see the island, and the *only* way to see some of its most dramatic areas and waterfalls. Tour prices usually include a videotape of your trip so you can relive the experience at home. Prices run from about $125 for a half-hour rain-forest tour to almost $400 for a two-hour mega-experience that includes a champagne toast on landing. Generally the 45- to 50-minute flights are the best value, and if you're willing to chance it, considerable discounts may be available if you call last minute.

It takes about 90 minutes to travel inside the volcano, then down to the village of Hāna. Some companies stop in secluded areas for refreshments. Helicopter-tour operators throughout the state come under sharp scrutiny for passenger safety and equipment maintenance. Don't be afraid to ask about a company's safety record, flight paths, age of equipment, and level of operator experience. Generally, though, if they're still in business they're doing something right.

Air Maui Helicopters. Air Maui prides itself on a perfect safety record, and provides 45- to 65-minute flights covering the waterfalls of the West Maui Mountains, Haleakalā Crater, Hāna, even the spectacular sea cliffs of Molokaʻi. Prices range from $217 to $286 with considerable discounts available on the Web site. ⊠*Kahului Heliport, Hangar 110, Kahului* ☎*877/238–4942 or 808/877–7005* ⊕*www.airmaui. com.*

Blue Hawaiian Helicopters. Blue Hawaiian has provided aerial adventures in Hawaiʻi since 1985, and has been integral in some of the filming Hollywood has done on Maui. Its AStar helicopters are air-conditioned and have noise-blocking headsets for all passengers. Flights are 30 to 65 minutes and cost $125 to $280. They also offer a fly–drive special to Hāna with Temptation Tours limo vans. ⊠*Kahului Heliport, Hangar 105, Kahului* ☎*808/871–8844* ⊕*www.bluehawaiian.com.*

Sunshine Helicopters. Sunshine offers tours of Maui and Moloka'i, as well as the Big Island, in its *Black Beauty* AStar or WhisperStar aircraft. A pilot-narrated videotape of your actual flight is available for purchase. Prices are $158 to $425 for 30 to 90 minutes. First-class seating is available for a fee. ⊠ *Kahului Heliport, Hangar 107, Kahului* 🕾 *808/871–0722 or 800/544–2520* ⊕ *www.sunshinehelicopters. com.*

HIKING

Hikes on Maui range from coastal seashore to verdant rain forest to alpine desert. Orchids, hibiscus, ginger, heliconia, and anthuriums grow wild on many trails, and exotic fruits like mountain apple, lilikoi (passion fruit), thimbleberry, and strawberry guava provide refreshing snacks for hikers. Ironically, much of what you see in lower altitude forests is alien, brought to Hawai'i at one time or another by someone hoping to improve upon nature. Plants like strawberry guava and ginger may be tasty, but they grow over native forest plants and have become serious, problematic weeds.

The best hikes get you out of the imported landscaping and into the truly exotic wilderness. Hawai'i possesses some of the world's rarest plants, insects, and birds. Pocket field guides are available at most grocery or drug stores and can really illuminate your walk. Before you know it you'll be nudging your companion and pointing out trees that look like something out of a Dr. Seuss book. If you watch the right branches quietly you can spot the same Honeycreepers or Happy-faced Spiders scientists have spent their lives studying.

HALEAKALĀ NATIONAL PARK

HALEAKALĀ CRATER

Fodor'sChoice ★ Hiking Haleakalā Crater is undoubtedly the best hiking on the island. There are 30 mi of trails, two camping areas, and three cabins. If you're in shape, you can do a day hike descending from the summit (along Sliding Sands Trail) to the crater floor. If you're in shape and have time, consider spending several days here amid the cinder cones, lava flows, and all that loud silence.

Going into the crater is like going to a different planet. In the early 1960s NASA actually brought moon-suited astronauts here to practice what it would be like to "walk on the moon." Today, on one of the many hikes—most moderate to strenuous—you'll traverse black sand and wild lava formations, follow the trail of blooming *'ahinahina* (silverswords), watch for *nēnē* (Hawaiian geese) as they fly above you, and witness tremendous views of big sky and burnt-red cliffs. If you're lucky enough to camp or stay in one of the cabins, you'll fall asleep under a wide screen of shooting stars, while the 'alauahio birds murmur around you like a litter of pups.

The best time to go into the crater is in the summer months, when the conditions are generally more predictable. Be sure to bring layered clothing—and plenty of warm clothes if you're staying overnight. It may be scorching hot during the day, but it gets mighty chilly after dark. Ask a ranger about water availability before starting your hike. Note that overnight visitors must get a permit at park headquarters before entering the crater; day-use visitors do not need a permit. Cabins are $70 per night, and fit 12 people. They book months in advance by lottery, though it's possible to get lucky due to last-minute cancellations. To reserve a cabin, write at least two months in advance to **Haleakalā National Park** (✉ *Box 369, Makawao, HI 96768* ☎ *808/572–4459*).

⇨ *For detailed information on hikes in the crater, see Haleakalā National Park in chapter 2, Exploring Maui.*

'OHE'O GULCH

A branch of Haleakalā National Park, 'Ohe'o Gulch is famous for its pools (the area is sometimes called the "Seven Sacred Pools"). Truth is, there are more than seven pools, and there's nothing sacred about them. The owner of the Hotel Hāna started calling the area "Seven Sacred Pools" to attract the masses to sleepy old Hāna. His plan worked and the name stuck, much to the chagrin of most Mauians. The Pools of 'Ohe'o is another name for them.

The best time to visit the pools is in the morning, before the crowds and tour buses arrive. Start your day with a vigorous hike. 'Ohe'o has some fantastic trails to choose from, including our favorite, the Pipiwai Trail *(see below)*. When you're done, nothing could be better than going to the pools, lounging on the rocks, and cooling off in the freshwater reserves.

You'll find 'Ohe'o Gulch on Route 31, 10 mi past Hāna town. All visitors must pay a $10 national park fee (per car not per person), which is valid for one week and can be used at Haleakalā's summit as well.

Important note: The road beyond 'Ohe'o Gulch to Kaupo was closed at this writing because of a 2006 earthquake that caused some instability and falling rocks. ■TIP➜**Check with officials at Haleakalā National Park (☎808-572-4400; dial 0 during the recorded message to speak to a representative during office hours) before traveling beyond 'Ohe'o Gulch.**

Pipiwai Trail. This moderate 2-mi trek upstream leads to the 400-

KEEP IN MIND

Wear sturdy shoes while hiking; you'll want to spare your ankles from a crash course in loose lava rock. When hiking near streams or waterfalls, be extremely cautious: flash floods can occur at any time. Do not drink stream water or swim in streams if you have open cuts; bacteria and parasites are not the souvenir you want to take home with you. Wear sunscreen, a hat, and layered clothing, and be sure to drink plenty of water (even if you don't feel thirsty). At upper elevations, the weather is guaranteed to be extreme—alternately chilly or blazing.

foot Waimoku Falls, pounding down in all its power and glory. Follow signs from the parking lot up the road, past the bridge overlook, and uphill into the forest. Along the way you can take side trips and swim in the stream's basalt-lined pools. The trail bridges a sensational gorge and passes onto a boardwalk through a mystifying forest of giant bamboo. This stomp through muddy and rocky terrain takes around three hours to fully enjoy. It's best

> **KALAUPAPA TRAIL**
>
> You can take an overnight trip to the island of Moloka'i for a day of hiking down to Kalaupapa Peninsula and back, by means of a 3-mi, 26-switchback trail. The trail is nearly vertical, traversing the face of some of the highest sea cliffs in the world. *See A Tale of Tragedy & Triumph in chapter 10, Moloka'i for more information.*

done early in the morning, before the touring crowds arrive (though it can never truly be called crowded). ⊠ *Trailhead: On highway toward 'Ohe'o bridge, near mile marker 42 ⊙ 3 hrs, 4 mi round-trip.*

Kahakai Trail. This easy ¼-mi hike (more like a walk) stretches between Kuloa Point and the Kipahulu campground. You'll see rugged shoreline views and can stop to gaze at the surging waves below. ⊠ *Trailhead: Kuloa Point ⊙ 15 mins, ½ mi round-trip.*

Kuloa Point Trail. An easy ½-mi walk, this trail takes you from the Kipahulu Visitor Center down to the Pools of 'Ohe'o at Kuloa Point. On the trail you pass native trees and precontact Hawaiian sites. Don't forget to wear your suit and bring your towel if you plan to take a dip in the pools. Keep in mind: no lifeguards are on duty and you'll want to stick to the pools—don't even think about swimming in the ocean. ⊠ *Trailhead: Kipahulu Visitor Center ⊙ 30 mins, 1 mi round-trip.*

Campsites. Down at the grassy sea cliffs at the Pools of 'Ohe'o, you can camp, no permit required, although you can stay only three nights. Toilets, grills, and tables are available, but there's no water and open fires are prohibited. For more information, call the Kipahulu Visitor Center. ☞ *Visitor Center: ☎ 808/248–7375 ⊕ www.nps.gov/hale.*

POLIPOLI FOREST

A good hiking area—and something totally unexpected on a tropical island—is Polipoli Forest (6,500 feet). During the Great Depression the government began a program to reforest the mountain, and soon cedar, pine, cypress, and even redwood took hold. Today, the area feels more like Vermont than Hawai'i. It's cold and foggy here, and often wet, but don't let that stop you from going. There's something about the enormity of the trees, the quiet mist and mysterious caves that will make you feel you've discovered an unspoken secret, and one you'll want to keep to yourself.

To reach the forest, take Route 37 all the way out to the far end of Kula. Then turn left at Route 377. After about a ½ mi, turn right at Waipoli Road. First you'll encounter switchbacks; after that the road is

Continued on page 114

HAWAI'I'S PLANTS 101

Hawai'i is a bounty of rainbow-colored flowers and plants. The evening air is scented with their fragrance. Just look at the front yard of almost any home, travel any road, or visit any local park and you'll see a spectacular array of colored blossoms and leaves. What most visitors don't know is that the plants they are seeing are not native to Hawai'i; rather, they were introduced during the last two centuries as ornamental plants, or for timber, shade, or fruit.

Hawai'i boasts nearly every climate on the planet, excluding the two most extreme: arctic tundra and arid desert. The Islands have wine-growing regions, cactus-speckled ranchlands, icy mountaintops, and the rainiest forests on earth.

Plants introduced from around the world thrive here. The lush lowland valleys along the windward coasts are predominantly populated by non-native trees including yellow- and red-fruited **guava**, silvery-leafed **kukui**, and orange-flowered **tulip trees**.

The colorful **plumeria flower**, very fragrant and commonly used in lei making, and the

giant multicolored **hibiscus flower** are both used by many women as hair adornments, and are two of the most common plants found around homes and hotels. The umbrella-like **monkeypod tree** from Central America provides shade in many of Hawai'i's parks including Kapiolani Park in Honolulu. Hawai'i's largest tree, found in Lahaina, Maui, is a giant **banyan tree.** Its canopy and massive support roots cover several acres. The native **o'hia tree**, with its brilliant red brush-like flowers, and the **hapu'u**, a giant tree fern, are common in Hawai'i's forests and are also used ornamentally in gardens and around homes.

Bougainvillea	Guava	Monkeypod Tree
Banyan Tree	O'hia Lehua	Tulip Tree
Plumeria	Pandanus	Hibiscus
Anthurium	Kukui Tree	Hapu'u Okina

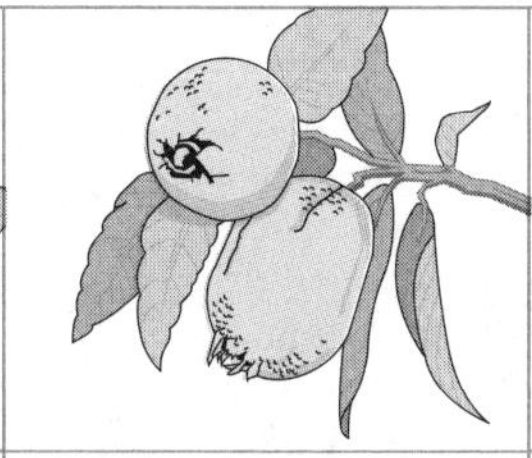

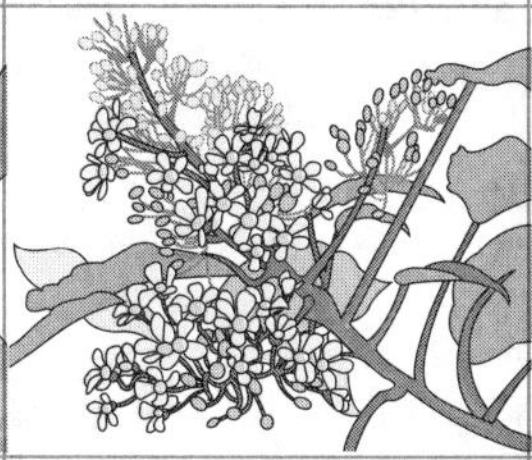

DID YOU KNOW?

Over 2,200 plant species are found in the Hawaiian Islands, but only about 1,000 are native. Of these, 282 are so rare, they are endangered. Hawai'i's endemic plants evolved from ancestral seeds arriving on the islands over thousands of years as baggage on birds, floating on ocean currents, or drifting on winds from continents thousands of miles away. Once here, these plants evolved in isolation creating many new species known nowhere else in the world.

just plain bad, but passable. Signs say that four-wheel-drive vehicles are required, though standard cars have been known to make it. Use your best judgment. There are great trails here for all levels, along with a small campground, and a cabin that you can rent from the Division of State Parks.

Important note: A major fire in January 2007 caused the closing of the Polipoli state park, with summer as the estimated time of reopening. Trail and campground conditions may have changed. ■TIP➔Be sure to check with the Division of State Parks or the Maui Visitor Bureau (800/525–6284) before visiting to prevent disappointment.

> **MOSQUITOES**
>
> Mosquitoes can be particularly pesky around pools and waterfalls—especially when the sun doesn't shine (dawn, dusk, and on overcast days). There's an easy solution: pack bug spray. It's a simple step that saves you lots of scratching later on. If you forget, ask to borrow some from a fellow hiker on the trail. People are pretty friendly on Maui and will be glad to help you out.

Write far in advance for the **cabin** (⌂ *Box 1049, Wailuku 96793* ☎ *808/244–4354*); for the campground, you can wait until you arrive in Wailuku and visit the **Division of State Parks** (⊠ *54 High St.* ☎ *808/984–8109*).

Boundary Trail. This 4-mi moderate trail begins just past the Kula Forest Reserve boundary cattle guard on Polipoli Road, and descends into the lower boundary southward, all the way to the Ranger's cabin at the junction of the Redwood and Plum Trails. Link it with these trails, and you've got a hearty 5-mi day hike. The trail crosses many scenic gulches, with an overhead of tall eucalyptus, pine, cedar, and plum trees. Peep through the trees for wide views of Kula and Central Maui. ⊠ *Trailhead: Polipoli Forest Campground* ☻ *3–4 hrs, 5-mi loop.*

Redwood Trail. This easy and colorful hike winds through redwoods and conifers past the short Tie Trail down to the old ranger's cabin. Although the views are limited, groves of trees and flowering bushes abound. At the end of the trail is an old cabin site and three-way junction with the Plum Trail and the Boundary Trail. ⊠ *Trailhead: From parking area at Polipoli campground, walk back up road ¼ mi and look to your left* ☻ *1–2 hrs, 3.4 mi round-trip.*

Upper Waiakoa Trail. This scenic albeit rugged trail starts at the Polipoli Access Road (look for trailheads) and proceeds up Haleakalā through mixed pine and past caves and thick shrubs. It crosses the land of Kaonoulu to the land of Waiakoa, where it reaches its highest point—7,800 feet. Here you'll find yourself in barren, raw terrain with fantastic views. At this point, you can either turn around, or continue on to the 3-mi Waiakoa Loop. Other than a cave shelter, there's no water or other facilities on either of these trails, so come prepared. ⊠ *Trailhead: Look for signs on Polipoli Access Rd.* ☻ *5–6 hrs, 14 mi round-trip.*

IN THE FOOTSTEPS OF KINGS

A much neglected hike is the coastal **Hoapili Trail** (☒ *Follow Mākena Alanui to end of paved road at La Pérouse Bay, walk through parking lot along dirt road, follow signs*) beyond the 'Āhihi-Kīna'u Natural Area Reserve. Named after a bygone Hawaiian king, it follows the shoreline, threading through the remains of ancient Hawaiian villages. The once-thriving community was displaced by one of Maui's last lava flows. Later, King Hoapili was responsible for overseeing the creation of an island-wide highway. This remaining section, a wide path of stacked lava rocks, is a marvel to look at and walk on, though it's not the easiest surface for the ankles. (It's rumored to have once been covered in grass.) You can wander over to the Hanamanioa lighthouse, or quietly ponder the rough life of the ancients.

Wear sturdy shoes and bring extra water. This is brutal territory with little shade and no facilities. Beautiful, yes. Accommodating, no.

'ĪAO VALLEY STATE PARK

★ In Hawaiian, 'Īao means "supreme cloud." When you enter this mystical valley in the middle of an unexpected rain forest, you'll know why. At 750 feet above sea level, the 10-mi valley clings to the clouds as if it's trying to cover its naked beauty. If you've been spending too many days in the sun, the cool shade and moist air may be just the welcome change you need.

One of Maui's great wonders, the valley is the site of a famous battle to unite the Hawaiian islands. Out of the clouds, the 'Īao Needle, a tall chunk of volcanic rock, stands as a monument to the long-ago lookout for Maui warriors. Today, there's nothing warlike about it: the valley is a peaceful land of lush, tropical plants, clear pools and a running stream, and easy, enjoyable walks.

To get to 'Īao Valley State Park, go through Wailuku and continue to the west end of Route 32. The road dead ends into the parking lot. The park is open daily 7 AM to 7 PM. Facilities are available. (For park information call ☎808/984–8109.)

'Īao Valley Trail. Anyone (including your grandparents) can take this easy hike from the parking lot at 'Īao Valley State Park. On your choice of two paved walkways, you can cross the 'Īao Stream and explore the junglelike area. Ascend the stairs up to the 'Īao Needle for spectacular views of Central Maui, or pause in the garden of Hawaiian heritage plants and marvel at the local youngsters hurling themselves from the bridge into the chilly pools below. ☒ *Trailhead: 'Īao Valley parking lot* ☋ *30 mins, ½ mi round-trip.*

GUIDED HIKES

☼ **Hawai'i Nature Center.** In 'Īao Valley, the Hawai'i Nature Center leads easy, interpretive hikes for children and their families. ☒ *875 'Īao Valley Rd., Wailuku* ☎ *808/244–6500* ⊕ *www.hawaiinaturecenter.org.*

CLOSE UP

Hawai'i Flora & Fauna

With all of its diverse climate zones, Hawai'i is home to a wide variety of plant life, from cacti to grape vines. The Islands have wine-growing regions, cactus-speckled ranchlands, icy mountaintops, and the rainiest forests on earth. The Galapagos has *nothing* on Hawai'i's biodiversity—more than 90% of Hawaiian plants and animals are endemic, meaning they exist nowhere else on earth. Most of the plants you see while walking around, however, aren't Hawaiian at all. Tropical flowers such as plumeria, orchids, red ginger, heliconia, and anthuriums are Asian or South American imports now growing wild on all the Islands.

Native Hawaiian plants are weird-looking, in the best sense. Take the silversword, for example. A giant, furry firework of a plant, it grows in one of the world's harshest climates: the summits of Haleakalā and Mauna Kea. Its 7-foot stalk, brimming with red or pale yellow flowers, blooms once and then dies. 'Ōhi'a trees—thought to be the favorite of Pele, the volcano goddess—bury their roots in fields of once-molten lava and sprout ruby pom-pom-like lehua blossoms. The deep yellow petals of 'ilima (once reserved for royalty) are tiny discs, which make the most elegant leis.

To match Hawai'i's unique flora, fantastic birds and insects evolved. Honeycreepers, distant relatives of the finch, have fabulously long, curved bills perfect for sipping nectar from lehua blossoms. The world's only carnivorous caterpillar can snatch a Hawaiian picture-wing fly from the air in less than a second. Hawai'i's state bird, the nēnē goose, is making a comeback from its former endangered status. It roams freely in parts of Maui, Kaua'i, and the Big Island. Pairs who mate for life are often spotted ambling across roads in Haleakalā or Hawai'i Volcanoes national park.

At the Kīlauea Point National Wildlife Refuge on Kaua'i, hundreds of Laysan albatross, wedge-tail shearwaters, red-footed boobies, and other marine birds glide and soar within photo-op distance of visitors to Kīlauea Lighthouse. Boobie chicks hatch in the fall and emerge from nests burrowed into cliff-side dirt banks and even under—any launching pad from which the fledgling flyer can catch the nearest air current.

Hawai'i's two native mammals are rare sights. Doe-eyed Hawaiian monk seals breed in the northwestern islands. With only 1,500 left in the wild, you probably won't catch many lounging on the beaches of Hawai'i's populated islands, though they have been spotted on the shores of Kaua'i in recent years. You can see rescued pups and adults along with Hawaiian green sea turtles at Sea Life Park and the Waikīkī Aquarium on O'ahu. The shy Hawaiian bat hangs out primarily at Kealakekua Bay on the Big Island.

Fodor's Choice **Hike Maui.** Hike Maui is the oldest hiking company on the Islands,
★ its rain forest, mountain ridge, crater, coastline, and archaeological-snorkel hikes are led by such knowledgeable folk as ethno-botanists and marine biologists. Prices range from $75 to $150 for hikes of 3 to 10 hours, including lunch (discounts are available for advance, online bookings). Hike Maui supplies waterproof day packs, rain ponchos, first-aid gear, water bottles, lunch and/or snacks for the longer hikes,

and transportation to the site. ☎ *808/879–5270* ⊕ *www.hikem-aui.com.*

FodorsChoice ★ **Friends of Haleakalā National Park.** This nonprofit offers day and overnight service trips into the crater, and in the Kipahulu region. The purpose of your trip, the service work itself, isn't too much—mostly removing invasive plants and light cabin maintenance. Chances are you'll make good friends and have more fun than on a hike you'd do on your own. Trip leader Farley, or one of his equally knowledgeable cohorts, will take you to places you'd never otherwise see, and teach you about the native flora and birds along the way. Bring your own water; share food in group dinners. Admission is free. ☎ *808/248–7660* ⊕ *www.fhnp.org.*

> **DAY HIKE CHECKLIST**
>
> ■ Water (at least 2 quarts per person)
>
> ■ Food—fruit and trail mix
>
> ■ Rain gear—especially if going into the crater
>
> ■ Hiking shoes with good ankle support
>
> ■ Layered clothing
>
> ■ Wide-brimmed hat and sunglasses
>
> ■ Sunscreen (SPF 30 or higher recommended)
>
> ■ Mosquito repellent

Maui Eco Adventures. For excursions into remote areas, Maui Eco Adventures is your choice. The ecologically minded company leads hikes into private or otherwise inaccessible areas. Hikes, which can be combined with kayaking, mountain biking, or sailing trips, explore botanically rich valleys in Kahakuloa and East Maui, as well as Hāna, Haleakalā, and more. Guides are botanists, mountaineers, boat captains, and backcountry chefs. Excursions are $80 to $160. ✉ *180 Dickenson St., Suite 101, Lahaina* ☎ *808/661–7720 or 877/661–7720* ⊕ *www.eco-maui.com.*

Maui Hiking Safaris. Hikes with Maui Hiking Safaris are limited to groups of eight or less. Excursions include hikes to waterfalls, Haleakalā, rain forests, and more. You can choose any two hikes to customize your own full-day tour. Hikes range from $60 to $140. ✉ *273 Leolani Pl., Pukalani* ☎ *808/573–0168 or 888/445–3963* ⊕ *www.mauihikingsafaris.com.*

Paths in Paradise. Paths in Paradise is a small company offering specialized hikes into wetlands, rain-forest areas, and the crater. The owner, RenateGassman-Duvall, is an expert birder and biologist. She helps hikers spot native honeycreepers feeding on lehua blossoms and supplies them with bird and plant check cards. Half-day hikes run $110, and full-day hikes are $135, with lunch and gear provided. ☎ *808/579–9294* ⊕ *www.hookipa.com/paths/index.htm.*

★ **Sierra Club.** A great avenue into the island's untrammeled wilderness is Maui's chapter of the Sierra Club. Rather than venturing out on your own, join one of the club's hikes into pristine forests and Valley Isle watersheds, or along ancient coastal paths. Several hikes a month are led by informative naturalists who carry first-aid kits and arrange waivers to access private land. Some outings include volunteer service, but most are just for fun. Bring your own food and water, sturdy shoes, and a suggested donation of $5—a true bargain. ✉ *Box 791180, Pāʻia* ☎ *808/579–9802* ⊕ *www.hi.sierraclub.org/maui.*

HORSEBACK RIDING

Several companies on Maui offer horseback riding that's far more appealing than the typical hourlong trudge over a dull trail with 50 other horses.

GUIDED RIDES

Charley's Trail Rides & Pack Trips. Rides with this company require a stout physical nature (but not a stout physique: riders must weigh less than 200 pounds). Overnight trips go from Kaupō, a *tiny* village nearly 20 mi past Hāna, up the slopes of Haleakalā, where you spend the night in the crater. Charley is a bona-fide *paniolo* (Hawaiian cowboy); overnight tours with him include meals, park fees, and camping supplies for $300 per person ($250 if you'd rather bring your own food), whereas day tours are available for $100 per person. Book several weeks in advance if you'd prefer a cabin instead of a tent. ☎ *808/248–8209* ⊕ *www.mauihikes.com.*

Fodor'sChoice ★ **Maui Stables.** Hawaiian-owned and run, this company provides a trip back in time, to an era when life moved more slowly and reverently—though galloping is allowed, if you're able to handle your horse! Educational tours begin at the stable in remote Kipahulu (near Hāna), and pass through several historic Hawaiian sites. Before heading up into the forest, your guides intone the words to a traditional *oli,* or chant, asking for permission to enter. By the time you reach the mountain pasture overlooking Waimoku Falls, you'll feel lucky to have been a part of the tradition. Both morning and afternoon rides are available at $150 per rider. ✉ *Between mile markers 40 and 41 on Hwy. 37, Hāna* ☎ *808/248–7799* ⊕ *www.mauistables.com.*

Fodor'sChoice ★ **Mendes Ranch.** Family-owned and run, Mendes operates out of the beautiful ranchland of Kahakuloa on the windward slopes of the West Maui Mountains. Two-hour morning and afternoon trail rides ($110) are available with an optional barbecue lunch ($20). Cowboys will take you cantering up rolling pastures into the lush rain forest to view some of Maui's biggest waterfalls. Mendes caters to weddings and parties and offers private trail rides on request. Should you need accommodations they have a home and bunk for rent right on the property. ✉ *Hwy. 340, Wailuku* ☎ *808/244–7320 or 808/871–8222* ⊕ *www. mendesranch.com.*

Piʻiholo Ranch. The local wranglers here will lead you on a rousing ride through family ranchlands—up hillside pastures, beneath a eucalyptus canopy, and past many native trees. Morning picnic rides are 3½ hours and include lunch. Morning and afternoon "country" rides are two hours. Their well-kept horses navigate the challenging terrain easily, but hold on when deer pass by! Prices are $120 to $160. Private rides and lessons are available. ⊠*End of Waiahiwi Rd., Makawao* ☎*808/357–5544* ⊕*www.piiholo.com.*

Pony Express Tours. Pony Express Tours offers trips on horseback into Haleakalā Crater. The half-day ride goes down to the crater floor for a picnic lunch; the full-day excursion covers 12 mi of terrain and visits some of the crater's unusual formations. Both are a great way to see the top of the dormant volcano. The company also offers one- and two-hour rides on the slopes of the Haleakalā Ranch. Prices range from $90 to $175. ☎*808/667–2200* ⊕*www.ponyexpresstours.com.*

ON THE SIDELINES

At the **Kapalua Jr. Vet/Sr. Tennis Championships** in May, players compete in singles and doubles. On Labor Day, the **Wilson Kapalua Open Tennis Tournament** calls Hawai'i's hitters to Kapalua's Tennis Garden and Village Tennis Center. Also at the Tennis Center, Women's International Tennis Association pros rally with amateurs at the **Kapalua Betsy Nagelsen Tennis Invitational** in December. All events are put on by the **Kapalua Tennis Club** (☎*808/669–5677*). The **Wailea Open Tennis Championship** is held at the Wailea Tennis Club (☎*808/879–1958*).

POLO

Polo is popular with the Upcountry *paniolos* (Hawaiian cowboys) on Maui. From April through June Haleakalā Ranch hosts "indoor" or arena contests on a field flanked by side boards. The field is on Route 377, 1 mi from Route 37. During the "outdoor" polo season, mid-August to the end of October, matches are held at Olinda Field, 1 mi above Makawao on Olinda Road. There's a $5 admission for most games, which start at 1:30 ᴏ- on Sunday. The **Manduke Baldwin Memorial Tournament** (☎*808/877–7744* ⊕*www.mauipoloclub.com*) occurs on Memorial Day and is a popular two-day event. The Maui Polo Club draws challengers from Argentina, England, South Africa, New Zealand, and Australia. For information, call or visit the Web site.

RODEOS

With dozens of working cattle ranches throughout the Islands, many youngsters learn to ride a horse before they can drive a car. Mauians love their rodeos and put on several for students at local high schools. *Paniolos* (Hawaiian cowboys) get in on the action, too, at three major annual events: the **Oskie Rice Memorial Rodeo,** usually staged the weekend after Labor Day; the **Cancer Benefit Rodeo** in April; and Maui's biggest event, drawing competitors from all the Islands as well as the U.S. mainland, the **4th of July Rodeo,** which comes with a full parade in Makawao town and other festivities that last for days.

TENNIS

Most courts charge by the hour but will let players continue after their initial hour for free, provided no one is waiting. In addition to the facilities listed below, many hotels and condos have courts open to non-guests for a fee. The best free courts are the five at the **Lahaina Civic Center** (⊠ *1840 Honoapi'ilani Hwy., Lahaina* ☎ *808/661–4685*), near Wahikuli State Park. They're available on a first-come, first-served basis.

Kapalua Tennis Garden. This complex, home to the Kapalua Tennis Club, serves the Kapalua Resort with 10 courts, 4 lighted for night play, and a pro shop. You'll pay $14 an hour if you're a guest, $16 if you're not. ⊠ *100 Kapalua Dr., Kapalua* ☎ *808/669–5677.*

Mākena Tennis Club. Mākena features six Plexipave courts, two of which are lighted for night play. Private lessons, rentals, ball machines, racquet stringing, and weekly clinics are available. ⊠ *Wailea Alanui Dr., Mākena* ☎ *808/879–8777.*

Wailea Tennis Club. The club has 11 Plexipave courts (its famed grass courts are, sadly, a thing of the past), lessons, rentals, and ball machines. On weekday mornings clinics are given to help you improve ground strokes, serve, volley, or doubles strategy. Rates are $12 per hour, per person, with three lighted courts available for night play. ⊠ *131 Wailea Ike Pl., Kīhei* ☎ *808/879–1958 or 800/332–1614.*

Shops & Spas

WORD OF MOUTH

"Don't miss the Maui swap meet, held every Saturday from 7 AM until noon. The local artists and local farmers bring all of their goods, and you can buy things for a fraction of the price you will find in the shops."

—Nancy 1013

"The spa at the Grande Wailea is out of this world if you want to splurge."

—KimF

SHOPS

By Shannon Wianecki

Whether you're searching for a dashboard hula dancer or an original Curtis Wilson Cost painting, you can find it on Front Street in Lahaina or at the Shops at Wailea. Art sales are huge in the resort areas, where artists regularly show up to promote their work. Alongside the flashy galleries are standards like Quicksilver and ABC store, where you can stock up on swim trunks, sunscreen, and flip-flops.

Don't miss the great boutiques lining the streets of small towns like Pā'ia and Makawao. You can purchase boutique fashions and art while strolling through these charming, quieter communities. Notably, several local designers—Tamara Catz, Sig Zane, and Maui Girl—all produce top-quality island fashions. In the neighboring galleries, local artisans turn out gorgeous work in a range of prices. Special souvenirs include rare hardwood bowls and boxes, prints of sea life, Hawaiian quilts, and blown glass.

Specialty food products—pineapples, coconuts, or Maui onions—and "Made in Maui" jams and jellies make great, less-expensive souvenirs. Cook Kwee's Maui Cookies have gained a following, as have Maui Potato Chips. Coffee sellers now offer Maui-grown-and-roasted beans alongside the better-known Kona varieties. Remember that fresh fruit must be inspected by the U.S. Department of Agriculture before it can leave the state, so it's safest to buy a box that has already passed inspection.

Business hours for individual shops on the island are usually 9 to 5, seven days a week. Shops on Front Street and in shopping centers tend to stay open later (until 9 or 10 on weekends).

WEST MAUI

SHOPPING CENTERS

Lahaina Cannery Mall. In a building reminiscent of an old pineapple cannery are 50 shops and an active stage. The mall hosts fabulous free events year-round (like the International Jazz Festival). Recommended stops include Na Hoku, purveyor of striking Hawaiian heirloom jewelry and pearls; Totally Hawaiian Gift Gallery; and Kite Fantasy, one of the best kite shops on Maui. An events schedule is on the Web site. ⊠ *1221 Honoapi'ilani Hwy., Lahaina* ☎ *808/661–5304* ⊕ *www.lahainacannery.com.*

Lahaina Center. Island department store Hilo Hattie Fashion Center anchors the complex and puts on a free hula show at 2 PM every Wednesday and Friday. In addition to Hard Rock Cafe, Warren & Anabelle's Magic Show, and a four-screen cinema, you can find a replica of an ancient Hawaiian village complete with three full-size thatch huts built with 10,000 feet of Big Island 'ōhi'a wood, 20 tons of *pili* grass, and more than 4 mi of handwoven coconut *senit* (twine). There's all that *and* validated parking. ⊠ *900 Front St., Lahaina* ☎ *808/667–9216.*

Whalers Village. Chic Whalers Village has a whaling museum and more than 50 restaurants and shops. Upscale haunts include Louis Vuitton, Ferragamo, Versace, and Chanel Boutique. The complex also offers some interesting diversions: Hawaiian artisans display their crafts daily; hula dancers perform on an outdoor stage weeknights from 7 to 8; and three films spotlighting whales and marine history are shown daily for free at the Whale Center of the Pacific. ⊠*2435 Kā'anapali Pkwy., Kā'anapali* ☎*808/661–4567.*

BOOKSTORES

Fodor'sChoice **Old Lahaina Book Emporium.** Down
★ a narrow alley you will find this bookstore stacked from floor to ceiling with new and antique finds. Spend a few moments (or hours) browsing the maze of shelves filled with mystery, sci-fi, nature guides, art, military history, and more. Collectors can scoop up rare Hawaiian memorabilia: playing cards, coasters, rare editions, and out-of-print-books chronicling Hawai'i's colorful past. ⊠*In the alley next door, 834 Front St., Lahaina* ☎*808/661–1399* ⊕*www.oldlahaina-bookemporium.com.*

CLOTHING

Hilo Hattie Fashion Center. Hawai'i's largest manufacturer of aloha shirts and mu'umu'u also carries brightly colored blouses, skirts, and children's clothing. ⊠*Lahaina Center, 900 Front St., Lahaina* ☎*808/661–8457.*

Honolua Surf Company. If you're not in the mood for a matching aloha shirt and mu'umu'u ensemble, check out this surf shop—popular with young men and women for surf trunks, casual clothing, and accessories. ⊠*845 Front St., Lahaina* ☎*808/661–8848.*

Maggie Coulombe. Maggie Coulombe's cutting-edge fashions have the style of SoHo and the heat of the Islands. The svelte, body-clinging designs are unique and definitely worth a look. ⊠*505 Front St., Lahaina* ☎*808/662–0696.*

GALLERIES

Lahaina Galleries. Works of both national and international artists are displayed at the gallery's two locations in West Maui. ⊠*828 Front St., Lahaina* ☎*808/667–2152* ⊠*In the Shops at Wailea, 3750 Wailea Alanui Dr., Wailea* ☎*808/874–8583.*

BEST MADE-ON-MAUI GIFTS

■ *Koa* jewelry boxes from **Maui Hands.**

■ Fish-shape sushi platters and bamboo chopsticks from the **Maui Crafts Guild.**

■ Black pearl pendant from **Maui Divers.**

■ Handmade Hawaiian quilt from **Hāna Coast Gallery.**

■ Jellyfish paperweight from **Hot Island Glassblowing Studio & Gallery.**

■ Fresh plumeria lei, made by you!

6

Lahaina Printsellers Ltd. Hawaiʻi's largest selection of original antique maps and prints pertaining to Hawaiʻi and the Pacific is available here. You can also buy museum-quality reproductions and original oil paintings from the Pacific Artists Guild. A second, smaller shop is at 505 Front Street. ⊠ *Whalers Village, 2435 Kāʻanapali Pkwy., Kāʻanapali* ☎ *808/667–7617.*

Martin Lawrence Galleries. Martin Lawrence displays the works of noted mainland artists, including Andy Warhol and Keith Haring, in a bright and friendly gallery. ⊠ *Lahaina Market Pl., Front St. and Lahainaluna Rd., Lahaina* ☎ *808/661–1788* ⊕ *www.martinlawrence.com.*

Village Gallery. This gallery, with two locations on the island, showcases the works of such popular local artists as Betty Hay Freeland, Wailehua Gray, Margaret Bedell, George Allen, Joyce Clark, Pamela Andelin, Stephen Burr, and Macario Pascual. ⊠ *120 Dickenson St., Lahaina* ☎ *808/661–4402* ⊠ *Ritz-Carlton, 1 Ritz-Carlton Dr., Kapalua* ☎ *808/669–1800* ⊕ *www.villagegalleriesmaui.com.*

JEWELRY

Jessica's Gems. Jessica's has a good selection of Hawaiian heirloom jewelry, and its Lahaina store specializes in black pearls. ⊠ *Whalers Village, 2435 Kāʻanapali Pkwy., Kāʻanapali* ☎ *808/661–4223* ⊠ *858 Front St., Lahaina* ☎ *808/661–9200.*

Lahaina Scrimshaw. Here you can buy brooches, rings, pendants, cuff links, tie tacks, and collector's items adorned with intricately carved sailors' art. ⊠ *845A Front St., Lahaina* ☎ *808/661–8820* ⊠ *Whalers Village, 2435 Kāʻanapali Pkwy., Kāʻanapali* ☎ *808/661–4034.*

Maui Divers. This company has been crafting gold and coral into jewelry for more than 20 years. ⊠ *640 Front St., Lahaina* ☎ *808/661–0988.*

CENTRAL MAUI

SHOPPING CENTERS

Kaʻahumanu Center. This is Maui's largest mall with 75 stores, a movie theater, an active stage, and a food court. The mall's interesting rooftop, composed of a series of manta ray–like umbrella shades, is easily spotted. Stop at Camellia Seed Shop for what the locals call "crack seed," a delicacy made from dried fruits, nuts, and lots of sugar. Other stops here include mall standards such as Macy's, Gap, and American Eagle Outfitters. ⊠ *275 Kaʻahumanu Ave., Kahului* ☎ *808/877–3369.*

Maui Mall. The anchor stores here are Longs Drugs and Star Market, and there's a decent Chinese restaurant, Dragon Dragon. The Tasaka Guri Guri Shop is an oddity—it's been around for nearly a hundred years, selling an ice-cream–likeconfection called "guri guri." The mall also has a whimsically designed 12-screen megaplex. ✉*70 Ka'ahumanu Ave., Kahului* ☎*808/872–4320.*

Maui Marketplace. On the busy stretch of Dairy Road, just outside the Kahului Airport, this behemoth marketplace couldn't be more conveniently located. The 20-acre complex houses several outlet stores and big retailers, such as Pier One Imports, Sports Authority, and Borders Books & Music. Sample local food at the Kau Kau Corner food court. ✉*270 Dairy Rd., Kahului* ☎*808/873–0400.*

CLOTHING

Bohemia. Tucked in a tiny mall next to Kahului Harbor, this consignment shop overflows with vintage Hawaiiana, as well as top-quality designer resale. ✉*101 Ka'ahumanu Ave., Kahului* ☎*808/893–2500.*

Hi-Tech. Stop here immediately after deplaning to stock up on surf trunks, windsurfing gear, bikinis, and sundresses. ✉*425 Koloa Rd., Kahului* ☎*808/877–2111.*

FodorśChoice
★ **Sig Zane.** Local clothing designer Sig Zane draws inspiration from island botanical treasures—literally. His sketches of Hawaiian flowers such as *puakenikeni* and *maile* decorate the brightly colored fabrics featured in his shop. The aloha shirts and dresses here are works of art—original and not too flashy. ✉*53 Market St., Wailuku* ☎*808/249–8997.*

FOOD SPECIALTIES

Maui Coffee Roasters. This café and roasting house near Kahului Airport is the best stop for Kona and Island coffees. The salespeople give good advice and will ship items. You even get a free cup of joe in a signature to-go cup when you buy a pound of coffee. ✉*444 Hāna Hwy., Unit B, Kahului* ☎*808/877–2877* ⊕*www.hawaiiancoffee.com.*

THE SOUTH SHORE

SHOPPING CENTERS

Azeka Place Shopping Center. Azeka II, on the *mauka* (toward the mountains) side of South Kīhei Road, has Longs Drugs (the place for slippers), the Coffee Store (the place for iced mochas), Who Cut the Cheese (the place for aged gouda), and the Nail Shop (the place for shaping, waxing, and tweezing). Azeka I, the older half on the *makai* (toward the ocean) side of the street, has a decent Vietnamese restaurant and Kīhei's post office. ✉*1280 S. Kīhei Rd., Kīhei* ☎*808/879–5000.*

Kīhei Kalama Village Marketplace. This is a fun place to investigate. Shaded outdoor stalls sell everything from printed and hand-painted T-shirts and sundresses to jewelry, pottery, wood carvings, fruit, and gaudily painted coconut husks—some, but not all, made by local craftspeople. ✉*1941 S. Kīhei Rd., Kīhei* ☎*808/879–6610.*

Rainbow Mall. This mall is one-stop shopping for condo guests—it offers video rentals, Hawaiian gifts, plate lunches, and a liquor store. ✉*2439 S. Kīhei Rd., Kīhei.*

Continued on page 128

ALL ABOUT LEIS

Leis brighten every occasion in Hawai'i, from birthdays to bar mitz-vahs to baptisms. Creative artisans weave nature's bounty—flowers, ferns, vines, and seeds—into gorgeous creations that convey an array of heartfelt messages: "Welcome," "Congratulations," "Good luck," "Farewell," "Thank you," "I love you." When it's difficult to find the right words, a lei expresses exactly the right sentiments.

WHERE TO BUY THE BEST LEIS

These florists carry a nice variety of leis: **A Special Touch** (Emerald Plaza, 142 Kupuohi St., Ste. F-1, Lahaina, 808/661–3455); **Kahului Florist** (Maui Mall, 70 E. Ka'ahumanu Ave., Kahului, 808/877–3951 or 800/711–8881); and **Wailea Flowers by Cora** (1280 S. Kīhei Rd., Ste. 126, Kīhei, 808/879–7249 or 800/339–0419). **Costco**, **Kmart**, **Wal-Mart**, and **Safeway** also sell leis, but their choices are usually limited to "basics" such as orchid, plumeria, and tuberose.

LEI ETIQUETTE

■ To wear a closed lei, drape it over your shoulders, half in front and half in back. Open leis are worn around the neck, with the ends draped over the front in equal lengths.

■ Pīkake, ginger, and other sweet, delicate blossoms are "feminine" leis. Men opt for cigar, crown flower, and carnation, which are sturdier and don't emit as much fragrance.

■ Leis are always presented with a kiss, a custom that supposedly dates back to World War II when a hula dancer fancied an officer at a U.S.O. show. Taking a dare from members of her troupe, she took off her lei, placed it around his neck, and kissed him on the cheek.

■ You shouldn't wear a lei before you give it to someone else. Hawaiians believe the lei absorbs your *mana* (spirit); if you give your lei away, you'll be giving away part of your essence.

ALL ABOUT LEIS

6

ORCHID

Growing wild on every continent except Antarctica, orchids—which range in color from yellow to green to purple—comprise the largest family of plants in the world. There are more than 20,000 species of orchids, but only three are native to Hawai'i—and they are very rare. The pretty lavender vanda you see hanging by the dozens at local lei stands has probably been imported from Thailand.

MAILE

Maile, an endemic twining vine with a heady aroma, is sacred to Laka, goddess of the hula. In ancient times, dancers wore maile and decorated hula altars with it to honor Laka. Today, "open" maile leis usually are given to men. Instead of ribbon, interwoven lengths of maile are used at dedications of new businesses. The maile is untied, never snipped, for doing so would symbolically "cut" the company's success.

'ILIMA

Designated by Hawai'i's Territorial Legislature in 1923 as the official flower of the island of O'ahu, the golden 'ilima is so delicate it lasts for just a day. Five to seven hundred blossoms are needed to make one garland. Queen Emma, wife of King Kamehameha IV, preferred 'ilima over all other leis, which may have led to the incorrect belief that they were reserved only for royalty.

PLUMERIA

This ubiquitous flower is named after Charles Plumier, the noted French botanist who discovered it in Central America in the late 1600s. Plumeria ranks among the most popular leis in Hawai'i because it's fragrant, hardy, plentiful, inexpensive, and requires very little care. Although yellow is the most common color, you'll also find plumeria leis in shades of pink, red, orange, and "rainbow" blends.

PĪKAKE

Favored for its fragile beauty and sweet scent, pīkake was introduced from India. In lieu of pearls, many brides in Hawai'i adorn themselves with long, multiple strands of white pīkake. Princess Kaiulani enjoyed showing guests her beloved pīkake and peacocks at Āinahau, her Waikīkī home. Interestingly, pīkake is the Hawaiian word for both the bird and the blossom.

KUKUI

The kukui (candlenut) is Hawai'i's state tree. Early Hawaiians strung kukui nuts (which are quite oily) together and burned them for light; mixed burned nuts with oil to make an indelible dye; and mashed roasted nuts to consume as a laxative. Kukui nut leis may not have been made until after Western contact, when the Hawaiians saw black beads from Europe and wanted to imitate them.

The Shops at Wailea. Stylish, upscale, and close to most of the resorts, this mall brings high fashion to Wailea. Luxury boutiques such as Gucci, Fendi, Cos Bar, and Tiffany & Co. have shops, as do less-expensive chains like Gap, Guess, and Tommy Bahama's. Several good restaurants face the ocean, and regular Wednesday-night events include live entertainment, art exhibits, and fashion shows. ⊠*3750 Wailea Alanui Dr., Wailea* ☎*808/891–6770.*

> **SIMPLE SOUVENIRS**
>
> **Take Home Maui.** The folks at this colorful grocery and deli will supply, pack, and deliver produce to the airport or your hotel. ⊠ *121 Dickenson St., Lahaina* ☎ *808/661–8067 or 800/545–6284.*

CLOTHING

Cruise. This upscale resort boutique has sundresses, swimwear, sandals, bright beach towels, and a few nice pieces of resort wear. ⊠*In the Grand Wailea, 3850 Wailea Alanui Dr., Wailea* ☎*808/875–1234.*

The Enchantress. Painted silk Sue Wong gowns and glittering tiaras command attention in the window of the Enchantress—the only boutique on the island where you can buy a fantasy wedding gown off the rack. Indulge the little girl within by flaunting a feather-fringed handbag, or hand-painted cowboy boots. It's true—Paris shops here. ⊠*The Shops at Wailea, 3750 Wailea Alanui Dr., Wailea* ☎*808/891–6360.*

Hilo Hattie Fashion Center. Hawai'i's largest manufacturer of aloha shirts and mu'umu'u also carries brightly colored blouses, skirts, and children's clothing. ⊠*297 Pi'ikea Ave., Kīhei* ☎*808/875–4545.*

Honolua Surf Company. If you're in the mood for colorful print tees and sundresses, check out this surf shop. It's popular with young men and women for surf trunks, casual clothing, and accessories. ⊠*2411 S. Kīhei Rd., Kīhei* ☎*808/874–0999.*

Sisters & Company. Opened by four sisters, this little shop has a lot to offer—current brand-name clothing such as Tamara Catz and ener-chi, locally made jewelry, beach sandals, and gifts. Sister No. 3, Rhonda, runs a tiny, ultrahip hair salon in back. ⊠*1913 S. Kīhei Rd., Kīhei* ☎*808/875–9888.*

Tommy Bahama's. It's hard to find a man on Maui who *isn't* wearing a TB–logo aloha shirt. For better or worse, here's where you can get yours. Make sure to grab a Barbados Brownie on the way out at the restaurant attached to the shop. ⊠*The Shops at Wailea, 3750 Wailea Alanui Dr., Wailea* ☎*808/879–7828.*

UPCOUNTRY, THE NORTH SHORE & HĀNA

CLOTHING

Biasa Rose. This boutique offers hip island styles for the whole family. The owners have also created unique gifts—pillows, napkins, photo albums—with batik fabrics they've acquired while traveling through Indonesia. ✉104 Hāna Hwy., Pā'ia ☎808/579–8602.

Collections. This eclectic boutique is brimming with pretty jewelry, humorous gift cards, Italian bags and sandals, yoga wear, and Asian print silks. ✉3677 Baldwin Ave., Makawao ☎808/572–0781.

Moonbow Tropics. If you're looking for an aloha shirt that won't look out of place on the mainland, make a stop at this little store, which sells the best-quality shirts on the island. ✉36 Baldwin Rd., Pā'ia ☎808/579–8592.

Fodor'sChoice ★ **Tamara Catz.** This Maui designer already has a world-wide following, and her sarongs and super-stylish beachwear have been featured in many fashion magazines. If you're looking for a sequined bikini or a delicately embroidered sundress, this is the place to check out. ✉83 Hāna Hwy., Pā'ia ☎808/579–9184.

SWIMWEAR **Hāna Hwy. Surf.** You can grab trunks and bikinis, and a board, if needed, at this surf shack on the North Shore. ✉149 Hāna Hwy., Pā'ia ☎808/579–8999.

Fodor'sChoice ★ **Maui Girl.** This is *the* place for swimwear, cover-ups, beach hats, and sandals. Maui Girl designs its own suits and imports teenier versions from Brazil as well. Tops and bottoms can be purchased separately, greatly increasing your chances of finding a suit that actually fits. ✉13 Baldwin Ave., Pā'ia ☎808/579–9266.

GALLERIES

★ **Hāna Coast Gallery.** One of the best places to shop on the island, this 3,000-square-foot gallery has fine art and jewelry on consignment from local artists. ✉Hotel Hāna-Maui, Hāna Hwy., Hāna ☎808/248–8636 or 800/637–0188.

Hāna Cultural Center. The center sells distinctive island quilts and other Hawaiian crafts. ✉4974 Uakea St., Hāna ☎808/248–8622.

Hot Island Glass. With furnaces glowing bright orange and loads of mesmerizing sculptures on display, this is an exciting place to visit. The working studio, set back from Makawao's main street in a little courtyard, is owned by a family of glassblowers. ✉3620 Baldwin Ave., Makawao

---

BEST BETS FOR SWIMWEAR

Hi-Tech. ✉425 Koloa Rd., Kahului ☎808/877–2111.

Honolua Surf Company. ✉845 Front St., Lahaina ☎808/661–8848 ✉2411 S. Kīhei Rd., Kīhei ☎808/874–0999.

Maui Girl. ✉13 Baldwin Ave., Pā'ia ☎808/579–9266.

Hāna Hwy. Surf. ✉149 Hāna Hwy., Pā'ia ☎808/579–8999.

☎ *808/572–4527* ⊕ *www.hotis-landglass.com.*

Fodor's Choice ★   **Maui Crafts Guild.** This is one of the more interesting galleries on Maui. Set in a two-story wooden building alongside the highway, the Guild is crammed with treasures. Resident artists craft everything in the store—from Norfolk-pine bowls to *raku* (Japanese lead-glazed) pottery to original sculpture. The prices are surprisingly low. Upstairs, gorgeous pieces of handcrafted hardwood furniture are on display. ⊠ *43 Hāna Hwy., Pā'ia* ☎ *808/579–9697.*

★   **Maui Hands.** This gallery shows work by dozens of local artists, including *paniolo-* (Hawaiian cowboy) theme lithographs by Sharon Shigekawa, who knows whereof she paints: she rides each year in the Kaupō Roundup. ⊠ *3620 Baldwin Ave., Makawao* ☎ *808/572–5194.*

JEWELRY

Master Touch Gallery. The exterior of this shop is as rustic as all the old buildings of Makawao, so there's no way to prepare yourself for the elegance of the handcrafted jewelry displayed within. Owner David Sacco truly has the "master touch." ⊠ *3655 Baldwin Ave., Makawao* ☎ *808/572–6000.*

GROCERY STORES ON MAUI

Foodland. In Kīhei town center, this is the most convenient supermarket for those staying in Wailea. It's open round-the-clock. ⊠ *1881 S. Kīhei Rd., Kīhei* ☎ *808/879–9350.*

Lahaina Square Shopping Center Foodland. This Foodland serves West Maui and is open daily from 6 AM to midnight. ⊠ *840 Waine'e St., Lahaina* ☎ *808/661–0975.*

Mana Foods. Stock up on local fish and grass-fed beef for your barbecue here. You can find the best selection of organic produce on the island, as well as a great bakery and deli at this typically crowded health-food store. ⊠ *49 Baldwin Ave., Pā'ia* ☎ *808/579–8078.*

Safeway. Safeway has three stores on the island open 24 hours daily. ⊠ *Lahaina Cannery Mall, 1221 Honoapi'ilani Hwy., Lahaina* ☎ *808/667–4392* ⊠ *170 E. Kamehameha Ave., Kahului* ☎ *808/877–3377* ⊠ *277 Piikea Ave., Kīhei* ☎ *808/891–9120.*

SPAS

Traditional Swedish massage and European facials anchor most spa menus, though you'll also find shiatsu, ayurveda, aromatherapy, and other body treatments drawn from cultures across the globe. *Lomi Lomi*, traditional Hawaiian massage involving powerful strokes down the length of the body, is a regional specialty passed down through generations. Many treatments incorporate local plants and flowers. *Awapuhi*, or Hawaiian ginger, and *noni*, a pungent-smelling fruit, are regularly used for their therapeutic benefits. *Limu*, or seaweed, and even coffee is employed in rousing salt scrubs and soaks. And this is just the beginning.

Fodor'sChoice
★ **The Spa at Four Seasons Resort.** The Four Seasons' hawklike attention to detail is reflected here. Thoughtful gestures like fresh flowers beneath the massage table (to give you something to stare at), organic herbal tea in the "relaxation room," and your choice of music begin to ease your mind and muscles before your treatment even begins. The spa is genuinely stylish and serene, and the therapists are among the best. Thanks to an exclusive partnership, the spa offers treatments created by celebrity skin-care specialist Kate Somerville. The "Ultimate Kate" is 80 minutes of super hydrating, collagen-increasing magic, incorporating light therapy and powerful, tingling products that literally wipe wrinkles away. ⊠ *3900 Wailea Alanui Dr., Wailea* ☎ *808/874–8000 or 800/334–6284* ⊕ *www.fourseasons.com* ☞ *$140 50-minute massage, $355 3-treatment packages; Hair salon, steam room. Gym with: cardiovascular machines, free weights, weight-training equipment. Services: aromatherapy, body wraps, facials, hydrotherapy, massage. Classes and programs: aquaerobics, meditation, personal training, Pilates, Spinning, tai chi, yoga.*

Fodor'sChoice
★ **Spa Grande, Grand Wailea Resort.**
Built to satisfy an indulgent Japanese billionaire, this 50,000-square-foot spa makes others seem like well-appointed closets. Slathered in honey and wrapped up in the steam room (if you go for the Ali'i honey steam wrap), you'll feel like royalty. All treatments include a loofah scrub and a trip to the *termé*, a hydrotherapy circuit including a Roman Jacuzzi, furo bath, plunge pool, powerful waterfall and Swiss jet showers, and five therapeutic baths. (Soak for 10 minutes in the moor mud to relieve sunburn or jellyfish stings.) To fully enjoy the baths, plan to arrive an hour before your treatment. Free

---

SPA TIPS

■ Arrive early for your treatment so you can enjoy the steam room and other amenities.

■ Bring a comfortable change of clothing and remove your jewelry.

■ Most spas are clothing-optional. If a swimsuit is required, you will be notified.

■ If you're pregnant, or have allergies, inform the receptionist before booking a treatment.

■ Your therapist should be able to explain the ingredients of products being used in your treatment. If anything stings or burns, say so.

6

with treatments, the termé is also available separately for $85 ($115 for non-hotel guests). At times—especially during the holidays—this wonderland can be crowded. ✉*3850 Wailea Alanui Dr., Wailea* ☎*808/875–1234 or 800/888–6100* ⊕*www.grandwailea.com* ⌇ *$165 50-minute massage, $350 half-day spa packages; Hair salon, hot tub, sauna, steam room. Gym with: cardiovascular machines, free weights, racquetball, weight-training equipment. Services: aromatherapy, body wraps, facials, hydrotherapy, massage, Vichy shower. Classes and programs: aquaerobics, cycling, Pilates, qigong, yoga.*

Fodor'sChoice ★ **The Spa at Hotel Hāna-Maui.** A bamboo gate opens into an outdoor sanctuary with a lava-rock pool and hot tub; at first glimpse this spa seems to have been organically grown, not built. The decor here can hardly be called decor—it's an abundant, living garden. Taro varieties, orchids, and ferns still wet from Hāna's frequent downpours nourish the spirit as you rest with a cup of jasmine tea, or take an invigorating dip in the plunge pool. Signature aromatherapy treatments utilize *Honua,* the spa's own sumptuous blend of sandalwood, coconut, ginger, and vanilla orchid essences. The Hāna Wellness package is a blissful eight hours of treatments, which can be shared between the family, or enjoyed alone. ✉*Hotel Hāna-Maui, Hāna Hwy., Hāna* ☎*808/270–5290* ⊕*www.hotelhanamaui.com* ⌇ *$140 60-minute massage, $395 spa packages; Hair salon, hot tubs (indoor and outdoor), sauna, steam room. Gym with: cardiovascular machines, free weights, weight-training equipment. Services: aromatherapy, body wraps, facials, hydrotherapy, massage. Classes and programs: meditation, Pilates, yoga.*

Spa Kea Lani, Fairmont Kea Lani Hotel Suites & Villas. This small spa is a little cramped, but nicely appointed: fluffy robes and Italian mints greet you upon arrival. We recommend the excellent *lomi lomi* massage—a series of long, soothing strokes combined with gentle stretching, or the *ili ili* hot stone therapy. Both treatments employ indigenous healing oils: rich *kukui* nut, kava, and *noni,* and tropical fragrances. Poolside massages by the divinely serene adult pool can be reserved on the spot. A fully-renovated, state-of-the-art, 1,440-square-foot fitness center is in the works. ✉*4100 Wailea Alanui Dr., Wailea* ☎*808/875–4100 or 800/659–4100* ⊕*www.kealani.com* ⌇ *$120 55-minute massage, $295 spa packages; Hair salon, steam room. Gym with: cardiovascular machines, free weights, weight-training equipment. Services: aromatherapy, body wraps, facials, hydrotherapy, massage, Vichy shower. Classes and programs: aquaerobics, yoga.*

Spa Moana, Hyatt Regency Maui. Spa Moana's oceanfront salon has a million-dollar view; it's a perfect place to beautify before your wedding or special anniversary. An older facility, it's spacious and well-appointed, offering traditional Swedish and Thai massage, reiki, and shiatsu, in addition to numerous innovative treatments such as the invigorating Ka'anapali coffee salt scrub, and the Royal Moana, an immune-boosting hot paraffin wrap combined with a facial and *kukui* nut oil scalp massage. For body treatments, the oceanfront rooms are a tad too warm—request one in back. ✉*200 Nohea Kai Dr., Lahaina* ☎*808/661–1234 or 800/233–1234* ⊕*www.maui.hyatt.com* ⌇ *$140*

50-minute massage, $378 all-day spa packages; Hair salon, hot tub, sauna, steam room. Gym with: cardiovascular machines, free weights, weight-training equipment. Services: aromatherapy, body wraps, facials, hydrotherapy, massage, Vichy shower. Classes and programs: aquaerobics, Pilates, tai chi, yoga.

★ **The Spa at the Westin Maui.** An exquisite 80-minute Lavender Body Butter treatment is the star of this spa's menu, thanks to a partnership with a local lavender farm. Other options include cabana massage (for couples, too) and water lily sunburn relief with green tea. The facility is flawless, and it's worth getting a treatment just to sip lavender lemonade in the posh ocean-view waiting room. The open-air yoga studio and the gym offer energizing workouts. Bridal parties can request a private area within the salon. ⊠ *Westin Kā'anapali, 2365 Kā'anapali Pkwy., Kā'anapali ☎ 808/667–2525 ⊕ www.westinmaui.com ☞ $125 50-minute massage, $280 day spa packages; Hair salon, hot tub, sauna, steam room. Gym with: cardiovascular machines, free weights, weight-training equipment. Services: aromatherapy, body wraps, facials, hydrotherapy, massage, Vichy shower. Classes and programs: aquaerobics, yoga.*

Waihua, Ritz-Carlton, Kapalua. If the stress of traveling has fried your nerves (or even if it hasn't), book a Waihua signature treatment such as "Harmony" or "Family Relations," which employs aromatherapy, hot stones, and massage. High-quality, handcrafted products enhance treatments inspired by Hawaiian culture, such as the *lomi lomi* massage with healing plant essences followed by a salt foot scrub. The newly refurbished facility offers superb services and a well-stocked boutique. Attention fitness junkies: personal DVD players are attached to the state-of-the-art cardiovascular machines. ⊠ *1 Ritz-Carlton Dr., Kapalua ☎ 808/669–6200 or 800/262–8440 ⊕ www.ritzcarlton. com ☞ $135 50-minute massage, $395 half-day spa packages; Hair salon, sauna, steam room. Gym with: cardiovascular machines, free weights, weight-training equipment. Services: aromatherapy, body wraps, facials, massage. Classes and programs: aquaerobics, nutrition, yoga.*

BUDGET-FRIENDLY SPAS

If hotel spa prices are a little intimidating, try **Spa Luna** (⊠ *810 Ha'ikū Rd., Ha'ikū* ☎ *808/575–2440*), a day spa, which is also an aesthetician's school. In the former Ha'ikū Cannery, it offers services ranging from massage to microdermabrasion. You can opt for professional services, but the student clinics are the real story here. The students are subject to rigorous training, and their services are offered at a fraction of the regular cost ($25 for a 50-minute massage).

6

Entertainment & Nightlife

WORD OF MOUTH

"We also went to the Feast at Lele and would give it thumbs up! We decided on the Feast because we wanted a table to ourselves and no buffet. The food was very good and the show was excellent. You will not be disappointed with this lūʻau."

—Spikeit

"Mulligans's is an Irish pub, notable for its live entertainment, which we enjoyed immensely."

—Iregeo

By Elaine Gast
Updated
by Amy
Westervelt

LOOKING FOR WILD ISLAND NIGHTLIFE? We can't promise you'll always find it here. This quiet island has little of Waikīkī's after-hours decadence, and the club scene (if you want to call it that) can be quirky, depending on the season and the day of the week. But sometimes Maui will surprise you with a big-name concert, outdoor festival, or special event, and it seems the whole island usually shows up for the party.

Before 10 PM, there's a lot to offer by way of lūʻau shows, dinner cruises, and tiki-lighted cocktail hours. Aside from that, you should at least be able to find some down-home DJ-spinning or the strum of acoustic guitars at your nearest watering hole. Lahaina and Kīhei are your best bets for action. Lahaina tries to uphold its reputation as a party town, and succeeds every Halloween when thousands of masqueraders converge for a Mardi Gras–style party on Front Street. Kīhei is a bit more local and can be something of a rough and rowdy crowd in parts. On the right night, both towns stir with activity, and if you don't like one scene, there's always next door.

Outside of Lahaina and Kīhei, you might be able to hit an "on" night in Pāʻia (North Shore) or Makawao (Upcountry), mostly on weekend nights. Your best bet? Pick up the free *MauiTime Weekly,* or Thursday's edition of the *Maui News,* where you'll find a listing of all your after-dark options, island-wide.

★ The **Maui Arts & Cultural Center** (⊠ *1 Cameron Way, above harbor on Kahului Beach Rd.* ☎ *808/242–2787*) is the hub of all high-brow arts and quality performances. Their events calendar features everything from rock to reggae to Hawaiian slack key, international dance and circus troupes, political and literary lectures, art films, cult classics—you name it. Each Wednesday (and occasionally Friday) evening, the MACC (as it's locally known) hosts movie selections from the Maui Film Festival. The complex includes the 1,200-seat Castle Theater, a 4,000-seat amphitheater for large outdoor concerts, the 350-seat McCoy Theater for plays and recitals, and a courtyard café offering pre-show dining and drinks. For information on current events, check the Events Box Office (☎ *808/242–7469* ⊕ *www.mauiarts.org*) or *Maui News.*

ENTERTAINMENT

LŪʻAU

A trip to Hawaiʻi isn't complete without a good lūʻau. With the beat of drums and the sway of hula, lūʻau give you a snippet of Hawaiian culture left over from a long-standing tradition. Early Hawaiians celebrated many occasions with lūʻau—weddings, births, battles, and more. The feasts originally brought people together as an offering to the gods, and to practice *hoʻokipa,* the act of welcoming guests. The word *lūʻau* itself refers to the taro root, a staple of the Hawaiian diet, which, when pounded, makes a grey, pudding-like substance called *poi.* You'll find *poi* at all the best feasts, along with platters of salty fish, fresh fruit, and *kālua* (baked underground) pork.

Lū'au are still held by locals today to mark milestones or as informal, family-style gatherings. For tourists, they are a major attraction, and for that reason, have become big business. Keep in mind—some are watered-down tourist traps just trying to make a buck, others offer a night you'll never forget. As the saying goes, you get what you pay for.
■ TIP→**Many of the best lū'au book weeks, sometimes months, in advance, so reserve early. Plan your lū'au night early on in your trip to help you get into the Hawaiian spirit.**

★ **The Feast at Lele.** "Lele" is an older, more traditional name for Lahaina. This feast redefines the lū'au by crossing it with island-style fine dining in an intimate beach setting. Each course of this succulent sit-down meal expresses the spirit of specific island cultures—Hawaiian, Samoan, Tongan, Tahitian—and don't forget dessert. Dramatic Polynesian entertainment accompanies the dinner, along with excellent wine and liquor selections. This is the most expensive lū'au on the island for a reason: Lele is top-notch. ✉505 Front St., Lahaina ☎808/667–5353 ⌕Reservations essential ⊕www.feastatlele.com ⌦$105 ⊘Nightly at sunset; 5:30 PM in winter, 6 PM in summer.

Fodor'sChoice **Old Lahaina Lū'au.** Many consider this the best lū'au on Maui; it's certainly the most traditional. Located right on the water, at the northern end of town, the Old Lahaina Lū'au is small, personal, and as authentic as it gets. Sitting either at a table or on a *lauhala* mat, you'll dine on all-you-can-eat Hawaiian cuisine: pork *laulau* (wrapped with taro sprouts in *tī* leaves), a'hi *poke* (pickled raw tuna, tossed with herbs and seasonings), *lomilomi* salmon (rubbed with onions and herbs), Maui-style mahimahi, *haupia* (coconut pudding), and more. At sunset the show begins a historical journey that relays key periods in Hawai'i's history, from the arrival of the Polynesians to the influence of the missionaries and, later, tourism. The tanned, talented performers will charm you with their music, chanting, and variety of hula styles (modern and *kahiko*, the ancient way of communicating with the gods). But if it's fire dancers you want to see, you won't find them here, as they aren't considered traditional. Although it's performed nightly, this lū'au sells out regularly. Make your reservations when planning your trip to Maui. You can cancel up until 10 AM the day of the scheduled show. ✉1251 Front St., makai (toward the ocean) of Lahaina Cannery Mall, Lahaina ☎808/667–1998 ⌕Reservations essential ⊕www.oldlahainaluau.com ⌦$89 Nightly at 5:30 PM in winter, 6 PM in summer.

DINNER & SUNSET CRUISES

There's no better place to see the sun set on the Pacific than from one of Maui's many boat tours. You can find a tour to fit your mood, as you can choose anything from a quiet, sit-down dinner to a festive, beer-swigging booze cruise.

Tours leave from Mā'alaea or Lahaina harbors. Be sure to arrive at least 15 minutes early (count in the time it will take to park). The dinner cruises typically feature music and are generally packed—which is great if you're feeling social, but you might have to fight for a good

Continued on page 141

MORE THAN A FOLK DANCE

Hula has been called "the heartbeat of the Hawaiian people." Also, "the world's best-known, most misunderstood dance." Both true. Hula isn't just dance. It is storytelling. No words, no hula.

Chanter Edith McKinzie calls it "an extension of a piece of poetry." In its adornments, implements, and customs, hula integrates every important Hawaiian cultural practice: poetry, history, genealogy, craft, plant cultivation, martial arts, religion, protocol. So when 19th-century Christian missionaries sought to eradicate a practice they considered depraved, they threatened more than just a folk dance.

With public performance outlawed and private hula practice discouraged, hula went underground for a generation, to rural villages. The fragile verbal link by which culture was transmitted from teacher to student hung by a thread. Even increasing literacy did not help because hula's practitioners were—and, to a degree, still are—a secretive and protected circle.

As if that weren't bad enough, vaudeville, Broadway, and Hollywood got hold of the hula, giving it the glitz treatment in an unbroken line from "Oh, How She Could Wicky Wacky Woo" to "Rock-A-Hula Baby." Hula became shorthand for paradise: fragrant flowers, lazy hours. Ironically, this development assured that hundreds of Hawaiians could make a living performing and teaching hula. Many danced 'auana (modern form) in performance; but taught kahiko (traditional), quietly, at home or in hula schools.

Today, 30 years after the cultural revival known as the Hawaiian Renaissance, language immersion programs have assured a new generation of proficient—and even eloquent—chanters, song-writers, and translators. Visitors can see more, and more authentic, hula than at any other time in the last 200 years.

Like the culture of which it is the beating heart, hula has survived.

Lei *po'o*. Head lei. In kahiko, greenery only. In 'auana, flowers.

Face emotes appropriate expression. Dancer should not be a smiling automaton.

Shoulders remain relaxed and still, never hunched, even with arms raised. No bouncing.

Eyes always follow leading hand.

Lei. Hula is rarely performed without a shoulder lei.

Arms and hands remain loose, relaxed, below shoulder level—except as required by interpretive movements.

Traditional hula skirt is loose fabric, smocked and gathered at the waist.

Hip is canted over weight-bearing foot.

Knees are always slightly bent, accentuating hip sway.

In kahiko, feet are flat. In 'auana, may be more arched, but not tiptoes or bouncing.

Kupe'e. Ankle bracelet of flowers, shells, or—traditionally—noise-making dog teeth.

MORE THAN A FOLK DANCE

7

BASIC MOTIONS

Speak or Sing

Moon or Sun

Grass Shack or House

Mountains or Heights

Love or Caress

At backyard parties, hula is performed in bare feet and street clothes, but in performance, adornments play a key role, as do rhythm-keeping implements.

In hula kahiko (traditional style), the usual dress is multiple layers of stiff fabric (often with a pellon lining, which most closely resembles *kapa*, the paper-like bark cloth of the Hawaiians). These wrap tightly around the bosom but flare below the waist to form a skirt. In pre-contact times, dancers wore only kapa skirts. Monarchy-period hula is performed in voluminous Mother Hubbard muʻumuʻu or high-necked muslin blouses and gathered skirts. Men wear loincloths or, for monarchy period, white or gingham shirts and black pants—sometimes with red sashes.

In hula ʻauana (modern), dress for women can range from grass skirts and strapless tops to contemporary tea-length dresses. Men generally wear aloha shirts, but sometimes grass skirts over pants or even everyday gear. (One group at a recent competition wore wetsuits to do a surfing song!)

SURPRISING HULA FACTS

■ Grass skirts are not traditional; workers from Kiribati (the Gilbert Islands) brought this custom to Hawaiʻi.

■ In olden-day Hawaiʻi, *mele* (songs) for hula were composed for every occasion—name songs for babies, dirges for funerals, welcome songs for visitors, celebrations of favorite pursuits.

■ Hula *maʻi* is a traditional hula form in praise of a noble's genitals; the power of the *ʻali* (royalty) to procreate gave *mana* (spiritual power) to the entire culture.

■ Hula students in old Hawaiʻi adhered to high standards: scrupulous cleanliness, no sex, daily cleansing rituals, certain food prohibitions, and no contact with the dead. They were fined if they broke the rules.

WHERE TO WATCH

■ Kāʻanapali Beach Hotel: Employees break into song at any excuse, teach daily hula lessons, and staff a free nightly hour-long hula show and torchlighting ceremony. ☎ 808/661-0011.

■ Feast of Lele: Nightly beachside lūʻau includes show that strives for authenticity. ☎ 866/244-5353.

■ Whalers Village: Twice-weekly free evening hula shows (usually Wednesday and Saturday, but check schedule). ☎ 808/661-4567.

■ Hula festivals: Festival of Hula, January, Lahaina Cannery Mall; Na Mele O Maui/Emma Farden Sharpe Hula Festival, December, Kāʻanapali Resort.

seat. You can usually get a much better meal at one of the local restaurants, and opt instead for a different type of tour. Most non-dinner cruises offer *pūpū* (appetizers) and an open bar, and sometimes a chocolate and champagne toast.

Winds are consistent in summer, but variable in winter—sometimes making for a rocky ride. If you're worried about sea sickness, you might consider a catamaran, which is much more stable than a monohull. Keep in mind, the boat crews are experienced in dealing with such matters. The best advice? Take Dramamine before the trip, and if you feel sick, sit in the shade (but not inside the cabin), place a cold rag or ice on the back of your neck, and *breathe* as you look at the horizon. In the worst-case scenario, aim downwind—and shoot for distance.

> ## STARGAZING
>
> For nightlife of a different sort, children and astronomy buffs should try stargazing at **Tour of the Stars**, a one-hour program held nightly on the roof or patio of the Hyatt Regency Maui. **Romance of the Stars**, with champagne and chocolate-covered strawberries, is held on Friday and Saturday nights at 11. Check-in at the hotel lobby 15 minutes prior to starting time. ✉ *Lahaina Tower, Hyatt Regency Maui Resort & Spa, 200 Nohea Kai Dr., Kā'anapali* ☎ *808/661–1234 Ext. 4727* 💲 *$20–$25* ⊘ *Nightly at 8, 9, and 10; Fri. and Sat. romantic program at 11.*

America II Sunset Sail. The star of this two-hour cruise is the craft itself— a 1987 America's Cup 12-meter class contender that will take you on a wild ride. This trip is all about the sail, so you can count out any cocktails or fancy food. But if it's adventure you're looking for, you will go fast, you will get wet … and you will have fun. Private charters available. ✉ *Slip 6, Lahaina Harbor, Lahaina* ☎ *808/667–2195* ⊕ *www. sailingonmaui.com* 💲 *$40* ⊘ *Daily 4–6* PM.

Kaulana Cocktail Cruise. This two-hour sunset cruise prides itself on its live music and festive atmosphere. Accommodating up to 100 people, the cruise generally attracts a younger, more boisterous crowd. *Pūpū*, such as meatballs, smoked salmon, and teriyaki pineapple, are served, and the open bar includes frozen drinks. ✉ *Lahaina Harbor, Lahaina* ☎ *808/667–9595* ⊕ *www.kaulana-of-maui.com* 💲 *$60* ⊘ *Weekdays 4:30–7:30* PM.

Pacific Whale Foundation Dinner or Cocktail Cruise. All aboard the sleek double-deck power catamaran *Ocean Quest* for a dinner of grilled steak and chicken, mahimahi, and Island Rum Macadamia Nut pie. This cruise holds up to 147 people, so it can be crowded. You might opt for the 50-foot catamaran sail on *Manute'a*, a relaxing "booze cruise," with hot and cold appetizers, live entertainment, and an open bar. ✉ *Ocean Discovery Store, 612 Front St., Lahaina* ☎ *808/249– 8811* ⊕ *www.pacificwhale.org* 💲 *$79 dinner cruise; cocktail cruises $40 (2 drinks included, cold appetizers), $50 (open bar, hot and cold* *appetizers)* ⊘ *Daily, call for seasonal check-in times. No cocktail cruise Fri.*

Paragon Champagne Sunset Sail. This 47-foot catamaran brings you a performance sail within a personal setting. Limited to groups of 24 (with private charters available), you can spread out on deck and enjoy the gentle trade winds. An easygoing, attentive crew will serve you hot and cold *pūpū*, such as grilled chicken skewers, spring rolls, and a veggie platter, along with beer, wine, mai

> **MAUI MIDNIGHT**
>
> If you want to see any action on Maui, head out early. Otherwise, you might be out past what locals call "Maui Midnight," where as early as 9 PM the restaurants close and the streets empty. What can you expect, though, when most people wake up with the sun? After a long, salty day of sea and surf, you might be ready for some shut-eye yourself.

tais, and champagne at sunset. This is one of the best trips around. ⊠ *Loading Dock, Lahaina Harbor* ☎ *808/244–2087* ⊕ *www.sailmaui. com* ⊠ *$51* ⊘ *Mon., Wed., Fri. evenings only; call for check-in times.*

Pride Charters. A 65-foot catamaran built specifically for Maui's waters, the *Pride of Maui* has a spacious cabin, dance floor, and large upper deck for unobstructed viewing. Evening cruises include cocktails and a buffet of *pūpū* such as grilled chicken, beef and veggie kebabs, and warm Asian wontons. ⊠ *Māʻalaea Harbor, Māʻalaea* ☎ *877/867–7433* ⊕ *www.prideofmaui.com* ⊠ *$50* ⊘ *Tues., Thurs., and Sat. 5–7:30 pm.*

Scotch Mist Charters. Sailing is at its best on this two-hour champagne cruise. The 25-passenger Santa Cruz 50 sloop *Scotch Mist II* will give you an intimate and exhilarating ride, with complimentary champagne, fresh pineapple, juice, beer, and wine. Private charters are available. ⊠ *Slip 2, Lahaina Harbor, Lahaina* ☎ *808/661–0386* ⊕ *www.scotchmistsailingcharters.com* ⊠ *$50* ⊘ *Daily, call for seasonal check-in times.*

Spirit of Lahaina Cocktail or Dinner Cruise. This double-deck, 65-foot catamaran offers you a choice of a full dinner cruise, featuring freshly grilled steak, mahimahi, and shrimp, or a cocktail cruise with appetizers, drinks, and dessert. Both cruises feature contemporary Hawaiian music and hula show. ⊠ *Slip 4, Lahaina Harbor* ☎ *808/662–4477* ⊕ *www. spiritoflahaina.com* ⊠ *$76 dinner cruise, $55 cocktail cruise* ⊘ *Daily 5–7:15 pm.*

FILM & THEATER

In the heat of the afternoon, a theater may feel like paradise. There are megaplexes showing first-run movies in Kukui Mall (Kīhei), Lahaina Center, and Maui Mall and Kaʻahumanu Shopping Center (Kahului). For live theater, check local papers for events and showtimes.

Maui Academy of Performing Arts. For over 30 years, this nonprofit performing-arts group has offered fine productions, as well as dance and drama classes for children and adults. Recent shows have included *Peter Pan,* the *Complete Works of William Shakespeare,* and the *Wizard of Oz.* Call ahead for performance venue. ✉*2027 Main St., Wailuku* ☎*808/244–8760* ⊕*www.mauiacademy.org* ▭*$10–$12.*

★ **Maui Film Festival.** In this ongoing celebration, the Maui Arts & Cultural Center features art-house films every Wednesday (and sometimes Friday) evening at 5 and 7:30 PM, accompanied by live music, dining, and poetry in the Candlelight Café. In summer an international week-long festival attracts big-name celebrities to Maui for cinema under the stars. ☎*808/579–9244 recorded program information* ⊕*www.mauifilmfestival.com.*

Maui OnStage. Located at the Historic ʻIao Theater, this nonprofit theater group stages four to six shows per season. Look for upcoming productions such as *Seussical* and *Go-Go Beach.* Each October, they hold an "Evening of Stars" Masquerade Ball, which can be a hoot of the costumed kind. ✉*ʻIao Theater, 68 N. Market St., Wailuku* ☎*808/242–6969* ⊕*www.mauionstage.com* ▭*$15–$20.*

★ ☾ **"ʻUlalena" at Maui Theatre.** One of Maui's hottest tickets, "ʻUlalena" is a 75-minute musical extravaganza that is well received by audiences and Hawaiian-culture experts alike. Cirque du Soleil–inspired, the ensemble cast (20 singer-dancers and a five-musician orchestra) mixes native rhythms and stories with acrobatic performance. High-tech stage wizardry gives an inspiring introduction to island culture. It has auditorium seating, and beer and wine are for sale at the concession stand. There are dinner-theater packages in conjunction with top Lahaina restaurants. ✉*878 Front St., Lahaina* ☎*808/661–9913 or 877/688–4800* ⊕*www.mauitheatre.com* ⌂*Reservations essential* ▭*$50–$70* ☾*Tues.–Sat. at 6:30 pm.*

Warren & Annabelle's. This is one show not to miss—it's serious comedy with an amazing sleight-of-hand. Magician Warren Gibson entices guests into his swank nightclub with red carpets and a gleaming mahogany bar, and plies them with à la carte appetizers (coconut shrimp, crab cakes), desserts (rum cake, crème brûlée), and "smoking cocktails." Then, he performs tableside magic while his ghostly assistant, Annabelle, tickles the ivories. This is a nightclub, so no one under 21 is allowed. ✉*Lahaina Center, 900 Front St., Lahaina* ☎*808/667–6244* ⊕*www.hawaiimagic.com* ⌂*Reservations essential* ▭*$50 or $86, including food and drinks* ☾*Mon.–Sat. at 5.*

BARS & CLUBS

Your best bet when it comes to bars on Maui? If you walk by and it sounds like it's happening, go in. If you want to scope out your options in advance, be sure to check the free *MauiTime Weekly,* found at most stores and restaurants, to find out who's playing where. *Maui News* also publishes an entertainment schedule in its Thursday edition of the

"Maui Scene." With an open mind (and a little luck), you can usually find a good scene for fun.

WEST MAUI

Cheeseburger in Paradise. This Front Street joint is known for—what else?—big beefy cheeseburgers (not to mention a great spinach-nut burger). This is a casual place to start your evening, as they usually have live music and big, fruity cocktails for happy hour. There's no dance floor, but the 2nd-floor balcony gives you a bird's-eye view of Lahaina's Front Street action. ⊠*811 Front St., Lahaina* ☎*808/661–4855.*

Hard Rock Cafe. You've seen one Hard Rock Cafe, you've seen them all. However, Maui's Hard Rock brings you Reggae Monday, featuring our beloved local reggae star Marty Dread ($5 cover, 10 PM). ⊠*Lahaina Center, 900 Front St., Lahaina* ☎*808/667–7400.*

Longhi's. This upscale, open-air restaurant is the spot on Friday nights, when there's usually live music and a bumping dance floor. Here you'll mingle with what locals call Maui's beautiful people, so be sure to dress your casual best ($5 cover, 10 PM). ⊠*Lahaina Center, 888 Front St., next to Hard Rock Cafe, Lahaina* ☎*808/667–2288.*

Moose McGillycuddy's. The Moose offers no-cover live or DJ music on most nights, drawing a young, mostly single crowd who come for the burgers, beer, and dance-floor beats. ⊠*844 Front St., Lahaina* ☎*808/667–7758.*

Pacific'O. Looking to stare longingly into your beloved's eyes? This is your place. This exclusive restaurant and martini bar brings you live jazz, right on the beach, from 9 to midnight on Friday and Saturday nights. Guest musicians—George Benson, for example—sometimes sit in. ⊠*505 Front St., Lahaina* ☎*808/667–4341.*

★ **Paradice Bluz.** Live local bands and comedians frequent the stage at this popular, underground West Maui hangout. This place is as close to a real night club as you'll find in Lahaina. It's dark and smoky, with a swanky lounge area, pool tables, and a decent lineup of bands and DJs. Expect to pay a hefty cover ($12 to $20). ⊠*744 Front St., Lahaina* ☎*808/667–5299.*

The Sly Mongoose. Off the beaten tourist path, the Sly Mongoose is the seediest dive bar in town, and one of the friendliest. The bartender will know your name

> **MAI TAI**
>
> Don't let your sweet tooth fool you. Maui's favorite drink—the mai tai—can be as lethal as it is sweet. The Original Trader Vic's recipe calls for 2 ounces of aged dark rum, mixed with almond syrup, orange curaçao, the juice of one lime, and (wouldn't you know it) rock-candy syrup. Mama's Fish House on the North Shore makes the best-tasting mai tai in town. Of course, in its lush, old-Hawai'i setting, Mama's could make just about any drink taste good.

and half your life history inside of 10 minutes, and she makes the strongest mai tai on the island. ⊠*1036 Limahana Pl., Lahaina* ☎*808/661–8097.*

THE SOUTH SHORE

Life's a Beach. This place brings in a young, rambunctious bunch looking to par-tay (read: meat market). But hey, if you dig lingerie contests and half-price Jägermeister shots, who are we to judge? Friday and Saturday is live music, Sunday is karaoke. ⊠*1913 S. Kīhei Rd., Kīhei* ☎*808/891–8010.*

Lulu's. Lulu's could be your favorite bar in any beach town. It's a second-story, open-air tiki and sports bar, with a pool table, small stage, and dance floor to boot. The most popular night is Salsa Thursday, with dancing and lessons until 11. Friday is country night; Saturday is house. ⊠*1945 S. Kīhei Rd., Kīhei* ☎*808/879–9944* ⊕*www.lulusmaui. com.*

★ **Mulligan's on the Blue.** Frothy pints of Guinness and late-night fish-and-chips—who could ask for more? Sunday nights feature foot-stomping Irish jams that will have you dancing a jig, and singing something about "a whiskey for me-Johnny." Thursdays and Fridays, Mulligan's also brings you the more mellow *Wailea Nights,* an inspired dinner show performed by members of the band "Hapa." ⊠*Blue Golf Course, 100 Kaukahi St., Wailea* ☎*808/874–1131* ⊕*www.mulligan-sontheblue.com.*

Tsunami. Located in one of Maui's most elite resorts, Tsunami's scene feels chic and electric. You can dance to DJ hip-hop, house, techno, and Top 40—or occasional live music. The place packs in a sophisticated crowd that spins on the dance floor under laser-beam lights. Weekend nights are the best, from 9:30 to 1. The dress code is strictly enforced—no jeans or shirts without a collar. $10 cover. ⊠*Grand Wailea Resort, 3850 Wailea Alanui Dr., Wailea* ☎*808/875–1234.*

UPCOUNTRY & THE NORTH SHORE

Casanova Italian Restaurant and Deli. Casanova can bring in some big acts, which in the past have included Kool and the Gang, Los Lobos, and Taj Majal. Most Friday and Saturday nights, though, it attracts a hip, local scene with live bands and eclectic DJs spinning house, funk, and world music. Don't miss the costume theme nights. Wednesday is for Wild Wahines (code for ladies drink half price), which can be more on the smarmy side. $5 to $15 cover. ⊠*1188 Makawao Ave., Makawao* ☎*808/572–0220* ⊕*www.casanovamaui.com.*

WHAT'S A LAVA FLOW?

Can't decide between a piña colada or strawberry daiquiri? Go with a Lava Flow—a mix of light rum, coconut and pineapple juice, and a banana, with a swirl of strawberry puree. Add a wedge of fresh pineapple and a paper umbrella, and mmm ... good. Try one at Lulu's in Kīhei.

7

Charley's. The closest thing to country Maui has to offer, Charley's is a down-home, dive bar in the heart of Pā'ia. It recently expanded its offerings to include disco, house, industry, and lounge nights. If you're lucky, you might even see Willy Nelson hanging here. ⊠*142 Hāna Hwy., Pā'ia* ☎*808/579–9453.*

Jacques. Jacques was once voted by locals as the "best place to see suspiciously beautiful people from around the world." On Friday nights, the crowd spills onto the cozy streets of Pā'ia, as funky DJs spin Latino, world lounge, salsa, and live jazz. ⊠*120 Hāna Hwy., Pā'ia* ☎*808/579–8844.*

Where to Eat

WORD OF MOUTH

"[Our best lunch was at] Mama's Fish House. Get the opakapaka
. . . We had it upcountry style, and it was superb."

—beanweb24

"Sure, it's not the crazy, so-special-it's stupid kind of place you'd
associate with gastronomic meccas, but Tastings blew me away
with impeccable flavor and fantastic service . . . too bad it's not
next door, because I'd be there every weekend."

—Ian M

WHERE TO EAT PLANNER

Fast Facts

Hours: Most restaurants are packed from 6 to 8 PM—the sunset hours. By 8:30 many dining rooms have quieted down, and by 9:30 most are closed. If the place has a rowdy bar (or karaoke machine), you may be able to get food until 10 or 11.

Dress: Maui's last jacket-required dining room closed years ago. This is paradise, after all. Wear what you like, but don't forget to bring a sweater or cover-up—many restaurants are open-air.

Tater tots: Even the fancy joints have a *keiki*, or kids' menu and box of crayons hidden somewhere.

Don't leave home without it: If you plan to purchase alcohol, bring your ID. The Maui County Liquor Commission requires employees at restaurants or stores to card all customers, whether they're 21 or 101 years of age.

No butts about it: Smoking is prohibited in Hawai'i restaurants, though some bars that serve food will turn a blind eye.

Got reservations?

Don't gamble. If you're dying to go to Mama's or the Old Lahaina Lūa'u, make your reservations before leaving home. Everywhere else can be squeezed into, at least at the bar, at the last minute.

A Tip

Here on "survivor island," most residents depend on tipped wages—18% to 20% is standard for quality service. But beware of hotels: adding an automatic gratuity is standard practice for room service. Check your check.

Keep in Mind

Unless a resort is noted for its culinary department (such as the Ritz-Carlton or Four Seasons), you may find hotel restaurants somewhat overpriced and underwhelming. Head out to a freestanding restaurant with a menu more varied and less astronomically priced.

What It Costs

If you want to dine well on the cheap, skip the touristy magazines and go for coupons advertised in the *Maui News*. Even upscale restaurants go half-price during the slow months (September through November). Ka'amaina discounts require a Hawai'i driver's license. Rather than feel left out, consider treating a local to dinner—you'll get their discount and directions to their secret surf spot.

	¢	$	$$	$$$	$$$$
RESTAURANTS	Under $10	$10–$17	$18–$26	$27–$35	Over $35

Restaurant prices are for a main course at dinner.

By Shannon
Wianecki

IN THE EARLY 1990S A few rebel Hawai'i chefs stopped ordering the standard expensive produce from the mainland and started sourcing local ingredients. Mixing the fruits and vegetables of Polynesia with classic European or Asian preparations, they spawned such dishes as 'ahi (yellowfin tuna) carpaccio, breadfruit soufflé, and liliko'i (passion fruit) cheesecake. Hawai'i Regional Cuisine was born and many of its innovators—Bev Gannon of Hali'imaile General Store, Roy Yamaguchi of Roy's, and Peter Merriman of Hula Grill, to name a few—continue to raise the culinary bar around the island. Savvy restaurateurs have followed the lead, many offering tasting menus with excellent wine lists. Because of Maui's outstanding natural resources—prime agricultural land and the adjoining Pacific Ocean—most menus are filled with healthy options so you can feel free to indulge. Fresh fish selections, bursting-ripe produce, and simple, stylized presentations characterize the very best. Expect to eat well at any price.

If you're hankering for ethnic or local-style cooking try wandering into the less-touristy areas such as Wailuku or Kahului. A good Hawaiian "plate lunch" will fulfill your daily requirement of carbohydrates: macaroni salad, two scoops of rice, and an entrée of, say, curry stew, teriyaki beef, or kālua (roasted in an underground oven) pig and cabbage.

WEST MAUI

LAHAINA

8

AMERICAN

$-$$ ✕ **Lahaina Coolers.** This breezy little café with a surfboard hanging from its ceiling serves such tantalizing fare as Evil Jungle Pasta (pasta with grilled chicken in spicy Thai peanut sauce) and linguine with prawns, basil, garlic, and cream. It also has pizzas, steaks, and burgers. Pastas are made fresh in-house. Don't be surprised to see a local fisherman walk through or a harbor captain reeling in a hearty breakfast. ⊠180 Dickenson St., Lahaina ☎808/661–7082 ▤AE, MC, V.

ECLECTIC

★ $-$$$$ ✕ **Mala Ocean Tavern.** Perched above the tide-tossed rocks, this breezy "ocean tavern" is wholly satisfying. Chef Mark Ellman's menu, composed of mostly organic and locally sourced ingredients, includes crisp and flavorful flatbreads and a hefty Kobe burger dripping with Maytag blue cheese. Best of all is the calamari, lightly battered and fried with lemon slices and served with a spicy mojo verde. This is a good place to try moi, the famed fish of Hawaiian royalty, wok-fried with ginger and spicy black-bean sauce. In the evening, the small bar is a coveted hangout. Those die-hard fans of the Caramel Miranda dessert at Avalon (Ellman's former restaurant) can find it here. ⊠1307 Front St., Lahaina ☎808/667–9394 ▤AE, MC, V.

FRENCH

★ **$$$–$$$$** ✕**Chez Paul.** Since 1975 this tiny roadside restaurant between Lahaina and Māʻalaea in Olowalu has been serving excellent French cuisine to a packed house of repeat customers. Such dishes as fresh local fish poached in white wine with shallots, cream, and capers typify the classical menu. If you can't resist foie gras, this

CHECK IT OUT

At press time, Chef Patrick Callarec, owner of Chez Paul, had plans to open a gourmet store and take-out window beside his popular Olowalu restaurant. Stop in for some *ʻono* (delicious) local grinds with French flair.

is the place to have it. The restaurant's offbeat exterior belies the fine art, linen-draped tables, and wine cellar within. Don't blink or you'll miss this small group of buildings huddled in the middle of nowhere. ⊠*Honoapiʻilani Hwy., 4 mi south of Lahaina, Olowalu* ☎*808/661–3843* ⌁*Reservations essential* ▤*AE, D, MC, V* ⊗*No lunch.*

$$$–$$$$ ✕**Gerard's.** Owner and celebrated chef Gerard Reversade started cook-
FodorsChoice ing at the age of 10, and at 12 he was baking croissants. He hon-
★ ors the French tradition with such exquisitely prepared dishes as rack of lamb in mint crust with thyme jus, and venison cutlets in a port sauce with confit of chestnuts, walnuts, fennel, and pearl onions. The menu changes once a year, but many favorites—such as the sinfully good crème brûlée—remain. A first-class wine list, a lovely room, and celebrity-spotting round out the experience. ⊠*Plantation Inn, 174 Lahainaluna Rd., Lahaina 96761* ☎*808/661–8939* ▤*AE, D, DC, MC, V* ⊗*No lunch.*

HAWAIIAN–PACIFIC RIM

$$$–$$$$ ✕**David Paul's Lahaina Grill.** Though the restaurant's namesake is only a
FodorsChoice consultant now, David Paul's is still a favorite. Beautifully designed, it's
★ adjacent to the elegant Lahaina Inn in a historic building on Lahain-aluna Road. The restaurant has an extensive wine cellar, an in-house bakery, and splashy artwork decorating the walls. The house somme-lier's suggestions keep up with the celebrated menu. Try the signature tequila shrimp and firecracker rice along with the scrumptious triple-berry pie. Demi portions are available at the bar. ⊠*127 Lahainaluna Rd., Lahaina 96761* ☎*808/667–5117* ⊕*www.lahainagrill.com* ▤*AE, DC, MC, V.*

$$$ ✕**Iʻo.** From its opening, this restaurant established itself as cutting edge in Lahaina, both for its theatrical interior designed by the artist Dado and for its contemporary Pacific Rim menu. Favorites include the lemongrass-coconut fish and nori-wrapped rare tuna, served with green-papaya salad, and the "Mad Hatter" appetizer: scallops drenched in lobster curry sauce. Desserts to savor are the Hawaiian Vintage Chocolate Mousse and the chocolate pâté with Kula strawber-ries. ⊠*505 Front St., Lahaina* ☎*808/661–8422* ▤*AE, D, DC, MC, V* ⊗*No lunch.*

¢–$ ✕**Aloha Mixed Plate.** Set right on the ocean, this funky open-air bar and restaurant is a great place for *ʻono grinds*—"good food" in Hawai-ian slang. Crispy coconut prawns, boca burgers, shoyu chicken, and kalua pork are favorite island comfort foods (these are the things local

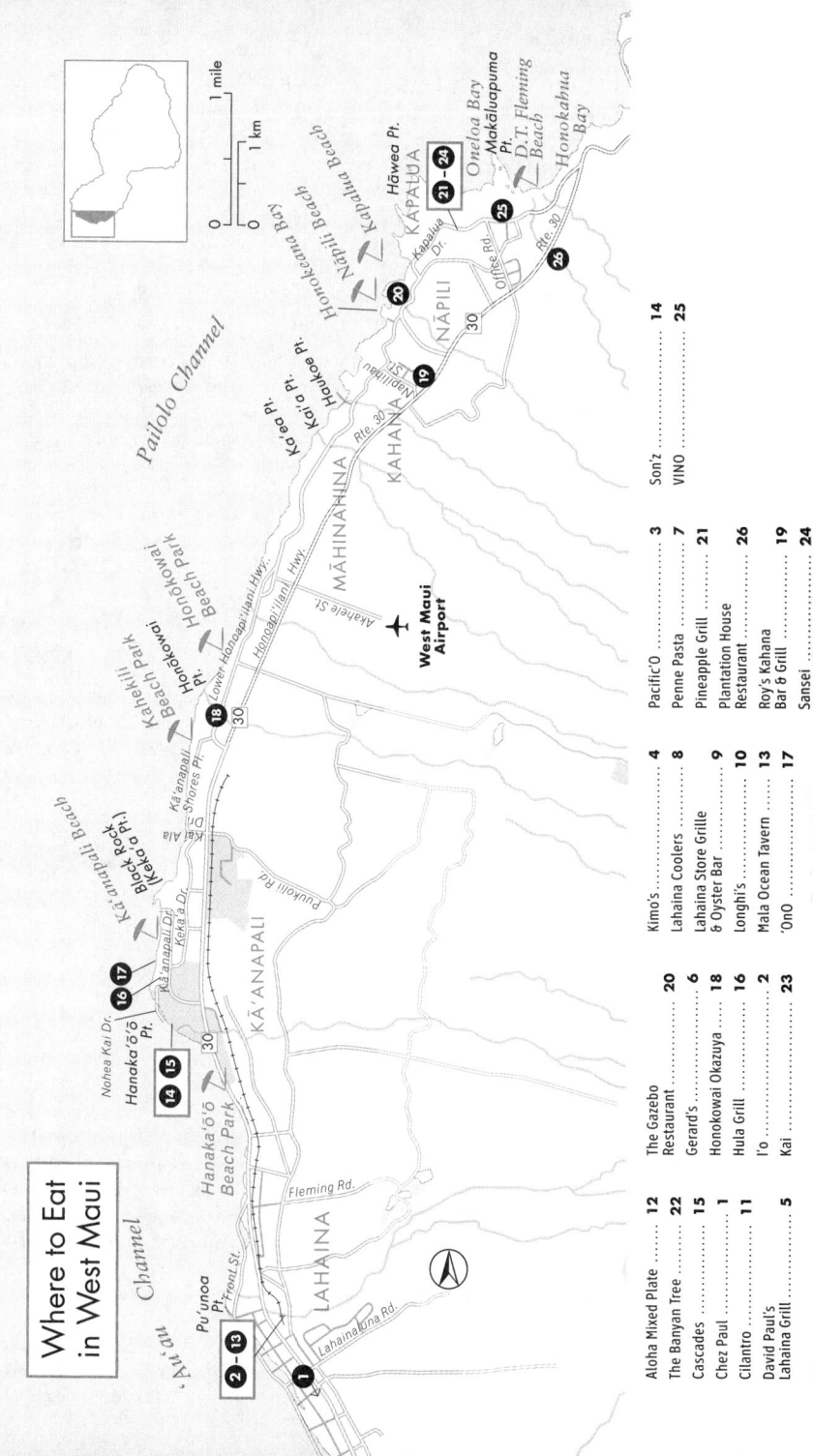

Where to Eat in West Maui

'Au'au Channel

Pailolo Channel

Pu'unoa Pt.
Front St.
LAHAINA
Lahaina Luna Rd.

Fleming Rd.
Hanaka'ō'ō Beach Park
Nohea Kai Dr.
Hanaka'ō'ō Pt.
Kā'anapali Beach
Black Rock (Keka'a Pt.)
Kā'anapali Dr.
Keka'a Dr.
Kai Ala Dr.
Kā'anapali Shores Pt.
KĀ'ANAPALI
Puukolii Rd.

Kahekili Beach Park
Honokōwai Pt.
Honokōwai Beach Park
Lower Honoapi'ilani Hwy.
Honoapi'ilani Hwy.

MĀHINAHINA
West Maui Airport
Akahele St.
KAHANA
Napilihau St.
Rte. 30

Ka'ea Pt.
Kai'a Pt.
Hau'oe Pt.
Honokeana Bay
Nāpili Beach
Kapalua Beach
Hāwea Pt.
NĀPILI
Office Rd.
Kapalua Dr.
Rte. 30

Onelua Bay
Makāluapuna Pt.
D.T. Fleming Beach
Honokahua Bay
KAPALUA

N
0   1 km
0   1 mile

Aloha Mixed Plate	12	
The Banyan Tree	22	
Cascades	15	
Chez Paul	1	
Cilantro	11	
David Paul's Lahaina Grill	5	
The Gazebo Restaurant	20	
Gerard's	6	
Honokowai Okazuya	18	
Hula Grill	16	
I'o	2	
Kai	23	
Kimo's	4	
Lahaina Coolers	8	
Lahaina Store Grille & Oyster Bar	9	
Longhi's	10	
Mala Ocean Tavern	13	
'OnO	17	
Pacific'O	3	
Penne Pasta	7	
Pineapple Grill	21	
Plantation House Restaurant	26	
Roy's Kahana Bar & Grill	19	
Sansei	24	
Son'z	14	
VINO	25	

kids daydream about when they're sent away to college). You too can indulge in these Hawaiian treats at this awesome outdoor location. ⊠ *1286 Front St., Lahaina* ☎ *808/661–3322* 🖃 *AE, D, DC, MC, V.*

¢–$ ✕ **Honokowai Okazuya.** Don't expect to sit down at this miniature restaurant sandwiched between a dive shop and a salon—this is strictly a take-out joint. You can order local plate lunches, Chinese, vegetarian, or sandwiches. The spicy eggplant is delicious, and the fresh chow fun noodles are bought up quickly. ⊠ *3600-D Lower Honoapi'ilani Hwy., Lahaina* ☎ *808/665–0512* 🖃 *No credit cards* ☺ *Closed Sun.*

ITALIAN

$$–$$$ ✕ **Longhi's.** A Lahaina establishment, Longhi's has been around since 1976, serving great Italian pasta as well as sandwiches, seafood, beef, and chicken dishes. The pasta is homemade and the in-house bakery turns out breakfast pastries, desserts, and fresh bread. Even on a warm day, you won't need air-conditioning with two spacious, breezy, open-air levels to choose from. The black-and-white tile floors are a classic touch. There's a second restaurant on the South Shore, at the Shops at Wailea. ⊠ *888 Front St., Lahaina* ☎ *808/667–2288* ⊠ *The Shops at Wailea, 3750 Wailea Alanui Dr., Wailea* ☎ *808/891–8883* 🖃 *AE, D, DC, MC, V.*

¢–$ ✕ **Penne Pasta.** Heaping plates of flavorful pasta and low-key, unintrusive service make this restaurant the perfect alternative to an expensive night out in Lahaina. The osso buco (Wednesday's special) is sumptuous, and the traditional salad niçoise overflows with generous portions of olives, peppers, garlic 'ahi, and potatoes. Couples should split a salad and entrée, as portions are large. ⊠ *180 Dickenson St., Lahaina* ☎ *808/661–6633* 🖃 *AE, D, DC, MC, V* ☺ *No lunch weekends.*

MEXICAN

★ ¢–$ ✕ **Cilantro.** At last! Mexican food to brag about on West Maui! The flavors of Old Mexico are given new life here, where the tortillas are hand-pressed and no fewer than nine chilies are used to create the salsas. Rotisserie chicken tacos with jicama slaw are both mouthwatering and healthy. The Mother Clucker flautas with crema fresca and jalapeño jelly are not to be missed. Look for owner Paris Nabavi's collection of dead soldiers—tortilla presses worn from duty, now hand-painted and displayed up on the wall. ⊠ *In Old Lahaina Center, 170 Papalaua Ave., Lahaina* ☎ *808/667–5444* 🖃 *AE, MC, V.*

SEAFOOD

★ $$–$$$$ ✕ **Pacific'O.** You can sit outdoors at umbrella-shaded tables near the water's edge, or find a spot in the breezy, marble-floor interior. The exciting menu features fresh 'ahi-and-ono tempura, in which the two kinds of fish are wrapped around *tobiko* (flying-fish roe), then wrapped in nori, and wok-fried. There's a great lamb dish, too—a whole rack of sweet New Zealand lamb, sesame-crusted and served with roasted macadamia sauce and Hawaiian chutney. Live jazz is played Friday and Saturday from 9 to midnight. ⊠ *505 Front St., Lahaina* ☎ *808/667–4341* 🖃 *AE, D, DC, MC, V.*

$–$$$$ ✕ **Kimo's.** On a warm Lahaina day, it's a treat to relax at an umbrella-shaded table on this restaurant's lānai, sip a mai tai, and watch sail-

Continued on page 156

AUTHENTIC TASTE OF HAWAI'I: LŪ'AU OR LAULAU?

The best place to sample Hawaiian food is at a backyard lū'au. Aunts and uncles are cooking, the pig is from a cousin's farm, and the fish is from a brother's boat.

But even locals have to angle for invitations to those rare occasions. So your choice is most likely between a commercial lū'au and a Hawaiian restaurant.

Most commercial lū'au will offer you little of the authentic diet; they're more about umbrella drinks, laughs, spectacle, and fun. Expect to spend some time and no small amount of cash.

For greater authenticity, folksy experiences, and rock-bottom prices, visit a Hawaiian restaurant (most are in anonymous storefronts in residential neighborhoods). Expect rough edges and some effort negotiating the menu.

In either case, much of what is known today as Hawaiian food would be as foreign to a 16th-century Hawaiian as risotto or chow mein. The pre-contact diet was simple and healthy—mainly raw and steamed seafood and vegetables. Early Hawaiians used earth ovens and heated stones to cook seafood, taro, sweet potatoes, and breadfruit and seasoned their food with sea salt and ground kukui nuts. Seaweed, fern shoots, sweet potato vines, coconut, banana, sugar cane, and select greens and roots rounded out the diet.

Successive waves of immigrants added their favorites to the ti leaf–lined table. So it is that foods as disparate as salt salmon and chicken long rice are now Hawaiian—even though there is no salmon in Hawaiian waters and long rice (cellophane noodles) is Chinese.

AT THE LŪʻAU: KĀLUA PORK

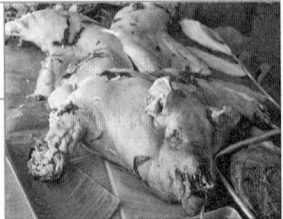

The heart of any lūʻau is the *imu*, the earth oven in which a whole pig is roasted. The preparation of an imu is an arduous affair for most families, who tackle it only once a year or so, for a baby's first birthday or at Thanksgiving, when many Islanders prefer to imu their turkeys. Commercial lūʻau operations have it down to a science, however.

THE ART OF THE STONE

The key to a proper imu is the *pohaku*, the stones. Imu cook by means of long, slow, moist heat released by special stones which can withstand a hot fire without exploding. Many Hawaiian families treasure their imu stones, keeping them in a pile in the back yard and passing them on through generations.

PIT COOKING

The imu makers first dig a pit about the size of a refrigerator, then lay down *kiawe* (mesquite) wood and stones, and build a white-hot fire that is allowed to burn itself out. The ashes are raked away, and the hot stones covered with banana and ti leaves. Well-wrapped in ti or banana leaves and a net of chicken wire, the pig is lowered onto the leaf-covered stones. *Laulau* (leaf-wrapped bundles of meats, fish, and taro leaves) may also be placed inside. Leaves—ti, banana, even ginger—cover the pig followed by wet burlap sacks (to create steam). The whole is topped with a canvas tarp and left to steam for the better part of a day.

OPENING THE IMU

This is the moment everyone waits for: The imu is unwrapped like a giant present and the imu keepers gingerly wrestle out the steaming pig. When it's unwrapped, the meat falls moist and smoky-flavored from the bone, looking and tasting just like Southern-style pulled pork, but without the barbecue sauce.

WHICH LŪʻAU?

The Feast at Lele. Top-notch value and price, great wine list.

Old Lahaina Lūʻau. Intimate and the most traditional; a perennial sell-out.

Outrigger Marriott Lūʻau. Imu ceremony and buffet.

MEA 'AI 'ONO.
GOOD THINGS TO EAT.

LAULAU
Steamed meats, fish, and taro leaf in ti-leaf bundles: fork-tender, a medley of flavors; the taro resembles spinach.

LOMI LOMI SALMON
Salt salmon in a piquant salad or relish with onions, tomatoes.

POI (DON'T CALL IT LIBRARY PASTE)
Islanders are beyond tired of jokes about poi, a paste made of pounded taro root.

Consider: The Hawaiian Adam is descended from *kalo* (taro). Young taro plants are called "keiki"—children. Poi is the first food after mother's milk for many Islanders. 'Ai, the word for food, is synonymous with poi in many contexts.

Not only that. We like it. "There is no meat that does-n't taste good with poi," the old Hawaiians said.

But you have to know how to eat it: with something rich or powerfully flavored. "It is salt that makes the poi go in," is another adage. When you're served poi, try it with a mouthful of smoky kālua pork or salty lomi lomi salmon. Its slightly sour blandness cleanses the palate. And if you don't like it, smile and say something polite. (And slide that bowl over to a local.)

Laulau

Lomi Lomi Salmon

Poi

E HELE MAI 'AI! COME AND EAT!

Hawaiian restaurants tend to be inconveniently located in well-worn storefronts with little or no parking, outfitted with battered tables and clattering Melmac dishes, open odd (and usually limited) hours and days, and often so crowded you have to wait. But they personify aloha, invariably run by local families who welcome tourists who take the trouble to find them.

Many are cash-only operations and combination plates are a standard feature: one or two entrées, a side such as chicken long rice, choice of poi or steamed rice and—if the place is really old-style—a tiny portion of coarse Hawaiian salt and some raw onions for relish.

Most serve some foods that aren't, strictly speaking, Hawaiian, but are beloved of

kama'āina, such as salt meat with watercress (preserved meat in a tasty broth), or *akubone* (skipjack tuna fried in a vinegar sauce).

Our two favorites: **Aloha Mixed Plate** and **A.K.'s Café**.

boats glide in and out of the harbor. Outstanding seafood is just one of the options here; also good are the Hawaiian-style chicken and pork dishes, and the burgers. Try the signature dessert, Hula Pie: vanilla-macadamia nut ice cream topped with chocolate fudge and whipped cream in an Oreo-cookie crust. ✉ *845 Front St., Lahaina* ☎ *808/661–4811* 🖃 *AE, DC, MC, V.*

KĀʻANAPALI

CONTINENTAL

★ $$$–$$$$ ✕**Sonʻz.** Descend the grand staircase into an amber-lit dining room that manages to be both spacious and intimate. Choose your evening's libation from one of 3,000 bottles of wine (the largest cellar in the state) while shielding your sourdough roll from the staring eyes of swans circling the waterfall-fed pool. Chef Geno Sarmiento's menu of goat-cheese ravioli, mint pesto-rubbed rack of lamb atop pumpkin gnocchi, and classic coq au vin has been drawing serious applause. ✉ *Hyatt Regency Maui, Kāʻanapali Beach Resort, 200 Nohea Kai Dr., Kāʻanapali* ☎ *808/661–1234* 🖃 *AE, D, DC, MC, V.*

HAWAIIAN–PACIFIC RIM

$–$$$ ✕**Cascades.** Above the Hyatt's wonderland swimming pools and beneath a canopy of interlocking *hau* trees, you can enjoy a sampler of island treats—pot stickers, teriyaki beef skewers, and *poke.* Toast to your good fortune with a kitschy tropical cocktail. If you've been out shopping late, you can order sushi and light fare until 10 PM. ✉ *Hyatt Regency Maui, Kāʻanapali Beach Resort, 200 Nohea Kai Dr., Kāʻanapali* ☎ *808/661–1234* 🖃 *AE, D, DC, MC, V.*

$–$$$ ✕**Hula Grill.** Genial chef-restaurateur Peter Merriman's bustling, family-oriented restaurant is in a re-created 1930s Hawaiian beach house, and every table has an ocean view. You can also dine on the beach, toes in the sand, at the Barefoot Bar, where Hawaiian entertainment is presented every evening. South Pacific snapper is baked with tomato, chili, and cumin aioli and served with a black bean, Maui onion, and avocado relish. Spareribs are steamed in banana leaves, then grilled with mango barbecue sauce over mesquitelike *kiawe* wood. ✉ *Whalers Village, 2435 Kāʻanapali Pkwy., Kāʻanapali* ☎ *808/667–6636* 🖃 *AE, DC, MC, V.*

$–$$$ ✕**ʻOnO.** This casual, fun restaurant features pūpū (known elsewhere in the world as tapas). This is a good place to bring the kids. They can munch away on the beef tenderloin kebabs while you sample the Hokkaido scallops and asparagus doused in a not-too-spicy Kim Chee cream. ✉ *Westin Maui Resort & Spa, 2365 Kāʻanapali Pkwy., Kāʻanapali* ☎ *808/667–2525* 🖃 *AE, DC, MC, V.*

NORTH OF KĀʻANAPALI

AMERICAN

¢ ✕**The Gazebo Restaurant.** Even locals will stand in line up to half an hour for a table overlooking the beach at this restaurant, an actual open-air gazebo. The food is standard diner fare, but it's thoughtfully prepared. Breakfast choices include macadamia-nut pancakes and Portuguese-sausage omelets. There are satisfying burgers and salads at lunch. The friendly hotel staff puts out coffee for those waiting in line.

✉*Nāpili Shores Resort, 5315 Lower Honoapiʻilani Hwy., Nāpili* ☎*808/669–5621* ▬*No credit cards* ⊘*No dinner.*

HAWAIIAN–PACIFIC RIM

★ $$$–$$$$ ✕**The Banyan Tree.** The tray of *dukka* (Middle Eastern spices) delivered with your bread should tell you that this elegant dining hall has something different to offer discerning palates. Chef Jojo Vasquez isn't the culinary maverick his predecessor was—so you won't find foie gras ice cream on the menu here any longer—but from the calamansi-splashed oysters to the pomegranate-glazed lamb chops, Vasquez hits the mark. The open-beam restaurant's subdued atmosphere is charged with the sounds of live world music. ✉*Ritz-Carlton, Kapalua, 1 Ritz-Carlton Dr., Kapalua* ☎*808/669–6200* ▬*AE, D, DC, MC, V.*

$$–$$$ ✕**Plantation House Restaurant.** It's hard to decide which is better here, the food or the view. Misty hills, grassy volcanic ridges lined with pine trees, and fairways that appear to drop off into the ocean provide an idyllic setting. The specialty is fresh island fish prepared according to different "tastes"—Upcountry Maui, Asian-Pacific, Provence, and others. The breeze through the large shuttered windows can be cool, so you may want to bring a sweater or sit by the fireplace. Breakfast here is a luxurious way to start your day. ✉*Plantation Course Clubhouse, 2000 Plantation Club Dr., past Kapalua* ☎*808/669–6299* ▬*AE, MC, V.*

★ $$–$$$ ✕**Roy's Kahana Bar & Grill.** Roy Yamaguchi's own sake brand ("Y") and Hawaiian-fusion specialties, such as shrimp with sweet-and-spicy chili sauce and miso yaki butterfish, keep regulars returning for more. Locals know to order the incomparable chocolate soufflé immediately after being seated. Both restaurants, in Kahana and Kīhei, are in supermarket parking lots—it's not the view that excites, it's the food. ✉*Kahana Gateway Shopping Center, 4405 Honoapiʻilani Hwy., Kahana* ☎*808/669–6999* ✉*Safeway Shopping Center, 303 Piʻikea Ave., Kīhei* ☎*808/891–1120* ▬*AE, D, DC, MC, V.*

$–$$$ ✕**Pineapple Grill.** Hawaiʻi regional cuisine finds superb expression here, Fodor'sChoice in dishes like seared ʻahi atop coconut-scented "forbidden" rice, and ★ braised short ribs garnished with just enough Maui pineapple relish to

8

heighten hidden lemongrass and anise flavors. Even more delicious? As a Maui Seafood Watch participant, the restaurant agrees to only serve seafood that has been harvested sustainably. So go on—order the Kona lobster. If the weather isn't too cold, the outdoor tables facing the West Maui Mountains can be even nicer than those with an ocean view. ✉ *200 Kapalua Dr., Kapalua 96761* ☎ *808/669–9600* 🖃 *AE, MC, V.*

SUSHI FOR ALL

On Maui, there's a sushi restaurant for everyone—even those who don't like sushi! Sansei has the most diverse menu: everything from lobster ravioli to sea urchin. People love designer rolls such as the "69"—unagi eel slathered in sweet sauce paired with crab, or the "caterpillar"—avocado and tuna wrapped around rice, complete with radish-sprout antennae!

ITALIAN

$–$$$$ ✕**VINO.** D.K. Kodama, the culinary mastermind behind Sansei, teamed up with Master Sommelier Chuck Furuya to create a strange child—an Italian tapas restaurant with a Japanese twist. The results have been hailed as, well, masterful. Set on the Kapalua golf course, the restaurant's active, somewhat noisy atmosphere encourages experimentation. Small plates of lamb chops, diver scallops, or plump shrimp atop Asian noodles with truffle butter are sure to tempt. Wines are served in Riedel stemware; flights can be sampled at the bar. ✉ *2000 Village Rd., Kapalua* ☎ *808/661–8466* 🖃 *AE, D, DC, MC, V.*

JAPANESE

★ **$–$$$$** ✕**Kai.** Master sushi chef Tadashi Yoshino sits at the helm of this intimate, ocean-view sushi bar, hidden behind the Lobby bar at the Ritz-Carlton, Kapalua. The menu includes sushi and hot Japanese entrées, but your best bet is to let Chef Yoshino design the meal. He might have yellowtail cheeks, fresh sea urchin, and raw lobster. He also makes lobster-head soup, a Japanese comfort food. The kitchen is open until 10 PM. ✉ *Ritz-Carlton, Kapalua, 1 Ritz-Carlton Dr., Kapalua* ☎ *808/669–6200* 🖃 *AE, D, DC, MC, V.*

¢–$$$ ✕**Sansei.** One of the best-loved restaurants on the island, Sansei is Japanese with a Hawaiian twist. Inspired dishes include *panko*-crusted
Fodor's Choice 'ahi (*panko* are Japanese bread crumbs), spicy fried calamari, mango-★ and-crab-salad roll, and a decadent foie gras *nigiri* (served on rice without seaweed) sushi. Desserts often use local fruit; the Kula-persimmon crème brûlée is stunning, and on special occasions, the tempura ice cream is worth the calories. The Kapalua location lost none of its intimacy and pizzazz by moving up the street. Both locations are popular karaoke hangouts, serving late-night sushi at half price. s*600 Office Rd., Lahaina, 96761* ✉ *600 Office Rd., Kapalua* ☎ *808/666–6286* ✉ *Kihei Town Center, 1881 S. Kihei Rd., Kihei, 96753* ☎ *808/879–0004* 🖃 *AE, D, MC, V* 🕐 *No lunch.*

SEAFOOD

$$–$$$ ✕**The Lahaina Store Grille & Oyster Bar.** Overlooking sparkling Lahaina Harbor, the rooftop tables at this restaurant are wonderfully romantic. Inside, antique fans, roaring 20s decor, and the giant etched mirror over the martini bar give a nod to this historic whaling town's past. Lunchtime grilled veggies, chicken, and burgers have added elegance with the mesmerizing view. At dinner, try six different oysters, on the half-shell or as shooters (our favorite), before diving into a fresh fillet. ✉*744 Front St., Lahaina* ☎*808/661–9090* ▭*AE, D, MC, V.*

THE SOUTH SHORE

Besides restaurants listed below, you'll find branches of Roy's, Sansei, and Longhi's in this area. For reviews of these establishments, *see* the West Maui section.

KĪHEI & NORTH

AMERICAN

$–$$$ **Cafe O Lei.** Once again, chef-owner Dana Pastula works her kitchen magic. Affordable, tasty dishes served at dinner and lunch include spicy chicken lettuce wraps (beloved by locals and tourists alike), crab cakes, and hefty salads. For dinner, order sushi from the bar in back, or roast duck and baked clams from the brick oven. Gauze curtains separate tables, which are nicely set with white linens and bright tableware. If you're looking for a midrange priced restaurant offering ample portions and flavor, this is it. ✉*1280 S. Kīhei Rd., Kīhei* ☎*808/891–1368* ▭*AE, MC, V.*

$–$$$ ✕**Māʻalaea Grill.** Large, open windows overlook Māʻalaea's small boat harbor and let the breeze into this casual seaside restaurant. The teak and bamboo furniture, exhibition kitchen, and walk-in wine cellar lend an air of sophistication to this otherwise happily relaxed locale. Enjoy a light but satisfying quinoa salad (the local favorite), *kiawe* grilled beef tenderloin, or shrimp prepared a variety of ways: coconut fried, sautéed Provencal, or garlic grilled with pesto. Live jazz music is performed Thursday through Sunday. ✉*In the Harbor Shops, 300 Māʻalaea Rd., Māʻalaea* ☎*808/243–2206* ▭*AE, MC, V.*

★ $–$$$ ✕**Tastings Wine Bar & Grill.** A wedge of a restaurant, this tiny epicurean mecca is tucked in behind a number of rowdy bars on South Kīhei Road. The owner-chef hails from Healdsburg, California, and he brought his highly regarded restaurant with him. The menu features "tastings" of oysters, risotto, lamb chops, and seared *opakapaka* (Hawaiian pink snapper) with a number of well-chosen wines by the bottle or glass. At the bar you can rub elbows with chefs and waiters from the island's best restaurants who come to spend their hard-earned tips here. ✉*1913 S. Kīhei Rd., Kīhei* ☎*808/879–8711* ⊕*www.tastingsrestaurant.com* ▭*AE, D, DC, MC, V.*

¢–$$$ ✕**Stella Blues.** Affordable Stella Blues wins die-hard fans for its unpretentious service and cuisine. Parked in humble Azeka's marketplace, the open-beam, warmly lit dining room is unexpectedly classy. The

8

menu is a major hit, especially with families. Comfort food of every sort is served at breakfast, lunch, and dinner—everything from Toby's Tofu Tia (a tofu and veggie-packed tortilla) to "Mama Tried" Meatloaf. The ample dessert tray is bound to tempt someone in your party, and if it doesn't the cocktails from the swank bar will. ⊠*1279 S. Kīhei Rd., Kīhei* ☎*808/874-3779* ⊟*AE, D, DC, MC, V.*

¢ ✕**Kihei Caffe.** People-watching is fun over a cup of coffee at this casual breakfast and lunch joint. Hearty, affordable portions will prepare you for a day of surfing across the street at Kalama Park. The bowl-shaped egg scramble is tasty and almost enough for two. The resident rooster may come a-beggin' for some of your muffin. This place closes at 8. ⊠*1945 S. Kīhei Rd., Kīhei* ☎*808/879-2230* ⊟*MC, V.*

ITALIAN

$$$–$$$$ ✕**Sarento's on the Beach.** The beachfront setting at this South Maui Italian restaurant is irresistible. Executive Chef George Gomes heads the kitchen. The menu features both traditional dishes—like penne Calabrese and seafood *fra diavolo*—as well as inventions such as swordfish saltimbocca, a strangely successful entrée with a prosciutto, Bel Paese cheese, radicchio, and porcini-mushroom sauce. The wine list includes some affordable finds. ⊠*2980 S. Kīhei Rd., Kīhei* ☎*808/875-7555* ⊟*AE, D, DC, MC, V* ⊗*No lunch.*

JAPANESE

★ ¢–$$ ✕**Hirohachi.** A stone's throw from the flashier Sansei, Hirohachi has been serving authentic Japanese fare for years. Owner Hiro has discerning taste: he buys only the best from local fishermen and imports many ingredients from Japan. Order with confidence even if you can't read the Japanese specials posted on the wall; everything on the menu is high quality. ⊠*1881 S. Kīhei Rd., Kīhei* ☎*808/875-7474* ⊟*AE, MC, V* ⊗*Closed Mon.*

SEAFOOD

$$–$$$$ ✕**Waterfront Restaurant.** At this harborside establishment, fresh fish is prepared in a host of sumptuous ways: baked in buttered parchment paper; imprisoned in ribbons of angel-hair potato; or topped with tomato salsa, smoked chili pepper, and avocado. The varied menu also lists an outstanding rack of lamb and veal scaloppine. Visitors like to come early to dine at sunset on the outdoor patio. Enter Mā'alaea at the Maui Ocean Center and then follow the blue WATERFRONT RESTAURANT signs to the third condominium. ⊠*50 Hau'oli St., Mā'alaea* ☎*808/244-9028* ⊟*AE, D, DC, MC, V* ⊗*No lunch.*

$–$$$ ✕**Blue Marlin Harborfront Grill & Bar.** This is a casual, less-expensive alternative to the Waterfront Restaurant. It's as much a bar as it is a grill, but the kitchen nonetheless sends out well-prepared, substantial servings of fresh fish, burgers, and salads. The sidewalk tables have a lovely view of the harbor. ⊠*Mā'alaea Harbor Village, at Old Mā'alaea Rd. and Honoapi'ilani Hwy., next to Maui Ocean Center, Mā'alaea* ☎*808/244-8844* ⊟*AE, MC, V.*

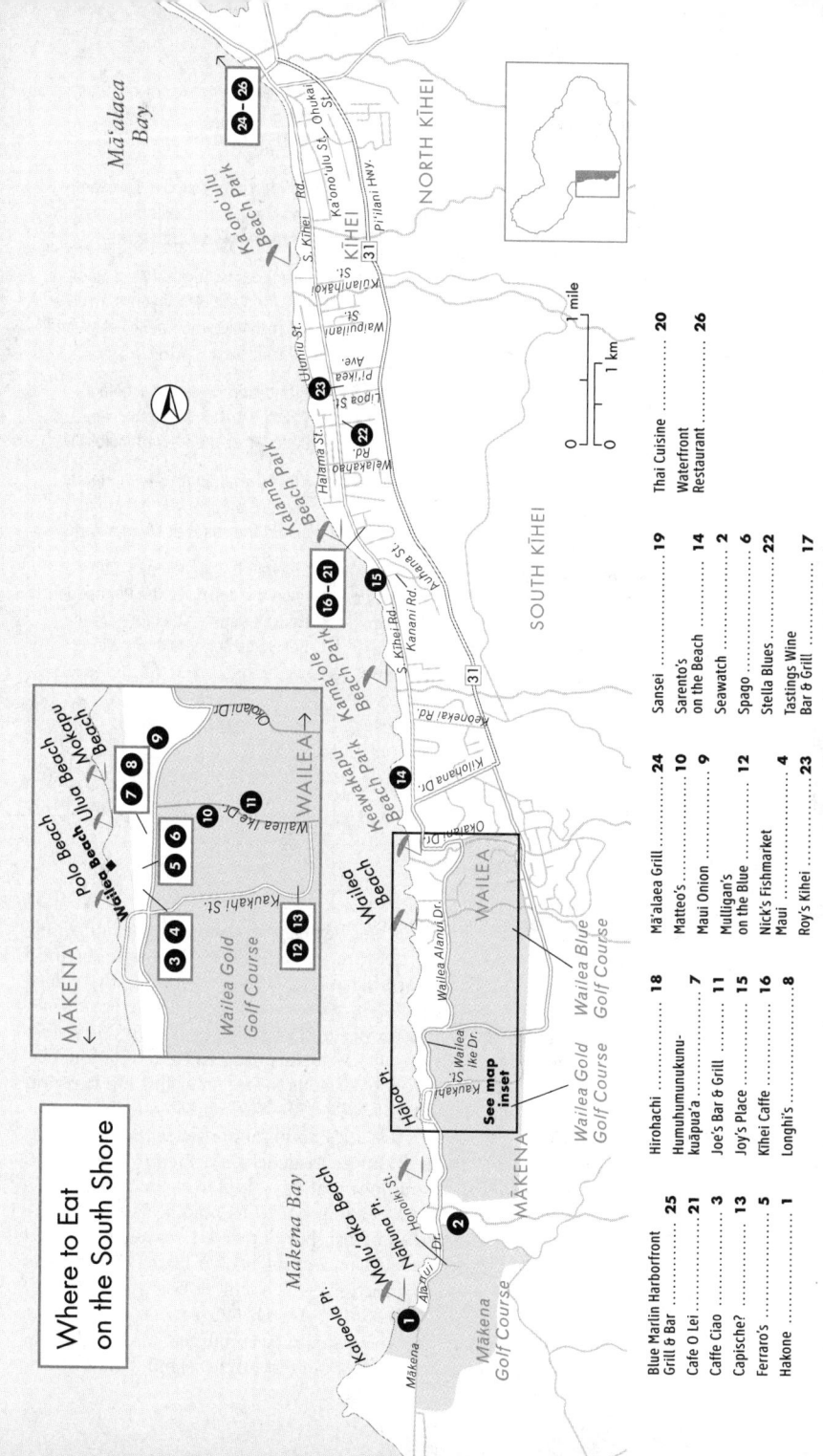

Where to Eat on the South Shore

Blue Marlin Harborfront Grill & Bar	25
Cafe O Lei	21
Caffe Ciao	3
Capische?	13
Ferraro's	5
Hakone	1

Hirohachi	18
Humuhumunukunu- kuāpua'a	7
Joe's Bar & Grill	11
Joy's Place	15
Kīhei Caffe	16
Longhi's	8

Mā'alaea Grill	24
Matteo's	10
Maui Onion	9
Mulligan's on the Blue	12
Nick's Fishmarket Maui	4
Roy's Kīhei	23

Sansei	19
Sarento's on the Beach	14
Seawatch	2
Spago	6
Stella Blues	22
Tastings Wine Bar & Grill	17

Thai Cuisine	20
Waterfront Restaurant	26

THAI

★ ¢–$ ✕**Thai Cuisine.** Fragrant tea and coconut-ginger chicken soup begin a satisfying meal at this excellent Thai restaurant. The care that goes into the decor here (reflected in the glittering Buddhist shrines, fancy napkin folds, and matching blue china) also applies to the cuisine. The lean and moist meat of the red-curry duck rivals similar dishes at resort restaurants, and the fried bananas with ice cream are wonderful. ⊠ *In Kukui Mall, 1819 S. Kīhei Rd., Kīhei* ☎ *808/875–0839* ▭ *AE, D, DC, MC, V.*

VEGETARIAN

¢–$ ✕**Joy's Place.** You may see Joy in the back, whipping up one of her fantastic, vitamin-packed soups. Her glowing skin and smile are testaments to her healthful, culinary wizardry. Try a sandwich or collard-green wrap filled with veggies and a creamy spread. If you have a hint of a cold, a spicy potion is available to ward it off. ⊠ *In Island Surf Bldg., 1993 S. Kīhei Rd., Suite 17, Kīhei* ☎ *808/879–9258* ▭ *MC, V.*

> ## BEST BETS FOR BREAKFAST
>
> **Colleen's** (Upcountry). Eavesdrop on surfers here, while munching on a scone or breakfast burrito.
>
> **Gazebo Restaurant** (West Maui). It's worth the wait if you're a sucker for coconut syrup, "*nēnē*" eggs, and a Pacific view.
>
> **Plantation House** (West Maui). Which is better, the crab cake Benedict or the view of Moloka'i?
>
> **Kihei Caffe** (South Shore). Hearty portions prepare you for surfing across the street at Kalama Park.
>
> **Seawatch** (South Shore). Continue the debate at the Plantation House's sister restaurant—are the Benedicts better with this view?

WAILEA & SOUTH SHORE

AMERICAN

$$–$$$$ ✕**Joe's Bar & Grill.** Owners Joe and Bev Gannon, who run the immensely popular Hāli'imaile General Store, have brought their flair for food home to roost in this comfortable treetop-level restaurant at the Wailea Tennis Club, where you can dine while watching court action from a balcony seat. With friendly service and such dishes as New York strip steak with caramelized onions, wild mushrooms, and Gorgonzola-cheese crumble, there are lots of reasons to stop in at this hidden spot. ⊠ *131 Wailea Ike Pl., Wailea* ☎ *808/875–7767* ▭ *AE, MC, V.*

$–$$$ ✕**Seawatch.** The Plantation House's South Shore sister restaurant has an equally good view, and almost as delicious a menu. Breakfast is especially nice here—the outdoor seating is cool in the morning, over-looking the parade of boats heading out to Molokini. The crab-cake Benedicts are a well-loved standard. For dinner, try seaweed-wrapped 'ahi with diver scallops awash in wasabi beurre blanc. Avoid seats above their private catering section, which can be noisy. ⊠ *100 Golf Club Dr., Wailea* ☎ *808/875–8080* ▭ *AE, D, DC, MC, V.*

$–$$ ✕**Maui Onion.** Forget the overrated Cheeseburger in Paradise in Lahaina—Maui Onion has the best burgers on the island, hands down, and phenomenal onion rings as well. They coat the onions in pancake batter, dip them in panko, then fry them until they're golden brown. ⊠*Renaissance Wailea, 3550 Wailea Alanui Dr., Wailea* ☎*808/879–4900*▭*AE, D, DC, MC, V.*

HAWAIIAN–PACIFIC RIM

$$$–$$$$ ✕**Humuhumunukunukuāpua'a.** Wrestle with the restaurant's formidable name—the name of the state fish—or simply watch the fish swim by in the 2,100-gallon tank at the bar. The thatch-roof building actually floats on a lagoon, creating an atmosphere that tends to outshine the food. We recommend skipping the dining room and enjoying *pūpū* at the bar. Try their signature 'ahi traps (delectable chunks of tempura-fried fish on lemongrass stalks) with an over-the-top cocktail. ⊠*Grand Wailea Resort, 3850 Wailea Alanui Dr., Wailea* ☎*808/875–1234*▭*AE, D, DC, MC, V.*

★ $$$–$$$$ ✕**Spago.** Celebrity chef and owner Wolfgang Puck wisely brought his fame to this gorgeous locale. Giant sea-anemone prints, modern-art-inspired lamps, and views of the shoreline give diners something to look at while waiting. The solid menu delivers with dishes like seared scallops with asparagus and *pohole* (fiddlehead fern) shoots, and "chinois" lamb chops with Hunan eggplant. The beef dish, with braised celery, Armagnac, and horseradish potatoes, may be the island's priciest—but devotees swear it's worth every cent. ⊠*Four Seasons Resort Maui at Wailea, 3900 Wailea Alanui Dr., Wailea* ☎*808/879–2999*▭*AE, D, DC, MC, V*☉*No lunch.*

IRISH

¢–$$ ✕**Mulligan's on the Blue.** If you're hankering for bangers and mash or shepherd's pie, stop in at this pub on Wailea's Blue golf course. You'll be greeted by a nearly all-Irish staff, and before you know it, you'll be sipping a heady pint of Guinness. The Wailea Nights dinner show is outstanding—and a terrific deal to boot. Breakfast is a good value for the area, and the view is one of the best. ⊠*100 Kaukahi St., Wailea* ☎*808/874–1131*▭*AE, D, DC, MC, V.*

ITALIAN

★ $$–$$$$ ✕**Capische?** Hidden up at the quiet Blue Diamond Resort, this restaurant is one local patrons would like kept secret. A circular stone atrium gives way to a small piano lounge, where you can find the best sunset view on the island. You can count on the freshness of the ingredients in superb dishes like the quail saltimbocca, and peppered 'ahi with squid-ink broth. Intimate and well conceived, Capische, with its seductive flavors and ambience, ensures a romantic night out. ⊠*Blue Diamond Resort, 555 Kaukahi St., Wailea* ☎*808/879–2224*▭*AE, D, DC, MC, V*☉*No lunch.*

★ $$–$$$$ ✕**Ferraro's.** Overlooking Wailea Beach, this outdoor restaurant is beautiful both day and night. For lunch, indulge in a lobster sandwich or salad niçoise. At dinner begin your feast with the crab lump-meat gazpacho while enjoying live classical music. Make use of the wine list's excellent Italian offerings and if Chef Paulo Vitaletti is offering one of his periodic tasting menus—such as the white Alba truffle promotion in fall—go for it. The service here is unparalleled. Occasionally you can catch celebrities gossiping at the bar. ⊠*Four Seasons Resort Maui at Wailea, 3900 Wailea Alanui Dr., Wailea* ☎*808/874–8000* ⊟*AE, D, DC, MC, V.*

$–$$$ ✕**Caffe Ciao.** Caffe Ciao brings Italy to the Fairmont Kea Lani. Authentic, fresh gnocchi and lobster risotto taste especially delicious in the open-air café, which overlooks the swimming pool. For casual European fare, try the poached-tuna salad, grilled panini, or pizza from the wood-burning oven. Locals have long known Caffe Ciao's sister deli as the sole source for discerning palates: family-oriented take-out food, delectable pastries, tapenades, and specialty kitchen items. ⊠*Fairmont Kea Lani, 4100 Wailea Alanui Dr., Wailea* ☎*808/875–4100* ⊟*AE, D, DC, MC, V.*

★ $–$$ ✕**Matteo's.** Chef Matteo Mitsura—a bona-fide Italian—may be heard singing as he pounds dough in the kitchen of this miraculous new pizzeria. (Trust us, discovering handsomely-sized Margherita and Portofino pizzas for $17 in Wailea is truly a miracle.) Handmade pastas are loaded with luxurious braised lamb, wild mushrooms, and fresh-shaved Parmesan. Located on the Wailea Blue golf course, the casual open-air restaurant benefits from gentle trade winds in the afternoon and a sky full of stars at night. ⊠*100 Wailea Ike Dr., Wailea* ☎*808/874–1234* ⊟*AE, D, MC, V.*

JAPANESE

$$–$$$$ ✕**Hakone.** The Japanese food served at this restaurant in the Maui Prince hotel has a great reputation. Each night, a different "Special Attraction Buffet" is served: Crazy Crab, Sake Sampler, or the Japanese buffet with numerous dishes of raw, cooked, hot, cold, sweet, and savory items. At $45, it's a good value for the quality of food presented. Impeccably fresh sushi, traditional cooked dishes, and an impressive sake list round out the menu. ⊠*Maui Prince, 5400 Mākena Alanui Rd., Mākena* ☎*808/874–1111* ⊟*AE, MC, V* ☉*No lunch.*

SEAFOOD

$$$–$$$$ ✕**Nick's Fishmarket Maui.** This romantic spot serves fresh seafood using the simplest preparations: mahimahi with Kula-corn relish, 'ahi pepper fillet, and *opakapaka* (Hawaiian pink snapper) with rock shrimp in a lemon-butter-caper sauce, to name a few. Everyone seems to love the Greek Maui Wowie salad made with local onions, tomatoes, avocado, feta cheese, and bay shrimp. The team service is formal—even theatrical—but it befits the beautiful food presentations and extensive wine list. ⊠*Fairmont Kea Lani, 4100 Wailea Alanui Dr., Wailea* ☎*808/879–7224* ⊟*AE, D, DC, MC, V* ☉*No lunch.*

CENTRAL MAUI

AMERICAN

¢ ✕**Maui Bake Shop.** Wonderful breads baked in old brick ovens (dating to 1935), hearty lunch fare, and irresistible desserts make this a popular spot in Central Maui. Baker José Krall was trained in France, and his wife, Claire, is a Maui native whose friendly face you often see when you walk in. Standouts include the focaccia and homemade soups. ✉ *2092 Vineyard St., Wailuku* ☎ *808/242–0064* ⊟ *AE, D, MC, V* ⊙ *Closed Sun. No dinner.*

CHINESE

¢–$$$ ✕ **Dragon Dragon.** Whether you're a party of 10 or 2, this is the place to share seafood-tofu soup, spareribs with garlic sauce, or fresh Dungeness crab with four sauces. Tasteful, simple decor complements the solid menu. The restaurant shares parking with the Maui Megaplex and makes a great pre- or post-movie stop. ✉ *In Maui Mall, 70 E. Ka'ahumanu Ave., Kahului* ☎ *808/893–1628* ⊟ *AE, D, MC, V.*

HAWAIIAN

¢–$ ✕ **A.K.'s Café.** Nearly hidden between auto-body shops and karaoke bars is this wonderful, bright café. Affordable, tasty entrées such as grilled tenderloin with wild mushrooms or garlic-crusted ono with ginger relish come with a choice of two sides. The flavorful dishes are healthy, too—Chef Elaine Rothermal previously instructed island nutritionists on how to prepare health-conscious versions of local favorites. Try the Hawaiian french-fried sweet potatoes, the steamed *ulu* (breadfruit), or the poi. ✉ *1237 Lower Main, Wailuku* ☎ *808/244–8774* ⊟ *D, MC, V* ⊙ *Closed Sun..*

ITALIAN

¢–$$ ✕ **Marco's Grill & Deli.** This convenient eatery outside Kahului Airport (look for the green awning) serves reliable Italian food that's slightly overpriced. Homemade pastas appear on the extensive menu, along with an unforgettably good Reuben sandwich and the best tiramisu on the island. The local business crowd fills the place for breakfast, lunch, and dinner. ✉ *444 Hāna Hwy., Kahului* ☎ *808/877–4446* ⊟ *AE, D, DC, MC, V.*

LATIN

$–$$$ ✕ **Mañana Garage.** Parked in downtown Kahului is this restaurant, which makes the most of its automobile theme—it's probably the only place you can have your wine served out of buckets with crankshaft stems. Under new ownership, the cuisine ranges from Cuban to Brazilian to Mexican, with "the owner's favorite sausages" thrown in for good measure. The bar turns out some mean south-of-the-border cocktails and there's lively music on the weekends. ✉ *33 Lono Ave., Kahului* ☎ *808/873–0220* ⊟ *AE, D, MC, V* ⊙ *No lunch weekends.*

BEST BETS FOR KEIKI (KIDS)

Hula Grill (Kā'anapali). You and your kids can dangle your feet in the sand at the "Barefoot Bar" fronting Kā'anapali Beach.

Maui Ocean Center (South Shore). What was the best exhibit? Decide over sandwiches and shakes at the aquarium's café.

Longhi's (Lahaina, South Shore). Though Longhi's doesn't have a kids' menu, the kitchen will whip up tyke-size noodle dishes on request.

Sugarcane Train (Lahaina). Why not wow the kids with a BBQ dinner aboard Maui's famed Sugarcane Train, the Lahaina–Kā'anapali & Pacific Railroad?

8

MENU GUIDE

Here's a primer on some menu language.

'ahi: yellowfin tuna.

aku: skipjack, bonito tuna.

'ama'ama: mullet; rare but tasty.

bento: a box lunch.

haupia: a light, gelatinlike dessert made from coconut.

imu: the underground ovens in which pigs are roasted for lū'au.

kālua: to bake underground.

kaukau: food.

kimchee: Korean dish of pickled cabbage made with garlic and hot peppers.

laulau: literally a bundle. Morsels of pork, chicken, butterfish, or other ingredients wrapped with young taro shoots in tī leaves for steaming.

liliko'i: passion fruit, a tart, seedy yellow fruit that makes delicious desserts and jellies.

limu: edible seaweed.

lomilomi: to rub or massage. *Lomilomi* salmon is fish rubbed with onions and herbs.

lū'au: a Hawaiian feast, also the leaf of the taro plant used in preparing such a feast.

mahimahi: mild-flavored dolphin-fish, not the marine mammal.

mai tai: potent rum drink with orange and lime juice; Tahitian for "good."

malasada: a Portuguese deep-fried doughnut dipped in sugar.

manapua: dough wrapped around diced pork.

manō: shark.

moi: fish once farmed and served only to Hawaiian royalty.

niu: coconut.

onaga: pink or red snapper.

ono: a long, slender mackerel-like fish; also called wahoo.

'opihi: a tiny shellfish, or mollusk, found on rocks; also called limpets.

pāpio: a young *ulua* or jack fish.

pohā: Cape gooseberry, often used in desserts.

poi: a paste made from pounded taro root.

poke: chopped, pickled raw tuna, tossed with seasonings.

saimin: long thin noodles and vegetables in broth.

tī: from the agave family. The leaves are used to wrap food while cooking.

uku: deep-sea snapper.

ulua: from the jack family, which also includes pompano and amberjack.

THAI

¢–$$ ✕**Saeng's Thai Cuisine.** Choosing a dish from the six-page menu here requires determination, but the food is worth the effort, and most dishes can be tailored to your taste buds: hot, medium, or mild. Begin with spring rolls and a dipping sauce, move on to such entrées as Evil Prince Chicken (cooked in coconut sauce with Thai herbs), or red-curry shrimp, and finish up with tea and tapioca pudding. Asian artifacts,

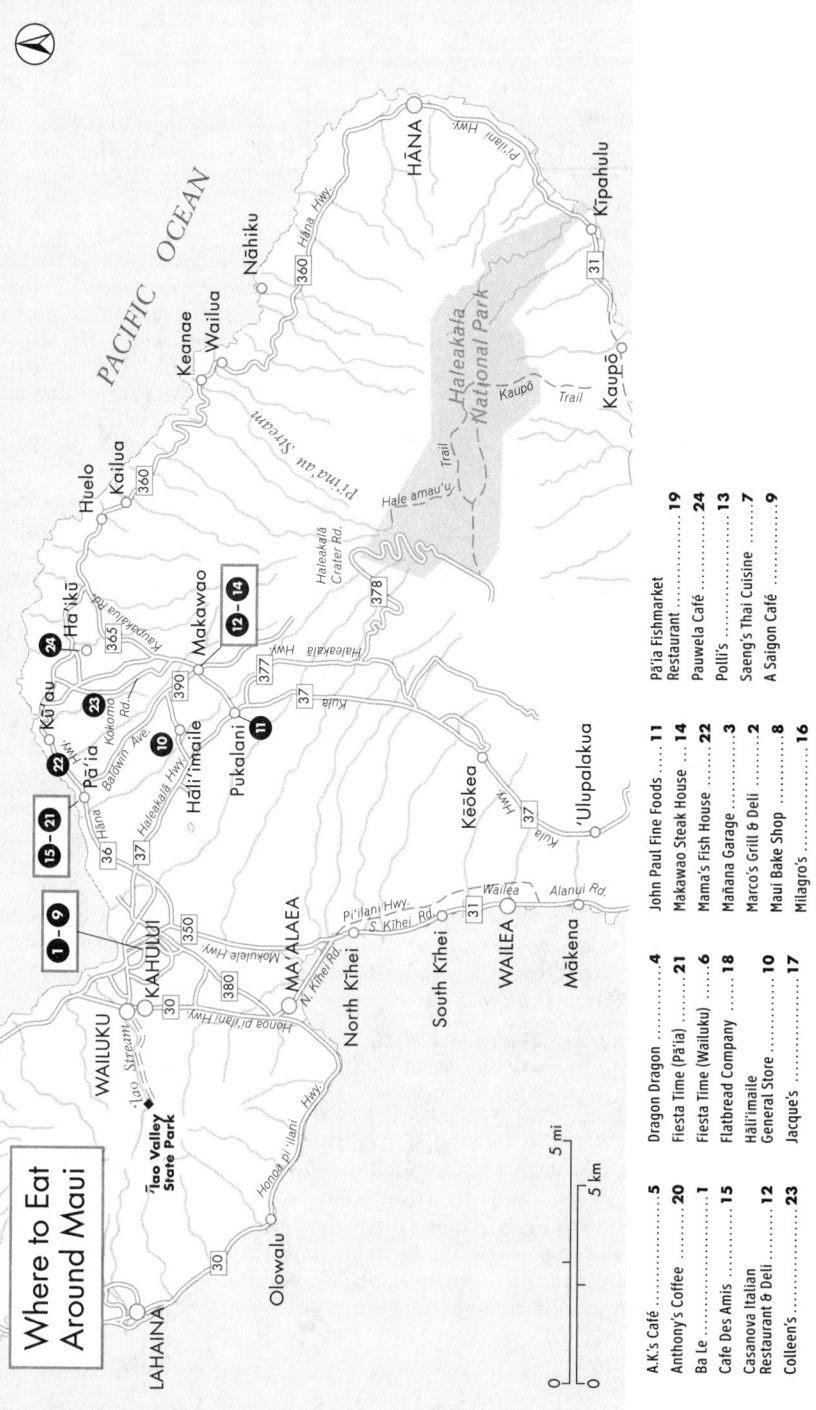

Where to Eat Around Maui

A.K.'s Café	....	**5**
Anthony's Coffee	....	**20**
Ba Le	....	**1**
Cafe Des Amis	....	**15**
Casanova Italian Restaurant & Deli	....	**12**
Colleen's	....	**23**

Dragon Dragon	....	**4**
Fiesta Time (Pāʻia)	....	**21**
Fiesta Time (Wailuku)	.....	**6**
Flatbread Company	....	**18**
Hāliʻimaile General Store	....	**10**
Jacque's	....	**17**

John Paul Fine Foods	.....	**11**
Makawao Steak House	...	**14**
Mama's Fish House	....	**22**
Mañana Garage	....	**3**
Marco's Grill & Deli	....	**2**
Maui Bake Shop	....	**8**
Milagro's	....	**16**

Pāʻia Fishmarket Restaurant	....	**19**
Pauwela Café	....	**24**
Polli's	....	**13**
Saeng's Thai Cuisine	.....	**7**
A Saigon Café	....	**9**

flowers, and a waterfall decorate the dining room, and tables
on a veranda satisfy lovers of the
outdoors. ✉*2119 Vineyard St.,
Wailuku* ☎*808/244–1567* ▭*AE,
MC, V.*

VIETNAMESE

★ ¢–$$ ✕**A Saigon Café.** The only store-
front sign announcing this small, delightful hideaway is one reading
OPEN. Once you find it, treat yourself to *banh hoi chao tom*, more com-
monly known as "shrimp pops burritos" (ground marinated shrimp,
steamed and grilled on a stick of sugarcane). Fresh island fish is always
available and vegetarian fare is well represented—try the green-papaya
salad. The white interior serves as a backdrop for Vietnamese carvings
in this otherwise unadorned space. Background music includes one-hit
wonders from the early '70s. ✉*1792 Main St., Wailuku* ☎*808/243–
9560* ▭*D, MC, V.*

¢ ✕**Ba Le.** Tucked into the mall's food court is the best, cheapest fast food
on the island. The famous soups, or *pho*, come laden with seafood or
rare beef, fresh basil, bean sprouts, and lime. Tasty sandwiches are
served on crisp French rolls—lemongrass chicken is a favorite. The
word is out, so the place gets busy at lunchtime, though the wait is
never long. ✉*Kau Kau Corner food court, Maui Marketplace, 270
Dairy Rd., Kahului* ☎*808/877–2400* ▭*AE, D, DC, MC, V.*

UPCOUNTRY

AMERICAN

¢–$$ ✕**John Paul Fine Foods.** Although not exactly a restaurant, this upscale
deli offers Upcountry diners a welcome alternative to cooking for
themselves. Owner John Paul's gorgeous plates of asparagus with
shaved Parmesan, slices of spice-rubbed prime rib, crab cakes, and
fancy "adult" mac and cheese are ready-made culinary delights—no
slaving over the stove necessary. The bright little shop even sells cut
stems to decorate the table. ✉*81 Makawao Ave., Pukalani* ☎*808/572–
1700* ▭*AE, D, MC, V.*

HAWAIIAN–PACIFIC RIM

★ $–$$$$ ✕**Hāli'imaile General Store.** What do you do with a lofty wooden build-
ing surrounded by sugarcane and pineapple fields that was a tiny
town's camp store in the 1920s? If you're Bev and Joe Gannon, you
invent a legendary restaurant. The Szechuan barbecued salmon and
Hunan-style rack of lamb are classics, as is the sashimi napoleon
appetizer: a tower of crispy wontons layered with 'ahi and salmon.
The back room houses a rotating art exhibit, courtesy of some of the
island's top artists. The restaurant even has its own cookbook. ✉*900
Hāli'imaile Rd., take left exit halfway up Haleakalā Hwy., Hāli'imaile*
☎*808/572–2666* ▭*MC, V.*

ITALIAN

$-$$$ ✕**Casanova Italian Restaurant & Deli.** This family-owned Italian dinner house is an Upcountry institution. The pizzas, baked in a brick wood-burning oven imported from Italy, are the best on the island, especially the *tartufo*, or truffle oil pizza. The daytime deli serves outstanding sandwiches and espresso. After dining hours, local and visiting entertainers heat up the dance floor. ✉*1188 Makawao Ave., Makawao* ☎*808/572–0220* ▭*D, DC, MC, V.*

MEXICAN

¢–$$ ✕**Polli's.** This Mexican restaurant not only offers standards such as enchiladas, chimichangas, and fajitas but will also prepare any item on the menu with seasoned tofu or vegetarian taco mix—and the meatless dishes are just as good as the real thing. A special treat are the *bunuelos*—light pastries topped with cinnamon, maple syrup, and ice cream. The intimate interior is plastered with colorful sombreros and other cantina knickknacks. ✉*1202 Makawao Ave., Makawao* ☎*808/572–7808* ▭*AE, D, DC, MC, V.*

STEAK

$$–$$$ ✕**Makawao Steak House.** A restored 1927 house on the slopes of Haleakalā is the setting for this *paniolo* (Hawaiian cowboy) restaurant, which serves consistently good prime rib, rack of lamb, and fresh fish. Three fireplaces, friendly service, and an intimate lounge create a cozy, welcoming atmosphere. ✉*3612 Baldwin Ave., Makawao* ☎*808/572–8711* ▭*D, DC, MC, V* ☻*No lunch.*

THE NORTH SHORE

8

AMERICAN

¢–$$ ✕**Colleen's.** Hidden up a jungly road in Ha'ikū, this is the neighborhood hangout for windsurfers, yoga teachers, and just plain beautiful people. For breakfast, the pastries tend to be jam-packed with berries and nuts, rather than butter and flakiness. Sandwiches are especially good, served on giant slices of homemade bread. For dinner you can't go wrong with the beef tenderloin salad or a piping hot pizza. ✉*In Hā'iku Cannery, 810 Kokomo Rd., Hā'iku* ☎*808/575–9211* ▭*AE, DC, MC, V.*

★ ¢–$$ ✕**Pā'ia Fishmarket Restaurant.** The line leading up to the counter of this tiny corner fishmarket attests to the popularity of the tasty fish sandwiches. Bench seating is somewhat grimy (you aren't the only one to have enjoyed fries here), but you really won't find a better fish sandwich. Don't bother with the other menu items—go for your choice of fillet served on a soft bun with a dollop of slaw and some grated cheese. As we say in Hawai'i, '*ono* (delicious)! ✉*2A Baldwin Ave., Pā'ia* ☎*808/579–8030* ▭*AE, DC, MC, V.*

¢ ✕**Anthony's Coffee.** This is a great place to eavesdrop on the local windsurfing crowd. The coffee is excellent—they roast their own beans. For breakfast, try the veggie benedict. Picnic lunches are available and there's an ice-cream counter. Bonus: free Wi-Fi. ✉*90 Hāna Hwy., Pā'ia* ☎*808/579–8340* ▭*AE, DC, MC, V* ☻*No dinner.*

WHERE TO WINE

Don't let the pineapple wine fool you: Maui residents can sip syrah with the best of them. At **Tastings Wine Bar & Grill** (✉ *1913 S. Kīhei Rd.* ☎ *808/879–8711*) on the South Shore, you can sample oysters, risotto, and steak with a number of wines by the bottle or glass. Small and smartly designed, this foodlover's hangout is tucked in between a number of rowdy bars in Kīhei. **Marc Aurel's Espresso & Wine Bar** (✉ *28 Market St., Wailuku* ☎ *808/244–0852*) has an even wider selection of wines by the glass. The impressive five-page wine menu reads like a novel and is complemented by Marc's own *tzatziki* (fresh cucumber dip) and a terrific assortment of cheeses. This favorite Wailuku watering hole is popular for *pau hanas*, or after-work drinks, so be sure to stop by before 9 PM.

In West Maui, try **VINO** (✉ *2000 Village Rd., Kapalua* ☎ *808/661–8466*) . Beloved island chef–restaurateur, D. K. Kodama (the force behind Sansei), opened this eclectic dining experience on the golf course, tweaking some of his favorite recipes and creating new ones to match his partner Master Sommelier Chuck Furuya's recommendations.

True connoisseurs might wrap their vacation around the **Kapalua Wine & Food Festival** (☎ *800/527–2782* ⊕ *www.kapaluamaui.com*). Since 1981, this extravaganza sponsored by Kapalua Resort has paired many of the island's top chefs with great wines from around the world. It kicks off in mid-July and events are spread out over four days.

¢ ✕**Pauwela Café.** Ultracasual and ultrafriendly, this spot just off Hāna Highway is worth the detour. Order a *kālua*-pork sandwich and a piece of coffee cake and pass the afternoon. The large breakfast burritos and homemade soups are also good. ✉ *375 W. Kuiaha Rd., off Hāna Hwy. past Ha'ikū Rd., Ha'ikū* ☎ *808/575–9242* ⊙ *No dinner.*

ECLECTIC

$–$$ ✕**Jacque's.** Jacque, an amiable French chef, won the hearts of the windsurfing crowd when he opened this hip, ramshackle bar and restaurant. French-Caribbean dishes like "*Jacque's Crispy Little Poulet*" (chicken) reveal the owner's expertise. The outdoor seating can be a little chilly at times; coveted spots at the sushi bar inside are snatched up quickly. On Friday nights, a DJ moves in and the dining room becomes a packed dance floor. ✉ *120 Hāna Hwy., Pā'ia* ☎ *808/579–8844* ⊟ *AE, D, MC, V.*

¢–$ ✕**Cafe Des Amis.** Papier-mâché wrestlers pop out from the walls at this small creperie. French crêpes with Gruyère, and Indian wraps with lentil curry are among the choices, all served with wild greens and sour cream or chutney on the side. The giant curry bowls are mild but tasty, served with delicious chutney. For dessert there are crêpes, of course, filled with chocolate, Nutella, cane sugar, or banana. ✉ *42 Baldwin Ave., Pā'ia* ☎ *808/579–6323* ⊟ *AE, D, MC, V.*

MEXICAN

¢–$$$ ✕**Milagro's.** Delicious fish tacos are found at this corner hangout, along with a selection of fine tequilas. Latin-fusion recipes ignite fresh fish and vegetables. The location at the junction of Baldwin Avenue and Hāna Highway makes people-watching under the awning shade a lot of fun. Lunch and happy hour (3 to 5) are the best values; the prices jump at dinnertime. ⊠*3 Baldwin Ave., Pā'ia* ☎*808/579–8755* ▤*AE, D, DC, MC, V.*

¢–$ ✕**Fiesta Time.** After a hard day of snorkeling, watching whales, and catching waves, little tastes better than a plate of fish tacos with rice and beans slathered in melted cheese and fresh salsa. At three locations, Fiesta Time can fill your belly with burritos, enchiladas, and chiles rellenos. The pickled vegetables available in take-home tubs are especially tasty. Decorated with fanciful Mexican murals, the Wailuku and Pā'ia locations have limited seating and are mainly takeout. The Mā'alaea restaurant serves alcohol. ⊠*In the Harbor Shops, 300 Mā'alaea Rd., Mā'alaea* ☎*808/244–5862* ⊠*1132 Lower Main St., Wailuku* ☎*808/249–8463* ⊠*Hāna Hwy., Pā'ia* ☎*808/579–8269* ▤*AE, MC, V.*

PIZZA

☼ ¢–$$ ✕**Flatbread Company.** This rambling restaurant with prayer flags strung from the ceiling and child-drawn menus has been a hit since opening its doors. The menu is comprised mainly of crisp, organic flatbreads shoveled from the clay oven, and includes vegan options. Partake in the "Punctuated Equilibrium," with Kalamata olives, and Surfing Goat cheese; or "Mopsy's Pork Pie" with *kalua* pork and homemade BBQ sauce. There's also a terrific mesclun salad dressed with arame seaweed and ginger-tamari vinaigrette. Portions are large and service is prompt and friendly, despite the near constant crowds. ⊠*375 Hāna Hwy., Pā'ia* ☎*808/579–8989. MC, V..*

SEAFOOD

★ $$$–$$$$ ✕**Mama's Fish House.** For years Mama's has been *the* destination for special occasions. A stone- and shell-engraved path leads you up to what would be, in an ideal world, a good friend's house. The Hawaiian nautical theme is hospitable and fun—the menu even names which boat reeled in your fish. Despite its high prices—even for Maui—the restaurant is nearly always full; dinner reservations start at 4:30 PM. If you're willing to fork over the cash, the daily catch baked in a creamy caper sauce or steamed in traditional lū'au leaves is outstanding, followed by the Polynesian Pearl—a gorgeous affair of chocolate mousse and passion-fruit cream. A tiny fishing boat is perched above the entrance to Mama's, about 1½ mi east of Pā'ia on Hāna Highway. ⊠*799 Poho Pl., Kū'au* ☎*808/579–8488* ⌕*Reservations essential* ▤*AE, D, DC, MC, V.*

8

Where to Stay

WORD OF MOUTH

"[Peace of Maui] is my favorite place to stay in Maui. Owners are friendly! I really enjoyed talking to others who were staying there. . . . Convenient to Haleakalā for hiking. I felt at home."

–Brian

"The stress melts off you the minute you walk through the door. The breakfast is fabulous. You feel like you have the run of the place. The Ho'oil House doesn't miss a beat."

–Debbie

WHERE TO STAY PLANNER

Resorts & Condos

The resorts are clustered along the leeward (west and south) shores, meaning they are hot and sunny in summer and hot and sunny in winter (with periodic downpours). Kāʻanapali (in West Maui) is the original resort community and has the most action, feeding off the old whaler's haunt, Lahaina town. Kapalua, farther north, is more private and serene, and catches a bit more wind and rain. On the South Shore, posh Wailea has excellent beaches and designer golf courses, each with a distinct personality.

If you can compromise on luxury, you will find convenient condos in West Maui (in Nāpili or Kahana) or on the South Shore (in Kīhei). Many are oceanfront and offer the amenities of a hotel suite without the cost. Furnishings can be a little scruffy, and rarely do condos have central air-conditioning—something to consider if you aren't used to sleeping in humidity.

Keep in Mind

Most resorts charge parking and facility fees. What once was complimentary is tacked on as a "resort fee." Thankfully, condos haven't followed suit yet—sometimes local calls are still free.

Apartment Rentals

Along with the condos listed in this chapter, which operate like hotels and offer hotel-like amenities, Maui has condos you can rent through central booking agents. Most agents represent more than one condo complex (some handle single-family homes as well), so be specific about price, space, facilities, and amenities. The following are multiproperty agents. **Destination Resorts** (✉ 3750 Wailea Alanui Dr., Wailea 96753 ☎ 866/384–1365 ⊕ www.drh-maui.com). **Maui Vacation Advisors** (✉ 360 Papa Pl., Suite 205, Kahului 96732 ☎ 808/871–7766 or 800/736–6284 ⊕ www.mauivacationadvisors.com).

What It Costs

The prices listed in this guide are the rack rates given by the hotels at this writing. Always ask about special packages and discounts. Note that in Hawaiʻi room prices can rise dramatically if a room has an ocean view. To save money, ask for a garden or mountain view.

	¢	$	$$	$$$	$$$$
HOTELS	Under $100	$100–$180	$181–$260	$261–$340	Over $340

Hotel prices are for two people in a double room in high season, including tax and service. Condo price categories reflect studio and one-bedroom rates.

B&Bs & Vacation Rentals

Most of the accommodations Upcountry and in Hāna are B&Bs or vacation rentals. Few offer breakfast, but most deliver seclusion and a countryside experience. If you're booking off the Internet, it pays to fact-check. Questions to ask before making the deposit: how far from the airport/beach/shops is it? Will I have a private bathroom and kitchen? Is there a phone and TV in the room?

By Shannon
Wianecki
Updated
by Wanda
Adams

MAUI'S ACCOMMODATIONS COME IN THREE SIZES: small, medium, and gargantuan. Small bed-and-breakfasts are personal and charming—often a few rooms or a cottage beside the owner's own home. They open a window into authentic island life. Medium-size condominiums are less personal (you won't see the owner out trimming the bougainvillea) but highly functional—great for longer stays or families who want no-fuss digs. The resorts are out of this world. They do their best to improve on nature, trying to re-create what is beautiful about Maui. And their best is pretty amazing. Opulent gardens, fantasy swimming pools with slides (some with swim-up bars), waterfalls, spas, and championship golf courses make it hard to work up the willpower to leave the resort and go see the real thing.

WEST MAUI

West Maui is a long string of small communities, beginning with Lahaina at the south end and meandering into Kā'anapali, Honokowai, Kahana, Nāpili, and Kapalua. Here's the breakdown on what's where: Lahaina is the business district with all the shops, shows, restaurants, historic buildings, churches, and rowdy side streets. Kā'anapali is all glitz: fancy resorts set on Kā'anapali Beach. Honokowai, Kahana, and Nāpili are quiet little nooks characterized by comfortable condos built in the late 1960s. All face the same direction and get the same consistently hot, humid weather. Kapalua, at the northern tip, faces windward, and has a cooler climate and slightly more rain.

LAHAINA

Lahaina doesn't have a huge range of accommodations, but it does make a great headquarters for active families, or those not looking to spend a bundle on resorts. One major advantage is the proximity of restaurants, shops, and activities—everything is within walking distance. It's a business district, however, and won't provide the same peace and quiet afforded by resorts or secluded vacation rentals. Still, Lahaina has a nostalgic charm, especially early in the morning before the streets have filled with visitors and vendors.

CONDOS & VACATION RENTALS

¢–$ 🏠 **Bambula Inn.** This casual sprawling house in a quiet Lahaina residential area has two studio apartments, one attached to the house and one freestanding. No breakfast is served; this is a move-in-and-hangout beach house. Just across the street is a small beach, and moored just offshore is a sailboat hand-built by the owner. He likes to take his guests out for whale-watching and sunset sails, no charge. He also provides snorkel equipment. This is a friendly, easygoing way to visit Lahaina. ⊠*518 Ilikahi St., Lahaina 96761* 🕾*808/667–6753 or 800/544–5524* 🖷*808/667–0979* ⊕*www.bambula.com* ➪*2 units* ⚑*In-room: no a/c (some), kitchen. In-hotel: no elevator* ⊟*AE, D, MC, V.*

WHERE TO STAY IN WEST MAUI

Hotels & Resorts

HOTEL NAME	Worth Noting	Cost $	Pools	Beach	Golf Course	Tennis Courts	Gym	Spa	Children's Programs	Rooms	Restaurants	Other	Location
6 Hyatt Regency Maui	130-ft water slide	410–725	1	yes	yes	6	yes	yes	3–12	815	4		Kāʻanapali
7 Kāʻanapali Beach Hotel	Hula & lei-making classes	205–345	1	yes	priv.					430	3		Kāʻanapali
18 Mauian Hotel	On Nāpili Bay	175–215	1	yes						44		no TVs	Nāpili
★ 20 Ritz-Carlton, Kapalua	Cultural education center	505–875	1	yes	priv.	10	yes	yes	5–12	470	3	shops	Kapalua
11 Royal Lahaina Resort	New tower wing	220–425	3	yes	priv.	11				516	3		Kāʻanapali
★ 10 Sheraton Maui	Nightly torch-lighting ritual	500–645	1	yes	priv.	3	yes	yes	5–12	510	2		Kāʻanapali
8 The Westin Maui Resort	The Heavenly Spa	485–750	5	yes	priv.	3	yes	yes	0–12	761	3		Kāʻanapali

Condos & Vacation Rentals

HOTEL NAME	Worth Noting	Cost $	Pools	Beach	Golf Course	Tennis Courts	Gym	Spa	Children's Programs	Rooms	Restaurants	Other	Location
2 Bambula Inn	Studio apartments	89–125								2		kitchens	Lahaina
7 Kāʻanapali Aliʻi	Great location	405–675	2	yes	yes	6				264		kitchens	Kāʻanapali
13 Mahana at Kāʻanapali	Spacious rooms	275–775	1	yes						145		kitchens	Honokowai
16 Mahina Surf	Free parking and phone	145–260	1							50		kitchens	Mahinahina
15 Makani Sands	Small private beach	180–435	1	yes						20		kitchens	Honokowai
12 Maui Eldorado	On golf course	279–349	3	yes	yes					258		kitchens	Kāʻanapali
★ 19 Nāpili Kai Beach Club	Outstanding beach	220–355	4	yes					6–12	162		kitchens	Nāpili
14 ResortQuest at Papakea Resort	Cultural classes	235–775	2			4			5–12	364		kitchens	Honokowai
17 Sands of Kahana	Kids' putting green	200–265	2	yes		3				162		kitchens	Kahana

B&Bs

HOTEL NAME	Worth Noting	Cost $	Pools	Beach	Golf Course	Tennis Courts	Gym	Spa	Children's Programs	Rooms	Restaurants	Other	Location
★ 1 Hoʻoilo House	Private outdoor showers	345	1							5		no kids	Lahaina
★ 4 Lahaina Inn	Historic property	165–210								12		no TVs	Lahaina
★ 5 The Makai Inn	Nice views	100–168								18		no A/C	Lahaina
★ 3 Plantation Inn	Gerard's restaurant	170–280	1							18	1		Lahaina

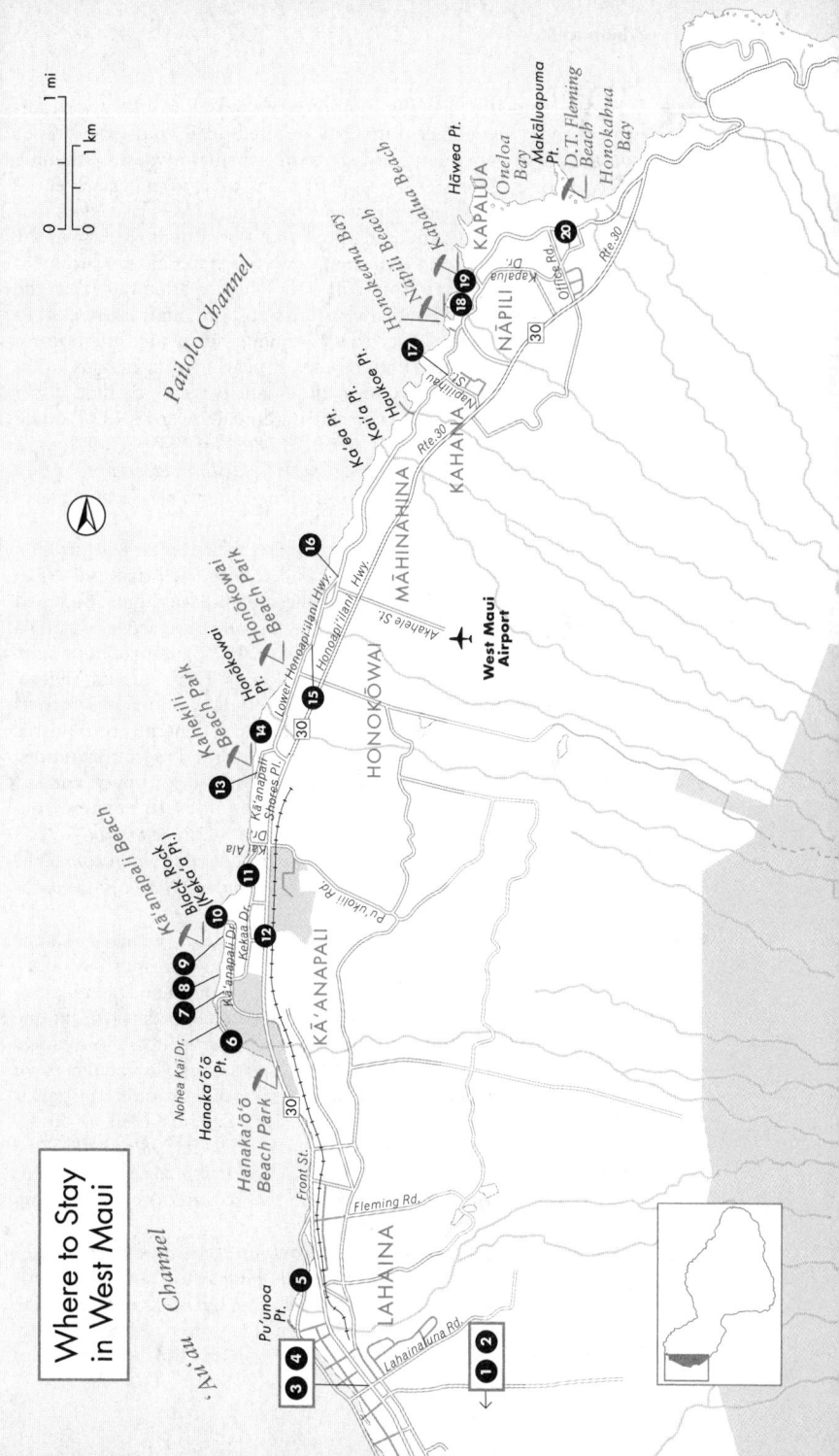

Where to Stay in West Maui

'Au'au Channel

Pailolo Channel

Pu'unoa Pt.

LAHAINA

Front St.

Lahainaluna Rd.

Fleming Rd.

Hanaka'ō'ō Beach Park

Nohea Kai Dr.

Hanaka'ō'ō Pt.

Kā'anapali Beach

Black Rock (Keka'a Pt.)

Kā'anapali Dr.

Kekaa Dr.

Pu'ukoli'i Rd.

KĀ'ANAPALI

Ka'anapali Shores Pt.

Kā'anapali Pkwy.

Kai Ala Dr.

Kahekili Beach Park

Honōkōwai Pt.

Honōkōwai Beach Park

Lower Honoapi'ilani Hwy.

Honoapi'ilani Hwy.

Akahele St.

West Maui Airport

HONOKŌWAI

MĀHINAHINA

KAHANA

Koʻea Pt.

Kaiʻa Pt.

Haukoe Pt.

Napilihau St.

Honokeana Bay

Nāpili Beach

Nāpili Bay

Hāwea Pt.

NĀPILI

Kapalua Dr.

Office Rd.

Kapalua Beach

Oneloa Bay

Makāluapuna Pt.

D.T. Fleming Beach

Honokahua Bay

KAPALUA

Rte. 30

Rte. 30

0   1 mi
0   1 km

B&BS

$$$$

Fodor's Choice

★

🖼 **Ho'oilo House.** If you really want to treat yourself to a luxurious get-away, spend a few nights at this Bali-inspired B&B. In the foothills of the West Maui Mountains, just south of Lahaina town, this stunning property brings the words "quiet perfection" to mind. As you enter the house your eye is immediately drawn to the immense glass doors that open onto a small but sparkling pool and a breathtaking view of the Pacific. Almost all of the furnishings and the materials used to build the house were imported from Bali. Two "conversation tables" in the common area are filled with Balinese cushions, providing great spots to snack, chat, or just relax. Each room is uniquely decorated and features traditional Balinese doors with mother-of-pearl inlay, a custom bed, a private lānai, a huge bathroom with a giant bathtub, an iPod docking station, and best of all—a private outdoor shower. ⊠ *138 Awaiku St., Lahaina 96761* ☎ *808/667–6669* 🖷 *808/661–7857* ⊕ *www.hooilo-house.com* ↝ *6 rooms* ♿ *In-room: safe, Wi-Fi, Ethernet. In-hotel: pool, public Wi-Fi, no kids under 16, no-smoking rooms, no elevator* ▤ *AE, MC, V.*

$–$$$ ★

🖼 **Plantation Inn.** Charm sets this inn apart, tucked into a corner of a busy street in the heart of Lahaina. Filled with Victorian and Asian furnishings, it's reminiscent of a southern plantation home. Secluded lānai draped with hanging plants face a central courtyard, pool, and a garden pavilion perfect for morning coffee. Each guest room or suite is decorated differently, with hardwood floors, French doors, slightly dowdy antiques, and four-poster beds. (We think number 10 is nicest.) Suites have kitchenettes and whirlpool baths. A generous breakfast is included in the room rate, and one of Hawai'i's best French restaurants, Gerard's, is on-site. Breakfast, coupled with free parking in downtown Lahaina, makes this a truly great value, even if it's 10 minutes from the beach. ⊠ *174 Lahainaluna Rd., Lahaina 96761* ☎ *808/667–9225 or 800/433–6815* 🖷 *808/667–9293* ⊕ *www.theplantationinn.com* ↝ *18 rooms* ♿ *In-room: refrigerator. In-hotel: restaurant, pool, no elevator* ▤ *AE, MC, V.*

$–$$ ★

🖼 **Lahaina Inn.** This antique jewel right in the heart of town is classic Lahaina—a two-story wooden building that will transport you back to the turn of the 20th century. The 10 small rooms and 2 suites shine with authentic period furnishings, including quilted bedcovers, antique lamps, and Oriental carpets. You can while away the hours in a wicker chair on your balcony, sipping coffee and watching Old Lahaina town come to life. An excellent continental breakfast is served in the parlor and the renowned restaurant, David Paul's Lahaina Grill, is downstairs. ⊠ *127 Lahainaluna Rd., Lahaina 96761* ☎ *808/661–0577 or 800/669–3444* 🖷 *808/667–9480* ⊕ *www.lahainainn.com* ↝ *10 rooms, 2 suites* ♿ *In-room: no TV. In-hotel: public Internet, no-smoking rooms, no elevator* ▤ *AE, D, MC, V.*

$

🖼 **The Makai Inn.** This pleasant oceanfront inn consists of 18 rooms, all at least 400 square feet, with four special "Hideaway" rooms with private lānai just 9 feet from the ocean. All are 1-bedroom except for the 2-bedroom "Pineapple Sweet." The furnishings aren't terribly attractive and you might find a smudge of red Lahaina dirt here and there

HONEYMOONER HIDEAWAY

After a barefoot wedding on the beach, honeymooners can slip away in style to Suite 301, a luxurious oceanfront room at the **Four Seasons Resort Maui at Wailea** (⊠ *3900 Wailea Alanui Dr., Wailea* ☎ *808/874–8000 or 800/334–6284* ⊕ *www.fourseasons.com/maui*) . Equipped with a butler's kitchen, concierge service, formal dining for 10, and a large private lawn, this suite is perfect for entertaining your wedding party. But forget them; the real draw is the hedonistic marble bathroom with its deep-soaking tub and eucalyptus rain shower. Room service will trail flower petals from your door to the tub, ending at a bottle of champagne. The haunt of celebrities, this suite must be booked far in advance.

Most locals, if asked, will say they'd like to retire in Keokea. They might even mention **The Star Lookout** (⊠ *622 Thompson Rd., Keokea* ☎ *907/346–8028* ⊕ *www.starlookout.com*) with a dreamy look in their eyes. Why? Hidden away halfway up Haleakalā, this charming 100-year-old perch is an ideal getaway. It's chilly enough in the evening to snuggle up, and in the morning it's brisk enough to enjoy jogging on the sleepy one-lane road. You can imagine typing out the first chapter of the "Great American Novel" while your partner sips coffee and the French doors let in a dizzying view of Maui from your bed. If you decide you never want to leave, the Star does offer monthly discounts.

For those who don't want to disappear entirely, the **Plantation Inn** (⊠ *174 Lahainaluna Rd., Lahaina* ☎ *808/667–9225 or 800/433–6815* ⊕ *www.theplantationinn.com*) is a good choice. Embedded in the action of Front Street, the charming old-world inn is an oasis of hospitality. We think the Southeast Asian decor in the deluxe room is the most romantic, with its dramatic four-poster bed. On-site, acclaimed restaurant Gerard's is a perfect destination for an anniversary dinner.

(there is no daily maid service and towels etc., are replaced only on request), but the lānai are perfect for daydreaming. Suzie, the landlord, lives on property, and keeps a flock of cheerful Java sparrows well fed; there's a lovely garden courtyard. ⊠ *1415 Front St., Lahaina 96761* ☎ *808/662–3200 or 808/870–9004* 📠 *808/661–9027* ⊕ *www.makaiinn.net* ⇄ *18 rooms* ♿ *In-room: no a/c (some), kitchen, no TV. In-hotel: laundry facilities, public Wi-Fi, no elevator* ⊟ *AE, MC, V.*

KĀʻANAPALI

Kāʻanapali is a playground—a long stretch of beach lined with over-the-top resorts, shopping, and restaurants. Expect top-class service here. Everything you could want is just a few steps from your room—including the calm waters of sun-kissed Kāʻanapali Beach. Wandering along the beach path between resorts is a recreational activity unto itself. Weather is dependably warm, and for that reason as well as all the others, Kāʻanapali is a popular—at times downright crowded—destination.

HOTELS & RESORTS

$$$$ **⛉Hyatt Regency Maui Resort & Spa.** Fantasy landscaping with splashing waterfalls, swim-through grottoes, a lagoonlike swimming pool, and a 130-foot waterslide wows guests of all ages at this active Kāʻanapali resort. Stroll through the lobby past museum-quality art, brilliant parrots, and … South African penguins (like we said, fantasy). It's not necessarily Hawaiian, but it is photogenic. At the southern end of Kāʻanapali Beach, this resort is in the midst of the action. Also on the premises is Spa Moana, an oceanfront, full-service facility. ⊠*200 Nohea Kai Dr., Kāʻanapali 96761* ☎*808/661–1234 or 800/233–1234* 🖷*808/667–4499* ⊕*www.maui.hyatt.com* ⬚*815   rooms* ⟆*In-room: safe, refrigerator, Ethernet. In-hotel: 4 restaurants, bars, golf courses, tennis courts, pool, gym, spa, beachfront, children's programs (ages 3–12)* ▭*AE, D, DC, MC, V.*

$$$$ **⛉Sheraton Maui Resort.** Set among dense gardens on Kāʻanapali's
FodorsChoice   best stretch of beach, the Sheraton offers a quieter, more understated
★   atmosphere than its neighboring resorts. The open-air lobby has a crisp, cool look with minimal furnishings and decor, and sweeping views of the pool area and beach. The majority of the spacious rooms come with ocean views; only one of the six buildings has rooms with mountain or garden views. The hotel has had a technology upgrade with 32-inch flat-screen TVs in all rooms and Bose stereo systems in suites; many of the public areas have been spruced up, as well. The swimming pool looks like a natural lagoon, with rock waterways and wooden bridges. Best of all, the hotel sits next to the 80-foot-high "Black Rock," from which divers leap in a nightly torch-lighting ritual. ⊠*2605 Kāʻanapali Pkwy., Kāʻanapali 97671* ☎*808/661–0031 or 888/488–3535* 🖷*808/661–0458* ⊕*www.starwood.com/hawaii* ⬚*510 rooms and suites* ⟆*In-room: safe, refrigerator. In-hotel: 2 restaurants, bar, tennis courts, pool, gym, spa, beachfront, children's programs (ages 5–12), laundry facilities, public Internet* ▭*AE, D, DC, MC, V.*

$$$$ **⛉The Westin Maui Resort & Spa.** The cascading waterfall in the lobby of this hotel gives way to an "aquatic playground" with 5 heated swimming pools, abundant waterfalls (15 at last count), lagoons complete with pink flamingos, and a premier beach. The water features combined with a spa and fitness center, and privileges at two 18-hole golf courses make this an active resort—great for families. Relaxation is by no means forgotten. Elegant dark-wood furnishings in the rooms accentuate the crisp linens of "Heavenly Beds." Rooms in the Beach Tower are newer but slightly smaller than those in the Ocean Tower. The 13,000-square-foot Heavenly Spa features 11 treatment rooms and a yoga studio. ⊠*2365 Kāʻanapali Pkwy., Kāʻanapali 96761* ☎*808/667–2525 or 888/488–3535* 🖷*808/661–5831* ⊕*www.starwood.com/hawaii* ⬚*761 rooms* ⟆*In-room: Ethernet. In-hotel: 3 restaurants, bar, pools, gym, spa, beachfront, children's programs (infant–12)* ▭*AE, D, DC, MC, V.*

$$–$$$$ **⛉Kāʻanapali Beach Hotel.** This somewhat rundown but still attractive, old-fashioned hotel is full of aloha. Locals say that it's one of the few resorts on the island where visitors can get a true Hawaiian experience. The vintage-style Mixed Plate restaurant, known locally for its

native cuisine program, has displays honoring the many cultural traditions represented by the staff: the employees themselves contributed
the artifacts. The spacious rooms are simply decorated in wicker and
rattan and face the beach beyond the courtyard. There are complimentary classes in authentic hula dancing, lei-making, and 'ukulele playing. The departure ceremony makes you want to come back. ✉*2525
Kā'anapali Pkwy., Kā'anapali 96761* ☎*808/661–0011 or 800/262–
8450* 🖶*808/667–5978* ⊕*www.kbhmaui.com* ➴*430 rooms* ⚬*In-room:
safe. In-hotel: 3 restaurants, bar, pool, beachfront* ⊟*AE, D, DC, MC,
V.*

$$–$$$$ 🏨**Royal Lahaina Resort.** The big news at Royal Lahaina Resort is the
newly renovated 12-story, 333-room tower offering Hawaiian canoe–
theme rooms with dark teak furnishings against light-colored walls.
The new rooms boast ocean and garden views from half-moon balco-
nies, plush "presidential" beds with 300-count Egyptian cotton linens,
sound systems with an iPod and MP3 docking station, and 32-inch,
high-definition flat-screen TVs. Visitors should be aware that reno-
vations continue through 2008 with work on the hotel's trademark
low-rise seaside cottages, on the grounds, and in the public areas. The
project upgrades the property from midprice to deluxe/luxury status.
Tennis buffs will be sorry to hear that the dozen tennis courts are going
in favor of a new condominium complex; two upgraded courts will
remain. Altogether, the aim is to return the resort to its glory days,
when, as the first property in the resort, it hosted millionaires and Hol-
lywood stars. ✉*2780 Keka'a Dr., Kā'anapali 96761* ☎*808/661–3611
or 800/447–6925* 🖶*808/661–3538* ⊕*www.hawaiianhotels.com* ➴*455
rooms* ⚬*In-room: Ethernet. In-hotel: 3 restaurants, tennis courts,
pools, beachfront* ⊟*AE, D, DC, MC, V.*

CONDOS & VACATION RENTALS

$$$$ 🏨**Kā'anapali Ali'i.** Four 11-story buildings are laid out so well that the
feeling of seclusion you'll enjoy may make you forget you're in a condo
complex. Instead of tiny units, you'll be installed in an ample one- or
two-bedroom apartment. All units have great amenities: a chaise in an
alcove, a sunken living room, a whirlpool, and a separate dining room,
though some of the furnishings are dated. It's the best of both worlds:
home-like condo living with hotel amenities—daily maid service, an
activities desk, small store with video rentals, and 24-hour front-desk
service. ✉*50 Nohea Kai Dr., Kā'anapali 96761* ☎*808/667–1400 or
800/642–6284* 🖶*808/661–1025* ⊕*www.classicresorts.com* ➴*264
units* ⚬*In-room: safe, kitchen. In-hotel: golf course, tennis courts,
pools, beachfront, laundry facilities* ⊟*AE, D, DC, MC, V.*

$$$–$$$$ 🏨**Maui Eldorado.** This fine condo complex, which wraps around the
Kā'anapali golf course's sixth fairway, offers several perks, most nota-
bly air-conditioning in the units and access to a fully outfitted beach
cabana on a semiprivate beach. The complex itself isn't exactly on
the beach—it's a quick golf-cart trip away. While resort guests get
scolded for dragging lounge chairs onto neighboring resort beaches,
here you can relax in luxury. Not only will you have beach chairs
at your disposal, but a full kitchen and lounge area at the cabana,
too. The privately managed units are tastefully decorated with modern

9

appliances and spacious bathrooms. Those overseen by the Outrigger aren't as up-to-date, but are still a good value for pricey Kāʻanapali. ⌧*2661 Kekaʻa Dr., Kāʻanapali 96761* ☎*808/661–0021* 🖷*808/661–5478* ⊕*www.lahainagrill.com/eldorado.htm* ⬒*258 units* ⬒*In-room: kitchen, Ethernet (some). In-hotel: golf course, pools, beachfront, concierge, laundry facilities* ▤*AE, D, DC, MC, V.*

NORTH OF KĀʻANAPALI (UPPER WEST SIDE)

The Upper West Side is how locals refer to the neighborhoods north of Kāʻanapali: Honokowai, Mahinahina, Kahana, Nāpili, and finally, Kapalua. They seamlessly blend into one another along Lower Honoapiʻilani Highway. Each has a few shops and restaurants and a secluded bay or two to call its own. Many visitors have found a second home here, at one of the condominiums nestled between beach-access roads and groves of mango trees. You won't get the stellar service of a resort, but you'll be among the locals here, in a relatively quiet part of the island. Be prepared for a long commute, if you're planning to do much exploring elsewhere on the island. Kapalua is the farthest town of them all, but well worth all the driving to stay at the elegant Ritz-Carlton, which is surrounded by misty greenery and overlooks beautiful D. T. Fleming Beach.

HOTELS & RESORTS

$$$$ ★   🏨 **Ritz-Carlton, Kapalua.** This elegant hillside property got a $95 million going-over in 2007 (reopening is set for early 2008) to give it more of a Hawaiian sense of place, including new furnishings in existing guest rooms and the creation of 107 one- and two-bedroom condominium residential suites, decorated in richly colored plantation-era themes. A new cultural education center was created; the spa was expanded; food and beverage outlets and the pool were all upgraded. Although not set directly on the sand, the resort does command ocean and mountain views and there is an almost-private beach. The multi-level pool and hot tubs are open 24 hours. The grounds are private and secluded, despite being in the midst of Kapalua's collection of hotels, shops, restaurants, and golf courses. A full-time cultural adviser, Clifford Naeʻole, educates employees and guests in Hawaiian traditions and conducts frequent ceremonies. This is a great jumping-off point for golfers—privileges are available at three championship courses, and the island of Lānaʻi, with its two renowned courses, is a quick ferry ride away. ⌧*1 Ritz-Carlton Dr., Kapalua 96761* ☎*808/669–6200 or 800/262–8440* 🖷*808/665–0026* ⊕*www.ritzcarlton.com/resorts/kapalua* ⬒*470 rooms* ⬒*In-room: safe, Wi-Fi. In-hotel: 6 restaurants, bar, tennis courts, pool, gym, spa, beachfront, children's programs (ages 5–12), laundry service* ▤*AE, D, DC, MC, V.*

$–$$ 🏨 **Mauian Hotel.** If you're looking for a quiet place to stay, this nostalgic hotel way out in Nāpili may be for you. The rooms have neither TVs nor phones—such noisy devices are relegated to the ʻOhana Room, where a continental breakfast is served daily. The simple two-story buildings date from 1959, but have been renovated with bright islander furnishings. Rooms include well-equipped kitchens. Best of all, the 2-acre property opens out onto lovely Nāpili Bay. ✉*5441 Lower Honoapi'ilani Hwy., Nāpili 96761* ☏*808/669–6205 or 800/367–5034* 🖷*808/669–0129* 🌐*www.mauian.com* 🛏*44 rooms* ⌂*In-room: no a/c, no phone, kitchen, no TV. In-hotel: pool, beachfront, laundry facilities, public Wi-Fi* ▭*AE, D, MC, V.*

CONDOS & VACATION RENTALS

$$$–$$$$ ⌂**Mahana at Kā'anapali.** Though the address claims Kā'anapali, this 12-story condominium complex is really in quiet, neighboring Honokowai. Spacious rooms and living areas can accommodate families easily. Built in 1974, the property has been regularly updated since, but the decor in individually owned units may vary. An elegant pool faces a sandy beach, which isn't, unfortunately, recommended for swimming because of the shallow reef. ✉*110 Kā'anapali Shores Pl., Honokowai 96761* ☏*808/661–8751* 🖷*808/661–5510* 🌐*www.themahana.com* 🛏*145 units* ⌂*In-room: safe, kitchen, dial-up, Wi-Fi (some). In-hotel: tennis courts, pool, beachfront, concierge, public Wi-Fi* ▭*AE, MC, V.*

$$–$$$$ ★ ⌂**Nāpili Kai Beach Club.** On 10 beautiful beachfront acres—the beach here is one of the best on the West Side for swimming and snorkeling—the Nāpili Kai draws a loyal following. Hawaiian-style rooms are done in sea-foam and mauve, with rattan furniture; shoji doors open onto the lānai. The rooms closest to the beach have no air-conditioning, but ceiling fans usually suffice. "Hotel" rooms have only mini-refrigerators and coffeemakers, whereas studios and suites have fully equipped kitchenettes. This is a family-friendly place, with children's programs and free classes in hula and lei-making. Packages that include a car, breakfast, and other extras are available if you stay five nights or longer. ✉*5900 Lower Honoapi'ilani Hwy., Nāpili 96761* ☏*808/669–6271 or 800/367–5030* 🖷*808/669–5740* 🌐*www.napilikai.com* 🛏*162 units* ⌂*In-room: no a/c (some), dial-up. In-hotel: pools, beachfront, concierge, children's programs (ages 6–12), laundry service* ▭*AE, MC, V.*

$$–$$$$ ⌂**ResortQuest at Papakea Resort.** Although this oceanfront condominium has no beach, there are several close by. And with classes on swimming, snorkeling, pineapple cutting, and more, you'll have plenty to keep you busy. Papakea has built-in privacy because its units are spread out among 11 low-rise buildings on some 13 acres of land; bamboo-lined walkways between buildings and fish-stocked ponds add to the serenity. Fully equipped kitchens and laundry facilities make longer stays easy here. There are air-conditioning units in the living rooms of each condo. ✉*3543 Lower Honoapi'ilani Hwy., Honokowai 96761* ☏*808/669–4848 or 800/922–7866* 🖷*808/922–8785* 🌐*www.resort-quest.com* 🛏*364 units* ⌂*In-room: kitchen, Wi-Fi. In-hotel: tennis courts, pools, children's programs (ages 5–12), laundry facilities* ▭*AE, MC, V.*

$$–$$$ ⌂**Sands of Kahana.** Meandering gardens, spacious rooms, and an on-site restaurant distinguish this large condominium complex. Primarily a time-share property, a few units are available as vacation rentals. The upper floors benefit from their height—matchless ocean views stretch away from private lānai. The oceanfront penthouse, which

9

accommodates up to eight, is a bargain at $435 during peak season. Kids can enjoy their own pool area near a putting green and ponds filled with giant koi. ✉*4299 Lower Honoapi'ilani Hwy., Kahana 96761* ☎*808/669–0400* 🖷*808/669–8409* ⊕*www.sands-of-kahana.com* 🛏*162 units* ☖*In-room: no a/c (some), kitchen, dial-up. In-hotel: restaurant, tennis courts, pools, beachfront, concierge* ▭*AE, MC, V.*

$–$$ 🏨**Mahina Surf.** Mahina Surf stands out from the many condo complexes lining the oceanside stretch of Honoapi'ilani Highway by being both well-managed and affordable. You won't be charged fees for parking, checkout, or local phone use, and discount car rentals are available. The individually owned units are typically overdecorated, but each one has a well-equipped kitchen and an excellent ocean view. The quiet complex is a short amble away from Honokowai's grocery shopping, beaches, and restaurants. ✉*4057 Lower Honoapi'ilani Hwy., Mahinahina 96761* ☎*808/669–6068 or 800/367–6086* 🖷*808/669–4534* ⊕*www.mahinasurf.com* 🛏*50 units* ☖*In-room: safe, kitchen, Ethernet (some). In-hotel: pool, concierge, laundry facilities* ▭*AE, MC, V.*

$–$$ 🏨**Makani Sands.** This centrally located, slightly older complex offers an economical way to see the West Side. Rooms have wide lānai, which hang over a small sandy beach below. The corner rooms (ending in 01) are best, with wraparound views. A small freshwater pool is available for cooling off. The back bedrooms may be noisy at night, as they're close to the road. ✉*3765 Lower Honoapi'ilani Hwy., Honokowai 96761* ☎*808/669–8223 or 800/227–8223* 🖷*808/665–0756* ⊕*www.makanisands.com* 🛏*26 units* ☖*In-room: kitchen, VCR, dial-up. In-hotel: pool, beachfront, laundry facilities* ▭*AE, MC, V.*

> ### CONDO COMFORTS
>
> **Foodland.** This large grocery store should have everything you need, including video rentals and a Starbucks. ✉*Old Lahaina Center, 845 Waine'e St., Lahaina* ☎*808/661–0975.*
>
> **Gaby's Pizzeria and Deli.** The friendly folks here will toss a pie for takeout. ✉*505 Front St., Lahaina* ☎*808/661–8112.*
>
> **The Maui Fish Market.** It's worth stopping by this little fish market for an oyster or a cup of fresh-fish chowder. You can also get live lobsters and fillets marinated for your barbecue. ✉*4405 Lower Honoapi'ilani Hwy., Honokowai* ☎*808/665–9895.*

THE SOUTH SHORE

The South Shore is composed of two main communities: resort-filled Wailea and down-to-earth Kīhei. In general, the farther south you go, the fancier the accommodations get. ■TIP➡**North Kīhei tends to have great prices but windy beaches scattered with seaweed. (Not a problem if you don't mind driving 5 to 10 minutes to save a few bucks.)** As you travel down South Kīhei Road, you can find condos both on and off inviting beach parks, and close to shops and restaurants. Once you hit Wailea, the opulence quotient takes a giant leap—perfectly groomed resorts gather around Wailea and Polo beaches. This resort wonderland mimics (some say improves upon) Kā'anapali. The two communities continuously compete over which is more exclusive and which has better weather—in our opinion it's a definite draw.

KĪHEI

If you're a beach lover, you won't find many disadvantages to staying in Kīhei. A string of welcoming beaches stretches from tip to tip. Snorkeling, boogie boarding, and barbecueing find their ultimate expression here. Affordable condos line South Kīhei Road; however, some find the busy traffic and the strip-mall shopping distinctly un-Maui and prefer quieter hideaways.

HOTELS & RESORTS

$-$$$

Fodor'sChoice
★

Mana Kai Maui. This unsung hero of South Shore hotels may be older than its competitors, but that only means it's closer to the beach—beautiful Keawakapu. Hotel rooms with air-conditioning are remarkably affordable for the location. Two-room condos with private lānai benefit from the hotel amenities, such as daily maid service and discounts at the oceanfront restaurant downstairs. Shoji screens and bamboo furniture complement the marvelous ocean views, which in winter are punctuated by the visiting humpback whales. ⊠2960 S. Kīhei Rd., Kīhei 96753 ☎808/879–2778 or 800/367–5242 ☎808/879–7825 ⊕www. crhmaui.com ⇆49 hotel rooms, 49 1-bedroom condos ⟂In-room: safe, refrigerator. In-hotel: restaurant, pool, beachfront ⊟AE, D, DC, MC, V.

$-$$

Maui Coast Hotel. You might never notice this elegant hotel because it's set back off the street. The standard rooms are fine—very clean and modern—but the best deal is to pay a little more for one of the suites. In these you'll get an enjoyable amount of space and jet nozzles in the bathtub. You can sample nightly entertainment by the large, heated pool or work out in the new fitness center until 10 PM. The 6-mi-long stretch of Kama'ole Beach I, II, and III is across the street. ⊠2259 S. Kīhei Rd., Kīhei 96753 ☎808/874–6284, 800/895–6284, or 800/426–0670 ☎808/875–4731 ⊕www.westcoasthotels.com ⇆265 rooms, 114 suites ⟂In-room: safe, refrigerator. In-hotel: 2 restaurants, tennis courts, pool, laundry service ⊟AE, D, DC, MC, V.

CONDOS & VACATION RENTALS

$-$$$$ ★

Hale Hui Kai. Bargain hunters who stumble across this small three-story condo complex will think they've died and gone to heaven. The beachfront units are older, but many of them have been renovated. Some have marble countertops in the kitchens and all have outstanding views. But never mind the interior; you'll want to spend all of your time outdoors—in the shady lava-rock lobby that overlooks a small pool perfect for kids, or on gorgeous Keawakapu Beach just steps away. Light sleepers should avoid the rooms just above the neighboring restaurant, Sarento's, but definitely stop in there for dinner. ⊠115 S. Kīhei Rd., Kīhei 96753 ☎808/879–1219 or 800/809–6284 ☎808/879–0600 ⊕www.halehuikaimaui.com ⇆40 units ⟂In-room: no a/c, safe,

9

WHERE TO STAY ON THE SOUTH SHORE

HOTEL NAME	Worth Noting	Cost $	Pools	Beach	Golf Course	Tennis Courts	Gym	Spa	Children's Programs	Rooms	Restaurants	Other	Location
Hotels & Resorts													
★ 4 Fairmont Kea Lani	Villas available	475–1,000	3	yes	priv.		yes	yes	5–12	450	3	shops	Wailea
★ 5 Four Seasons Resort	Luxurious	440–880	1	yes	priv.	2	yes	yes	5–12	380	3		Wailea
6 Grand Wailea Resort	Spa Grande	675–955	3	yes	priv.		yes	yes	5–12	779	5	shops	Wailea
★ 14 Mana Kai Maui	Great prices	125–330	1	yes						98			Kihei
16 Maui Coast Hotel	Beach across the street	175–235	1							379	2		Kihei
★ 1 Maui Prince	Secluded beach	375–575	2	yes	yes	6			5–12	310	4		Mākena
7 Wailea Beach Marriott Resort and Spa	Package deals avail.	349–429	3	yes	priv.			yes	5–12	516	3		Wailea
Condos & Vacation Rentals													
10 Amanda and George's Wonderful Wailea	1-BR suite	120	2			4				1		kitchens	Wailea
★ 13 Hale Hui Kai	Oceanfront lounge	180–385	1	yes						40		kitchens	Kihei
15 Kama'ole Sands	Beach across the street	210–525	1			4				309	1	kitchens	Kihei
17 Luana Kai	Poolside BBQs	129–299	1			4				113		no A/C	Kihei
★ 2 Mākena Surf	Secluded gated community	300–1,399	2	yes	priv.					71		kitchens	Wailea
18 Maui Sunseeker Resort	Beach across the street	145–215								4		kitchens	Kihei
★ 3 Polo Beach Club	Location, location, location	550–695	1	yes	priv.					71		kitchens	Wailea
★ 9 Wailea 'Ekahi	Studios available	180–925	4	yes	priv.					300		kitchens	Wailea
★ 8 Wailea 'Elua	Gated Community	180–925	2	yes	priv.					150		kitchens	Wailea
★ 11 Wailea 'Ekolu	Hillside view	180–925	2	no	priv.					160		kitchens	Wailea
B&Bs													
12 Eva Villa	360° views from rooftop	135–175	1							3		kitchens	Wailea

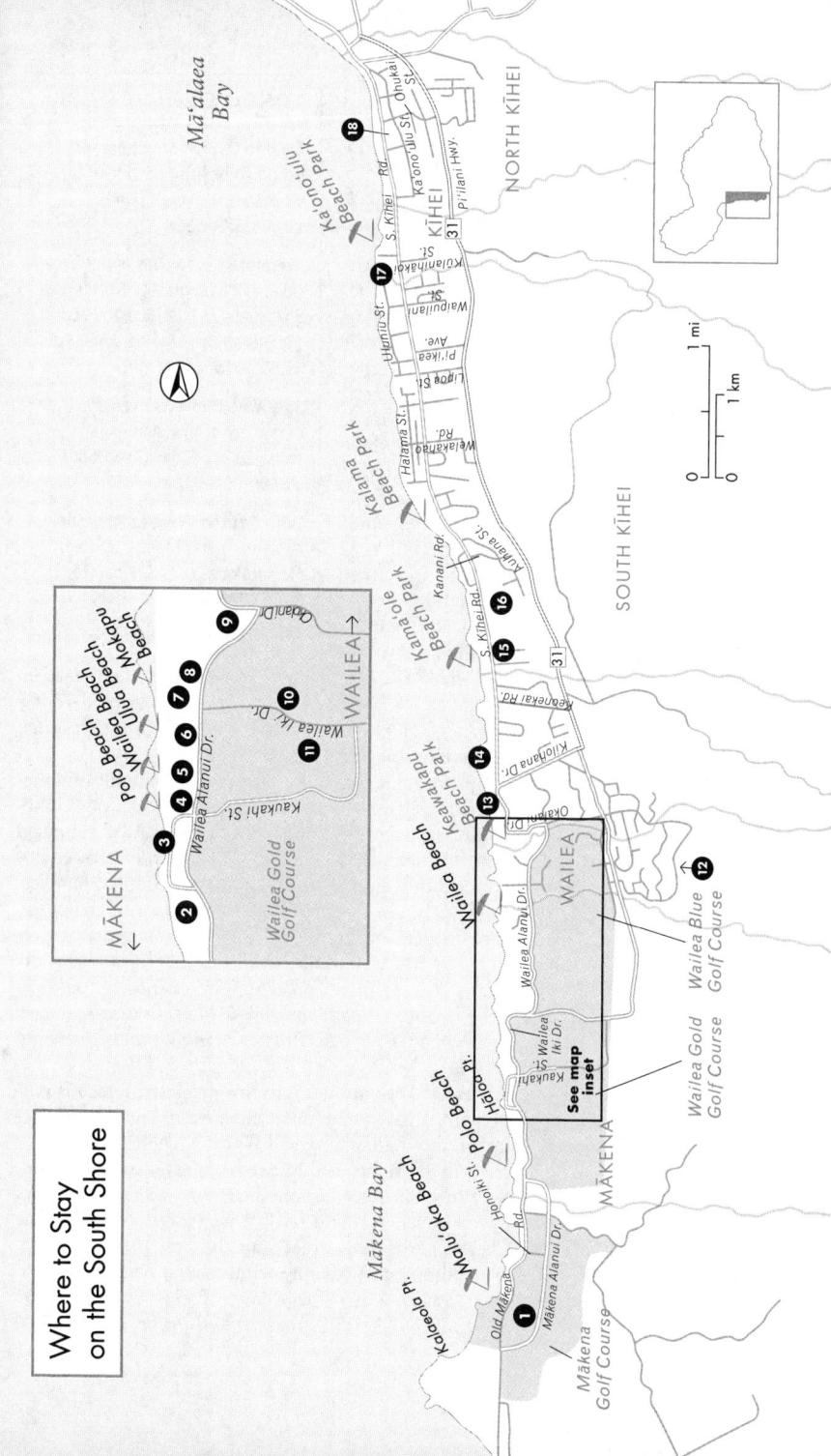

Where to Stay on the South Shore

Ma'alaea Bay

Mākena Bay

Kalaeola Pt.

Malu'aka Beach

Old Mākena

Honoiki St.

Polo Pt.

Hāloa Pt.

Mākena Alanui Dr.

Mākena Golf Course

MĀKENA

Wailea Gold Golf Course

Wailea Iki Dr.

Kaukahi St.

See map inset

WAILEA

Wailea Alanui Dr.

Wailea Blue Golf Course

Wailea Gold Golf Course

Okalani Dr.

Kilohana Dr.

Keonekai Rd.

S. Kihei Rd.

Piilani Hwy. 31

Kanani Rd.

Kiipahu St.

SOUTH KĪHEI

Wailea Beach

Keawakapu Beach Park

Kama'ole Park Beach Park

Kalama Park Beach Park

Kihei Rd.

Welakahao Rd.

Halama St.

Lipoa St.

Pi'ikea Ave.

Uluniu St.

Waipuilani St.

Kūlanihāko'i St.

Ke ono 'ulu St.

S. Kihei Rd.

Ka'ono'ulu Beach Park

Ohukai

NORTH KĪHEI

KĪHEI

MĀKENA Polo Beach Beach Wailea Beach 'Ulua Mokapu Beach

Wailea Alanui Dr.

Kaukahi St.

Okani Dr.

WAILEA

Wailea Gold Golf Course

Wailea Iki Dr.

0   1 km
0   1 mi

kitchen, VCR. In-hotel: pool, beachfront, laundry faciliti-es ☐*AE, D, DC, MC, V.*

$$$ 🏨**Kama'ole Sands.** "Kam" Sands is a good choice for the active traveler; there are tennis and volleyball courts to keep you in shape, and the ideal family beach (Kama'ole III) waits across the street. Eleven four-story buildings wrap around 15 acres of grassy slopes with swimming pools, a small waterfall, and BBQs. Condos are equipped with modern conveniences, but there's a relaxed, almost retro feel to the place. All units have kitchens, laundry facilities, and private lānai. The property has a 24-hour front desk and an activities desk. ■**TIP→Attention home owners: privately owned house-trade options are available at www.**

kamaole-sands.com. ⊠ *2695 S. Kīhei Rd., Kīhei 96753* ☎ *808/874–8700 or 800/367–5004* 🖷 *808/879–3273* ⊕ *www.castleresorts.com* ⤳ *309 units* ♿ *In-room: no a/c (some), kitchen, VCR (some), dial-up. In-hotel: restaurant, tennis courts, pool* ☐ *AE, D, DC, MC, V.*

$–$$$ 🏨**Luana Kai.** Set-up house at this North Kīhei condominium-by-the-sea. Units are older with slightly dated furnishings, but each one comes with everything you need to make yourself at home: a fully equipped kitchen with dishwasher, laundry facilities, TV, VCR, and stereo equipment. There are three different room plans, suited for couples, families, or friends traveling together. The pool area is a social place, with five gas grills, a full outdoor kitchen, and Jacuzzis. The property adjoins a grassy county park with tennis courts, and the beach is a short way down the road. ⊠ *940 S. Kīhei Rd., Kīhei 96753* ☎ *808/879–1268 or 800/669–1127* 🖷 *808/879–1455* ⊕ *www.luanakai.com* ⤳ *113 units* ♿ *In-room: no a/c (some), kitchen, VCR, Wi-Fi. In-hotel: tennis courts, pool, no elevator* ☐ *AE, DC, MC, V.*

$–$$ 🏨**Maui Sunseeker Resort.** The care put into this property, which is particularly popular with a gay and lesbian clientele, is already noticeable from the sign on the road. This small North Kīhei hotel is a great value for the area and is private and relaxed. You can opt for a simple but attractively furnished studio, one-bedroom, or two-bedroom penthouse; all have kitchenettes and full baths, as well as BBQs. The 4-mi stretch of beach across the street isn't the best for swimming, but it's great for strolling and watching windsurfers, whales (in winter), and sunsets. ⊠ *551 S. Kīhei Rd., Kīhei 96753* ☎ *808/879–1261 or 800/532–6284* 🖷 *808/874–3877* ⊕ *www.mauisunseeker.com* ⤳ *16* *units* ☍ *In-room: VCR (some). In-hotel: laundry facilities, public Internet, no elevator* ═MC, V.

WAILEA & MĀKENA

Wailea is warm, serene, and luxurious. Less action-packed than West Maui resorts, the properties here tend to focus on ambience—little thoughtful details and big scenery. Nightlife is pretty much nil, save for a few swank bars and a boisterous Irish pub. But you'll have your choice of sandy beaches with good snorkeling. Farther south, Mākena is a little less developed, a little more wild; more stars can be seen here at night. Expect everything—even bottled water—to double in price when you cross the line from Kīhei to Wailea.

HOTELS & RESORTS

$$$$
Fodor's Choice
★

Fairmont Kea Lani Hotel Suites & Villas. Gleaming white spires and tiled archways are the hallmark of this stunning resort. Spacious suites have microwaves, stereos, and marble bathrooms. But the villas are the real lure. Each is two-story and has a private plunge pool, two (or three) large bedrooms, a laundry room, and a fully equipped kitchen—BBQ and margarita blender included. Best of all, maid service does the dishes. A fantastic haven for families, the villas are side by side in a sort of miniature neighborhood. Request one on the end, with an upstairs sundeck. The resort offers good dining choices, a gourmet deli, and a small, almost private beach. ⊠ *4100 Wailea Alanui Dr., Wailea 96753* ☎ *808/875–4100 or 800/882–4100* ☐ *808/875–1200* ⊕ *www.kealani. com* ⟳ *413 suites, 37 villas* ☍ *In-room: refrigerator, VCR, dial-up. In-hotel: 3 restaurants, bar, pools, gym, spa, beachfront, children's programs (ages 5–12)* ═AE, D, DC, MC, V.

$$$$
Fodor's Choice
★

Four Seasons Resort Maui at Wailea. Impeccably stylish, subdued, and relaxing describe most Four Seasons properties; this one fronting award-winning Wailea beach is no exception. Thoughtful luxuries—like Evian spritzers poolside and room-service attendants who toast your bread in-room—earned this Maui favorite its reputation. The property has an understated elegance, with beautiful floral arrangements, courtyards, and private cabanas. Most rooms have an ocean view (avoid those over the parking lot in the North Tower), and you can find terry robes and whole-bean coffee grinders in each. Choose between three excellent restaurants, including Wolfgang Puck's Spago. The recently renovated spa is small but expertly staffed. Honeymooners: request Suite 301, with its round tub and private lawn. Recently added: Flight Bites lunch boxes upon departure; poolside spa mini-treatments. ⊠ *3900 Wailea Alanui Dr., Wailea 96753* ☎ *808/874–8000 or 800/334–6284* ☐ *808/874–6449* ⊕ *www.fourseasons.com/maui* ⟳ *380 rooms* ☍ *In-room: safe, refrigerator, Ethernet. In-hotel: 3 restaurants, bars, tennis courts, pool, gym, spa, beachfront, bicycles, children's programs (ages 5–12)* ═AE, D, DC, MC, V.

$$$$
Grand Wailea Resort. With all rooms renovated in 2007, "Grand" is no exaggeration for this opulent, sunny 40-acre resort. Elaborate water features include a "canyon riverpool" with slides, caves, a Tarzan swing, and a water elevator. Tropical garden paths meander past

artwork by Léger, Warhol, Picasso, Botero, and noted Hawaiian artists—sculptures even hide in waterfalls. Spacious ocean-view rooms are outfitted with stuffed chaises, comfortable desks, and oversize marble bathrooms. Spa Grande, renovated and upgraded in 2007, is the island's most comprehensive spa facility, offering you everything from mineral baths to massage. For kids, Camp Grande has a full-size soda fountain, game room, and movie theater. Although not the place to go for quiet or for especially attentive service, the property is astounding. ⊠ *3850 Wailea Alanui Dr., Wailea 96753* ☎ *808/875–1234 or 800/888–6100* 🖷 *808/874–2442* ⊕ *www.grandwailea.com* ⏎779 *rooms* ☝ *In-room: safe, dial-up. In-hotel: 5 restaurants, bars, pools, gym, spa, beachfront, children's programs (ages 5–12)* ⊟ *AE, D, DC, MC, V.*

$$$$ ★ 🛈**Maui Prince.** This isn't the most luxurious resort on the South Shore—it could actually use a face-lift—but it has many pluses that more than make up for the somewhat dated decor. The location is superb. Just south of Mākena, the hotel is on a secluded piece of land surrounded by two magnificent golf courses and abutting a beautiful, near-private beach. The pool area is simple (two round pools), but surrounded by beautiful gardens that are quiet and understated compared to the other big resorts. The attention given to service is apparent from the minute you walk into the open-air lobby—the staff is excellent. Rooms on five levels all have ocean views (in varying degrees) and surround the courtyard, which has a Japanese garden with a bubbling stream. ⊠ *5400 Mākena Alanui Rd., Mākena 96753* ☎ *808/874–1111 or 800/321–6284* 🖷 *808/879–8763* ⊕ *www.princeresortshawaii.com* ⏎ *310 rooms* ☝ *In-room: safe, VCR, Ethernet, Wi-Fi. In-hotel: 4 restaurants, golf courses, tennis courts, pools, beachfront, children's programs (ages 5–12)* ⊟ *AE, DC, MC, V.*

$$$$ 🛈**Wailea Beach Marriott Resort & Spa.** The Marriott (formerly the Outrigger) was built before current construction laws were put in place, so rooms sit much closer to the crashing surf than at most resorts. Wailea Beach is a few steps away, as are the Shops at Wailea. In 2007, the hotel completed a $60 million renovation with redesigned guest rooms, a new 10,000-square-foot Mandara Spa, and a redesigned Hula Moons Restaurant & Bar. Public spaces showcase a remarkable collection of Hawaiian and Pacific Rim artifacts. All of the spacious rooms have private lānai and are styled with a tropical theme. There are golf privileges at three nearby courses, as well as tennis privileges at the Wailea Tennis Club. ⊠ *3700 Wailea Alanui Dr., Wailea 96753* ☎ *808/879–1922 or 800/922–7866* 🖷 *808/874–8331* ⊕ *www.marriothawaii.com* ⏎ *516 rooms* ☝ *In-room: safe, dial-up. In-hotel: 3 restaurants, pools, spa, beachfront, children's programs (ages 5–12), laundry service* ⊟ *AE, D, DC, MC, V.*

CONDOS & VACATION RENTALS

$$$$ ★ 🛈**Polo Beach Club.** This wonderful, old eight-story property lording over a hidden section of Polo Beach somehow manages to stay under the radar. From your giant corner window, you can look down at the famed Fairmont Kea Lani villas, and know you've scored the same great locale at a fraction of the price. Individually owned apart-

ments are well cared for and feature top-of-the-line amenities, such as stainless-steel kitchens, marble floors, and valuable artwork. An underground parking garage keeps vehicles out of the blazing Kīhei sun. ✉*3750 Wailea Alanui Dr., Wailea 96753* ☎*808/879–1595 or 800/367–5246* 🖷*808/874–3554* ⊕*www.mauiownercondos.com* ⬙*71 units* ⛾*In-room: kitchen, VCR, Wi-Fi. In-hotel: pool, beachfront, laundry facilities, no-smoking rooms* ▤*AE, MC, V.*

$$$–$$$$ ★ 🏨**Mākena Surf.** For travelers who've done all there is to do on Maui and just want simple, luxurious relaxation, this is the spot. The security-gate entrance gives way to manicured landscaping dotted with palm trees. The secluded complex is designed so that it's hard to tell they're actually three-story buildings. Water aerobics and tennis clinics are regularly offered. "B" building is oceanfront; "A," "C," and "G" are the best value, just a bit farther from the shore. Privacy envelops the grounds—which makes the place a favorite with visiting celebrities. ✉*3750 Wailea Alanui Dr., Wailea 96753* ☎*808/879–1595 or 800/367–5246* 🖷*808/874–3554* ⊕*www.drhmaui.com* ⬙*107 units* ⛾*In-room: safe, kitchen, VCR, Wi-Fi. In-hotel: tennis courts, pools, beachfront, laundry facilities* ▤*AE, MC, V.*

$–$$$$ 🏨**Wailea 'Ekahi, 'Elua, and 'Ekolu.** The Wailea Resort started out with
Fodor's Choice three upscale condominium complexes named, appropriately, 'Ekahi,
★ 'Elua, and 'Ekolu (One, Two, and Three). The individually owned units, managed by Destination Resorts Hawai'i, represent some of the best values in this high-class neighborhood. All benefit from daily housekeeping, air-conditioning, high-speed Internet, free long distance, lush landscaping, and preferential play at the neighboring world-class golf courses and tennis courts. You're likely to find custom appliances and sleek furnishings befitting the million-dollar locale. ■TIP➔**The concierges here will stock your fridge with groceries—even hard-to-find dietary items—for a nominal fee.** 'Ekolu, farthest from the water, is the most affordable, and benefits from a hillside view; 'Ekahi is a large V-shape property focusing on Keawakapu Beach; 'Elua has 24-hour security and overlooks Ulua Beach. ✉*3750 Wailea Alanui Dr., Wailea 96753* ☎*808/879–1595 or 800/367–5246* 🖷*808/874–3554* ⊕*www.drhmaui.com* ⬙*594 units* ⛾*In-room: kitchen, VCR, Wi-Fi. In-hotel: pools, beachfront, laundry facilities* ▤*AE, MC, V.*

$ 🏨**Amanda and George's Wonderful Wailea Condominium.** Exceptionally tasteful decor (lovely artwork) makes this one-bedroom suite live up to its name. The view is of a wooded ravine, and the location is outstanding—near the Blue golf course, it's a quick drive (or seven-minute jog) to the South Shore's best beaches, restaurants, and shops. Amenities include use of the two pools and Jacuzzis on the grounds and access to the famed Wailea Tennis Club (for a fee). ✉*At Grand Champions, Wailea Ike Pl. #25, Wailea 96753* ☎*808/891–2214* ⊕*www.travelmaui.com/condo_rental/wailea* ⬙*1 unit* ⛾*In-room: kitchen. In-hotel: pools, laundry facilities* ▤*No credit cards.*

9

FAMILY REUNION HEADQUARTERS

For adventurous families, the lovely cottage at **Peace of Maui** (⊠ *1290 Hali'imaile Rd., Hali'imaile* ☎ *808/572–5045 or 888/475–5045* ⊕ *www.peaceofmaui.com*) makes a great headquarters. The casual digs are affordable and less than 15 minutes from most everything (on the North Shore, that is). We can't say enough about the friendliness of the owners here—you'll want to adopt them into your family. Call far in advance to make sure you can rent the whole shebang ($120 a night).

Kama'ole Sands (⊠ *2695 S. Kīhei Rd., Kīhei96753* ☎ *808/874–8700 or 800/367–5004* ⊕ *www.castleresorts.com*) is an easy spot for launching family activities. Two-bedroom units

have everything a family needs: kitchens, laundry facilities, and pool access. The complex is across the street from Kam III beach park to boot—a great place for family barbecues, Frisbee championships, or kite-flying contests.

On the other end of the spectrum there are the villas at the **Fairmont Kea Lani Hotel Suites & Villas** (⊠ *4100 Wailea Alanui Dr., Wailea* ☎ *808/875–4100 or 800/882–4100* ⊕ *www.kealani.com*). Twice as luxurious (and about six times more costly), a two-story villa is a posh hangout zone for the family. In-laws and cousins can book suites, and activities focus around the villa with its fully equipped kitchen, plunge pool, and BBQ.

B&BS

$ 🏨 **Eva Villa.** A waterfall and lilies provide an elegant welcome at this B&B in the residential neighborhood above Wailea. Three modern, 600-square-foot suites come furnished with queen-size beds and sleeper sofas, kitchens stocked with continental breakfasts, and access to the pool and Jacuzzi. Rick and Dale Pounds, the congenial owners who live on-property, even provide guests with a farewell CD of island photos and music. The real treasure, however, is the 360-degree ocean and mountain view from the rooftop patio, accompanied by a telescope. ⊠ *815 Kumulani Dr., Wailea 96753* ☎ *808/874–6407* ⊕ *www.mauibnb.com* 🛏 *3 suites* ⚬ *In-room: cable TV, kitchen. In-hotel: pool, laundry facilities, public Internet, no elevator. MC, V.*

CENTRAL MAUI

Kahului and Wailuku, the industrial centers that make up Central Maui, are not known for their lavish accommodations. The exceptions, of course, make the rule, and the few listed below meet some travelers' needs perfectly.

B&BS

$–$$ 🏨 **Old Wailuku Inn.** This historic home, built in 1924, may be the ulti-

Fodor'sChoice ★ mate Hawaiian B&B. Each room is decorated with the theme of a Hawaiian flower, and the flower motif is worked into the heirloom Hawaiian quilt on each bed. Other features include 10-foot ceilings, floors of native hardwoods, and (depending on the room) delightful bathtubs and Swiss jet showers. The 1st-floor rooms have private gardens. A hearty breakfast is included. ⊠*2199 Kahoʻokele St., Wailuku 96793* ☎*808/244–5897 or 800/305–4899* ⊕*www.mauiinn.com* ⤿*7 rooms* ⌂*In-room: VCR, dial-up. In-hotel: no elevator* ▤*AE, D, DC, MC, V.*

HOSTELS

¢ 🏨 **Banana Bungalow Maui Hostel.** A typical lively and cosmopolitan hostel, Banana Bungalow offers the cheapest accommodations on the island. Private rooms have one queen or two single beds; bathrooms are down the hall. Dorm rooms are available for $22 per night. Free daily tours to waterfalls, beaches, and Haleakalā Crater make this a stellar deal. (Yes, the tours are *free*.) The property's amenities include free high-speed Internet access in the common room, kitchen privileges, a Jacuzzi, and banana trees ripe for the picking. Though it's tucked in a slightly rough-around-the-edges corner of Wailuku, the old building has splendid mountain views. ⊠*310 N. Market St., Wailuku 96793* ☎*808/244–5090 or 800/846–7835* ⊕*www.mauihostel.com* ⤿*38 rooms* ⌂*In-room: no a/c, kitchen. In-hotel: laundry facilities, public Internet, no elevator* ▤*MC, V.*

UPCOUNTRY

Upcountry accommodations (those in Kula, Makawao, and Haliʻimaile) are on country estates and are generally small, privately owned vacation rentals, or B&Bs. At high elevation, these lodgings offer splendid views of the island, temperate weather, and a "getting away from it all" feeling—which is actually the case, as most shops and restaurants are a fair drive away, and beaches even farther. You'll definitely need a car here.

HOTELS & RESORTS

$ 🏨 **Kula Lodge.** This hotel isn't typical for Hawaiʻi: the lodge inexplicably resembles a chalet in the Swiss Alps, and two units even have gas fireplaces. Charming and cozy in spite of the nontropical ambience, it's a good spot for a romantic stay. Units are in two wooden cabins; four have lofts in addition to the ample bed space downstairs. On 3 acres, the lodge has startling views of Haleakalā and two coasts, enhanced by the surrounding tropical gardens. The property has an art gallery and a protea store that will pack flowers for you to take home; next door you'll find a gourmet and gift shop. ⊠*Haleakalā Hwy., Rte. 377* ⌂*R.R. 1, Box 475, Kula 96790* ☎*808/878–2517 or 800/233–1535* ⌂*808/878–2518* ⊕*www.kulalodge.com* ⤿*5 units* ⌂*In-room: no a/c, no phone, no TV. In-hotel: restaurant, no elevator* ▤*AE, MC, V.*

CONDOS & VACATION RENTALS

$$$–$$$$ ★ 🏨 **Aloha Cottages.** The two secluded cottages on this property, the Bali Bungalow and the Thai Treehouse, are perfect for honeymooners or anyone else seeking a romantic getaway. The property abounds with tropical plants allowing each cottage complete privacy. Intricate woodwork and furnishings, all imported from Bali, add a touch of

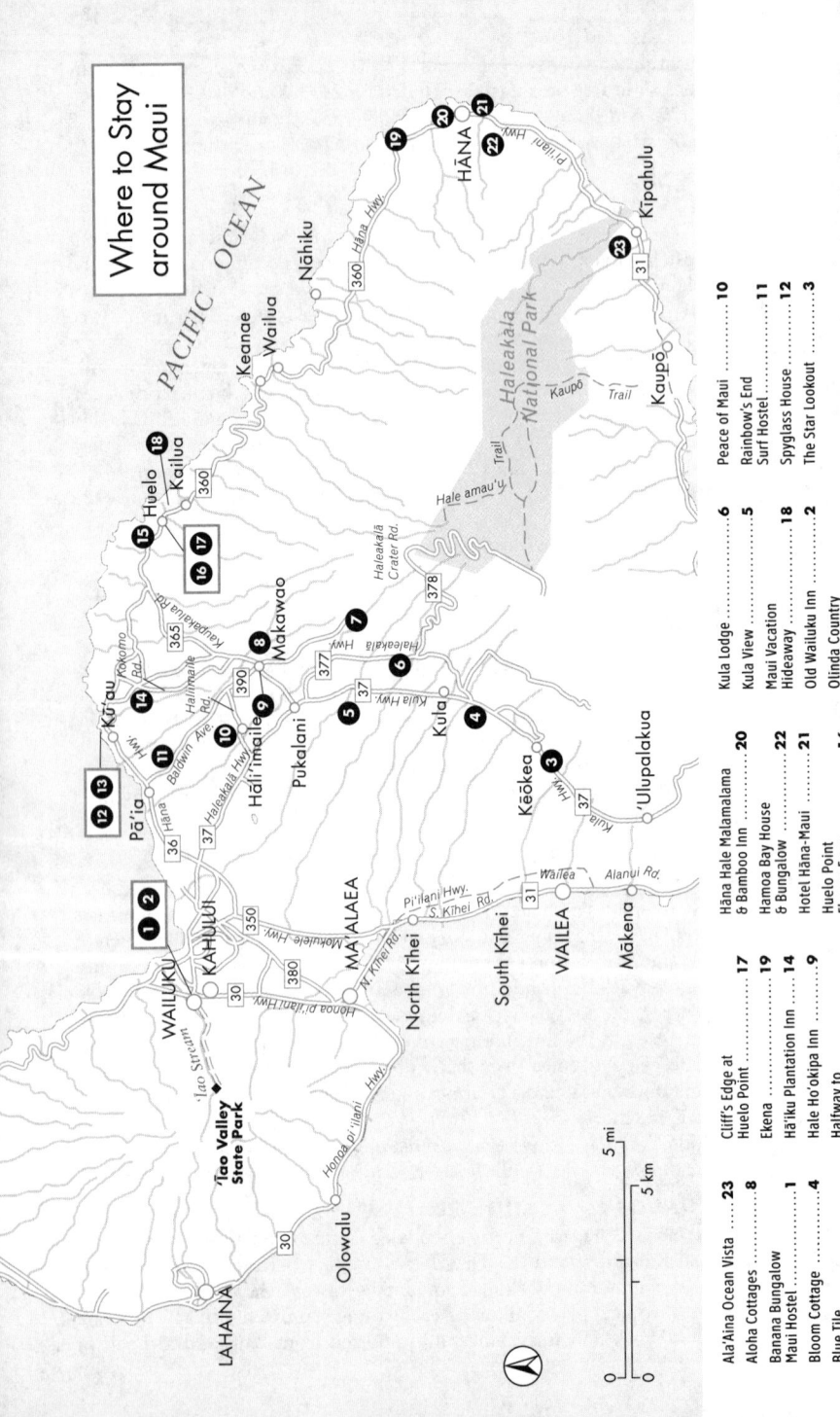

Where to Stay around Maui

PACIFIC OCEAN

Haleakalā National Park

ʻĪao Valley State Park

exoticism to the interiors. Each cottage has a large comfortable bed, fully equipped kitchen, and outdoor hot tub on a private lānai. Ranjana, your hostess, is happy to assist you with planning activities and booking restaurants. She can also arrange for a private massage, yoga lessons, or even a candlelight dinner in the "Lotus House" on the property. The restaurants and shops of Makawao are a short drive away. ⊠*1879 Olinda Rd., Makawao 96768* ☎*808/573–8500* ⊕*www.alo-hacottage.com* ⇨*2 cottages* ⚲*In-room: no a/c, kitchen, DVD, dial-up. In-hotel: no kids under 18, no elevator* ☰*MC, V.*

$$ 🍴**The Star Lookout.** Hidden away halfway up Haleakalā, this charming 100-year-old perch is an ideal getaway. With a view of most of the Valley Isle, this retreat is remote, serene, and deliciously temperate—you'll want to snuggle up, rather than blast the air-conditioning. Up to six people can be accommodated in this inventively designed house, but four is more comfortable, and two is downright romantic. Snipping a few fresh herbs from the garden will make cooking while on vacation all the more fun. ⊠*622 Thompson Rd., Keokea 96790* ☎*907/346–8028* ⊕*www.starlookout.com* ⇨*1 unit* ⚲*In-room: no a/c, kitchen, VCR, no elevator* ☰*No credit cards.*

B&BS

$–$$$ 🍴**Olinda Country Cottages & Inn.** This restored Tudor home and adjacent cottages are so far up Olinda Road above Makawao you'll keep thinking you must have passed them. The Inn, which sits amid an 8½-acre protea farm surrounded by forest and some wonderful hiking trails, has five accommodations: two upstairs bedrooms with private baths; the downstairs Pineapple Sweet; a romantic cottage, which looks like a dollhouse from the outside; and best of all, Hidden Cottage, which has a private hot tub. Bring warm clothes—the mountain air can be chilly. Breakfast is served in the common living room. ⊠*2660 Olinda Rd., Olinda 96768* ☎*800/932–3435* 🖷*808/572–1453* ⊕*www.mauibnb-cottages.com* ⇨*3 rooms, 2 cottages* ⚲*In-room: no a/c. In-hotel: no elevator* ☰*No credit cards.*

$ 🍴**Bloom Cottage.** The name comes from the abundance of roses and other flowers that surround this well-run, classic B&B. The property consists of a main house and separate cottage. This is life in the slow lane, with quiet, privacy, and a living-room fireplace for when the evenings are nippy. The furnishings are very Ralph Lauren, with a cowhide flourish suited to this ranch-country locale. The 1906 house has three rooms and is good for four to six people willing to share a single bathroom. The cottage is ideal for a couple. ⊠*229 Kula Hwy., Kula 96790* ☎*808/579–8282* 🖷*661/393–5015* ⊕*www.hookipa.com/bloom_cottage.html* ⇨*1 house, 1 cottage* ⚲*In-room: no a/c, kitchen, VCR, Wi-Fi. In-hotel: laundry facilities, no-smoking rooms, no elevator* ☰*AE, D, MC, V.*

$ 🍴**Hale Ho'okipa Inn.** This handsome 1924 Craftsman-style house in the heart of Makawao town is a good base for excursions to the crater or to Hāna. The owner has furnished it with antiques and fine art, and allows guests to peruse her voluminous library of Hawai'i-related books. The house is divided into three single rooms, each prettier than the next, and the South Wing, which sleeps four and includes the

9

kitchen. There's also a separate cottage on the property, which sleeps two to four. All rooms have private claw-foot baths. This inn has a distinct plantation-era feel with squeaky wooden floors and period furnishings to boot. ⊠*32 Pakani Pl., Makawao 96768* ☎*808/572–6698* ⊟*808/572–2580* ⊕*www.maui-bed-and-breakfast.com* ➪*3 rooms, 1 suite, 1 cottage* ♿*In-room: no a/c (some), no elevator* ⊟*No credit cards.*

CONDO COMFORTS

Head to **Pukalani Terrace Center** (⊠*55 Pukalani St., Pukalani*) for pizza, a bank, post office, hardware store, and Starbucks. There's also a **Foodland** (☎*808/572–0674*), which has fresh sushi and a good seafood section in addition to the usual grocery store fare, and **Paradise Video** (☎*808/572–6200*).

$ ⛭ **Kula View.** This affordable home-away-from-home sits in peaceful, rural Kula. At an elevation of 2,000 feet, the climate is pleasantly temperate. Guests stay in the entire upper floor of a tastefully decorated house with a private entrance, deck, and gardens. A commanding view of Haleakalā stretches beyond the French doors. The hostess provides an "amenity basket," a very popular continental breakfast, advice on touring, and even beach towels or warm clothes for your crater trip. ⊠*600 Holopuni Rd., Kula 96790* ☎*808/878–6736* ⊕*www.kulaview.com* ➪*1 room* ♿*In-room: no a/c, kitchen, no elevator* ⊟*No credit cards.*

¢–$ ⛭ **Peace of Maui.** This Upcountry getaway is ideal for budget-minded travelers who want to be out and active all day. Well situated for accessing the rest of the island, it's only 15 minutes from Kahului and less than 10 from Pā'ia, Ha'ikū, and Makawao. Six modest double rooms in a "lodge" have pantries and minirefrigerators. The kitchen, two bathrooms, and living room are shared. An amply equipped separate cottage (including fresh-cut flowers) sleeps four to six and overlooks the North Shore and the West Maui Mountains. You'll have sweeping views of rainbow-washed pineapple fields here. If you're lucky, the family dog will sit near the Jacuzzi while you relax after a hard day's adventuring. ⊠*1290 Hali'imaile Rd., Hali'imaile 96768* ☎*808/572–5045 or 888/475–5045* ⊕*www.peaceofmaui.com* ➪*6 rooms with shared bath, 1 cottage* ♿*In-room: no a/c, refrigerator. In-hotel: public Internet, no elevator* ⊟*No credit cards.*

THE NORTH SHORE

A string of unique accommodations starts in the North Shore surf town of Pā'ia, passes through tiny Kū'au, then winds along the rain-forested Hāna Highway through Ha'ikū and Huelo. Many are ocean-front—not necessarily beachfront—with tropical gardens overflowing with ginger, bananas, and papayas. Some have heart-stopping views or the type of solitude that seeps in, easing your tension before you know it. Several have muddy driveways and nightly bug symphonies. This is a rain forest, after all. Brief, powerful downpours let loose frequently here, especially in Ha'ikū and Huelo. You'll need a car to enjoy staying on the North Shore.

CONDOS & VACATION RENTALS

$$–$$$$ 🏠**Cliff's Edge at Huelo Point.** Perched on a 300-foot cliff overlooking Waipio Bay, you can sometimes spot turtles swimming below this 2-acre multi-million-dollar estate. The guesthouses are resplendent, with well-equipped kitchens, entertainment systems, and large bathtubs. But it's the heart-stopping views from the private hot tubs that keep regulars coming back. The Bali cottage is wildly popular, decked out entirely in elegant Balinese imports. In the main house, the Penthouse and King suite each have breathtaking views, private entrances, lānai, and kitchenettes. You're free to pick fruit and flowers from the lush grounds. You'll be far from it all out here, in a remote paradise. ⊠*Door of Faith Rd., Huelo* 🖂*Box 1095, Ha'ikū 96708* 📞*808/572–4530* ⊕*www.cliffsedge.com* 🛏*2 rooms, 2 houses* ♿*In-room: kitchen, Wi-Fi. In-hotel: pool, no kids under 13, no elevator* 🖃*AE, MC, V.*

$ 🏠**Maui Vacation Hideaway.** The warm ocean breeze rolls through these pretty rentals, shooing the mosquitoes away. The decor is both whimsical and calming—expect colorfully painted walls and sheer curtains. The saltwater pool is fed by a waterfall. Fully equipped kitchens and Wi-Fi make these studios an ideal home away from home. Allergy-prone travelers can relax here—no chemicals or pesticides are used on the property. This is a perfect spot if you want quiet, gorgeous scenery, and don't mind being a fair drive from civilization. ⊠*240 N. Holokai Rd., Ha'ikū 96708* 📞*808/572–2775* 📠*808/573–2775* ⊕*www.mauivacationhideaway.com* 🛏*3 units* ♿*In-room: no a/c, kitchen, VCR, Wi-Fi. In-hotel: pool, laundry facilities, no elevator. MC, V.*

$ 🏠**Spyglass House.** This eccentric old beach property is somewhere Pippi Longstocking might have lived after cashing in her pirate father's gold: splendid views of the Pacific, stained-glass windows, wood floors, even a room called the "Crow's Nest." Rooms in the main house are a tad classier and larger, with better views than those in the Dolphin house, but all are nice. The two houses can be rented together, accommodating up to 20 for special occasions. Your hostess, Poni, is a singer-songwriter and avid surfer who may fill you in on the weekly surf report. ⊠*367 Hāna Hwy., Kū'au 96779* 📞*808/579–8608 or 800/475–6695* ⊕*www.spyglassmaui.com* 🛏*6 rooms* ♿*In-room: no a/c, kitchen. In-hotel: no elevator* 🖃*MC, V.*

¢–$ 🏠**Halfway to Hāna House.** A private studio on Maui's lush rural north coast, this serene retreat includes a two-person hammock, surrounding organic gardens, and great ocean views. It's a short walk from here to natural pools, waterfalls, and hiking areas. The room comes with optional continental breakfast and a well-supplied kitchenette—all the equipment you need to do your own thing. ⊠*Hāna Hwy., Huelo* 🖂*Box 675, Ha'ikū 96708* 📞*808/572–1176* 📠*808/572–3609* ⊕*www.halfwaytohana.com/paradise.html* 🛏*1 unit* ♿*In-room: no a/c, kitchen. In-hotel: no elevator* 🖃*No credit cards.*

9

B&BS

$$$–$$$$ 🏨**Huelo Point Flower Farm.** Amid verdant foliage, this cluster of architecturally impressive houses faces dramatic Waipio Bay. Three of the four rentals have cathedral ceilings; all have amazing views. The **Main House,** with a sunken tub in the master bath and a large patio with a private hot tub, accommodates up to eight. The two-bedroom **Guesthouse** has floor-to-ceiling glass windows, a spacious patio, and a private hot tub facing the ocean. The small **Gazebo Cottage** has a half bath, kitchenette, and an outdoor shower. Set back from the cliff, the **Carriage House** has a loft bedroom with a queen-size bed, a den with a double bed, and two spacious decks. An organic orchard and Olympic-size ozonated pool are special treats. Don't try to find this secluded rental at night—it's next door to the Cliff's Edge at the end of a long, partly paved road. ✉ *Door of Faith Rd. off Hāna Hwy., Huelo* 📪 *Box 1195, Pā'ia 96779* ☎ *808/572–1850* ⊕ *www.maui.net/~huelopt* ➴ *4 units* ♿ *In-room: no a/c, VCR. In-hotel: pool, no elevator* ➾ *AE, MC, V.*

¢–$$ 🏨**Blue Tile Beach House.** This large house is reminiscent of a Mediterranean villa with fountains, arched doorways, and yes, lots of blue tile. It sits on Tavares Bay, a tiny, semiprivate surfing beach. The two suites have plenty of extras: spacious living areas, carved wood, granite countertops, multijet showers, and Jacuzzis—one even has a sauna. The individual rooms are small, tasteful, and privy to the immensely relaxing grounds. A large, two-story lobby in the center of the house can be booked for special functions. The house can also be booked as a whole. ✉ *459 Hāna Hwy., Kū'au 96779* ☎ *808/579–8608 or 888/579–6446* ⊕ *www.beachvacationmaui.com* ➴ *2 suites, 4 rooms* ♿ *In-room: no a/c. In-hotel: beachfront, no elevator* ➾ *MC, V.*

$ ★ 🏨**Ha'ikū Plantation Inn.** Water lilies and a shade tree bedecked in orchids greet you at this forested bend in the road. A remnant of Ha'ikū's plantation history, this gracious estate was built in 1870 for the company doctor. A feeling of wellness persists—revered Hawaiian healer Kahu Lyons Na'one teaches traditional medicine and *ho'oponopono,* literally "making right," on-site. A small massage *hale* stands beside a thatched-roof gazebo in a lush garden of *ulu* (breadfruit), *liliko'i* (passion fruit), sugarcane, bananas, and pineapple. Rooms are uncluttered and charming, with private baths; the Plumeria room has a clawfoot tub. ✉ *555 Ha'ikū Rd., Ha'ikū 96708* ☎ *808/575–7500* ⊕ *www.haikuleana.net* ➴ *4 rooms* ♿ *In-room: no a/c, kitchen. In-hotel: no elevator* ➾ *AE, MC, V.*

CONDO COMFORTS

The **Ha'ikū Cannery** (✉ *810 Ha'ikū Rd., Ha'ikū*) is home to **Ha'ikū Grocery** (☎ *808/575–9291*), a somewhat limited grocery store where you can find the basics: veggies, meats, wine, snacks, and ice cream. **88-Cent Video** (☎ *808/575–2723*) is also here, along with a laundromat, bakery, and hardware store. The post office is across the street.

HOSTELS

¢ 🏠**Rainbow's End Surf Hostel.** "Rainbow" is right: the kitchen in this colorful hostel is painted a cheery fuchsia with lime trim. A quick stroll from Pā'ia's shops, beaches, and restaurants, this active place is a cheap headquarters for surfers and adventurers. A giant wooden longboard decorates the hallway and surfboards can be stored out back. Free Internet access is available in the cozy (if sometimes hot) common area. Built in the 1940s, the home's shared bathrooms and kitchen areas are humble, but never dirty. Make sure to get a room with a good cross-breeze; the midday heat can be stifling. ⊠*221 Baldwin Ave., Pā'ia 96779* 🕾*808/579–9057* ⊕*www.mauigateway.com/~riki* ⟳*3 four-person dorm rooms, 3 private rooms* ⚐*In-room: no a/c, kitchen, VCR. In-hotel: public Internet, no elevator. No credit cards.*

HĀNA

Why stay in Hāna when it's so far from everything? In a world where everything moves at high speed, Hāna still travels on horseback, ambling along slowly enough to smell the fragrant vines hanging from the trees. But old-fashioned and remote do not mean tame—this is a wild coast, known for heart-stopping scenery and downpours. Leave city expectations behind: the single grocery may run out of milk, and the only videos to rent may be several years old. The dining options are slim. ■ TIP➔If you're staying for several days, or at a vacation rental, stock up on groceries before you head out to Hāna. Even with these inconveniences, Hāna is a place you won't want to miss.

HOTELS & RESORTS

$$$$ 🏠**Hotel Hāna-Maui.** Tranquility envelops Hotel Hāna's ranch setting,
Fodor'sChoice with its unobstructed views of the Pacific. Small, secluded, and quietly
★ luxurious, this property is a departure from the usual resort destinations. Spacious rooms (680 to 830 square feet) have bleached-wood floors, authentic kapa-print fabric furnishings, and sumptuously stocked minibars at no extra cost. Spa suites and a heated *watsu* (massage performed in warm water) pool complement a state-of-the-art spa-and-fitness center. The Sea Ranch Cottages with individual hot tubs are the best value. Horses nibble wild grass on the sea cliff nearby. A shuttle takes you to beautiful Hāmoa Beach. ⊠*Hāna Hwy.,* ⌂*Box 9, Hāna 96713* 🕾*808/248–8211 or 800/321–4262* 🖷*808/248–7264* ⊕*www.hotelhanamaui.com* ⟳*19 rooms, 47 cottages, 1 house* ⚐*In-room: no TV, dial-up, refrigerator. In-hotel: 2 restaurants, bar, tennis courts, pools, gym, spa, beachfront, public Internet, no elevator* ☰*AE, D, DC, MC, V.*

CONDOS & VACATION RENTALS

$$–$$$$ 🏠**Ekena.** "Ekena" means Garden of Eden, and the grounds here are full of tropical fruit trees and exotic flowers. A hillside location makes for commanding views of the ocean. There are two houses, each with a fully equipped kitchen. Jasmine, the smaller of the two, is suited to parties of two. The main house, Sea Breeze, is huge (2,600 square feet), with two large suites, but occupancy is restricted to a maximum

9

of four people. ✉ *Off Hāna Hwy.* ✆ *Box 728, Hāna 96713* 📠 *808/248–7047* ⊕ *www. maui.net/~ekena* ↪ *2 units* ☝ *In-room: no a/c, kitchen, DVD. In-hotel: laundry facilities, no kids under 14, no elevator* ▭ *No credit cards.*

$$-$$$ ★   ⛨ **Hamoa Bay House & Bungalow.** This Balinese-inspired property is sensuous and secluded—a private sanctuary in a fragrant jungle. There are two buildings: the main house is 1,300 square feet and contains two bedrooms; one of them is a suite set apart by a breezeway. There is a screened veranda with an ocean view and an outdoor lava-rock shower accessible to all guests. The 600-square-foot bungalow is a treetop perch with a giant bamboo bed and a hot tub on the veranda. Hamoa Beach is a short walk away. ✉ *Hāna Hwy.* ✆ *Box 773, Hāna 96713* 📞 *808/248–7884* 📠 *808/248–7047* ⊕ *www.hamoabay.com* ↪ *2 units* ☝ *In-room: kitchen, VCR. In-hotel: laundry facilities, no kids under 14, no-smoking rooms, no elevator* ▭ *No credit cards.*

B&BS

$–$$ ⛨ **Hāna Hale Malamalama & Bamboo Inn.** If you want lots of nature and little distraction, this place is perfect. The two duplexes and three cottages overlook a natural spring-fed fish pond and the remains of a *heiau* (an ancient Hawaiian stone platform once used as a place of worship). A black-sand beach, surrounded by lush tropical forest is steps away. Accommodations are simple but clean with rustic bamboo furniture, full kitchens, large bathrooms, and private lānai. Don't be surprised to find a few ants or lizards; they come with all the scenery. A continental breakfast is served in the "lobby," a Polynesian-style, open-air hut. The roar of the ocean and the rustling of palm trees add a soothing backdrop to the stunning setting. *Off Uakea Rd.* ✆ *Box 374, Hāna 96713* 📞 *808/248–8211* ⊕ *www.hanahale.com* ↪ *4 rooms, 3 cottages* ☝ *In-room: no a/c, kitchen, DVD, dial-up. In-hotel: no-smoking rooms, no elevator* ▭ *MC, V.*

$ ⛨ **Alāa'ina Ocean Vista.** This B&B is on the grounds of an old banana plantation past 'Ohe'o Gulch (about a 40-minute drive from Hāna). Banana trees still populate the property alongside mango, papaya, and avocado trees. There's also a Balinese garden, complete with a lotus-shape pond. The single room has a private lānai with an outdoor kitchenette, outdoor shower (there's

---

SHOPPING IN HĀNA

Hasegawa General Store. Hāna's one-stop shopping option is charming, ramshackle Hasegawa's. Buy fishing tackle, hot dogs, ice cream, and eggs here. You can rent videos and buy the newspaper, which isn't always delivered on time. Check out the bulletin board for local events. ✉ *5165 Hāna Hwy.* ☎ *808/248–8231.*

B & BS

Additional B&Bs on Maui can be found by contacting **Bed & Breakfast Hawai'i** (☎ *808/733–1632* ⊕ *www.bandb-hawaii.com*) . **Bed and Breakfast Honolulu** (☎ *808/595–7533 or 800/288–4666* ⊕ *www.hawaiibnb.com*) is another good source.

a regular shower in the room as well), and astonishing views of the coastline. Sam and Mercury, a mother-daughter team, live in the main house on-site and are available to give tips and advice about exploring the area. This is a simple, back-to-nature kind of spot. ⊠*Off Hwy. 31, 10 mi past Hāna* ⬧*SR 184-A, Hāna 96713* ☎*808/248–7824 or 877/216–1733* ⊕*www.hanabedandbreakfast.com* ⬧*1   room* ⬧*In-room: no a/c, kitchen. In-hotel: no elevator* ⊟*No credit cards.*

Moloka'i

WORD OF MOUTH

"It was a beautiful experience, and we really didn't do anything. Beautifully boring. We walked to the beach twice a day . . . read our books a lot, walked a lot, played golf once, looked for whales, talked to a few people . . . and just hung out. I'd go again in a heartbeat."

—pdx

WELCOME TO MOLOKA'I

TOP 5
Reasons to Go

1 **Kalaupapa Peninsula:** Hike or take a mule ride down the world's tallest sea cliffs to a fascinating, historic community.

2 **Hike to a Waterfall in Hālawa:** A guided hike through private property takes you past ancient ruins and restored taro patches.

3 **Deep-Sea Fishing:** Sport fish are plentiful in these waters, as are gorgeous views of several islands.

4 **Nature:** Deep valleys, sheer cliffs, and the untamed ocean are the main attractions on Moloka'i.

5 **Pāpōhaku Beach:** This 3-mi stretch of sand is one of the most sensational beaches in all of Hawai'i.

■ TIP→ Directions on the island are often given as *mauka* (toward the mountains) and *makai* (toward the ocean).

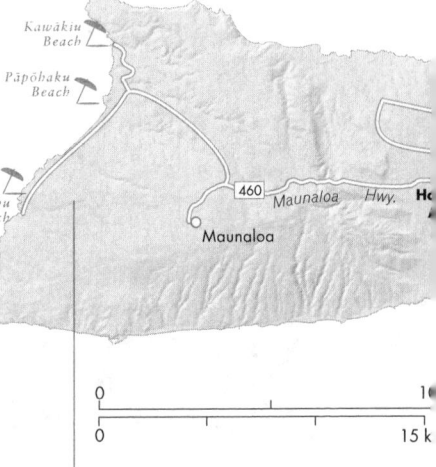

The most arid part of the island, the West End has two inhabited areas: the coastal stretch includes a few condos and luxury homes, and the largest beaches on the island. Nearby, the hilltop hamlet of Maunaloa boasts the finest accommodation on the island, the Lodge at Moloka'i Ranch.

Getting Oriented

Shaped like a long bone, Moloka'i is only about 10 mi wide on average, and four times that long. The North Shore thrusts up from the sea to form the tallest sea-cliffs on Earth, while the South Shore slides almost flat into the water, then fans out to form the largest shallow-water reef system in the United States. Surprisingly, the highest point on Moloka'i rises only to about 4,000 feet.

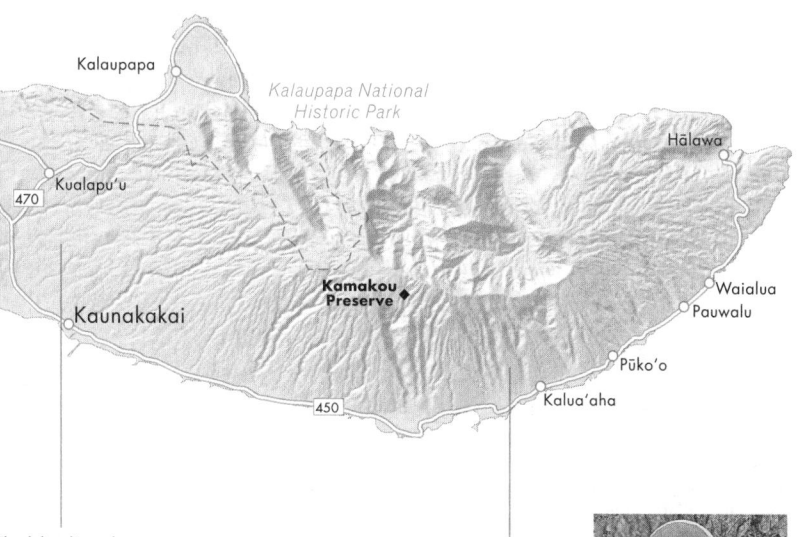

The island's only true town, Kaunakakai, with its mile-long wharf, lies in Central Moloka'i. Nearly all the island's eateries and stores are in or close to Kaunakakai. Highway 470 crosses the center of the island, rising to the top of the sea-cliffs and the Kalaupapa overlook.

The scenic drive around the East End passes through the green pastures of Pu'u O Hoku Ranch and climaxes with a descent into Hālawa Valley. The farther east you go, the lusher the island gets.

MOLOKA'I PLANNER

What You Won't Find on Moloka'i

Moloka'i is a great place to be outdoors. And that's a good thing, because with only about 7,000 residents Moloka'i has very little of what you would call "indoors." There are no tall buildings, no traffic lights, no street lights, no stores bearing the names of national chains, and almost nothing at all like a resort. Among the Hawaiian Islands, Moloka'i has distinguished itself as the one least interested in attracting tourists. At night the whole island grows dark, creating a velvety blackness and a wonderful, rare thing called silence.

Where to Stay

Moloka'i appeals most to travelers who appreciate genuine Hawaiian ambience rather than swanky digs. Aside from the upscale Lodge at Moloka'i Ranch, most hotel and condominium properties range from adequate to funky. Visitors who want to lollygag on the beach should choose one of the condos or home rentals at the West End. Locals tend to choose Hotel Moloka'i, located seaside just 2 mi from Kaunakakai, with its on-site restaurant, bar, and live music. Travelers who want to immerse themselves in the spirit of the island should seek out a bed-and-breakfast or cottage, the closer to the East End the better.

Additional planning details are listed in Moloka'i Essentials at the end of this chapter.

Timing Is Everything

If you're keen to explore Moloka'i's beaches, coral beds, or fishponds, summer is your best bet for non-stop calm seas and sunny skies. For a real taste of Hawaiian culture, plan your visit around a festival. In January, islanders and visitors compete in ancient Hawaiian games at the Ka Moloka'i Makahiki Festival. The Moloka'i Ka Hula Piko, an annual daylong event in May, draws the state's premiere hula troupes, musicians, and storytellers to perform. The Festival of Lights includes an Electric Light Parade down the main street of Kaunakakai in December. While never crowded, the island is busier during these events—book accommodations and transportation six months in advance.

Will It Rain?

Moloka'i's weather mimics that of the other islands: mid- to low 80s year-round, slightly rainier during winter. Because the island's accommodations are clustered at low elevation or along the leeward coast, warm weather is a dependable constant for visitors (only 15 to 20 inches of rain fall each year on the coastal plain). As you travel up the mountainside, the weather changes with bursts of forest-building downpours.

Cell Phones and the Internet

Communication with the outside world is a real challenge on Moloka'i. Most of the island lies outside the range of many cell-phone services. Even regular telephone service, at Hotel Moloka'i for example, can be unreliable. Travelers who absolutely need to stay in touch with home or the office should get a room at the Lodge at Moloka'i Ranch.

By Paul Wood
Updated by
Joana Varawa

MOLOKA'I IS GENERALLY THOUGHT OF as the last bit of "real" Hawai'i. Tourism has been held at bay by the island's unique history (Moloka'i was once occupied solely by a leper's colony), despite the fact that the longest white-sand beach in Hawai'i can be found along its western shore. With working ranches and sandy beaches to the west, sheer sea cliffs to the north, and a rainy, lush eastern coast, Moloka'i offers a bit of everything, including a peek at what the islands were like 50 years ago. The sign at the airport says it all, SLOW DOWN, YOU'RE IN MOLOKA'I.

Only 38 mi long and 10 mi wide at its widest point, Moloka'i is the fifth-largest island in the Hawaiian archipelago. Eight thousand residents call Moloka'i home, nearly 40% of whom are Hawaiian.

GEOLOGY

Roughly 1½ million years ago two large volcanoes—Kamakou in the east and Maunaloa in the west—broke the surface of the Pacific Ocean and created the island of Moloka'i. Shortly thereafter a third and much smaller caldera, Kauhako, popped up to form the Makanalua Peninsula on the north side. After hundreds of thousands of years of rain, surf, and wind, an enormous landslide on the north end sent much of the mountain into the sea, leaving behind the sheer sea cliffs that make Moloka'i's North Shore so spectacularly beautiful.

HISTORY

In 1886, Moloka'i's Makanalua Peninsula, surrounded on three sides by the Pacific and accessible only by a steep, switchback trail, seemed the ideal place to exile people cursed with leprosy. The first patients were thrown into the waters and left for seven years with no facilities, shelter, or supplies. In 1893 a missionary named Father Damien arrived and created Moloka'i's famous leper's colony. Though the disease is no longer contagious, many patients chose to stay in their longtime home, and the colony still has roughly 100 residents. Visitors are welcome, but must pay $40 for a tour operated by Damien Tours of Kalaupapa.

THE BIRTHPLACE OF HULA

Legend has it that Laka, goddess of the hula, gave birth to the dance on Moloka'i, at a sacred place in Ka'ana. The island recognizes the birth of this sacred dance with a celebration called Ka Hula Piko every year during the third weekend in May. When Laka died, it is believed that her remains were secretly hidden somewhere beneath the hill Pu'u Nana. The hula was finally established, the work of Laka was complete, and the dance has flourished ever since throughout Hawai'i.

10

EXPLORING MOLOKA'I

The first thing to do on Moloka'i is to drive everywhere. It's a feat you can accomplish in a day. Basically you have one 40-mi west–east highway (two lanes, no stop lights) with three side trips: the little west end town of Maunaloa; the Highway 470 drive (just a few miles) to the top of the North Shore and the overlook of Kalaupapa Peninsula; and the short stretch of shops in Kaunakakai town. After you learn the general lay of the land, you can return for in-depth experiences.

WEST MOLOKA'I

The region is largely made up of the 53,000-acre Moloka'i Ranch. The rolling pastures and farmlands are presided over by Maunaloa, a dormant volcano crowned by a sleepy little former plantation town of the same name. West Moloka'i has another claim to fame: Pāpōhaku, the island's best beach.

MAIN ATTRACTIONS

❶ Kaluako'i Hotel and Golf Club. This late-1960s resort passed through several owners, and the hotel itself is now closed, awaiting its next incarnation. Some very nice condos are still operating here, however. Stroll the grounds—an impressive 6,700 acres of beachfront property, including the newly revived golf course and 5 mi of coastline. ⊠*Kaluako'i Rd., Maunaloa* ☎*808/552–2555 or 888/552–2550.*

❷ Pāpōhaku Beach. The most splendid stretch of golden white sand on Moloka'i, Pāpōhaku is also the island's largest beach—it stretches 3 mi along the western shore. Even on busier days you're likely to see only a handful of other people. If the waves are high, swimming is dangerous. ⊠*Kaluako'i Rd.; 2 mi beyond Kaluako'i Hotel and Golf Club.*

ALSO WORTH SEEING

★ **❸ Maunaloa.** This sleepy town was developed in 1923 to house the workers on the island's pineapple plantation. Although the fields of golden fruit have gone fallow, some of the old dwellings still stand, anchoring the West End of Moloka'i. A few colorful local characters run the town businesses (including a kite shop, an import art and jewelry gallery, and an eclectic general store) along the short main street. This is also the headquarters for Moloka'i Ranch. ⊠*Western end of Maunaloa Hwy., Rte. 460.*

CENTRAL MOLOKA'I

Most residents live centrally, near the island's one and only true town, Kaunakakai. It's just about the only place on the island to get food and supplies. It *is* Moloka'i. Go into the shops along and around Ala Mālama Street. Buy stuff. Talk with people. Take your time and you'll really enjoy being a visitor.

MAIN ATTRACTIONS

➐ Coffees of Hawai'i. Visit the headquarters of a 500-acre plantation of Moloka'i coffee. The espresso bar serves java in artful ways, freshly made sandwiches, and *liliko'i* (passion fruit) cheesecake. The gift shop offers a wide range of Moloka'i handicrafts and memorabilia, and, of course, coffee. Call in advance to ask about various tours (fee) of the plantation. ⊠ *Farrington Hwy., off Rte. 470, Kualapu'u* ☎ *800/709–2326 or 808/567–9023* ⊕ *www.coffeesofhawaii.net.* Café and gift shop weekdays 8–5, Sat. 8–4, Sun 8–2.

➏ Kalaupapa, *See* A Tale of Tragedy and Triumph, *page 213–216.*

★ **⑫ Kaunakakai.** Kaunakakai looks like a 1940's movie set. Along the one-block main drag is a cultural grab bag of restaurants and shops. Many people are friendly and willing to supply directions. The preferred dress is shorts and a tank top, and no one wears anything fancier than a cotton skirt or aloha shirt. ⊠ *Rte. 460, about 3 blocks north of Kaunakakai Wharf.*

Fodor's Choice **Moloka'i Mule Ride.** Mount a friendly mule and wind along a 3-mi, 26-switchback trail to reach the town of Kalaupapa. The path was built ★ in 1886 as a supply route for the settlement below. Once in Kalaupapa, you can take a guided tour of the town and have a picnic lunch. The trail is very steep, down some of the highest sea cliffs in the world. Only those in good shape should attempt the ride, as two hours each way on a mule can take its toll. The entire event takes seven hours. Make reservations ahead of time, as spots are limited. The same outfit can arrange for you to hike down or fly in, or some combination of a hike in and fly out. F *See A Tale of Tragedy and Triumph special feature, below, for more information.* ⊠ *100 Kala'e Hwy., Rte. 470, Kualapu'u* ☎ *808/567–6088* ⊕ *www.muleride.com* ☑ *$185* ☼ *Mon.–Sat. 8–3:30.*

★ **➎ Pālā'au State Park.** One of the island's few formal recreation areas, this cool retreat covers 233 acres at a 1,000-foot elevation. A short path through an ironwood forest leads to **Kalaupapa Lookout,** a magnificent overlook with views of the town of Kalaupapa and the 1,664-foot-high sea cliffs protecting it. Informative plaques have facts about leprosy, Father Damien, and the colony. The park is also the site of **Kauleonānāhoa** (the phallus of Nānāhoa)—women in old Hawai'i would come to the rock to enhance their fertility. It is still a sacred site, so be respectful. The park is well maintained, with trails, camping facilities, rest rooms, and picnic tables. ⊠ *Take Rte. 460 west from Kaunakakai and then head mauka (toward the mountains) on Rte. 470, which ends at park* ☎ *No phone* ☑ *Free* ☼ *Daily dawn–dusk.*

10

➑ Purdy's Macadamia Nut Farm. Moloka'i's only working macadamia-nut farm is open for educational tours hosted by the knowledgeable and entertaining owner. A family business on Hawaiian homestead land in Ho'olehua, the farm takes up 1½ acres with a flourishing grove of some 50 trees more than 70 years old. Taste a delicious nut right out of its shell or home roasted, and dip it into macadamia-blossom honey; then buy some at the shop on the way out. Look for Purdy's sign behind

Moloka'i

PACIFIC OCEAN

Kaiwi Channel

TO O'AHU →

Kawaiihau Bay

Kawākiu Beach

Kapukahehu Bay

Kepuhi Beach

Pāpōhaku Beach

1 Kaluako'i Hotel and Golf Club

Kaluako'i Rd.

2

Lā'au Pt.

TO LĀNA'I ←

3 **Maunaloa**

Maunaloa Hwy.

Ho'olehua Airport

Purdy's Macadamia Nut Farm

Ho'olehua

Coffees of Hawai'i

8 **7** **4**

Kualapu'u

470

Maunaloa Hwy.

5

R.W. Meyer Sugar Mill and Moloka'i Museum

Church Row

9

Kapuāiwa Coconut Grove **10**

Kaunakakai Wharf

Kaunakakai **11** **12**

Kamiloloa Heights

13 **Kaloko'eli Fishpond**

One Ali'i Beach Park

Kaiwi Channel

Kalohi Channel

Kalaupapa Airfield

Kalaupapa Peninsula

6 **Kalaupapa**

Pālā'au State Park

Kamakou Preserve

Kawela

Kamehameha V. Hwy.

Church of St. Joseph's

Smith and Bronte Monument

14 **Kamalō**

450

'Ualapu'e

Kalua'aha

Pūko'o

450

Pauwalu

Honouliwai Taro Patch Farm

15 Mokuho'oniki Island

16 **Pu'u o Hoku Ranch**

17 **Hālawa Valley**

Moa'ula Falls

Hālawa Beach Park

Wailau Trail

Walalva Beach Park

Pailolo Channel

TO MAUI →

0   10 miles

0   15 km

Moloka'i High School. ⊠*Lihi-pali Ave., Ho'olehua* ☎*808/567–6601* 🖂*Free* ⊙*Tues.–Fri. 9:30–3:30, Sat. 10–2.*

④ R. W. Meyer Sugar Mill and Moloka'i Museum. Built in 1877, this three-room mill has been reconstructed as a testament to Moloka'i's agricultural history. Some of the equipment may still be in working order, including a mule-driven cane crusher, redwood evaporat-

ing pans, some copper clarifiers, and a steam engine. A small museum with changing exhibits on the island's early history and a gift shop are on-site as well. The facility serves as a campus for Elderhostel educational programs. ⊠*Rte. 470, 2 mi southwest of Pālā'au State Park, Kala'e* ☎*808/567–6436* 🖂*$2.50* ⊙*Mon.–Sat. 10–2.*

ALSO WORTH SEEING

⑨ Church Row. Standing together along the highway are several houses of worship with primarily native Hawaiian congregations. Notice the unadorned, boxlike style of architecture so similar to missionary homes. ⊠*Mauka (toward the mountains) side of Rte. 460, 5½ mi southwest of airport.*

⑩ Kapuāiwa Coconut Grove. At first glance this looks like a sea of coconut trees. Close-up you can see that the tall, stately palms are planted in long rows leading down to the sea. This is one of the last surviving royal groves planted by Prince Lot, who ruled Hawai'i as King Kamehameha V from 1863 until his death in 1872. The park is closed for renovations but you can park on the side of the road and walk in to the beach. Watch for falling coconuts. ⊠*Makai (toward the ocean) of Rte. 460, 5½ mi south of airport.*

⑪ Kaunakakai Wharf. Docks, once bustling with barges exporting pineapples, now host boats shipping out potatoes, tomatoes, baby corn, herbs, and other produce. The wharf is also the starting point for excursions, including fishing, sailing, snorkeling, whale-watching, and scuba diving. ⊠*Rte. 450 and Ala Mālama St.; drive makai (toward the ocean) on Kaunakakai Pl., which dead-ends at wharf.*

10

EAST MOLOKA'I

On the beautifully undeveloped east end of Moloka'i, you can find ancient fishponds, a magnificent coastline, splendid ocean views, and a fertile valley that's been inhabited for 14 centuries. The east is flanked by Mt. Kamakou, the island's highest point at 4,961 feet, and home to the Nature Conservancy's Kamakou Preserve. Mist hangs over waterfall-filled valleys, and ancient lava cliffs jut out into the sea.

MAIN ATTRACTIONS

⑰ Hālawa Valley. As far back as ⅟ₛ 650 a busy community lived in this
Fodor'sChoice valley, the oldest recorded habitation on Moloka'i. Hawaiians lived in
★ a perfectly sustainable relationship with the valley's resources, growing taro and fishing until the 1960s, when cultural changes plus an
enormous flood wiped out the taro patches and forced the old-timers to abandon their traditional lifestyle. Now a new generation of
Hawaiians has returned and begun the challenging work of restoring
the taro fields. Much of this work involves rerouting stream water
to flow through carefully engineered level ponds called *lo'i*. The taro
plants with their big dancing leaves grow in the submerged mud of the
lo'i, where the water is always cool and flowing. Hawaiians believe
that the taro plant is their ancestor and revere it both as sustenance
and as a spiritual necessity. The Hālawa Valley Cooperative gives tours
of this restoration project and leads hikes through the valley, which
is home to two sacrificial temples, many historic sites, and the 3-mi
trail to Moa'ula Falls, a 250-foot cascade. The $75 fee ($45 for children) goes to support the restoration work. ⊠*Eastern end of Rte.
450* ☎*808/553–9803* ⊕*www.gomolokai.com.*

⑮ Honouliwai Taro Patch Farm. Although they are not reviving an entire
valley and lifestyle like the folks in Hālawa, Jim and Lee Callahan are
reviving taro cultivation on their small farm watered by a year-round
spring. The owners provide 1½-hour tours so visitors can experience
all phases of taro farming, from planting to eating. Lee was raised in
Thailand, so she uses a traditional Southeast Asian farm device—a
plow-pulling water buffalo named Bigfoot. Tours are available every
day, but you must call for an appointment when you are on the island.
⊠*East of mile marker 20, mauka (toward the mountains), where sign
says "Honouliwai Is a Beautiful Place to Be"* ☎*808/558–8922* ⊕*www.
angelfire.com/film/chiangmai/index.html* ⊠*$20.*

★ **⑬ Kaloko'eli Fishpond.** With its narrow rock walls arching out from the
shoreline, Kaloko'eli is typical of the numerous fishponds that define
southern Moloka'i. Many of them were built around the 13th century under the direction of powerful chiefs. This early type of aqua-
culture, particular to Hawai'i, exemplifies the ingenuity of precontact
Hawaiians. One or more openings were left in the wall, where gates
called *makaha* were installed. These gates allowed seawater and tiny
fish to enter the enclosed pond but kept larger predators out. The tiny
fish would then grow too big to get out. At one time there were 62
fishponds around Moloka'i's coast. ⊠*Rte. 450, about 6 mi east of
Kaunakakai.*

**OFF THE
BEATEN
PATH**
★
Kamakou Preserve. Tucked away on the slopes of Mt. Kamakou,
Moloka'i's highest peak, the 2,774-acre preserve is a dazzling wonderland full of wet *'ōhi'a* (hardwood trees of the myrtle family, with
red blossoms called *lehua* flowers) forests, rare bogs, and native trees
and wildlife. Guided hikes, limited to eight people, are held on the
first Saturday of each month; reserve well in advance. You can visit
the park without a tour, but you need a good four-wheel-drive vehicle,
and the Nature Conservancy requests that you sign in at the office

Continued on page 217

Father Damien's Church, St. Philomena

A TALE OF TRAGEDY & TRIUMPH

For those who crave drama, there is no better destination than Moloka'i's Kalaupapa Peninsula—but it wasn't always so. For 100 years this remote strip of land was "the loneliest place on earth," a feared place of exile for those suffering from leprosy (now known as Hansen's Disease).

The world's tallest sea cliffs, rain-chiseled valleys, and tiny islets dropped like exclamation points along the coast emphasize the passionate history of the Kalaupapa Peninsula. Today, it's impossible to visit this stunning National Historic Park and view the evidence of human ignorance and heroism without responding. You'll be tugged by emotions—awe and disbelief for starters. But you'll also glimpse humorous facets of everyday life in a small town. Whatever your experience here may be, chances are you'll return home feeling that the journey to present-day Kalaupapa is one you'll never forget.

THE SETTLEMENT'S EARLY DAYS

Father Damien with patients outside St. Philomena church.

IN 1865, PRESSURED BY FOREIGN RESIDENTS, the Hawaiian Kingdom passed "An Act to Prevent the Spread of Leprosy." Anyone showing symptoms of the disease was to be permanently exiled to Kalawao, the north end of Kalaupapa Peninsula—a spot walled in on three sides by nearly impassable cliffs. The peninsula had been home to a fishing community for 900 years, but those inhabitants were evicted and the entire peninsula declared settlement land.

The first 12 patients were arrested and sent to Kalawao in 1866. People of all ages and many nationalities followed, taken from their homes and unceremoniously dumped on the isolated shore. Officials thought the patients could become self-sufficient, fishing and farming sweet potatoes in the stream-fed valleys. That was not the case. Settlement conditions were deplorable.

Father Damien, a Belgian missionary, was one of four priests who volunteered to serve the leprosy settlement at Kalawao on a rotating basis. His turn came first; when it was up, he refused to leave. He is cred-ited with turning the settlement from a merciless exile to a place where hope could be heard in the voices of his recruited choir. He organized the building of the St. Philomena church, nearly 300 houses, and a home for boys. A vocal advocate for his adopted community, he pestered the church for supplies, administered medicine, and oversaw the nearly daily funerals. Sixteen years after his arrival, in 1889, he died from the effects of leprosy, having contracted the disease during his service. Known around the world for his sacrifice, Father Damien was beatified by the Catholic Church in 1995, achieving the first step toward Sainthood.

Mother Marianne heard of the mission while working at a hospital in Syracuse, New York. Along with six other Franciscan Sisters, she volunteered to work with those with leprosy in the Islands. They sailed to the desolate Kalaupapa Peninsula in November of 1888. Like the Father, the Sisters were considered saints for their tireless work. Mother Marianne stayed at Kalaupapa until her death in 1918; she was beatified by the Catholic Church in 2005.

VISITING KALAUPAPA TODAY

Kalaupapa Peninsula

FROZEN IN TIME, Kalaupapa's one-horse town has bittersweet charm. Signs posted here and there remind residents when the bank will be open (once monthly), where to pick up lost sunglasses, and what's happening at the tiny town bar. The town has the nostalgic, almost naive ambience expected from a place almost wholly segregated from modern life.

About 30 former patients remain at Kalaupapa (by choice, as the disease is controlled by drugs and the patients are no longer carriers), but many travel frequently to other parts of the world and all are over the age of 60. Richard Marks, the town sheriff and owner of Damien Tours, will likely retire soon, as will the elderly postmistress. They haven't, however, lost their chutzpah. Having survived a lifetime of prejudice and misunderstanding, Kalaupapa's residents aren't willing to be pushed around any longer—several recently made the journey to Honolulu to ask for the removal of a "rude and insensitive" superintendent.

To get a feel for what their lives were like, visit the National Park Service Web site (⊕ www.nps.gov/kala/docs/start.htm) or buy one of several heartbreaking memoirs at the park's library-turned-bookstore.

THE TRUTH ABOUT HANSEN'S DISEASE

■ A cure for leprosy has been available since 1941. Multi-drug therapy, a rapid cure, has been available since 1981.

■ With treatment, none of the disabilities traditionally associated with leprosy need occur.

■ Most people have a natural immunity to leprosy. Only 5% of the world's population is even susceptible to the disease.

■ There are still about 500,000 new cases of leprosy each year; at least two-thirds are in India.

■ All new cases of leprosy are treated on an outpatient basis.

■ The term "leper" is offensive and should not be used. It is appropriate to say "a person is affected by leprosy" or "by Hansen's Disease."

GETTING HERE

The Kalaupapa Trail and Peninsula are all part of Kalaupapa National Historic Park (☎ 808/567–6802 ⊕ www.nps.gov/kala/), which is open every day but Sunday. Keep in mind, there are no public facilities (except an occasional restroom) anywhere in the park. Pack your own food and water, as well as light rain gear, sunscreen, and bug repellent.

Hiking: Hiking allows you to travel at your own pace and stop frequently for photos—not an option on the mule ride. The hike takes about 1 hour down and 1½ hours up. You'll want to hit the trail by 8 AM to avoid a trail hazard—fresh mule poop.

Mule-Skinning: You'll be amazed as your mule trots up to the edge of the switch-back, swivels on two legs, and com-

Kalaupapa Beach & Peninsula

THE KALAUPAPA TRAIL

Unless you fly (flights are available through Moloka'i Air Shuttle, ☎ 808/567–6847), the only way into Kalaupapa National Historic Park is on a dizzying switchback trail. The switchbacks are numbered—26 in all—and descend 1,700 feet to sea level in just under 3 mi. The steep trail is more of a staircase, and most of the trail is shaded. Keep in mind, however, that footing is uneven and there is little to keep you from pitching over the side. If you don't mind heights, you can stare straight down to the ocean for most of the way. *Access Kalaupapa Trail off Hwy. 470 near the Kalaupapa Overlook. There is ample parking near end of Hwy. 470.*

TO HIKE OR TO RIDE?

There are two ways to get down the Kalaupapa Trail: in your hiking boots, or on a mule.

pletes a sharp-angled turn—26 times. The guides tell you the mules can do this in their sleep, but that doesn't take the fear out of the first few switchbacks. Make reservations well in advance. *Moloka'i Mule Ride* ☎ 808/567–6088 ⊕ *www.muleride.com.*

IMPORTANT PERMIT INFORMATION

The only way to visit Kalaupapa settlement is on a tour. Book through Damien Tours (☎ 808/567–6171) if you're hiking or flying in; Moloka'i Mule Ride (☎ 808/567–6088) if you're riding. Daily tours are offered Monday through Saturday. Be sure to reserve in advance. Visitors ages 16 and under are not allowed at Kalaupapa, and photographing patients without their explicit permission is forbidden.

and get directions first. ⊠*The
Nature Conservancy, 23 Pueo
Pl.,   Kualapu'u* ☎*808/553–
5236* ⊕*www.nature.org* ✉*Free;
donation for guided hike, $10
members, $25   nonmembers,
includes 1-yr membership.*

ALSO WORTH SEEING

⑭ **Kamalō.** A natural harbor used
by small cargo ships during the
19th century and a favorite fishing spot for locals, this is also the
site of the **Church of St. Joseph's,**

READY FOR A SNACK

Stop for a coffee, sandwich, and
homemade pastry at **Stanley's
Coffee Shop & Gallery** (⊠*125
Puali St.* ☎*808/553–9966*), at
the east end of Kaunakakai. Sit
in a cool booth and admire the
original art on the walls, or use
their Internet service to check
your mail.

a tiny white church built by Father Damien in the 1880s. The door is
usually unlocked. Slip inside and sign the guestbook. The congregation
keeps this church in beautiful condition. ⊠*Rte. 450, about 11 mi east
of Kaunakakai, makai (toward the ocean).*

**NEED A
BREAK?** The best place to grab a snack or picnic supplies is **Mana'e Goods &
Grinds** (⊠*Rte. 450, 16 mi east of Kaunakakai, Puko'o* ☎*808/558–
8498 or 558–8186*). It's the only place on the east end where you can
find essentials such as ice and bread, and not-so-essentials such as
burgers and shakes. Try a refreshing smoothie while here.

⑯ **Pu'u O Hoku Ranch.** A 14,000-acre private spread in the highlands of
East Moloka'i, Pu'u O Hoku was developed in the 1930s by wealthy
industrialist Paul Fagan. Route 450 cuts right through this rural gem
with its pastures and grazing horses and cattle. As you drive along,
enjoy the splendid views of Maui and Lāna'i. The small island off the
coast is Mokuho'oniki, a humpback-whale nursery where the military practiced bombing techniques during World War II. The ranch
offers horseback-trail rides, two guest cottages, and a retreat facility
for groups. If you love seclusion you will love it here. ⊠*Rte. 450 about
25 mi east of Kaunakakai* ☎*808/558–8109* ⊕*www.puuohoku.com.*

10

BEACHES

Moloka'i's unique geography gives the island plenty of drama and spectacle along the shorelines but not so many places for seaside basking
and bathing. The long North Shore consists mostly of towering cliffs
that plunge directly into the sea and is inaccessible except by boat, and
even then only in the summer. Much of the South Shore is enclosed by
a huge reef that stands as far as a mile offshore and blunts the action
of the waves. Within this reef you will find a thin strip of sand, but the
water here is flat, shallow, and clouded with silt. This reef area is best
suited to pole fishing, kayaking, or learning how to windsurf.

The big, fat, sandy beaches lie along the west end. The largest of
these—one of the largest in the Islands—is Pāpōhaku Beach, which
fronts a grassy park shaded by a grove of *kiawe* (mesquite) trees. These
stretches of West End sand are generally unpopulated. ■TIP➔**The soli-**

tude can be a delight, but it should also be a caution; the sea here can be treacherous. At the east end, where the road hugs the sinuous shoreline, you encounter a number of pocket-size beaches in rocky coves, good for snorkeling. Don't venture too far out however, or you may find yourself caught in dangerous currents. The road ends at Hālawa Valley with its unique double bay.

If you need beach gear, head to Moloka'i Fish and Dive at the west end of Kaunakakai's only commercial strip or rent kayaks from Moloka'i Outdoors also in Kaunakakai.

All of Hawai'i's beaches are free and public. Camping, by permit, is permitted at Pāpōhaku and One Ali'i beach parks. None of the beaches on Moloka'i have telephones or lifeguards, and they're all under the jurisdiction of the **Department of Parks, Land and Natural Resources** (✉ *Box 1055, 90 Ainoa St., Kaunakakai 96748* ☎ *808/553–3204*).

WEST MOLOKA'I

Moloka'i's west end looks across a wide channel to the island of O'ahu. Crescent-shaped, this cup of coastline holds the island's best sandy beaches as well as the most arid and sunny weather. This side of the island is largely uninhabited and few signs of development mark the coast besides a few condos, the Kaluako'i Resort (now closed), and a handful of ocean-view homes. Remember: all beaches are public property, even those that front developments, and most have public access roads. Beaches below are listed from north to south.

Kawākiu Beach. Seclusion is the reason to come to this remote beach, accessible only by four-wheel drive or a 45-minute walk. The white-sand beach is beautiful. ⚠**Rocks and undertow can make swimming extremely dangerous at times, so use caution.** ✉ *Past Ke Nani Kai condos on Kaluako'i Rd., look for dirt road off to right. Park here and hike in or, with 4WD, drive along dirt road to beach* ☞ *No facilities.*

Kepuhi Beach. Kaluako'i Hotel is closed but its restored golf course is open, and so is this ½-mi of ivory white sand. The beach shines beautifully against the turquoise sea, black outcroppings of lava, and magenta bougainvillea flowers of the resort's landscaping. When the sea is perfectly calm, lava ridges in the water make good snorkeling spots. With any surf at all, however, the water around these rocky places churns and foams, wiping out visibility and making it difficult to avoid being slammed into the jagged rocks. ✉ *Kaluako'i Hotel and Golf Club, Kaluako'i Rd.* ☞ *Toilets, showers.*

> ### GUIDED TOURS
>
> **Moloka'i Off-Road Tours and Taxi.** Visit Hālawa Valley, Kalaupapa Lookout, Maunaloa town, and other points of interest in the comfort of an air-conditioned van on four- or six-hour tours. Pat and Alex Pua'a, your personal guides, will even help you mail a coconut back home. Tours start at $95 per person, two person minimum, and usually begin at 9 AM. Charters are also available. ☎ *808/553–3369.*

Fodor's Choice ★ **Pāpōhaku Beach.** One of the most sensational beaches in Hawai'i, Pāpōhaku is a 3-mi-long strip of light golden sand, the longest of its kind on the island. ■TIP→**Some places are too rocky for swimming, so look carefully before entering the water and go in only when the waves are small (generally in summer).** There's so much sand here that Honolulu once purchased barge-loads in order to replenish Waikiki Beach. A shady beach park just inland is the site of the Ka Hula Piko Festival of Hawaiian Music and Dance, held each year in May. The park is also a great sunset-facing spot for a rustic afternoon barbecue. Camping is allowed with a permit, available from the Department of Parks, Land and Natural Resources in Kaunakakai. ⊠*Kaluako'i Rd.; 2 mi south of Kaluako'i Hotel and Golf Club* ⚲*Toilets, showers, picnic tables, grills/firepits.*

> ## BEACH SAFETY
>
> Unlike protected shorelines such as Kā'anapali on Maui, the coasts of Moloka'i are exposed to rough sea channels and dangerous rip currents. The ocean tends to be calmer in the morning and in summer. No matter what the time, however, always study the sea before entering. Unless the water is placid and the wave action minimal, it's best to simply stay on shore. Don't underestimate the power of the ocean. Protect yourself with sunblock. Cool breezes make it easy to underestimate the power of the sun as well.

Kapukahehu Bay. Locals like to surf just out from this bay in a break called Dixie's or Dixie Maru. The sandy protected cove is usually completely deserted on weekdays but can fill up when the surf is up. The water in the cove is clear and shallow with plenty of well-worn rocky areas. These conditions make for excellent snorkeling, swimming, and boogie boarding on calm days. ⊠*Drive about 3½ mi south of Pāpōhaku Beach to end of Kaluako'i Rd.; beach-access sign points to parking* ⚲*No facilities.*

CENTRAL MOLOKA'I

The South Shore is mostly a huge, reef-walled expanse of flat saltwater edged with a thin strip of gritty sand and stones, mangrove swamps, and the amazing system of fishponds constructed by the chiefs of ancient Moloka'i. From this shore you can look out across glassy water to see people standing on top of the sea—actually, way out on top of the reef—casting fishing lines into the distant waves. This is not a great area for beaches, but is interesting in its own right.

One Ali'i Beach Park. Clear, close views of Maui and Lāna'i across the Pailolo Channel dominate One Ali'i Beach Park (*One* is pronounced *o-nay,* not *won*), the only decent beach park on the island's south-central shore. Moloka'i folks gather here for family reunions and community celebrations; the park's tightly trimmed expanse of lawn could accommodate the entire island population. Swimming within the reef is perfectly safe, but don't expect to catch any waves. ⊠*Rte. 450, east of Hotel Moloka'i* ⚲*Toilets, showers, picnic tables.*

EAST MOLOKA'I

The east end unfolds as a coastal drive with turnouts for tiny cove beaches—good places for snorkeling, shore-fishing, or scuba exploring. Rocky little Mokuho'oniki Island marks the eastern point of the island and serves as courting grounds and a nursery for humpback whales in the winter. The road loops around the east end, then descends and ends at Hālawa Valley.

Waialua Beach Park. This arched strip of golden sand, a roadside pull-off near mile marker 20, also goes by the name Twenty Mile Beach. The water here, protected by the flanks of the little bay, is often so clear and shallow (sometimes too shallow) that even from land you can watch fish swimming among the coral heads. ■ TIP➔This is the most popular snorkeling spot on the island, a pleasant place to stop on the drive around the east end. ⊠ *Drive east on Rte. 450 to mile marker 20* ☞ *No facilities.*

Hālawa Beach Park. The vigorous water that gouged the steep, spectacular Hālawa Valley, also carved out two bays side by side. Coarse sand and river rock has built up against the sea along the wide valley mouth, creating some protected pool areas that are good for wading or floating around. Most people come here just to hang out and absorb the beauty of this remote valley. All of the property in the valley is private, so do not wander without a guide. Sometimes you'll see people surfing, but it's not wise to entrust your safety to the turbulent open sea along this coast. ⊠ *Drive east on Rte. 450 to dead-end* ☞ *Toilets.*

WATER SPORTS & TOURS

Moloka'i's shoreline topography limits opportunities for water sports. The North Shore is all sea cliffs; the South Shore is largely encased by a huge, taming reef. ■ TIP➔Open-sea access at west-end and east-end beaches should be used with caution because seas are rough, especially in winter. Generally speaking, there's no one around—certainly not lifeguards—if you get into trouble. For this reason alone, guided excursions are recommended. At least be sure to ask for advice from outfitters or residents. Two kinds of water activities predominate: kayaking within the reef area, and open-sea excursions on charter boats, most of which tie up at Kaunakakai Wharf.

BOOGIE BOARDING, BODYSURFING & SURFING

You rarely see people boogie boarding or bodysurfing on Moloka'i and the only surfing is for advanced wave riders. The best spots for boogie boarding, when conditions are safe (occasional summer mornings), are the west end beaches, especially Kepuhi Beach at the old Kaluako'i Hotel. Or seek out waves at the east end around mile marker 20.

Two companies offer good surf–snorkel excursions—for advanced surfers only—with guides when the conditions are right. **Moloka'i Fish and Dive** (⊠ *downtown Kaunakakai, the Ranch at Maunaloa, or the*

Hotel Moloka'i Activities Desk ☎*808/553–5926* ⊕*molokaifishanddive.com*) is the island's main resource for all outdoor activities. **Fun Hogs Sportfishing** (✉*Kaunakakai Wharf* ☎*808/567–6789*) takes people to good wave action on its charter boat *Ahi.*

FISHING

For Moloka'i people, as in days of yore, the ocean is more of a larder than a playground. It's common to see residents fishing along the shoreline or atop the South Shore reef, using poles or lines. If you'd like to try your hand at this form of local industry, go to **Moloka'i Fish and Dive** (✉*Hotel Moloka'i Activities Desk* ☎*808/553–5926* ⊕*molokaifishanddive.com*) for gear and advice.

Deep-sea fishing by charter boat is a great Moloka'i adventure. The sea channels here, though often rough and windy, provide gorgeous views of several islands. The big sport fish are plentiful in these waters, especially mahimahi, small marlin, and various kinds of tuna. Generally speaking, boat captains will customize the outing to your interests, share a lot of information about the island, and let you keep some or all of your catch. That's Moloka'i style—personal and friendly.

BOATS & CHARTERS

Alyce C. The six-passenger, 31-foot cruiser runs excellent sportfishing excursions. The cost for the boat is $450 for a nine-hour trip, $400 for five to six hours. Shared charters are available for six passengers maximum. Gear is provided. It's a rare day when you don't snag at least one memorable fish. ✉*Kaunakakai Wharf* ☎*808/558–8377* ⊕*www.alycecsportfishing.com.*

Fun Hogs Sportfishing. Trim and speedy, the 27-foot flybridge sportfishing boat named *Ahi* offers half-day ($400), six-hour ($500), and full-day ($600) sportfishing excursions. Skipper Mike Holmes also provides one-way or round-trip journeys to Lāna'i, as well as (in winter only) sunset cruises. ✉*Kaunakakai Wharf* ☎*808/567–6789.*

Moloka'i Action Adventures. Walter Naki's Moloka'i roots go back forever, and he knows the island intimately. What's more, he has traveled (and fished) all over the globe, and he's a great talker. He will create customized fishing and hunting expeditions and gladly share his wealth of experience. If you want to explore the north side under the great sea cliffs, this is the way to go. His 21-foot Boston Whaler is usually seen at the mouth of Hālawa Valley, in the east end. ☎*808/558–8184.*

10

KAYAKING

Moloka'i's South Shore is enclosed by the largest reef system in the United States—an area of shallow, protected sea that stretches over 30 mi. This reef gives inexperienced kayakers an unusually safe, calm environment for shoreline exploring. ⚠ **Outside the reef, Moloka'i waters are often rough and treacherous. Kayakers out here should be strong, experienced, and cautious.**

The **South Shore Reef** area is superb for flat-water kayaking any day of the year. It's best to rent a kayak from Moloka'i Outdoors in Kaunakakai and slide into the water from Kaunakakai Wharf, on either side. Get out in the morning before the wind picks up and paddle east, exploring the ancient Hawaiian fishponds. When you turn around to return, you'll usually get a push home by the wind, which blows strong and westerly along this shore in the afternoon.

Independent kayakers who are confident about testing their skills in rougher seas can launch at the west end of the island from **Hale O Lono Harbor** (at the end of a long, bumpy, private dirt road from Maunaloa town). At the east end of the island, enter the water near mile marker 20 or beyond and explore in the direction of Mokuho'oniki Island. ■ TIP➡ **Kayaking anywhere outside the South Shore Reef is safe only on calm days in summer.**

EQUIPMENT RENTALS & LESSONS

Moloka'i Fish and Dive. At the west end of Kaunakakai's commercial strip, this all-around outfitter provides guided kayak excursions inside the South Shore Reef. One excursion paddles through a dense mangrove forest and explores a huge, hidden ancient fishpond. One bonus of going with guides: if the wind starts blowing hard, they tow you back with their boat. The fee is $89 for the half-day trip. Check at the store (on Ala Mālama Street) for numerous other outdoor activities. ⊠ *61 Ala Mālama St., Kaunakakai* ☎ *808/553–5926* ⊕ *molokaifishanddive.com.*

Moloka'i Outdoors. This is the place to rent a kayak for exploring on your own. Kayaks rent for $15 an hour, and extra paddles are also available. ⊠ *40 Ala Mālama St., Kaunakakai* ☎ *808/553–4477.*

SAILING

Moloka'i is a place of strong predictable winds that make for good and sometimes rowdy sailing. The island views in every direction are stunning. Kaunakakai Wharf is the home base for all of the island's charter sailboats.

Gypsy Sailing Adventures. The 33-plus-foot ocean-going catamaran *Star Gypsy* has a large salon, three staterooms, and a fully equipped galley. They do any kind of sailing you want—"any kind of adventure that's prudent and safe"—from two-hour explorations of Moloka'i's huge reef (stopping at otherwise inaccessible coves and beaches) to interisland cruising (Maui and Lāna'i). In summer, this company does two-day trips that explore the island's North Shore (for experienced sailors only). Full days cost $550 to $750, depending on the amount of catering involved. Half days are $300. Six person maximum; prices are for the whole boat. ⊠ *Kaunakakai Wharf* ☎ *808/553–4328.*

SCUBA DIVING

Moloka'i Fish and Dive is the only PADI-certified purveyor of scuba gear, training, and dive trips on Moloka'i. Shoreline access for divers is extremely limited, even nonexistent in winter. Boat diving is the way to go. Without guidance, visiting divers can easily find themselves in risky situations with wicked currents. Proper guidance, though, opens an undersea world rarely seen.

Moloka'i Fish and Dive. Owners Tim and Susan Forsberg can fill you in on how to find dive sites, rent you the gear, or hook you up with one of their PADI-certified dive guides to take you to the island's best underwater spots. Their 32-foot dive boat, the *Ama Lua,* is certified for 18 passengers and can take 8 divers and gear. Two tank dives lasting about five hours cost $155 with gear, $135 if you bring your own. They know the best blue holes and underwater-cave systems, and they can take you swimming with hammerhead sharks. ⊠*61 Ala Mālama St., Kaunakakai* ☎*808/553–5926* ⊕*molokaifishanddive.com.*

> ### ACTIVITY SPECIALISTS
>
> There are basically two activity vendors on the island who book everything: **Moloka'i Fish and Dive** (⊠*61 Ala Mālama, Kaunakakai* ☎*808/553–5926* ⊕*molokaifishanddive.com*), who also have desks at the Lodge at Moloka'i Ranch, and the Hotel Moloka'i; and **Moloka'i Outdoors** (⊠*40 Ala Mālama, Kaunakakai* ☎*877/553–4477*). Be sure to book well in advance because not all activities are offered daily.

SNORKELING

During the times when swimming is safe—mainly in summer—just about every beach on Moloka'i offers good snorkeling along the lava outcroppings in the island's clean and pristine waters. Certain spots inside the South Shore Reef are also worth checking out.

BEST SPOTS

Kepuhi Beach. In winter, the sea here is deadly. But in summer, this ½-mi-long beach offers plenty of rocky nooks that swirl with sea life. The presence of outdoor showers is a bonus. Take Kaluako'i Road all the way to the west end. Park at Kaluako'i Resort (it's closed) and walk through the open-air lobby area to the beach.

Waialua Beach Park. A thin curve of sand rims a sheltered little bay loaded with coral heads and aquatic life. The water here is shallow—sometimes so shallow that you bump into the underwater landscape—and it's crystal clear. To find this spot, head to the east end on Route 450, and pull off near mile marker 20. When the sea is calm, you'll find several other good snorkeling spots along this stretch of road.

EQUIPMENT RENTALS & DIVE TOURS

Rent snorkel sets from either Moloka'i Outdoors, or Moloka'i Fish and Dive in Kaunakakai *(F see box, Activity Specialists, above).* Rental fees are nominal—$6 a day. All the charter boats carry snorkel gear and include dive stops.

10

Fun Hog Sportfishing. Mike Holmes, captain of the 27-foot power boat *Ahi,* knows the island waters intimately, likes to have fun, and is willing to arrange any type of excursion—for example, one dedicated entirely to snorkeling. His 2½-hour snorkel trips leave early in the morning and explore rarely seen fish and turtle posts outside the reef west of the wharf. Bring your own food and drinks; the trips cost $65 per person. ✉ *Kaunakakai Wharf* ☎ *808/567–6789.*

WHALE-WATCHING

Maui gets all the credit for the local wintering humpback-whale population. Most people don't realize that the big cetaceans also come to Moloka'i. Mokuho'oniki Island at the east end serves as a whale nursery and playground, and the whales pass back and forth along the South Shore. This being Moloka'i, whale-watching here will never involve floating amid a group of boats all ogling the same whale.

Alyce C. Although this six-passenger sportfishing boat is usually busy hooking mahimahi and marlin, the captain gladly takes three-hour excursions to admire the humpback whales. The price is $75 per person, depending on the number of passengers in the group. ✉ *Kaunakakai Wharf* ☎ *808/558–8377* ⊕ *www.alycecsportfishing.com.*

Ama Lua. This 32-foot dive boat, certified for up to 18 passengers, can take you out to see the whales, and is respectful of their privacy and the laws that protect them. A 2½-hour whale-watch is $70 per person and departs from Kaunakakai Wharf at 7 AM during whale season, roughly from December to April. Call Moloka'i Fish and Dive for reservations or information. ✉ *91 Ala Mālama St., Kaunakakai* ☎ *808/553–5926 or 808/552–0184* ⊕ *molokaifishanddive.com.*

Fun Hogs Sportfishing. The *Ahi,* a flybridge sportfishing boat, takes 2½-hour whale-watching trips in the morning from December to April. The cost is $75 per person. Bring your own snacks and drinks. ✉ *Kaunakakai Wharf* ☎ *808/567–6789.*

Gypsy Sailing Adventures. Being a catamaran, the *Star Gypsy* can drift silently under sail and follow the whales without disturbing them. Captain Richard Messina and crew share a lot of knowledge about the whales and pride themselves on being ecologically-minded. The 2½-hour trip costs $75 and includes soft drinks and water. ✉ *Kaunakakai Wharf* ☎ *808/658–0559.*

GOLF, HIKING & OUTDOOR ACTIVITIES

BIKING

Street biking on this island is a dream for pedalers who like to eat up the miles. Moloka'i's few roads are long, straight, and extremely rural. You can really stretch out and go for it—no traffic lights and most of the time no traffic. If you don't happen to be one of those athletes who always travels with your own customized cycling tool, you can rent something from **Moloka'i Bicycle** (☎*808/553–3931*) in Kaunakakai.

EQUIPMENT RENTALS & TOURS

East End Trails. Moloka'i Bicycle will take mountain bikers out to two-wheel the expansive east end spread of Pu'u O Hoku Ranch. You might ride along an eastern ridge rimming Hālawa Valley to four waterfalls and a remote pool for swimming, or pedal on sea cliffs to a secluded beach. ☎*808/553–3931 Moloka'i Bicycle.*

Na'iwa Mountain Trails. Guides from Moloka'i Fish and Dive take biking extremists on a gorgeous but challenging adventure in Na'iwa—the remote central mountains—for convoluted forest courses, daredevil verticals (if you want), and exhilarating miles at the brink of the world's tallest sea cliffs. ✉*61 Ala Mālama St., Kaunakakai*☎*808/553–5926*⊕*molokaifishanddive.com.*

Single-Track Trails at Moloka'i Ranch. Moloka'i Ranch, headquartered in the small town of Maunaloa, was once known for some of the best mountain-bike experiences in the world, but lately the trails have deteriorated and are overgrown. Expect to have to hoist your bike over a locked gate. If you want to try anyway, Moloka'i Fish and Dive runs the activity desk at the Ranch, and has a rental shop with older mountain bikes and related two-wheel gear. ✉*61 Ala Mālama St., Kaunakakai*☎*808/553–5926*⊕*molokaifishanddive.com.*

GOLF

Although golf is good on Moloka'i, there isn't much of it—just two courses and a total of 27 holes.

Ironwood Hills Golf Course. Like the other nine-hole plantation-era courses with which it shares lineage, Ironwood Hills is not for everyone. It helps if you like to play laid-back golf with locals and can handle the occasionally rugged conditions. On the plus side, most holes here offer lovely views of the ocean. Fairways are *kukuya* grass and run through pine, ironwood, and eucalyptus trees. Carts are rented, but there's not always someone there to rent you a cart—in which case, there's a wooden box for your green fee (honor system), and happy walking. ✉*Kala'e Hwy., Box 182, Kualapu'u* ⚑*9 holes. 3,088 yds. Par 35. Green Fee: $20*⛳*Facilities: Putting green, golf carts, pull carts.*

★ **Kaluako'i Golf Course.** Kaluako'i Golf Course, associated with the Lodge at Moloka'i Ranch, has more ocean frontage than any other Hawai'i course. Ted Robinson (1976) was given a fantastic site and created some excellent holes, starting with the par-5 first, with the beach on the right from tee to green. The front nine are generally flat, never running far from the sea, and providing dramatic views of the island of O'ahu; the back nine wind through rolling hills and dense forest. You can check-in and pay your green fee at the clubhouse on the course, or book at Moloka'i Ranch. ✉*Moloka'i Ranch, Box 259, Maunaloa*☎*808/552–0255*⊕*www.molokairanch.com* ⚑*18   holes.*

10

6,200 yds. Par 72. Green Fee: $80 ☞ Facilities: Driving range, putting green, golf carts, rental clubs.

HIKING

Rural and rugged, Moloka'i is an excellent place for hiking. Roads and developments are few, so the outdoors is always beckoning. The island is steep, so hikes often combine spectacular views with hearty physical exertion. Because the island is small, you can traverse quite a bit of it on foot and come away with the feeling of really knowing the place. And you won't see many other people around. Just remember that much of what may look like deserted land is private property, so be careful not to trespass without permission or an authorized guide.

BEST SPOTS

Kalaupapa Trail. You can make a day of hiking down to Kalaupapa Peninsula and back by means of a 3-mi, 26-switchback trail. The trail is nearly vertical, traversing the face of some of the highest sea cliffs in the world. So be sure you are in excellent condition for this hike. You will have to hook up with Damien Tours to see the peninsula, however. *F See* A Tale of Tragedy and Triumph *earlier in this chapter.*

Kamakou Preserve. Four-wheel drive is essential for this half-day (minimum) journey into the Moloka'i highlands. The Nature Conservancy of Hawai'i manages the 2,774-acre Kamakou Preserve, one of the last stands of Hawai'i's native plants and birds. A long, rough dirt road, which begins not far from Kaunakakai town, leads to the preserve. The road is not marked, so you must check in with the **Nature Conservancy's Moloka'i office** (⊠*At Moloka'i Industrial Park about 3 mi west of Kaunakakai, 23 Pueo Pl.* ☎*808/553–5236* ⊕*www.nature.org*), for directions. Let them know that you plan to visit the preserve, and pick up the informative 24-page brochure with trail maps.

On your way up to the preserve, be sure to stop at Waikolu Overlook, which gives a view into a precipitous North Shore canyon. Once inside the preserve, various trails are clearly marked. The trail of choice—and you can drive right to it—is the 1½-mi boardwalk trail through Pēpē'ōpae Bog, an ecological treasure. Organic deposits here date back at least 10,000 years, and the plants are undisturbed natives. This is the landscape of prediscovery Hawai'i and can be a mean trek. ■TIP➜**Wear long pants and bring rain gear. Your shoes ought to provide good traction on the slippery, narrow boardwalk and muddy trails.**

Kawela Cul-de-Sacs. Just east of Kaunakakai, three streets—Kawela One, Two, and Three—jut up the mountainside from the Kamehameha V Highway. These roads end in cul-de-sacs that are also informal trailheads. Rough dirt roads work their way from here to the top of the mountain. The lower slopes are dry, rocky, steep, and austere. (It's good to start in the cool of the early morning.) A hiker in good condition can get all the way up into the high forest in two or three hours. There's no park ranger and no water fountain. These are not for the casual stroller. But you will be well rewarded.

GUIDED HIKES

Fodor'sChoice **Hālawa Valley Cultural Waterfall Hike.** Hālawa is a gorgeous, steep-walled
★ valley carved by two rivers and rich in history. Site of the earliest Polynesian settlement on Moloka'i, Hālawa sustained island culture with
its ingeniously designed *lo'i*, or taro fields. In the 1960s, because of
changing cultural conditions and a great flood, the valley became der-
elict. Now Hawaiian families are restoring the *lo'i* and taking visitors
on guided walks through the valley, which includes two of Moloka'i's
luakini heiau (sacred temples). Half-day visits, starting at at 9:30 AM or
2 PM cost $75 (less for children) and support the work of restoration.
Call ahead to book your visit. Bring water, food, and insect repellent,
and wear shores that can get wet. ☎*808/553–9803 or 808/274–
9303* ⊕*www.gomolokai.com* ✉*$75.*

Historical Hikes of West Moloka'i. This company has six guided hikes,
ranging from two to six hours. The outings focus on Moloka'i's cultural past, and take you to sites such as an ancient quarry, an early
fishing village, or high sea cliffs where Hawaiian chiefs played games
during the traditional *Makahiki* (harvest festival) season. Backpacks
are provided, as is lunch on intermediate and advanced hikes. Guides
Lawrence and Catherine Aki are knowledgeable and passionate about
Hawaiian culture. ✉*The Lodge at Moloka'i Ranch Activity Desk,
Maunaloa Hwy., Maunaloa* ☎*808/552–2797, 808/553–9803, or
800/274–9303* ⊕*www.gomolokai.com* ✉*$45–$125.*

HORSEBACK RIDING

Pu'u O Hoku Ranch. Set on the prow of the island's Maui-facing east
end, this ranch keeps a stable of magnificent, amiable horses that are
available for trail rides starting at $55 an hour. The peak experience is
a four-hour beach ride ($120) that culminates at a secluded cove where
the horses are happy to swim, rider and all. Bring your own lunch.
This is a good experience for people with little or no horse skills. They
match skill-levels with appropriate steeds. ✉*Rte. 450, 20 mi east of
Kaunakakai* ☎*808/558–8109* ⊕*www.puuohoku.com.*

10

SHOPPING

Moloka'i has one main commercial area: Ala Mālama Street in
Kaunakakai. There are no department stores or shopping malls, and
the clothing available is typical island wear. A handful of family-run
businesses line the main drag of Maunaloa, a rural former plantation
town. Most stores in Kaunakakai are open Monday through Saturday
between 9 and 6. In Maunaloa most shops close by 4 in the afternoon
and all day Sunday.

ARTS & CRAFTS

The **Big Wind Kite Factory and Plantation Gallery** (✉*120 Maunaloa Hwy.,
Maunaloa* ☎*808/552–2364*) has custom-made appliquéd kites you can
fly or display. Designs range from hula girls to tropical fish. Also in
stock are kite-making kits, paper kites, minikites, and wind socks. Ask

to go on the factory tour, or take a free kite-flying lesson. The gallery is adjacent to and part of the kite shop and carries locally made crafts, Hawaiian books and CDs, Asian import jewelry and fabrics, and an elegant line of women's linen clothing.

Moloka'i Artists & Crafters Guild (⊠*110 Ala Mālama St., Kaunaka-kai* ☎*808/553–8018*), a small shop above the America Savings Bank downtown, has locally made folk art like dolls, clay flowers, hula skirts, aloha-print visors, and children's wear. They also carry original and Giclee prints, jewelry, and Father Damien keepsakes.

★ **Moloka'i Fine Arts Gallery** (⊠*In the Moore Business center on the corner of King Kamehameha V Hwy., 2 Kamoi St. Suite 300, Kaunaka-kai* ☎*808/553–8520*) only represents artists who live on the island, including world-class talent in photography, wood carving, ceramics, and Hawaiian musical instruments. This business actively supports the community by showcasing local talents.

CLOTHING

Casual, knockabout island wear is sold at **Imports Gift Shop** (⊠*82 Ala Mālama St., Kaunakakai* ☎*808/553–5734*), across from Kanemitsu Bakery. **Moloka'i Island Creations** (⊠*62 Ala Mālama St., Kaunaka-kai* ☎*808/553–5926*) carries exclusive swimwear, beach cover-ups, sun hats, and tank tops. **Moloka'i Surf** (⊠*130 Kamehameha V Hwy., Kaunakakai* ☎*808/553–5093*) is known for its wide selection of Moloka'i T-shirts, swimwear, and sports clothing.

GROCERY STORE

Friendly Market Center (⊠*90 Ala Mālama St., Kaunakakai* ☎*808/553–5595*) is the best-stocked supermarket on the island. Its slogan—"Your family store on Moloka'i"—is truly credible: hats, T-shirts, and sun-and-surf essentials keep company with fresh produce, meat, groceries, liquor, and sundries. Locals say the food is fresher here than at the other major supermarket. It's open weekdays 8:30 AM to 8:30 PM and Saturday 8:30 AM to 6:30 PM.

Victuals and travel essentials are available at the **Maunaloa General Store** (⊠*200 Maunaloa Hwy., Maunaloa* ☎*808/552–2346*). It's convenient for guests staying at the nearby condos of the Kaluako'i Resort area and for those wishing to picnic at one of the west-end beaches. The store sells meat, produce, dry goods, and drinks—and even fresh donuts on Sunday morning. It's open Monday through Saturday 8 AM to 6 PM and Sunday 8 AM to noon.

Misaki's Inc. (⊠*78 Ala Mālama St., Kaunakakai* ☎*808/553–5505*), in business since 1922, has authentic island allure. Pick up housewares and beverages here, as well as your food staples, Monday through Saturday 8:30 AM to 8:30 PM, and Sunday 9 AM to noon.

Don't let the name **Moloka'i Wines 'n' Spirits** (⊠*77 Ala Mālama St., Kaunakakai* ☎*808/553–5009*) fool you. Along with a surprisingly good selection of fine wines and liquors, the store also carries gourmet cheeses and snacks. It's open Sunday through Thursday 9 AM to 8 PM, Friday and Saturday until 9.

ISLAND GOODS & JEWELRY

Imports Gift Shop (✉ *82 Ala Mālama St., Kaunakakai ☎808/553–5734*) sells a small collection of 14-karat-gold chains, rings, earrings, and bracelets, plus a jumble of Hawaiian quilts, pillows, books, and postcards. It also carries stunning Hawaiian heirloom jewelry, a unique style of gold jewelry, inspired by popular Victorian pieces, that has been crafted in Hawai'i since the late 1800s. It's made to order.

Moloka'i Island Creations (✉ *62 Ala Mālama St., Kaunakakai ☎808/553–5926*) carries its own unique line of jewelry, including sea opal, coral, and silver, as well as other gifts and resort wear.

SPORTING GOODS

Moloka'i Bicycle (✉ *80 Mohala St., Kaunakakai ☎808/553–3931 or 800/709–2453 ⊕www.bikehawaii.com/molokaibicycle*) rents and sells mountain and road bikes as well as jogging strollers, kids' trailers, helmets, and racks. It supplies maps and information on biking and hiking and will drop off and pick up equipment for a fee nearly anywhere on the island. Call or stop by Wednesday from 3 PM to 6 PM or Saturday from 9 AM to 2 PM to arrange what you need.

Moloka'i Fish and Dive (✉ *61 Ala Mālama St., Kaunakakai ☎808/553–5926 ⊕molokaifishanddive.com*) is *the* source for sporting needs, from snorkel rentals to free and friendly advice. These folks handle all activities for the Lodge at Moloka'i Ranch and can book most other activities on the island. This is also a good place to pick up original-design Moloka'i T-shirts, water sandals, books, and gifts.

ENTERTAINMENT & NIGHTLIFE

Local nightlife consists mainly of gathering with friends and family, sipping a few cold ones, strumming 'ukuleles and guitars, singing old songs, and talking story. Still, there are a few ways to kick up your heels. Pick up a copy of the weekly *Moloka'i Times* and see if there's a church supper or square dance. The bar at the Hotel Moloka'i is always a good place to drink. They have live music by island performers every night, and Moloka'i may be the best place to hear authentic, old time, non-professional Hawaiian music. Don't be afraid to get up and dance should the music move you. The "Aloha Friday" weekly gathering here, from 4 to 6 PM, always attracts a couple dozen old-timers with guitars and 'ukuleles. This impromptu, feel-good event is a peak experience for any Moloka'i trip. The Paddler's Inn in Kaunakakai has live music every night. It's open until 2 AM on weekends.

Movie fans can head to **Maunaloa Town Cinemas** (✉ *Maunaloa Hwy., Maunaloa ☎808/552–2707*). Folks from all around Moloka'i come here nightly for current blockbusters.

10

WHERE TO EAT

During a week's stay, you might easily hit all the dining spots worth a visit, then return to your favorites for a second round. The dining scene is fun because it's a microcosm of Hawai'i's diverse cultures. You can find locally grown vegetarian foods, spicy Filipino cuisine, and Hawaiian fish with a Japanese influence—such as 'ahi or *aku* (types of tuna), mullet, and moonfish grilled, sautéed, or mixed with seaweed and eaten raw as *poke* (marinated raw fish). Most eating establishments are on Ala Mālama Street in Kaunakakai, with pizza, pasta, and ribs only a block away. What's more, the price is right.

WHAT IT COSTS				
	¢	$	$$	$$$	$$$$
RESTAURANTS	under $10	$10–$17	$18–$26	$27–$35	over $35

Restaurant prices are for a main course at dinner.

WEST MOLOKA'I

$–$$$$ ✕**Maunaloa Room.** Dining here is as "upscale" as you can find on the island, with appetizers such as local yellowfin tuna carpaccio. Entrées follow a steak-and-seafood theme, and the catch of the day can be prepared with *alae* (a pale-orange salt found in Moloka'i and Kaua'i). Inside, wagon-wheel chandeliers with electric candles typify the hotel restaurant's ranch ambience. A dinner on the outside deck is soothing and peaceful. Weekends are busy so make reservations in advance. ✉*The Lodge at Moloka'i Ranch, 8 Maunaloa Hwy., Maunaloa* ☎*808/660–2725* ▭*AE, MC, V.*

★ **¢–$$$** ✕**Paniola Lounge.** Lighter fare is available here at the bar at the Moloka'i Ranch, where you can watch sports movies while you eat, or sit on the deck with a view of rolling hills and deep blue sea. For lunch try the Won Ton Mein, or cowboy-sized hamburgers. In the evening the menu is enhanced by a rock-shrimp crab cake that is too good to miss, sliced New York steak with camp fries, and a Hawaiian *pūpū* platter for two that includes pork, ribs, chicken wings, and sashimi. If you sit on the veranda you can listen to the music from the Great Room during the dinner hour. ✉*The Lodge at Moloka'i Ranch, 8 Maunaloa Hwy., Maunaloa* ☎*808/660–2725* ▭*AE, MC, V.*

CENTRAL MOLOKA'I

★ **$–$$** ✕**Oceanfront Dining Room.** This is *the* place to hang out on Moloka'i. Locals relax at the bar listening to live music every night, or they come in for theme-night dinners (posters around town tell you what's in store for the week). Service is brisk and friendly, the food is good, and the atmosphere casual. Prime-rib specials on Friday and Saturday nights draw a crowd. Try the broiled baby-back ribs smothered in barbecue sauce, or the vegetarian stir-fry. Every Friday from 4 to 6 PM Moloka'i's *kūpuna* (old-timers) bring their instruments here for a lively Hawaiian jam session, a wonderful experience of grassroots aloha spirit. ✉*Hotel*

Moloka'i, Kamehameha V Hwy., Kaunakakai ☎808/553–5347 ⊟*AE, DC, MC, V.*

¢–$$ ✕ **Kamuela's Cookhouse.** Kamuela's is the only eatery in rural Kualapu'u and a local favorite. This laid-back diner is a classic refurbished green-and-white plantation house; inside, paintings of hula dancers and island scenes enhance the simple furnishings. Typical fare is a plate of chicken or pork *katsu* served with rice. Try their mahi burger or chicken stir-fry with fresh vegetables. It's across the street from the Kualapu'u Market. ✉*Farrington Hwy., 1 block west of Rte. 470, Kualapūu* ☎808/567–9655 ⊟*No credit cards* ⊘*Closed Sun. and Mon..*

¢–$$ ✕ **Moloka'i Pizza Cafe.** A cheerful, busy restaurant, Moloka'i Pizza is a popular gathering spot for families. Pizza, sandwiches, salads, pasta, fresh fish, and homemade pies are simply prepared and tasty. Kids keep busy on a few little coin-operated rides and their art decorates the walls. ✉*Kaunakakai Pl. on Wharf Rd., Kaunakakai* ☎808/553–3288 ⊟*No credit cards.*

¢–$$ ✕ **Paddler's Inn.** A roomy, comfortable restaurant with an extensive menu, Paddler's Inn is right in Kaunakakai town but on the ocean side of Kamehameha V Highway. There are three eating areas—standard restaurant seating, a shady cool bar, and an open-air courtyard where you can sit at a counter eating *poke* (raw, marinated cubes of fish) and drinking beer while getting cooled with spray—on hot days—from an overhead misting system. The food is a blend of island-style and standard American fare (fresh *poke* every day; a prime rib special every Friday night). There's live entertainment every Wednesday and local bands play on weekends. ✉*10 Mohala St., Kaunakakai* ☎808/553–5256 ⊟*AE, DC, MC, V.*

¢ ✕ **Kanemitsu Bakery and Restaurant.** Stop for morning coffee with fresh-baked bread or a taste of *lavosh,* a pricey flatbread flavored with sesame, taro, Maui onion, Parmesan cheese, or jalapeño. Or try the round Moloka'i bread—a sweet, pan-style white loaf that makes excellent cinnamon toast. Be prepared to wait, and settle down into Moloka'i time. ✉*79 Ala Mālama St., Kaunakakai* ☎808/553–5855 ⊟*No credit cards* ⊘*Closed Tues..*

Fodor'sChoice
★

¢ ✕ **Moloka'i Drive Inn.** Fast food Moloka'i-style is served at a walk-up counter. Hot dogs, fries, and sundaes are on the menu, but residents usually choose the foods they grew up on, such as *saimin* (thin noodles and vegetables in broth), plate lunches, shave ice (snow cone), and the beloved *loco moco* (rice topped with a hamburger and a fried egg, covered in gravy). ✉*857 Ala Mālama St., Kaunakakai* ☎808/553–5655 ⊟*No credit cards.*

¢ ✕ **Outpost Natural Foods.** A well-stocked store, Outpost is the heart of Moloka'i's health-food community. At the counter you can get fresh juices and delicious sandwiches geared toward the vegetarian palate. It's a great place to pick up local produce and all the ingredients you need for a picnic lunch. ✉*70 Makaena St., Kaunakakai* ☎808/553–3377 ⊟*AE, MC, V* ⊘*Closed Sat. No dinner.*

¢ ✕ **Oviedo's.** This modest lunch counter specializes in *adobos* (stews) with traditional Filipino spices and sauces. Try the tripe, pork, or beef *adobo* for a taste of tradition. Locals say that Oviedo's makes the best

10

roast pork in the state. You can eat in or take out. ✉ *145 Ala Mālama St., Kaunakakai* ☎ *808/553–5014* ▭ *No credit cards* ⊘ *No dinner.*

¢ ✕**Stanley's Coffee Shop & Gallery.** The high ceiling and open space in this shop make for a cool place to sit at an old-fashioned booth and refresh yourself. Coffee, pastries, sandwiches, waffles for breakfast, salads, and—yes—cigars (though smoking is not allowed inside, anywhere in Hawai'i) are available. The walls are adorned with original paintings done in a sophisticated art-school manner, and there is Internet access and an upstairs gallery. ✉ *125 Puali St., Kaunakakai* ☎ *808/553–9966* ▭ *MC, V* ⊘ *Closed Sun.*

¢ ✕**Sundown Deli.** This clean little rose-color deli focuses on freshly made takeout food. Sandwiches come on half-a-dozen types of bread, and the Portuguese bean soup and chowders are rich and filling. ✉ *145 Ala Mālama St., Kaunakakai* ☎ *808/553–3713* ▭ *No credit cards* ⊘ *Closed Sun. No dinner.*

WHERE TO STAY

The coastline along Moloka'i's west end has ocean-view condominium units and luxury homes available as vacation rentals. In the hills above, little Maunaloa town offers the semiluxurious Lodge at Moloka'i Ranch and the oddly luxurious seaside tents at Kaupoa Beach Village. Central Moloka'i offers seaside condominiums and the icon of the island—Hotel Moloka'i. The only lodgings on the east end are some guest cottages in magical settings and the ranch house at Pu'u O Hoku. The Moloka'i Visitor's Association ☎ *800/800–6367* has a brochure with up-to-date listing of all vacation rentals.

WHAT IT COSTS					
	¢	$	$$	$$$	$$$$
HOTELS	under $100	$100–$180	$181–$260	$261–$340	over $340

Hotel prices are for two people in a double room in high season, including tax and service. Condo price categories reflect studio and one-bedroom rates.

WEST MOLOKA'I

HOTELS & RESORTS

$$$$ 🏨**The Lodge at Moloka'i Ranch.** Moloka'i's only high-end accommoda-
Fodor'sChoice tion is this Old West–style lodge. The atmosphere is low-key, with most
★ guests either lazing around the heated pool or out sightseeing. Ranching memorabilia and artwork adorn guest-room walls, with each of the 22 luxury rooms individually decorated. All rooms have private lānai and some have skylights. An impressive stone fireplace warms up the central Great Room, and there's a billiards room for pleasant socializing during cool Moloka'i evenings. Pathways and flowering shrubs delineate the grounds. The ranch shuttle takes guests down to Kaupoa Beach Village and a white-sand beach. An Outfitters Center offers a gift shop, activities, bike rentals, and a photo history of the

property. ✉ *Maunaloa Hwy., Box 259, Maunaloa 96770* ☎ *888/627–8082* ⊕ *www.molokairanch.com* ➷ *22 rooms* ☍ *In-room: safe, refrigerator, dial-up. In-hotel: restaurant, bar, pool, gym, spa, children's programs (ages 5–12)* ⊟ *AE, D, MC, V.*

$$$–$$$$ ★ 🏕 **Kaupoa Beach Village.** This dream-come-true campground consists of two-bedroom canvas bungalows, mounted on wooden platforms. Don't let the presence of ecotravelers fool you—the tenta-lows are unexpectedly luxurious, with a private deck, self-composting flush toilets, and private, outdoor, solar-heated showers. Breakfast, lunch, and dinner are served family-style in an open-air pavilion (price not included in room rate). A pristine white-sand beach fronts the property. Extensive activities, including snorkeling, kayaking, clay shooting, and horseback riding, are available. ✉ *Maunaloa Hwy., Box 259, Maunaloa 96770* ☎ *888/627–8082* ⊕ *www.molokairanch.com* ➷ *40 units* ☍ *In-room: no a/c, no phone, no TV. In-hotel: restaurant, beachfront, water sports, airport shuttle, no elevator* ⊟ *AE, D, MC, V.*

CONDOS & VACATION RENTALS

$$–$$$$ 🏠 **Hale Aloha.** This spacious four-bedroom, three-bath vacation rental is on 12 secluded acres, has ocean views, and is surrounded by woodlands and an orchard. Wood floors stretch the length of the house, connecting the two kitchens. A wraparound porch leads to a gazebo-covered hot tub. Rooms are open and simple, with wood-beam ceilings. The managers of this property, 1-800-Moloka'i, also handle a number of other West End condos available for as little as $100 a night. ✉ *Kaluako'i Rd., Box 20, Maunaloa 96770* ☎ *800/665–6524 or 808/552–2222* ⊕ *www.molokai.tv* ➷ *1 unit* ☍ *In-room: no a/c, kitchen, VCR. In-hotel: pool, no elevator* ⊟ *AE, MC, V.*

★ **$–$$$** 🏠 **Paniolo Hale.** Perched high on a ledge overlooking the beach, Paniolo Hale is one of Moloka'i's best condominium properties. Some units have spectacular ocean views. Studios and one- or two-bedroom units all have beautiful screened lānai, well-equipped kitchens, and washers and dryers. Rooms are tidy and simple and some are quite lovely. The property fronts the back nine of the Kaluako'i Golf Course and is a stone's throw from the Kaluako'i Hotel and Golf Club. ✉ *Lio Pl., Box 1979, Kaunakakai 96748* ☎ *808/553–8334 or 800/367–2984* 🖷 *808/553–3783* ⊕ *www.molokai-vacation-rental.net* ➷ *77 units* ☍ *In-room: kitchen, laundry facilities. In-hotel: golf course, pool, no elevator* ⊟ *AE, MC, V.*

$ 🏠 **Ke Nani Kai.** These pleasant one- and two-bedroom condo units have ocean views and use of the pool and other facilities at the former Kaluako'i Hotel and Golf Club. Furnished lānai have flower-laden trellises and the spacious interiors are decorated with rattans and pastels. Each unit has a washer-dryer unit and a fully equipped kitchen. The beach is just across the road. ✉ *Kaluako'i Rd., Box 289, Maunaloa 96770* ☎ *808/553–8334 or 800/367–2984* 🖷 *808/553–3783* ⊕ *www. molokai-vacation-rental.net* ➷ *120 units* ☍ *In-room: no a/c, kitchen. In-hotel: golf course, tennis courts, pool, laundry facilities, no elevator* ⊟ *AE, D, DC, MC, V.*

10

CENTRAL MOLOKA'I

HOTELS & RESORTS

★ **$-$$ Hotel Moloka'i.** Friendly staff members embody the aloha spirit at this local favorite. The low-slung buildings are arranged in a landscaped tropical setting. Simple, airy furnishings with white rattan accents fill the rooms, and there are basket swings on some of the upstairs lānai. The lower-priced rooms are small and plain. The Oceanfront Dining Room serves breakfast, lunch, dinner, and libations—with entertainment nightly. Ask about deals in conjunction with airlines and rental-car companies when you make your reservation. There is an activities desk in the lobby. ⊠ *Kamehameha V Hwy., Box 1020, Kaunakakai 96748* ☎ *808/553–5347* 🖷 *808/553–5047* ⊕ *www. hotelmolokai.com* 🖙 *45 rooms* ⚐ *In-room: no a/c. In-hotel: restaurant, pool, laundry facilities, no elevator* ▭ *AE, D, DC, MC, V.*

CONDOS & VACATION RENTALS

$$ ⌂ **Moloka'i Shores.** Some of the units in this oceanfront, three-story condominium complex have a view of the water. One-bedroom, one-bath units or two-bedroom, two-bath units all have full kitchens and furnished lānai, which look out on 4 acres of manicured lawns. There's a great view of Lāna'i in the distance. ⊠ *1000 Kamehameha V Hwy., Box 1887, Kaunakakai 96748* ☎ *808/553–5954 or 800/535–0085* ⊕ *www.marcresorts.com* 🖷 *800/633–5085* 🖙 *100 units* ⚐ *In-room: no a/c, kitchen. In-hotel: pool, no elevator* ▭ *AE, D, MC, V.*

★ **$** ⌂ **Wavecrest.** This oceanfront condominium complex is convenient if you want to explore the east side of the island—it's 13 mi east of Kaunakakai. Individually decorated one- and two-bedroom units have full kitchens. Each has a furnished lānai, some with views of Maui and Lāna'i. Be sure to ask for an updated unit when you reserve. The 5-acre oceanfront property has access to a beautiful reef and excellent snorkeling and kayaking. ⊠ *Rte. 450 near mile marker 13* 🖅 *Moloka'i Vacation Rentals, Box 1979, Kaunakakai 96748* ☎ *800/367–2984 or 808/553–8334* 🖷 *808/553–3784* ⊕ *www.Molokai-vacation-rental. net* 🖙 *126 units* ⚐ *In-room: no a/c, kitchen. In-hotel: tennis courts, pool, beachfront, no elevator* ▭ *V.*

EAST MOLOKA'I

CONDOS & VACATION RENTALS

$ 　**Dunbar Beachfront Cottages.** These two spotlessly clean two-bedroom, one-bath cottages with complete kitchens—each with its own secluded beach—are set about a ¼ mi apart. The beach is good for swimming and snorkeling during the summer months and great for whale-watching in winter. Covered lānai have panoramic vistas of Maui, Lāna'i, and Kaho'olawe across the ocean. ⊠*King Kamehameha V Hwy., at mile marker 18* ⚡*HC01, Box 738, Kaunakakai 96748* ☎*808/558–8153 or 800/673–0520* ⊕*www.molokai-beachfront-cottages.com* ⇔*2 cottages* ⚙*In-room: no a/c, kitchen, DVD. In-hotel: beachfront, no-smoking rooms, no elevator* ▭*No credit cards.*

$ 　**Kamalō Plantation Cottage.** Located in a lush tropical garden in the middle of a five-acre property, this studio cottage has a full kitchen, a bedroom alcove with a king-size bed, dining and living areas, and a full bath. It's only a 5-minute walk from the ocean and has great views. Swimming beaches are just a seven-minute drive east. ⊠*East of Kaunakakai off Rte. 450* ⚡*HC 01, Box 300, Kaunakakai 96748* ☎*808/558–8236* ⊕*www.molokai.com/kamalo* ⇔*1 unit* ⚙*In-room: no a/c, kitchen. In-hotel: no elevator* ▭*No credit cards.*

$ 　**Moanui Beach House.** This two-bedroom house, with a king-size bed in each bedroom, has a full kitchen, dining area, living room, a full bath upstairs, and a half bath downstairs. It's right in front of one of Moloka'i's best snorkeling beaches and has fantastic views from the decks. Prices are for single/double occupancy; there is an extra fee of $50 per night for each additional person. This rental is owned by the same people who have the Kamalō Plantation Cottage. ⊠*East of Kaunakakai off Rte. 450* ⚡*HC 01, Box 300, Kaunakakai 96748* ☎*808/558–8236* ⊕*www.molokai.com/kamalo* ⇔*1 cottage* ⚙*In-room: no a/c, kitchen. In-hotel: no elevator* ▭*No credit cards.*

> ## GROCERY STORES
>
> **Friendly Market Center** (⊠*93 Ala Mālama St., Kaunakakai* ☎*808/553–5595*) is the best-stocked supermarket on the island. **Misaki's Inc.** (⊠*78 Ala Mālama St., Kaunakakai* ☎*808/553–5505*) is a good spot for housewares, beverages, and food staples. **Moloka'i Wines 'n' Spirits** (⊠*77 Ala Mālama St., Kaunakakai* ☎*808/553–5009*) carries a good selection of fine wines and liquors, as well as gourmet cheese and snacks.

10

$ 　**Pu'u O Hoku Ranch.** At the east end of Moloka'i, near mile marker 25, lie these three ocean-view accommodations, on 14,000 isolated acres of pastures and forest. This is a remote and serene location for people who want to get away. One country cottage has two bedrooms, basic wicker furnishings, and *lau hala* (natural fiber) woven matting on the floors. An airy four-bedroom cottage has a small deck and a somewhat Balinese air. For large groups—family reunions, for example—the Ranch has a lodge with 11 rooms, 9 bathrooms, and a large kitchen. The full lodge goes for $1,250 nightly (rooms are not available on an individual basis). Inquire about horseback riding on the property. ⊠*Rte. 450, Box 1889, Kaunakakai 96748* ☎*808/558–8109* 🖶*808/558–8100* ⊕*www.puuohoku.com* ⇌*1 2-bedroom cottage, 1 4-bedroom cottage, 11 rooms in lodge* ⇧*In-room: no a/c, kitchen. In-hotel: pool, no elevator* ⊟*MC, V.*

MOLOKA'I ESSENTIALS

TRANSPORTATION

BY AIR

If you're flying in from the mainland United States, you must first make a stop in Honolulu. From there, it's a 25-minute trip to the Friendly Isle.

AIRPORTS Moloka'i's transportation hub is Ho'olehua Airport, a tiny airstrip 8 mi west of Kaunakakai and about 18 mi east of Maunaloa. An even smaller airstrip serves the little community of Kalaupapa on the North Shore.

Information Ho'olehua Airport (☎*808/567-6140*). **Kalaupapa Airfield** (☎*808/567-6331*).

CARRIERS Island Air, the puddle-jumper arm of Aloha Airlines, provides daily flights between Moloka'i and O'ahu or Maui on its 37-passenger de Haviland Dash-8 aircraft. Pacific Wings operates chartered flights on its nine-passenger Cessna between O'ahu and Moloka'i.

If you fly into the airstrip at Kalaupapa, you must book a ground tour with Damien Tours before you depart. Pacific Wings and Moloka'i Air Shuttle fly from Honolulu to Kalaupapa. Paragon Air runs charter flights from Maui to Kalaupapa.

Contacts Island Air (☎*800/323-3345* ⊕*www.islandair.com*). **Moloka'i Air Shuttle** (☎*808/567-6847 in Honolulu*). **Pacific Wings** (☎*808/873-0877 or 888/575-4546* ⊕*www.pacificwings.com*).

TO & FROM
THE AIRPORT From Ho'olehua Airport, it takes about 10 minutes to reach Kaunakakai and 25 minutes to reach the west end of the island by car. There's no public bus.

Shuttle service for two passengers costs about $18 from Ho'olehua Airport to Kaunakakai. A trip to Moloka'i Ranch costs $28, divided by the number of passengers. For shuttle service, call Moloka'i Off-Road Tours and Taxi, or Moloka'i Outdoors.

Contacts Moloka'i Off-Road Tours and Taxi (☎*808/553-3369*). **Moloka'i Outdoors** (☎*808/553-4227* ⊕*www.molokai-outdoors.com*).

BY CAR

If you want to explore Moloka'i from one end to the other, it's best to rent a car. With just a few main roads to choose from, it's a snap to drive around here.

The gas stations are in Kaunakakai and Maunaloa. When you park your car, be sure to lock it—thefts do occur. Drivers must wear seat belts or risk a $75 fine. Children under three must ride in a federally approved child passenger-restraint device, easily leased at the rental agency. Ask your rental agent for a free *Moloka'i Drive Guide.*

CAR RENTAL Budget maintains a counter near the baggage-claim area at the airport. Dollar also has offices at Ho'olehua Airport, and your rental car can be picked up in the parking lot. Expect to pay $40 to $50 per day for a standard compact and $50 to $70 for a midsize car. Rates are seasonal and may run higher during the peak winter months. Make arrangements in advance because there may not be cars available when you walk in. If you're flying on Island Air or Hawaiian Airlines, see whether fly-drive package deals are available—you might luck out on a less-expensive rate. Hotels and outfitters might also offer packages.

Locally owned Island Kine Rent-a-Car offers airport or hotel pickup and sticks to one rate year-round for vehicles in a broad spectrum from two- and four-wheel drives to 11-passenger vans.

Major Agencies Budget (☎ 808/451–3600 or 800/527–7000 ⊕ www.budget. com). **Dollar** (☎ 800/367–7006 ⊕ www.dollar.com).

Local Agencies Island Kine Rent-a-Car (☎ 808/553–5242 ⊕ www.molokai-car-rental.com).

BY FERRY

The Moloka'i Ferry crosses the channel every day between Lahaina (Maui) and Kaunakakai, making it easy for West Maui visitors to put Moloka'i on their itineraries. Keep in mind that the ferry is an older vessel that has had some mechanical difficulties in the past, and the crossing can be very rough in strong trade-wind weather, especially on the return trip. The 1½-hour trip takes passengers but not cars, so arrange ahead of time for a car rental or tour at the arrival point. The easiest way to do this is to contact Moloka'i Outdoors, who will arrange your transportation and lodgings.

Contact Moloka'i Ferry (☎ 808/667–2585 ⊕ www.molokaiferry.com).

10

CONTACTS & RESOURCES

EMERGENCIES

Round-the-clock medical attention is available at Moloka'i General Hospital. Severe cases or emergencies are often airlifted to Honolulu.

Emergency Services Ambulance and general emergencies (☎ 911). **Coast Guard** (☎ 808/552–6458 on O'ahu). **Fire** (☎ 808/553–5601 in Kaunakakai, 808/567–6525 at Ho'olehua Airport). **Police** (☎ 808/553–5355).

Hospital Moloka'i General Hospital (✉ 280A Puali St., Kaunakakai ☎ 808/553–5331).

VISITOR INFORMATION

There's tourist information available in kiosks and stands at the airport in Ho'olehua or at the Moloka'i Visitors Association. The Moloka'i Visitors Association has a brochure that lists a number of activity vendors and accommodations. Call them for a copy before you leave home. Be sure to book all activities well in advance because not every activity is available every day. Plan ahead and you will have a happier visit.

Information **Maui Visitors Bureau** (⬦ *On Maui: 1727 Wili Pa Loop, Wailuku 96793* ☎ *808/244–3530* ⊕ *www.visitmaui.com*). **Moloka'i Visitors Association** (✉ *12 Kamoi St., Suite 200, Hwy., Box 960, Kaunakakai 96748ADDRESS* ☎ *808/553–3876 or 800/800–6367* ⊕ *molokai-hawaii.com*).

Lāna'i

WORD OF MOUTH

"If you are going for golf or tennis or lazing around in the sun, it is wonderful. Other than that, it is very, very low-key with minimal shopping and no evening activities."

—breckgal

"The day we went [to Polihua Beach] it was only us and three locals who were fishing. The sand is so soft, and the water is crystal clear."

—alex

WELCOME TO LĀNA'I

Polihua Beach

TOP 5
Reasons to Go

1 Seclusion & Serenity: Lāna'i is small: local motion is slow motion. Go home rested instead of exhausted.

2 Garden of the Gods: Walk amid the eerie red-rock spires that ancient Hawaiians believed to be the home of the spirits.

3 A Dive at Cathedrals: Explore underwater pinnacle formations and mysterious caverns lit by shimmering rays of light.

4 Dole Square: Hang out in the shade of the Cook Pines and talk story with the locals.

5 Lāna'i Pine Sporting Clays & Archery Range: Play a Pacific William Tell, aiming your arrow at a pineapple.

■ TIP→ Directions on the island are often given as *mauka* (toward the mountains) and *makai* (toward the ocean).

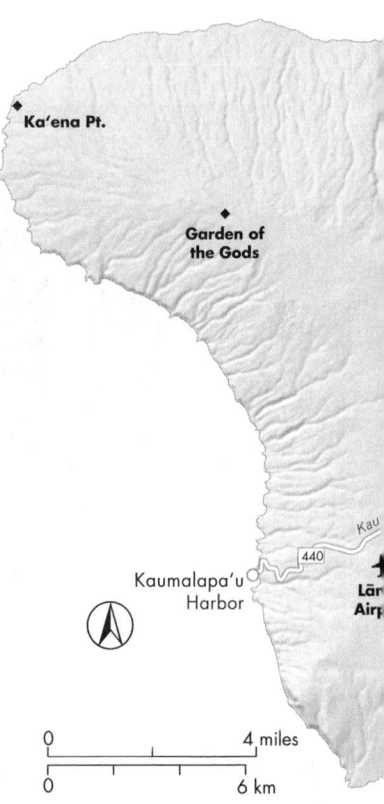

Ka'ena Pt.

Garden of
the Gods

Kau

440

Kaumalapa'u
Harbor

Lā
Air

0   4 miles
0   6 km

Hulopo'e Beach   *Garden of the Gods*

Getting Oriented

Unlike the other Hawaiian islands with their tropical splendors, Lāna'i looks like a desert: kiawe trees right out of Africa, red-dirt roads that glow molten at sunset, and a deep blue sea that literally leads to Tahiti. Lāna'ihale (house of Lāna'i), the mountain that bisects the island, is carved into deep canyons by rain and wind on the windward side, and the dryer leeward side slopes gently to the sea, where waves pound against surf-carved cliffs.

Spinner Dolphins

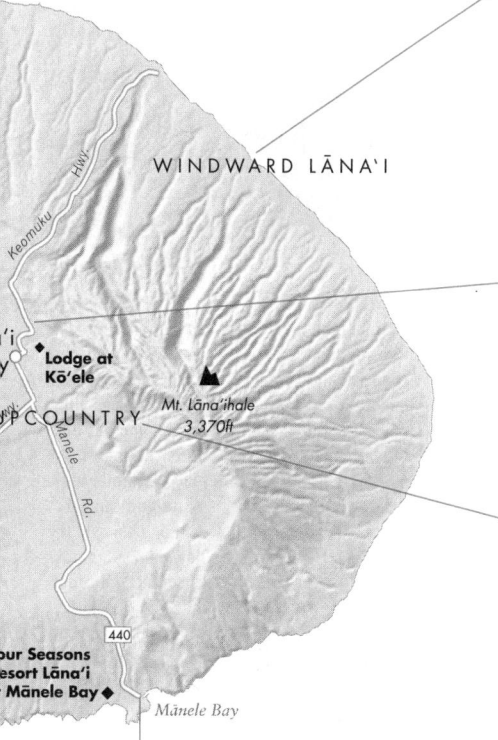

Windward Lāna'i is the long white sand beach at the base of Lāna'ihale. Now uninhabited, it was once occupied by thriving Hawaiian fishing villages and a sugar-cane plantation.

WINDWARD LĀNA'I

Lodge at Kō'ele

UPCOUNTRY

Mt. Lāna'ihale 3,370ft

Hwy

Keomuku

Manele

Rd.

440

our Seasons
esort Lāna'i
Mānele Bay

Mānele Bay

Lāna'i City is really a tiny plantation village. Locals hold conversations in front of Dole Park shops and from their pickups on the road, and kids ride bikes in colorful impromptu parades while cars wait for them.

Cool and serene, Upcountry is graced by Lāna'i City, towering Cook Pine trees, and misty mountain vistas.

Lāna'i Pine Archery

The more developed beach side of the island, Mānele Bay and harbor is where it's happening: swimming, picnicking, off-island excursions, and boating are all concentrated in this very accessible area.

LĀNA'I PLANNER

Sunsets and Moonrises

One of the best ways to tap into Lāna'i's Pacific Island pace is to take the time not just to watch the sun set but also to watch the moon rise. The best sunset-viewing spots are the veranda at The Lodge, the grassy field past the Lodge's tennis courts, Hulopo'e Beach, and the Challenge at Mānele clubhouse. For full moons, nothing beats the trail that leads to Pu'u Pehe or the many stopping places along Keōmoko Road.

Navigating Without Signs

Lāna'i has no traffic, no traffic lights, and only three paved roads. Bring along a good topographical map, study it, and keep in mind your directions. Stop from time to time and re-find landmarks and gauge your progress. Distance is better measured in the condition of the road than in miles. Watch out for other jeep drivers who also don't know where they are. Never drive to the edge of lava cliffs, as rock can give way under you.

Timing Is Everything

Whales are seen off Lāna'i's shores from December through April. A Pineapple Festival on the 4th of July Saturday in Dole Park features local food, Hawaiian entertainment, a pineapple eating and cooking contest and fireworks. Buddhists hold their annual outdoor Obon Festival honoring departed ancestors with joyous dancing, food booths, and taiko drumming in early July. Lāna'i celebrates the statewide Aloha Festivals in mid-October with a hometown parade, car contests, more food, and more music. Beware hunting season weekends—from mid-February through mid-May, and mid-July through mid-October. Most of the private lodging properties are booked way in advance.

Car Rentals

Renting a four-wheel-drive vehicle is expensive but almost essential. There are only 30 mi of paved road on the island. The rest of your driving takes place on bumpy, muddy, secondary roads, which generally aren't marked. Be sure to make reservations far in advance of your trip, because Lāna'i's fleet of vehicles is limited.

Will It Rain?

As higher mountains on Maui capture the trade-wind clouds, Lāna'i receives little rainfall and has a desert ecology. It's always warmer at the beach and can get cool or even cold (by Hawaiian standards) Upcountry. Consider the wind direction when planning your day. If it's blowing a gale on the windward beaches, head for the beach at Hulopo'e or check out Garden of The Gods. Overcast days, when the wind stops or comes lightly from the southwest, are common in whale season. Try a whale-watching trip or the windward beaches.

Additional planning details are listed in Lāna'i Essentials at the end of this chapter.

By Joana
Varawa
Updated
by Shannon
Wianecki

WITH NO TRAFFIC OR TRAFFIC lights and miles of open space, Lāna'i seems lost in time. The tiny plantation town is really a village, where locals hold conversations around Dole Park and from their pickups on the road, and kids ride bikes in impromptu parades. The two resorts on the island are now run by the Four Seasons. If you yearn for a beach with amenities, a luxury resort, and golf course, the Four Seasons Resort Lāna'i at Mānele Bay beckons from the shoreline. Upcountry, the luxurious Lodge at Kō'ele provides cooler pleasures. This leaves the rest of the 100,000-acre island open to explore.

Small (141 square mi) and sparsely populated, Lāna'i is the smallest inhabited Hawaiian Island. Lāna'i City has just 3,000 residents, and no one lives elsewhere on the island. Though it may seem a world away, Lāna'i is separated from Maui and Moloka'i by two narrow channels, and easily accessed by boat from either island.

FLORA & FAUNA

Lāna'i bucks the "tropical" trend of the other Hawaiian Islands with African keawe trees, cock pines, and eucalyptus in place of palm trees, red dirt instead of black lava rock, and deep blue sea where you might expect shallow turquoise bays. Abandoned pineapple fields are overgrown with drought-resistant grasses, Christmas berry and lantana; native plants, *a'ali'i* and *'ilima,* are found in uncultivated areas. Axis deer from India dominate the ridges, and wild turkeys lumber around the resorts. Whales can be seen December through April and a family of resident spinner dolphins drops in regularly at Hulopo'e Bay.

ON LĀNA'I TODAY

Despite its fancy resorts, Lāna'i still has that sleepy old Hawai'i feel. Residents are a mix of just about everything—Hawaiian/Chinese/German/Portuguese/Filipino/Japanese/French/Puerto Rican/English/Norwegian, you name it. The plantation was divided into ethnic camps which helped retain cultural cuisines. Potluck dinners feature sashimi, Portuguese bean soup, *laulau* (morsels of pork, chicken, butterfish, or other ingredients wrapped with young taro shoots in tī leaves), potato salad, teriyaki steak, chicken *hekka* (a gingery Japanese chicken stir-fry), and Jell-O. The local language is pidgin, a mix of words as complicated and rich as the food. In recent years, David Murdock's plan to pay for the resorts by selling expensive homes next to them has met with opposition from locals.

THE GHOSTS OF LĀNA'I

Lāna'i has a reputation for being haunted (at one time by "cannibal spirits") and evidence abounds: a mysterious purple *lehua* at Keahialoa; the crying of a ghost chicken at Kamoa; Pohaku O, a rock that calls at twilight; and remote spots where cars mysteriously stall, and lights are seen at night. Tradition has it that Pu'upehe (an offshore sea stack) was a child who spoke from the womb, demanding *awa* root. A later story claims it is the grave of a woman drowned in a cave at the nearby cliffs. Hawaiians believe that places have *mana* (spiritual power), and Lāna'i is far from an exception.

EXPLORING LĀNA'I

Lāna'i has an ideal climate year-round, hot and sunny at the sea and a few delicious degrees cooler Upcountry. In Lāna'i City, the nights and mornings can be almost chilly when a mystic fog or harsh trade winds settle in. Winter months are known for *slightly* rougher weather—periodic rain showers and higher surf.

You can easily explore Lāna'i City and the island's two resorts without a car; just hop on the hourly shuttle. To access the rest of this untamed island, you'll need to rent a four-wheel-drive. Take a map, be sure you have a full tank, and bring a snack and plenty of water. Ask the rental agency or your hotel's concierge about road conditions before you set out. If the roads are impassable (as they often are after heavy rains) you may be able to negotiate a refund for your rental car.

The main road in Lāna'i, Route 440, refers to both Kaumalapau Highway and Mānele Road. On the Islands, the directions *mauka* (toward the mountains) and *makai* (toward the ocean) are often used.

LĀNA'I CITY, GARDEN OF THE GODS & MĀNELE BAY

Pineapples once blanketed the Pālāwai, the great basin south of Lāna'i City. Before that it was a vast dryland forest; now most of it is fenced-in pasture or a game-bird reserve, and can only be viewed from the Mānele Road. Although it looks like a volcanic crater, it isn't. Some say that the name Pālāwai is descriptive of the mist that sometimes fills the basin at dawn and looks like a huge shining lake.

The area northwest of Lāna'i City is wild; the Garden of the Gods is one of its highlights.

MAIN ATTRACTIONS

❺ **Garden of the Gods.** This preternatural plateau is scattered with boulders of different sizes, shapes, and colors, the products of a million years of wind erosion. Time your visit for sunset, when the rocks begin to glow—from rich red to purple—and the fiery globe sinks to the horizon. Magnificent views of the Pacific Ocean, Moloka'i, and, on clear days, O'ahu provide the perfect backdrop for photographs.

FodorśChoice
★

The ancient Hawaiians shunned Lāna'i for hundreds of years, believing the island was the inviolable home of spirits. Standing beside the oxide-red rock spires of this strange, raw landscape, you might be tempted to believe the same. This lunar savannah still has a decidedly eerie edge; but the shadows disappearing on the horizon are those of Mouflon sheep and axis deer, not the fearsome spirits of lore. According to tradition, the spirits were vanquished by Kā'ulula'au, a chief's son from Maui who was exiled here for destroying his father's prized breadfruit groves. The clever boy outwitted and exhausted the spirits, and announced their banishment with a giant bonfire. ✉*From Stables at Kō'ele, follow dirt road through pasture, turn right at crossroad marked by carved boulder, head through abandoned fields and iron-wood forest to open red-dirt area marked by a carved boulder.*

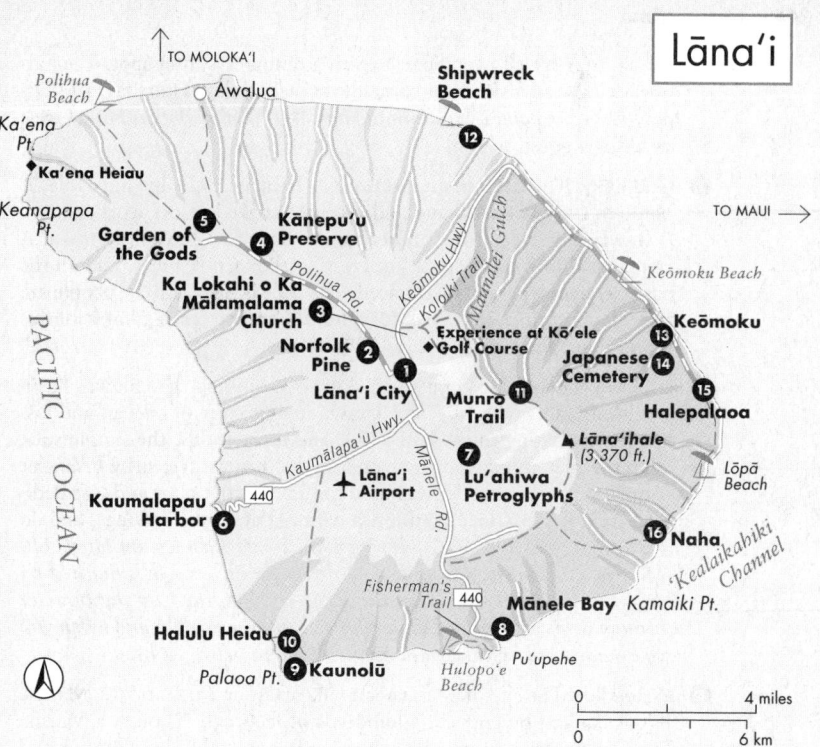

Lāna'i

TO MOLOKA'I
Polihua Beach
Awalua
Shipwreck Beach
Ka'ena Pt.
Ka'ena Heiau
Keanapapa Pt.
Garden of the Gods ❺
Kānepu'u Preserve ❹
Polihua Rd.
Ka Lokahi o Ka Mālamalama Church ❸
Norfolk Pine ❷
Lāna'i City ❶
Kaumālapa'u Hwy.
Lāna'i Airport
Kaumalapau Harbor ❻
440
Halulu Heiau ❿
Palaoa Pt.
Kaunolū ❾
Hulopo'e Beach
PACIFIC OCEAN
Keōmoku Hwy.
Maunalei Gulch
Kōloiki Trail
Experience at Kō'ele ◆Golf Course
Keōmoku Beach
Keōmoku ⓭
Japanese Cemetery ⓮
Halepalaoa ⓯
Munro Trail ⓫
Lāna'ihale (3,370 ft.)
Lu'ahiwa Petroglyphs ❼
Mānele Rd.
Lōpā Beach
Naha ⓰
'Kealaikahiki Channel
TO MAUI →
Fisherman's Trail 440
Mānele Bay ⑧ Kamaiki Pt.
Pu'upehe
0   4 miles
0   6 km

❸ **Ka Lokahi o Ka Mālamalama Church.** This picturesque church was built in 1938 to provide services for Lāna'i's growing population—for many people, the only other Hawaiian church, in coastal Keōmuku, was too far away. A classic structure of preplantation days, the church had to be moved from its original Lāna'i Ranch location when the Lodge at Kō'ele was built. Sunday services are still held, in Hawaiian and English; visitors are welcome, but are requested to attend quietly. ⊠*Left of entrance to Lodge at Kō'ele.*

❹ **Kānepu'u Preserve.** Kānepu'u is the largest example of a rare native dryland forest dominated by Hawaiian sandalwood, olive, and ebony trees. Thanks to a partnership between the Nature Conservancy of Hawai'i and landowners Castle & Cooke Resorts, the 590-acre remnant forest is protected from the hungry axis deer and Mouflon sheep that have nibbled the landscape beyond its fence to a barren moonscape. More than 45 native plant species, including *na'u*, the endangered Hawaiian gardenia, can be seen here. A short self-guided loop trail, with eight signs illustrated by local artist Wendell Kaho'ohalahala, reveals this ecosystem's beauty and the challenges it faces. ⊠*Polihua Rd., 6 mi north of Lāna'i City.*

❻ **Kaumalapau Harbor.** Built in 1926 by the Hawaiian Pineapple Company, which later became Dole, this is Lāna'i's principal seaport. The cliffs that flank the western shore are as much as 1,000 feet tall. Water activities aren't allowed here, but it's a dramatic sunset spot. The harbor is closed to visitors on barge days: Wednesday, Thursday, and Friday. ⊠ *From Lāna'i City follow Hwy. 440 (Kaumalapau Hwy.) west as far as it goes.*

❶ Lāna'i City. This tidy plantation town, built in 1924 by Jim Dole, is home to old-time residents and recently arrived resort workers, and is slowly changing from a quiet rural village to a busy little town. A simple grid of roads here is lined with stately Cook pines, and all the basic services a person might need. The pace is slow and the people are friendly. Visit the **Lāna'i Arts & Cultural Center** to get a glimpse of this island's creative abundance. ⊠ *339 7th Ave..*

❼ Lu'ahiwa Petroglyphs. On a steep slope overlooking the Pālāwai Basin are 34 boulders with carvings. Drawn in a mixture of ancient and historic styles dating to the late 1700s and early 1800s, the simple stick figures depict animals, people, and mythic beings. A nearby *heiau*, or temple, no longer visible, was used to summon the rains and was dedicated to the god Kāne. Do not draw on or deface the carvings, and do not add to the collection. ⊠ *From Lāna'i City turn left on Hwy. 440 (Mānele Rd.) and continue to first dirt road on your left, marked by large carved boulder and sign. Follow road marked by the boulder through fields; do not go left uphill but continue straight and when you see boulders on hillside, park and walk up to petroglyphs.*

❽ Mānele Bay. The site of a Hawaiian village dating from AD 900, Mānele Bay is flanked by lava cliffs hundreds of feet high. Though a Marine Life Conservation District, it's the island's only public boat harbor and was the location of most post-contact shipping until Kaumalapau Harbor was built in 1926. The ferry to and from Maui also pulls in here. Public restrooms, water, and picnic tables make it a nice pit stop—you can watch the boating activity as you rest and refuel.

Just offshore you can catch a glimpse of **Pu'upehe.** Often called Sweetheart Rock, the isolated 80-foot-high islet carries a sad Hawaiian legend that is probably not true. The rock is said to be named after Pehe, a woman so beautiful that her husband, afraid that others would steal her away, kept her hidden in a sea cave. One day, while Pehe was alone, the surf surged into the cave and she drowned. Her grief-stricken husband buried her on the summit of this rock and then jumped to his own death. A more authentic, if less romantic, story is that the enclosure on the summit is a shrine to birds, built by bird-catchers. Archaeological investigation has revealed that the enclosure was not a burial place. ⊠ *From Lāna'i City follow Hwy. 440 (Mānele Rd.) south to bottom of hill and look for harbor on your left.*

ALSO WORTH SEEING

❿ Halulu Heiau. The well-preserved remains of an impressive *heiau* at Kaunolu village, which was actively used by Lāna'i's earliest residents, attest to this spot's sacred history. As late as 1810, this hilltop temple was considered a place of refuge, where those who had broken *kapu* (taboos) were forgiven and where women and children could find safety in times of war. If you explore the area, be very respectful, take nothing with you and leave nothing behind. This place is hard to find, so get someone to mark a map for you. The road is alternately rocky, sandy, and soft at the bottom. ⊠*From Lāna'i City follow Hwy. 440 west toward Kaumalapau Harbor. Pass airport, then look for carved boulder on hill on your left. Turn left on dirt road, follow it to another carved boulder, then head downhill.*

❾ **Kaunolū.** Close to the island's highest cliffs, Kaunolū was once a prosperous fishing village. This important archaeological site includes a major *heiau*, terraces, stone floors, and house platforms. The impressive 90-foot drop to the ocean through a gap in the lava rock is called **Kahekili's Leap.** Warriors would make the dangerous jump into the shallow 12 feet of water below to show their courage. The road is very rocky then gets sandy at the bottom. ⊠*From Lāna'i City follow Hwy. 440 (Kaumalapau Hwy.) west past the airport turnoff; at carved boulder on hill, turn left onto Kaupili, an unmarked dirt road; continue until you reach the second carved boulder and then head makai (toward the ocean) 3 mi to village.*

❷ **Norfolk Pine.** More than 100 feet high, this majestic pine tree was planted here, at the former site of the manager's house, in 1875. Almost 30 years later, George Munro, then the ranch manager, would observe how, in foggy weather, water collected on its foliage, forming a natural rain. This fog drip led Munro to supervise the planting of Cook pines along the ridge of Lāna'ihale and throughout the town in order to add to the island's water supply. ⊠*Entrance of Lodge at Kō'ele.*

WINDWARD LĀNA'I

The eastern section of Lāna'i is wild and untouched. An inaccessible *heiau*, or temple, is the only trace of human habitation, with the exception of stacks of rocks marking old shrines, and trails. Four-wheel drive is a must to explore this side of the isle, and be prepared for hot, rough conditions. Pack a picnic lunch and bring plenty of drinking water.

MAIN ATTRACTIONS

★ **⓫** **Munro Trail.** This 9-mi jeep trail along a fern- and pine-clad narrow ridge was named after George Munro, manager of the Lāna'i Ranch Co., who began a reforestation program in the 1950s to restore the island's much-needed watershed. The trail climbs **Lāna'ihale** (House of Lāna'i), which, at 3,370 feet, is the island's highest point; on clear days you'll be treated to a panorama of canyons and almost all of the Hawaiian Islands. ■TIP➔**The one-way road gets very muddy, and trade winds can be strong. A sheer drop-off in some sections requires an attentive driver. Keep an eye out for hikers along the way.** You can also hike the Munro Trail (⇨ *Hiking later in this chapter*), though it's a difficult trek: it's steep, the ground is uneven, and there's no water. ⊠*From Lodge at Kō'ele head north on Keōmuku Hwy. for 1¼ mi, then turn right onto dirt road; trailhead is ½ mi past cemetery on right.*

★ **⓬** **Shipwreck Beach.** The rusting World War II tanker off this 8-mi stretch of sand adds just the right touch to an already photogenic beach.

Maui is visible in the distance, and Moloka'i lies just across beautiful but unrelenting Kalohi Channel. Strong trade winds have propelled innocent vessels onto the reef since at least 1824, when the first shipwreck was recorded. Some believe that the unknown Navy oiler you see stranded today, however, was intentionally scuttled. To see petroglyphs of warriors and dogs decorating dark-red boulders, follow the painted rocks and signs at the end of the road south about 200 yards. ■ TIP→ The water is unsafe for swimming; stick to beachcombing. ⊠ *End of Keōmuku Hwy. heading north.*

ALSO WORTH SEEING

⓯ Halepalaoa. Named for the whale bones that once washed ashore here, Haleapalaoa, or house of whale ivory, was the site of the wharf used by the short-lived Maunalei Sugar Company to ship cane in 1899. Some say the sugar company failed because the sacred stones of nearby **Kahe'a Heiau** were used for the construction of the cane railroad. Angry gods turned the drinking water salty, forcing the sugar company to close after just two years in 1901. The remains of the *heiau,* once an important place of worship for the people of Lāna'i, are now hard to find through the *kiawe* (mesquite) overgrowth. There's good public beach access here and clear shallow water for swimming, but no other facilities. ⊠ *6½ mi southeast from where Keōmuku Hwy. dead-ends at Shipwreck Beach, on dirt road running along north shore.*

⓮ Japanese Cemetery. In 1899 sugar came to this side of Lāna'i. A plantation took up about 2,400 acres and seemed a profitable proposition, but that same year, disease wiped out the labor force. This authentic Buddhist shrine commemorates the Japanese workers who died. ⊠ *6½ mi southeast from where Keōmuku Hwy. dead-ends at Shipwreck Beach, on dirt road running along north shore.*

⓭ Keōmuku. There's an eerie beauty about Keōmuku, with its faded memories and forgotten homesteads. During the late 19th century, this busy Lāna'i community of some 900 to 2,000 residents served as the headquarters of Maunalei Sugar Company. After the company failed, the land was used for ranching, but by 1954 the area lay abandoned. Its church, **Ka Lanakila O Ka Mālamalama,** was built in 1903. It has been partially restored by volunteers, and visitors often leave some small token, a shell or faded lei, as an offering. ⊠ *5 mi along unpaved road southeast of Shipwreck Beach.*

⓰ Naha. An ancient rock-walled fishpond—visible at low tide—lies here, where the sandy shorelines end and the cliffs begin their rise along the island's shores. The beach is a frequent resource for local fisherfolk. ■ TIP→ Treacherous currents make this a dangerous place for swimming. ⊠ *East side of Lāna'i, at end of dirt road that runs from end of Keōmuku Hwy. along eastern shore.*

BEACHES

Lāna'i offers miles of secluded white-sand beaches on its windward side, and the moderately developed Hulopo'e Beach, which is adjacent to the Four Seasons Resort Lāna'i at Mānele Bay. Hulopo'e is accessible by car or hotel shuttle bus; to reach the windward beaches you'll need a four-wheel-drive vehicle. Offshore reef, rocks, and coral make swimming on the windward side problematic, but it's fun to splash around in the shallow water. Driving on the beach itself is illegal and can be dangerous. Beaches in this chapter are listed alphabetically.

THE COASTAL ROAD

Road conditions can change overnight and become impassable due to rain in the uplands. Car-rental agencies should be able to give you updates before you hit the road. Many of the spur roads leading to the windward beaches from the coastal dirt road cross private property and are closed off by chains. Look for open spur roads with recent tire marks (a fairly good sign that they are safe to drive on). It's best to park on firm ground and walk in to avoid getting your car mired in the sand.

Fodor'sChoice **Hulopo'e Beach.** A short stroll from the Four Seasons Resort Lāna'i at
★ Mānele Bay, Hulopo'e is considered one of the best beaches in all of Hawai'i. The sparkling crescent of this Marine Life Conservation District beckons with calm waters safe for swimming almost year-round, great snorkeling reefs, tide pools, and, sometimes, spinner dolphins. A shady, grassy beach park is perfect for picnics. If the shore break is pounding, or if you see surfers riding big waves, stay out of the water. In the afternoons, watch Lāna'i High School students heave outrigger canoes down the steep shorebreak and race one another just offshore. ✉️ *From Lāna'i City follow Hwy. 440 (Mānele Rd.) south to bottom of hill; turn right, road dead-ends at beach's parking lot* ☞ *Toilets, showers, picnic tables, grills, parking lot.*

Lōpā Beach. A popular surfing spot for locals, Lōpā is also an ancient fishpond. With majestic views of West Maui and Kaho'olawe, this remote, white-sand beach is a great place for a picnic. ⚠️**Don't let the sight of surfers fool you: the channel's currents are too strong for swimming.** ✉️ *East side of Lāna'i, 7 mi south down a dirt road that runs from end of Keōmuku Hwy. along eastern shore* ☞ *No facilities.*

★ **Polihua Beach.** This often-deserted beach gets a star for beauty with its long, wide stretch of white sand and clear views of Moloka'i. The dirt road to get here can be bad with deep, sandy places (when it rains it's impassable), however, and frequent high winds whip up sand and waves. ■**TIP→**Strong currents and a sudden drop in the ocean floor make swimming dangerous. On the northern end, the beach ends at a rocky lava cliff with some interesting tide pools. Polihua is named after the sea turtles that lay their eggs in the sand. Do not drive on the beach and endanger their nests. Curiously, wild bees sometimes gather around your car for water at this beach. To get rid of them, put out water some place away from the car and wait a bit. ⊠ *Windward Lāna'i, 11 mi from Lāna'i City, past Garden of the Gods* ☞ *No facilities.*

Shipwreck Beach. Beachcombers come to this fairly accessible beach for shells and washed-up treasures; photographers for great shots of Moloka'i, just across the 9-mi-wide Kalohi Channel; and walkers for the long stretch of sand. It may still be possible to find glass-ball fishing floats but more common is waterborne debris from the Moloka'i channel. Kaiolohia, its Hawaiian name, is a favorite local diving spot. ■ TIP → An offshore reef and rocks in the water mean that it's not for swimmers, though you can play in the shallow water on the shoreline. ⊠ *North shore, 10 mi north of Lāna'i City at end of Keōmuku Hwy.* ☞ *No facilities.*

WATER SPORTS & TOURS

BOAT TOURS & CHARTERS

Trilogy Oceansports Lāna'i. If you're staying in Lāna'i and want to play on the ocean, Trilogy is your outfitter.

A 2½-hour blue-water snorkeling and adventure rafting trip includes lessons, equipment, and a hot barbecue lunch at the Trilogy Pavilion when you return to Mānele harbor. Tours are offered Monday, Tuesday, Thursday, and Friday; costs are $95 for adults and $47 for kids 15 and under.

On Wednesday you can opt for a Snorkel and Sail on a large catamaran, departing at 11:15 AM. This trip is perfect if you want to spend your early morning over a leisurely breakfast. The three-hour sail includes the barbecue lunch and a cruise up the coast to a remote snorkel site. The tour costs $125 for adults, $62 for children.

Serious divers should go for Trilogy's two-tank dive; location depends on the weather. You must be certified, so don't forget your documentation. The $169 fee includes a light breakfast of cinnamon rolls and coffee. Beginners (minimum age 12) can try a one-tank introductory dive for $95. You'll wade into Hulopo'e Bay with an instructor at your side; actual dive time is 20 to 30 minutes. Certified divers can choose a 35- to 40-minute wade-in dive at Hulopo'e for $95.

If that's not enough, sign up for a blue-water dolphin watch, whale-watching sail, or a sunset cruise. You can book trips through your hotel concierge, but try online first, where discounts are often available. ☎ 888/628–4800 ⊕ *www.sailtrilogy.com.*

DEEP-SEA FISHING

Some of the best sportfishing grounds in Maui County are off the southwest shoreline of Lāna'i. Pry your eyes open and go deep-sea fishing in the early morning, with departures at 6 or 6:30 AM from Mānele Harbor. Console yourself with the knowledge that Maui fishers have to leave an hour earlier to get to the same prime locations. Peak seasons are spring and summer, although good catches have been landed year-round. Mahimahi, *ono* (which means delicious in Hawaiian), *'ahi,* and marlin are prized catches and preferred eating.

Fish-N-Chips. This 32-foot Hatteras Sport Fisher with tuna tower will get you to the fishing grounds in comfort, and Captain Jason will do everything except reel in the big one for you. Plan on trolling along the south coast for *ono* and around the point at Kaunolu for mahi or marlin. A trip to the offshore buoy often yields skipjack tuna or big *'ahi,* and the captain and crew are always open to a bit of bottom fishing. Fishing gear, sodas, and water are included. Let them know if you would like breakfast or lunch for an additional charge. A four-hour charter (six-passenger maximum) will set you back $625; each additional hour costs $110. You can keep up to a third of all fish caught. Shared charters on Sunday and Wednesday are $130 per person. Book with the concierge at your resort or call directly. ☏*808/565–7676.*

KAYAKING

Lāna'i's southeast coast offers leisurely paddling inside the windward reef. Curious sea turtles and friendly manta rays may tag along for company. There are miles of scenic coastline with deserted beaches on the inside reef to haul up on for an informal picnic. When the wind comes from the southwest, the windward coast is tranquil. Kayaking along the leeward cliffs is more demanding with rougher seas and strong currents. No kayaking is permitted in the Marine Conservation District at Hulopo'e Bay.

Early mornings tend to be calmer. The wind picks up as the day advances. Expect strong currents along all of the coasts. Experience on the water is advised, and knowing how to swim is essential. ■ TIP➔ **There's one major drawback to kayaking on Lāna'i: you'll have to travel with your own kayak or arrange for a Maui vendor to meet you on the island, as there are no kayak rentals or guides on Lāna'i.**

SCUBA DIVING

When you have a dive site such as Cathedrals—with eerie pinnacle formations and luminous caverns—it's no wonder that scuba-diving buffs consider exploring the waters off Lāna'i akin to having a religious experience.

Just outside of Hulop'oe Bay, the boat dive site **Cathedrals** was named the best cavern dive site in the Pacific by *Skin Diver* magazine. Shimmering light makes the many openings in the caves look like stained-glass windows. A current generally keeps the water crystal clear, even if it's turbid outside. In these unearthly chambers, large *ulua* and small reef shark add to the adventure. **Sergeant Major Reef,** off Kamaiki Point, is named for big schools of yellow- and black-striped *manini* (Sergeant Major fish) that turn the rocks silvery as they feed. The site is made up of three parallel lava ridges, a cave, and an archway, with rippled sand valleys between the ridges. Depths range 15 to 50 feet.

Trilogy *(see Boat Tours & Charters, above)* is the only company running boat dives from Lāna‘i.

SNORKELING

Snorkeling is the easiest ocean sport available on the island, requiring nothing but a snorkel, mask, fins, and good sense. Borrow equipment from your hotel or purchase some in Lāna‘i City if you didn't bring your own. Wait to enter the water until you are sure no big sets are coming; and observe the activity of locals on the beach. If little kids are playing in the shore break, it's usually safe to enter.

> ### HOW TO GET WET
>
> Never turn your back on the ocean seems easy advice to remember, but many forget it. Much to the amusement of water-smart locals, hundreds of visitors get smashed trying to wade in backwards through breaking waves, wearing fins, mask, and snorkel. Wading in facing the waves is equally dangerous, so always swim in past the breakers, and in the comparative calm put on your fins, then mask and snorkel.

Hulopo‘e Beach is an outstanding snorkeling destination. The bay is a State of Hawai‘i Marine Conservation District and no spearfishing or diving is allowed. Schools of *manini* feeding on the coral coat the rocks with flashing silver, and you can view *kala, uhu,* and *papio* in all their rainbow colors. As you wade in from the sandy beach, the best snorkeling is toward the left. Beware of rocks and surging waves. When the resident spinner dolphins are in the bay, it's courteous to watch them from the shore. If swimmers and snorkelers go out, the dolphins may leave and be deprived of their necessary resting place. Another wade-in snorkel spot is just beyond the break wall at **Mānele Small Boat Harbor.** Enter over the rocks just past the boat ramp. ■TIP→It's dangerous to enter if waves are breaking.

Book with Trilogy *(see Boat Tours & Charters, above)* for snorkel sails.

SURFING

Surfing the near-empty sets of waves on Lāna‘i can be truly enjoyable. Quality, not quantity, characterizes this isle's few breaks. Be considerate of the locals—surfing takes the place of megaplex theaters and pool halls here, serving as one of the island's few recreational luxuries.

Don't try to Hang Ten at **Hulop‘oe Bay** without watching the conditions for a while. When it "goes off," it's a tricky left-handed shore break that requires some skill. The southeast-facing breaks at **Lōpā Beach** are inviting for beginners. Give them a try during summer, when the swells roll in nice and easy.

Lāna‘i Surf School. Nick and his wife Nanea offer the only surf instruction and board rentals on the island. Sign up for their "4X4 Safari"—a four-hour adventure that includes hard- or soft-top boards, snacks, transportation to "secret spots," and plenty of local anecdotes. Experienced riders can rent short or longboards overnight for $58 with a $125 deposit. ☎808/306–9837 ⊕ *www.lanaisurfsafari.com.*

GOLF, HIKING & OUTDOOR ACTIVITIES

BIKING

Many of the same red-dirt roads that invite hikers are excellent for biking, offering easy flat terrain and long clear views. There's only one hitch: you may have to bring your own bike, as there are no rentals or tours for non-resort guests available.

A favorite biking route is along the fairly flat red-dirt road northward from Lāna'i City through the old pineapple fields to Garden of the Gods. Start your trip on Keōmuku Highway in town. Take a left just before the Lodge's tennis courts, and then a right where the road ends at the fenced pasture, and continue on to the north end and the start of Polihua and Awalua dirt roads. If you're really hardy you could bike down to Polihua Beach and back, but it would be a serious all-day trip. In wet weather these roads turn to slurry and are not advisable. Go in the early morning or late afternoon because the sun gets hot in the middle of the day. Take plenty of water, spare parts, and snacks.

For the exceptionally fit, it's possible to bike from town down the Keōmuku Highway to the windward beaches and back, or to bike the Munro Trail (⇨ *see Hiking, below).* Experienced bikers also bike up and down the Mānele Highway from Mānele Bay to town.

CAMPING

Camping isn't encouraged outside Lāna'i's one official campground at Hulopo'e: the island is privately owned; islanders are keen on privacy; and, unless you know about local conditions, camping on the beach can be hazardous.

Fodor'sChoice **Castle & Cooke Resorts Campground.** The inviting, grassy campground at
★ Hulopo'e Beach has shade trees, clean restrooms, BBQ grills, beachside showers, and a big grass lawn, perfect for Frisbee. All of that *and* it happens to be a stone's throw from one of the best beaches in the state. (Camping on the beach itself is reserved for residents only.) Buy charcoal in Lāna'i City, as well as basic camping supplies and food. Cutting firewood is not allowed. It is possible to walk from Mānele Harbor to the campground. Call in advance; it's $20 for a permit, plus a $5 fee per person per night (three-night limit). ☎808/565–3975 *for permits and advance reservations.*

GOLF

Lāna'i has just three courses and a total of 45 holes (not counting an 18-hole putting course), but all three are good and offer very different environments and challenges. The two resort courses, especially, are so different, it's hard to believe they're on the same island, let alone just 20 minutes apart by resort shuttle.

Cavendish Golf Course. At this unique nine-holer, there's no phone, no clubhouse, no starter, just a slotted wooden box on the first tee requesting a monetary donation—go ahead, be generous!—to help with maintenance costs. The course is a legacy of the plantation era, designed in 1947 by E. B. Cavendish, superintendent of factory guards, and is used by locals for Sunday tournaments and popular skins games. Holes run through chutes of stately Norfolk pines, and most greens are elevated. ⊠ *Call Lodge at Kō'ele for directions* ☎ *Box 862, Lāna'i City 96763* 🏌 *9 holes. 3,071 yds. Par 36. Green Fee: Donation* ☞ *No facilities.*

The Challenge at Mānele. Designed by Jack Nicklaus (1993), this course sits right over the water of Hulopo'e Bay. Built on lava outcroppings, the course features three holes on cliffs that use the Pacific Ocean as a water hazard. The five-tee concept challenges the best golfers—tee shots over natural gorges and ravines must be precise. This unspoiled natural terrain is a stunning backdrop, and every hole offers ocean views. ⊠ *1 Challenge Dr., Lāna'i City* ☎ *808/565–2222* ⊕ *www.go-lanai.com* 🏌 *18 holes. 6,310 yds. Par 72, slope 126. Green Fee: hotel guests $190, non-guests $225* ☞ *Facilities: Driving range, putting green, golf carts, rental clubs, pro shop, lessons, restaurant, bar.*

The Experience at Ko'ele. This challenging Greg Norman (1991) layout begins at an elevation of 2,000 feet. The front nine moves dramatically through ravines wooded with pine, koa, and eucalyptus trees; seven lakes and streams with cascading waterfalls dot the course. No other course in Hawai'i offers a more incredible combination of highland terrain, inspired landscape architecture, and range of play challenges. ⊠ *Kaimuko Dr., Lāna'i City* ☎ *808/565–4653* ⊕ *www.go-lanai.com* 🏌 *18 holes. 6,310 yds. Par 72, slope 134. Green Fee: hotel guests $190, non-guests $225* ☞ *Facilities: Driving range, putting green, golf carts, rental clubs, pro shop, lessons, restaurant, bar.*

HIKING

Only 30 mi of Lāna'i's roads are paved. But red-dirt roads and trails, ideal for hiking, will take you to sweeping overlooks, isolated beaches, and shady forests. Don't be afraid to leave the road to follow deer trails, but make sure to keep your landmarks in clear sight so you can always retrace your steps. Or take a self-guided walk through Kāne Pu'u, Hawai'i's largest native dryland forest. You can explore the Munro Trail over Lāna'ihale with views of plunging canyons, or hike along an old, coastal fisherman trail or across Koloiki Ridge. Wear hiking shoes, a hat, and sunscreen, and carry plenty of water.

BEST SPOTS

Koloiki Ridge. This marked, moderate trail starts behind the Lodge at Kōʻele and takes you along the cool and shady Munro Trail to overlook the windward side, with impressive views of Maui, Molokaʻi, Maunalei Valley, and Naio Gulch. The average time for the 5-mi round-trip is three hours. Bring snacks and water, and take your time.

Lānaʻi Fisherman Trail. Local fishermen still use the Lānaʻi Fisherman Trail to get to their favorite fishing spots. The trail takes about 1½ hours to hike and follows the rocky shoreline below the Four Seasons Resort at Lānaʻi Mānele Bay, along cliffs bordering the golf course. Caves and tide pools beckon beneath you, but be careful climbing down. The marked trail entrance begins at the west end of Hulopoʻe Beach. Keep your eyes open for spinner dolphins cavorting offshore and the silvery flash of fish feeding in the pools below you. The condition of the trail varies with weather and frequency of maintenance.

Munro Trail. This is the real thing: a strenuous 9-mi trek that begins behind the Lodge and follows the ridge of Lānaʻihale through the rain forest. The island's most demanding hike, it has an elevation gain of 1,400 feet and leads to a lookout at the island's highest point, Lānaʻihale. It's also a narrow dirt road; watch out for careening jeeps. The trail is named after George Munro, who supervised the planting of Cook pine trees and eucalyptus wind breaks. Mules used to wend their way up the mountain carrying the pine seedlings. Unless you arrange for someone to pick you up at the trail's end, you have a long boring hike back through the Palawai Basin to return to your starting point. The top is often cloud-shrouded and can be windy and muddy, so check conditions before you start.

Puʻu Pehe Trail. Beginning to the left (facing the ocean) of Hulopoʻe Beach, this trail travels a short distance around the coastline, and then climbs up a sharp, rocky rise. At the top, you're level with the offshore stack of Puʻu Pehe and can overlook miles of coastline in both directions. The trail is not difficult, but it's hot and steep. ⚠ **Never go next to the edge, as the cliff can easily give way.** The hiking is best in the early morning or late afternoon, and it's a perfect place to look for whales in season (December–April). Wear shoes; this is not a hike for sandals or slip-ons.

HORSEBACK RIDING

Stables at Kōʻele. The subtle beauty of the high country slowly reveals itself to horseback riders. Sunset rides, private saunters, and two-hour adventures traverse leafy trails with scenic overlooks. There's a fancy horse-drawn carriage for romantic couples and well-trained horses for riders of all ages and skill levels. Prices start at $85 for one hour and climb to $150 for a two-hour private ride. Book rides at the Lodge at Kōʻele. ☎808/565–4424.

SPORTING CLAYS & ARCHERY

★ **Lānaʻi Pine Sporting Clays and Archery Range.** Outstanding rustic terrain, challenging targets, and a well-stocked pro shop make this sporting-clays course top-flight in the expert's eyes. Sharpshooters can complete the meandering 14-station course, with the help of a golf cart, in 1½ hours. There are group tournaments, and even kids can enjoy skilled instruction at the archery range and compressed air-rifle gallery. The $45 archery introduction includes an amusing "pineapple challenge"—contestants are given five arrows with which to hit a pineapple target. The winner takes home a crystal pineapple as a nostalgic souvenir of the old Dole Plantation days. Guns and ammunition are provided with the lessons. ⊠ *Just past Cemetery Rd. on windward side of island, first left off Keōmuku Hwy.* ☎ *808/559–4600.*

SHOPPING

A miniforest of Cook pine trees in the center of Lānaʻi City surrounded by small shops and restaurants, Dole Park is the closest thing to a mall on Lānaʻi. Except for the high-end resort boutiques and pro shops, it provides the island's only shopping. A morning or afternoon stroll around the park offers an eclectic selection of gifts and clothing, plus a chance to chat with residents. Friendly general stores are straight out of the 1920s, and new galleries and a boutique have original art and fashions for men, women, and children. The shops close on Sunday and after 5 PM, except for the general stores, which are open a bit later.

GENERAL STORES

International Food and Clothing Center. You may not find everything the name implies, but this old-fashioned emporium does stock items for your everyday needs, from fishing gear to beer. It's a good place for last-minute camping supplies. ⊠ *833 ʻIlima Ave., Lānaʻi City* ☎ *808/565–6433.*

Lānaʻi City Service. In addition to being a gas station, auto-parts store, and car-rental operation, this outfit sells Hawaiian gift items, sundries, T-shirts, beer, sodas, and bottled water in the **Plantation Store.** Open 7 to 7 daily for gas and sundries; auto-parts store open weekdays 7 AM to 4 PM. ⊠ *1036 Lānaʻi Ave., Lānaʻi City* ☎ *808/565–7227.*

Pine Isle Market. This is one of Lānaʻi City's two supermarkets, stocking everything from cosmetics to canned vegetables. It's a great place to buy fresh fish. Look at the photos of famous local fish and fishermen over the beer case. Closed Sunday and during lunch hours from noon to 1:30 PM. ⊠ *356 8th St., Lānaʻi City* ☎ *808/565–6488.*

Richard's Shopping Center. Richard Tamashiro founded this store in 1946, and the Tamashiro clan continues to run the place. Along with groceries, the store has a fun selection of Lānaʻi T-shirts. Richard's has a good selection of what they call "almost" fine wines, and a few gourmet food items. ⊠ *434 8th St., Lānaʻi City* ☎ *808/565–6047.*

Sergio's Oriental Store. Sergio's, the closest thing to a Costco on Lāna'i, has Filipino sweets and pastries, case-loads of sodas, water, juices, family-size containers of condiments, and frozen fish and meat. Open 8 to 8 daily. ⊠ *831-D Houston St., Lāna'i City* ☎ *808/565–6900.*

SPECIALTY STORES

Dis 'n Dat. This tiny, jungle-green shop packs in thousands of art, gift, and jewelry items in a minuscule space enlivened by a glittering crystal ceiling. Fanciful garden ornaments, serene Buddhas, and Asian antiques add to the charm. ⊠ *418 8th St., Lāna'i City* ☎ *808/565–9170* ⊕ *www. suzieo.com.*

Gifts with Aloha. Casual resort wear is sold alongside a great collection of Hawaiiana books and the work of local artists, including ceramic ware, *raku* (Japanese-style lead-glazed pottery), fine handblown glass, and watercolor prints. Look for a complete selection of Hawaiian music CDs and Lāna'i-designed Stone Shack shirts. ⊠ *363 7th St., Lāna'i City* ☎ *808/565–6589.*

Jordanne Fine Art Studio. Take a piece of historic Lāna'i home: Jordanne Weinstein's affordable, whimsical portraits of rural island life and soy candles decorated with gold-leaf pineapples make terrific souvenirs. Stop into her bright studio just off of Dole Park, where she paints on-site. ⊠ *850 Fraser St., Lāna'i City* ☎ *808/563–0088.*

Lāna'i Arts and Cultural Center. Local artists practice and display their crafts at this dynamic center. Workshops in the pottery, photography, woodworking, and painting studios welcome visitors, and individual instruction may be arranged. The center's gift shop sells original art and unique Lāna'i handicrafts. The art center sponsors a monthly movie night outdoors in Dole Park. Check the center's Web site for schedule. Closed Sunday and Monday. ⊠ *337 7th Ave., Lāna'i City* ☎ *808/565–7503* ⊕ *www.lanaiart.org.*

Local Gentry. This tiny, classy store has clothing for every need, from casual men's and women's beachwear to evening resort wear, shoes, jewelry, and hats. A small selection of fashionable children's apparel is also available. Proprietor Jenna Gentry will mail your purchases for the cost of the postage. ⊠ *363 7th St., Lāna'i City* ☎ *808/565–9130.*

Mike Carrol Gallery. The dreamy, soft-focus oil paintings of resident painter Mike Carroll are showcased along with wood bowls, and koa 'ukulele by Warren Osako, and fish-print paper tapestries by Joana Varawa. Local photographer Ron Gingerich, island artist Cheryl McElfresh, and jeweler Susan Hunter are also featured. ⊠ *443 7th St., Lāna'i City* ☎ *808/565–7122.*

SPAS

If you're looking for rejuvenation, the whole island could be considered a spa, though the only spa facilities are at the Mānele Bay Hotel or the Health Center at the Lodge at Kō'ele. For a quick polish in town, try one of the following local spots. **Island Images** (☎ *808/565–7870*) offers haircuts, waxing, and eyebrow shaping with threads (an ancient technique). **Highlights** (☎ 808/565–7207) offers hair, nails, and makeup services. **Nita's In Style** (☎ 808/565–8082) features hair-care services.

Lodge at Kō'ele's Healing Arts Center. Adjacent to the Lodge's pool and Jacuzzis, this bright, modest center provides cardiovascular equipment and free weights. Pump iron and watch yourself in the floor-to-ceiling mirrors or look out at the formal gardens and majestic trees. A single massage room offers specialty treatments and massages. ⊠ *Lodge at Kō'ele* ☎ *808/565–7300* ⊕ *www.fourseasons.com/manelebay* ☞ *$145 50-minute massage. Gym with: cardiovascular machines, free weights. Services: aromatherapy, body wraps, hot-rock massage, facials, chemical peel, lash and brow tinting, herbal-therapy consulting. Classes and programs: yoga.*

The Spa at Mānele. State-of-the-art pampering enlists a panoply of oils and unguents that would have pleased Cleopatra. The Spa After Hours Experience relaxes you in private services including a neck and shoulder massage and a 50-minute treatment of your choice. Then melt down in the sauna or steam room, finish off with a scalp massage and light *pūpū* (snacks), and ooze out to your room. The *Ali'i* banana-coconut scrub and pineapple-citrus polish treatments have inspired their own cosmetic line. Massages in private *hale* (houses) in the courtyard gardens are available for singles or couples. A tropical fantasy mural, granite stone floors, eucalyptus steam rooms, and private cabanas set the scene for indulgence. ⊠ *Four Seasons Resort Lāna'i at Mānele Bay* ☎ *808/565–2000* ⊕ *www.fourseasons.com/manelebay* ☞ *$145 50-minute massage; $340 per person 2-hour Spa After Hours Experience (2-person minimum). Gym with: cardiovascular equipment, free weights. Services: aromatherapy, reflexology, body wraps, facials, pedicures, hair salon, hair care, nails, waxing. Classes and programs: yoga, tai chi, aquaerobics, hula classes, guided hikes, personal training.*

ENTERTAINMENT & NIGHTLIFE

Lāna'i is certainly not known for its nightlife. Fewer than a handful of places stay open past 9 PM. At the resorts, excellent piano music or light live entertainment makes for a quiet, romantic evening. Another romantic alternative is star-watching from the beaches or watching the full moon rise in all its glory.

Four Seasons Resort Lāna'i at Mānele Bay. Hale Aheahe (House of Gentle Breezes), the classy open-air lounge, with upscale pūpū and complete bar, offers musical entertainment Tuesday through Saturday evenings from 5:30 to 9:30. Darts, pool, and shuffleboard competitions are riotous fun. There's a Saturday *keiki* (kids) hula show in the grand lobby at 2:30. ☎ 808/565–7700.

Hotel Lāna'i. A visit to the small, lively bar here is an opportunity to visit with locals. Last call is at 9. ☎ 808/565–7211.

Lāna'i Theater and Playhouse. This 153-seat, 1930s landmark presents first-run movies Friday through Tuesday, with showings at 6:30 and 8:30. This is also the venue that shows films from the Hawai'i Film Festival. ⊠ *465 7th Ave., Lāna'i City* ☎ *808/565-7500.*

Lodge at Kō'ele. The cozy cocktail bar stays open until 11 PM. The Lodge also features quiet piano music in its Great Hall every evening from 7 to 10, as well as special performances by well-known Hawaiian entertainers and local hula dancers. The Saturday afternoon *keiki* (kids) hula show is at 12:30. ☎ *808/565-7300.*

WHERE TO EAT

Lāna'i's own version of Hawai'i regional cuisine draws on the fresh bounty provided by local hunters and fishermen, combined with the skills of well-trained chefs. The upscale menus at the Lodge at Kō'ele and the Four Seasons Resort at Lāna'i Mānele Bay encompass European-inspired cuisine and innovative preparations of quail, 'ahi, wild deer, and boar. Lāna'i City's eclectic ethnic fare runs from construction-worker-size local plate lunches to Cajun ribs and pesto pasta. Keep in mind that Lāna'i "City" is really just a small town; restaurants sometimes choose to close the kitchen early.

WHAT IT COSTS					
	¢	$	$$	$$$	$$$$
RESTAURANTS	under $10	$10–$17	$18–$26	$27–$34	over $35

Prices are for one main course at dinner.

MĀNELE BAY

★ $$–$$$$ ✕ **'Ihilani.** The fine dining room at the Four Seasons Resort Lāna'i at Mānele Bay shimmers with crystal chandeliers and gleaming silver in a serene setting illuminated by floor-to-ceiling etched-glass doors. Executive chef Oliver Beckert offers an upscale version of Italian comfort food designed around fresh local fish. Puna goat-cheese ravioli with pine nuts and baby vegetables, and *onaga* (red snapper) served alla puttanesca, with artichoke puree, and a spicy tomato and caper sauce, are good choices. Service is nonintrusive but attentive. ⊠ *Four Seasons Resort Lāna'i at Mānele Bay* ☎ *808/565-2296* ⚲ *Reservations essential* ▤ *AE, DC, MC, V* ☉ *No lunch, Closed Sun. and Mon.*

$$–$$$$ ✕ **The Challenge at Mānele Clubhouse.** This terraced restaurant has a stunning view of the legendary Pu'u Pehe offshore island, which only enhances its imaginative fare. Tuck into a Hulop'e Bay prawn BLT, pan-seared *opakapaka*, or pad thai noodles with shrimp and crab in a macadamia-nut curry sauce. Specialty drinks add to the informal fun. ⊠ *Four Seasons Resort Lāna'i at Mānele Bay* ☎ *808/565-2290* ▤ *AE, DC, MC, V* ☉ *No dinner.*

$$–$$$$ ✕ **The Ocean Grill Bar & Restaurant.** Poolside at the Four Seasons Resort Lāna'i at Mānele Bay, the Ocean Grill offers informal lunch and din-

ner in a splendid setting. The big umbrellas are cool and cheerful, and bamboo-inspired uphol-stered chairs in yellow and green are deliciously comfortable. If you're a coffee drinker, a Kona Cappuccino Freeze by the pool is a must. Favorite lunch items include the *kālua* (pit-roasted) pork and cheese quesadilla, or the rare 'ahi tuna *salade Niçoise* with fresh island greens. The din-ner menu includes a combination of small and large plates that lean toward the healthy side. Try the wok-fried buckwheat noodles

> ## FOOD WITH A VIEW
>
> Don't miss a meal at the Chal-lenge at Mānele clubhouse, overlooking Hulopo'e Bay. Day or night, the view is spectacular. Palm trees frame a vista of the white-sand beach with the rocky headland of Pu'u Pehe (Sweet-heart Rock) punctuating the lu-minous sky. At night, with the full moon scattering sequins on the sea, it's enough to get you singing the whole score of *South Pacific*.

with plump Tiger shrimp or lemongrass steamed *onaga* (red snapper) served with a refreshing carrot-miso vinaigrette. The view of Hulopo'e Bay is stunning and the service is Four Seasons' brand of cool aloha. ⊠ *Four Seasons Resort Lāna'i at Mānele Bay* 🕾 *808/565–2000* ▤ *AE, DC, MC, V.*

$$–$$$ ✕ **Four Seasons Hulopo'e Court.** Hulopo'e Court offers an extensive break-fast buffet, lunch, and dinner in airy comfort. Retractable awnings shade the terrace, which overlooks the wide sweep of the bay. Indoors, comfy upholstered chairs, cream walls, stylish wood paneling, and modernized Hawaiian decor create an almost equally inviting back-drop. At breakfast, fresh baked pastries and made-to-order omelets ensure your day will start well. For dinner, the daily fish special, the baked Pacific prawns stuffed with Dungeness crab, or Kurobuta pork chops marinated in hoisin sauce with Lāna'i pineapple relish are all local favorites. The chocolate cake is perfect. ⊠ *Four Seasons Resort Lāna'i at Mānele Bay* 🕾 *808/565–2290* ⚭ *Reservations essential* ▤ *AE, DC, MC, V* ☻ *No lunch.*

UPCOUNTRY & LĀNA'I CITY

$$$$ ✕ **Formal Dining Room.** Reflecting the Lodge's country-manor elegance,
Fodor's Choice this romantic octagonal restaurant is one of the best in the state. Inti-
★ mate tables are clustered close to a roaring fireplace with room between for private conversation. Expanding on Hawai'i regional cuisine, the changing menu includes the signature rack of lamb (expertly done, with rosemary au jus and a slender potato croquette) and crispy seared *moi* (a fish once reserved for Hawaiian chiefs). Start with tiny roasted quail on baby greens and finish with a warm pear soufflé (ordered in advance). A master sommelier provides exclusive wine pairings and the service is flawless. ⊠ *Lodge at Kō'ele* ℗ *Box 631380, Lāna'i City 96763* 🕾 *808/565–7300* ⚭ *Reservations essential* Jacket required ▤ *AE, DC, MC, V* ☻ *No lunch.*

$–$$$ ✕ **Henry Clay's Rotisserie.** With the only bar and comparatively fine dining in Lāna'i City, this is a lively spot, right at the Hotel Lāna'i. Louisiana-style ribs, Cajun-style shrimp, and gumbo add up to what chef Henry Clay Richardson calls "American country," but he brings it back home with island venison and locally caught fish. A fireplace and paintings by local artists add to the upcountry feel. Large parties can be accommodated and are sometimes quite noisy. ⊠ *Hotel Lāna'i, 828 Lāna'i Ave., Lāna'i City* ☎ *808/565–4700* ⌂ *Reservations essential* ▭ *MC, V.*

$–$$$ ✕ **The Terrace.** Floor-to-ceiling glass doors open onto formal gardens and lovely vistas of the mist-clad mountains. Breakfast, lunch, and dinner are served in an informal atmosphere with attentive service. Try poached eggs on crab cakes to start the day and a free-range strip loin with pesto mashed potatoes to finish it. The soothing sounds of the grand piano in the Great Hall in the evening complete the ambience. ⊠ *Lodge at Kō'ele* ☎ *808/565–7300* ▭ *AE, DC, MC, V.*

$–$$ ✕ **The Experience at Ko'ele Clubhouse.** The clubhouse overlooks the emerald greens of the golf course. Sit inside and watch sports on the TV, or on the terrace to enjoy the antics of lumbering wild turkey families. The grilled fresh-catch sandwich is accompanied by fries; the succulent hamburgers are the best on the island. Salads and sandwiches, beer and wine, soft drinks, and some not very inspiring desserts complete the menu. ⊠ *Lodge at Kō'ele* ☎ *808/565–4605* ▭ *AE, DC, MC, V* ⊗ *No dinner.*

$–$$ ✕ **Pele's Other Garden.** Mark and Barbara Zigmond's colorful little eatery is a deli and bistro all in one. For lunch, deli sandwiches or daily hot specials reward an arduous hike. At night the restaurant turns into an intimate tablecloth-dining bistro, complete with soft jazz music. A nice wine list enhances an Italian-inspired menu. Start with bruschetta, then choose from a selection of pasta dishes or pizzas. ⊠ *811 Houston St., Lāna'i City* ☎ *808/565–9628 or 888/764–3354* ▭ *AE, DC, MC, V.*

¢–$ ✕ **Blue Ginger Café.** This cheery eatery is a Lāna'i City institution. Owners Joe and Georgia Abilay have made this place into one of the town's most popular hangouts with consistent, albeit simple, food. Locally inspired paintings and photos line the walls inside, while the town passes the outdoor tables in parade. For breakfast, try the Portuguese sausage omelet with rice or fresh pastries. Lunch selections range from burgers and pizza to Hawaiian staples such as *musubi* (fried Spam wrapped in rice and seaweed). Try a shrimp stir-fry for dinner. ⊠ *409 7th Ave., Lāna'i City* ☎ *808/565–6363* ▭ *No credit cards.*

¢–$ ✕ **565 Café.** Named after the only telephone prefix on Lāna'i, this is a convenient stop for anything from pizza to a Pālāwai chicken-breast sandwich on fresh-baked foccacia. Make a quick stop for plate lunches or try a picnic *pūpū* (appetizer) platter of chicken *katsu* to take along for the ride. If you need a helium balloon for a party, you can find that here, too. The patio and outdoor tables are kid-friendly, and an outdoor Saturday afternoon flea market adds to the quirkiness. ⊠ *408 8th St., Lāna'i City* ☎ *808/565–6622* ▭ *No credit cards* ⊗ *Closed Sun.*

¢ ✕ **Lāna'i Coffee.** A block off Dole Park, you can sit outside on the large deck, sip cappuccinos, and watch the slow-pace life of the town slip by. Bagels with lox, deli sandwiches, and pastries add to the caloric content, while blended espresso shakes and gourmet ice cream complete the old-world illusion. Caffeine-inspired specialty items make good gifts and souvenirs. ⊠604 'Ilima St., Lāna'i City ☎808/565–6962 ⊘ Closed Sun.

WHERE TO STAY

Though Lāna'i has few properties, it does have a range of price options. Four Seasons manages both the Lodge at Kō'ele and Four Seasons Resort Lāna'i at Mānele Bay. Although the room rates are different, guests can partake of all the resort amenities at both properties. If you're on a budget, seek out a bed-and-breakfast or consider the Hotel Lāna'i. House rentals, a great option for families, give you a feel for everyday life on the island. In hunting seasons, from mid-February through mid-May, and from mid-July through mid-October, most of the private properties are booked way in advance.

WHAT IT COSTS					
	¢	$	$$	$$$	$$$$
HOTELS	under $100	$100–$180	$181–$260	$261–$340	over $340

Hotel prices are for two people in a double room in high season, including tax and service. Condo price categories reflect studio and one-bedroom rates.

HOTELS & RESORTS

☾ $$$$ **Four Seasons Resort Lāna'i at Mānele Bay.** With the added benefits
Fodor'sChoice bestowed by Four Seasons management, this ornate resort overlooking
★ Hulopo'e Bay now ranks among the state's best. The architecture combines Mediterranean and Asian elements; elaborate life-size paintings of Chinese court officials, gold brocade warrior robes, and artifacts decorate the open-air lobbies. Courtyard gardens separate two-story guest-room buildings. Ground-floor rooms are best—opening right up onto a lawn overlooking Hulopo'e Beach—though spectacular coastline vantages are had just about anywhere on the property. Adults can indulge in Evian spritzes by the pool while *keiki* (children) hunt for crabs and play 'ukulele. Teens have their own cybercafé. At night, everyone can meet for shuffleboard and darts in Hale Ahe Ahe—the swank game room. A state-of-the-art fitness center overlooks the sea, and an adjacent movement studio offers daily classes. ⌂ Box 631380, 1 Mānele Bay Rd., Lāna'i City 96763 ☎808/565–2000 or 800/321–4666 ☎808/565–2483 ⊕ www.fourseasons.com/manelebay ⟳215 rooms, 21 suites ⌂ In-room: safe, DVD, Ethernet. In-hotel: 3 restaurants, room service, bars, refrigerator, golf course, tennis courts, pool, gym, spa, children's programs (ages 5–13), laundry service, public Internet, no-smoking rooms, ☐ AE, DC, MC, V.

$$$–$$$$ **Lodge at Kō'ele.** In the highlands edging Lāna'i City, this grand coun-
Fodor'sChoice try estate, managed by Four Seasons, exudes luxury and quiet romance.
★ Secluded by old pines, 1½ mi of paths meander through formal gardens with a huge reflecting pond, a wedding gazebo, and an orchid greenhouse. Afternoon tea is served in front of the immense stone fireplaces

beneath the high-beamed ceilings of the magnificent Great Hall. The music room lounge is a relaxing haven after a day on the Lodge's golf course or sporting-clays range. A long veranda, furnished with wicker lounge chairs, looks out over rolling green pastures toward spectacular sunsets. ⌂*Box 631380, 1 Keōmuku Hwy., Lāna'i City 96763* ☎*808/565–7300 or 800/321–4666* 🖷*808/565–3868* ⊕*www.lodgeatkoele.com* 🖙*84 rooms, 12 suites* ⚟*In-room: safe, Ethernet. In-hotel: 2 restaurants, room service, bar, refrigerator, golf course, tennis courts, pool, gym, bicycles, children's programs (ages 5–12), laundry service, no-smoking rooms,* ▭*AE, DC, MC, V.*

$ 🖳**Hotel Lāna'i.** Built in 1923 to house visiting pineapple executives, this 10-room inn was once the only accommodation on the island. The recently refurbished plantation-inspired rooms, with country quilts, light pine woods, and local art, make it seem like you're staying in someone's home. Rooms with porches overlooking the pine trees and Lāna'i City are especially nice. The restaurant has a small bar. A self-serve continental breakfast with fresh-baked breads is served on the veranda and is included in the rate. ✉*828 Lāna'i Ave., Lāna'i City 96763* ☎*808/565–7211 or 800/795–7211* 🖷*808/565–6450* ⊕*www.hotellanai.com* 🖙*10 rooms, 1 cottage* ⚟*In-room: no a/c, no TV. In-hotel: restaurant, no-smoking rooms* ▭*AE, MC, V.*

CONDOS & VACATION RENTALS

All vacation rentals are in Lāna'i City, where altitude and prevailing trade winds replace air-conditioning. During hunting seasons, rentals are booked months—possibly years—in advance.

$ 🖳**Sheila Black.** A log-cabin cottage next to the Blacks' residence on "Haole Hill" is available as a vacation rental. This simply furnished, family-friendly, two-bedroom, two-bath cottage offers a fully equipped kitchen with all appliances, linens, pine trees, and country peace. It can accommodate up to seven, with extra beds in the living room ($15 extra per night per additional person over four). ✉*656 Pu'ulani Pl., 96763* ☎*808/565–6867* 🖷*808/565–7695* ✉ *adblack@aloha.net* 🖙*1 unit* ⚟*In-room: no a/c, kitchen. In-hotel: no-smoking rooms, no elevator* ▭*No credit cards.*

¢ 🖳**McOmber Enterprises.** Five different houses in Lāna'i City are available as short-term economy vacation rentals. They can accommodate two to eight persons. Kitchens are fully furnished and equipped, and linens are supplied. ⌂*Box 630646, 96763* ☎*808/565–6071* ✉ *mcomber@aloha.net* 🖙*5 houses* ⚟*In-room: no a/c, no phone, kitchen, no TV (some). In-hotel: laundry facilities, no-smoking rooms, no elevator* ▭*No credit cards.*

B&BS

$ 🖳**Dreams Come True.** Michael and Susan Hunter rent out a four-bedroom, four-bathroom plantation home in the heart of Lāna'i City, available in its entirety or as individual guest rooms. Antiques gleaned from many trips through South Asia add to the atmosphere. Some rooms have canopy beds, and each has its own marble bath with whirlpool tub. The living room has a TV and VCR, and the kitchen is available for guest use. There's also a veranda and garden. Enjoy the Hunters' company and gather information about the island each morning, when a home-cooked full breakfast becomes a special occasion. They will arrange vehicle rental and book activities, too. ✉ *1168 Lāna'i St., Lāna'i City 96763* ☎*808/565–6961 or 800/566–6961* 🖷*808/565–7056* ⊕*www.circumvista.com/dreamscometrue.html* ↩*3 rooms* ⚐*In-room: no a/c, no phone. In-hotel: laundry facilities, public Internet, no-smoking rooms, no elevator* ⊟*AE, D, MC, V.*

¢   ⌨**Hale Moe.** Momi Suzuki has turned her three-bedroom suburban home into a peaceful Japanese-inspired retreat. This serenely furnished B&B has a well-tended garden with expansive views of the distant ocean. There's a TV in the living room and a kitchen available for guest use. Help yourself to coffee and continental breakfast on the sunny deck. Momi will advise you on what to do; sometimes her jeep is available for rent. You can rent individual rooms or secure the three-bedroom, three-bath house for $300 a night with a limit of eight people. ⌂*Box 630196, 96763* ☎*808/565–9520* ⊕*staylanai.com* ↩*3 rooms* ⚐*In-room: no a/c, no phone (some), no TV (some). In-hotel: no-smoking rooms, no elevator* ⊟*No credit cards.*

LĀNA'I ESSENTIALS

TRANSPORTATION

BY AIR

You can reach Lāna'i from O'ahu's Honolulu International Airport via Island Air. Island Air offers several flights daily on 18-passenger Dash-6s and 37-seat Dash-8s; round-trip tickets start at $150. Royal Hawaiian Air Service has two daily flights to and from Honolulu. Traveling from other islands requires a stop in Honolulu and a transfer to Island Air; book through Aloha Airlines.

AIRPORT   The airport has a federal agricultural inspection station so that guests departing to the mainland can check luggage directly.

INFORMATION   **Lāna'i Airport** (☎*808/565–6757*).

TO & FROM   Lāna'i Airport is a 10-minute drive from Lāna'i City. If you're staying
THE AIRPORT   at the Hotel Lāna'i, the Lodge at Kō'ele, or the Four Seasons Resort Lāna'i at Mānele Bay, you'll be met by a shuttle, which serves as transportation between the resorts and Lāna'i City for the length of your stay (the fee is included in your room rate). See the resort receptionist at the airport. Dollar will pick you up if you're renting a car or jeep. Call from the red courtesy phone at the airport.

BY CAR

There are only 30 mi of paved road on the island. Keōmuku Highway starts just past the Lodge at Kō'ele and runs north to Shipwreck Beach. Mānele Road (Highway 440) runs south down to Mānele Bay

11

and Hulopo'e Beach. Kaumalapau Highway (also Highway 440) heads west to Kaumalapau Harbor. The rest of your driving takes place on bumpy, muddy, secondary roads, which generally aren't marked.

You'll never find yourself in a traffic jam, but it's easy to get lost on the unmarked dirt roads. Before heading out, ask for a map at your hotel desk. Always remember *mauka* (toward the mountain) and *makai* (toward the ocean) for basic directions. If you're traveling on dirt roads, take water. People still drive slowly, wave, and pull over to give each other lots of room. The only gas station on the island is in Lāna'i City, at Lāna'i City Service (open 7 to 7 daily).

CAR RENTAL Renting a four-wheel-drive vehicle is expensive but almost essential if you'd like to explore beyond the resorts and Lāna'i City. Make reservations far in advance of your trip, because Lāna'i's fleet of vehicles is limited. Lāna'i City Service, a subsidiary of Dollar Rent A Car, is open daily 7 to 7. Jeep Wranglers and minivans go for $139 a day, full-size cars are $80, and compact cars are about $60. Sometimes a better deal (with fewer restrictions on where you can drive) can be found by booking through B&B owners.

INFORMATION **Lāna'i City Service** (✉ *Lāna'i Ave. at 11th St.* ☎ *808/565–7227 or 800/533–7808*).

BY FERRY
Expeditions' ferries cross the channel five times daily, departing from Lahaina on Maui and Mānele Bay Harbor on Lāna'i. The crossing takes 45 minutes and costs $25 each way. Be warned: passage can be rough, especially during winter. On the flip side, you'll see plenty of whales along the way.

INFORMATION **Expeditions** (☎ *808/661–3756 or 800/695–2624* ⊕ *www.go-lanai.com*).

TO & FROM If you are staying at the Four Seasons Resort Lāna'i at Mānele Bay or THE HARBOR the Lodge at Kō'ele, transportation from the harbor is almost effortless; the resort staff accompanies you on the boat, and shuttles stand ready to deliver you and your belongings to either resort. If you aren't staying with the Four Seasons, it's pretty much the same drill—the bus drivers will herd you onto the appropriate bus and take you into town for $10 round-trip. Advance reservations aren't necessary (or even possible), but be prepared for a little confusion on the dock.

INFORMATION **Lāna'i City Service** (✉ *Lāna'i Ave. at 11th St.* ☎ *808/565–7227 or 800/533–7808*).

BY SHUTTLE
A shuttle transports hotel guests between the Hotel Lāna'i, the Lodge at Kō'ele, the Four Seasons Resort Lāna'i at Mānele Bay, and the airport. A $25 fee covers all transportation during the length of stay.

CONTACTS & RESOURCES

EMERGENCIES

In an emergency, dial **911** to reach an ambulance, the police, or the fire department. The Lāna'i Family Clinic, part of the Straub Clinic & Hospital, is the island's health-care center. It's open weekdays from 8 to 5 and closed on weekends. There's a limited pharmacy. In emergencies, call 911 or go to the emergency room of the hospital next door.

INFORMATION **Straub Clinic & Hospital** (⊠ *628 7th St., Lāna'i City* ☎ *808/565-6423 clinic, 808/565-6411 hospital).*

VISITOR INFORMATION

Lāna'i Visitor's Bureau is your best bet for general information and maps. Feel free to stop in at their office, next to the Post Office, between 8 AM and 4 PM. The Maui Visitors Bureau also has some information on the island.

INFORMATION **Lāna'i Visitor's Bureau** (⊠ *431 7th St., Suite A, Lāna'i City 96763* ☎ *808/565-7600)* .**Maui Visitors Bureau** (☎ *808/244-3530* ⊕ *www.visitlanai.com).*

UNDERSTANDING MAUI

HAWAI'I AT A GLANCE

FAST FACTS

Nickname: Aloha State
Capital: Honolulu
State song: "Hawai'i Pono'i"
State bird: The nēnē, an endangered land bird and variety of goose
State flower: Yellow Hibiscus Brackenridgii
State tree: Kukui (or candlenut), a Polynesian-introduced tree
Administrative divisions: There are four counties with mayors and councils: City and County of Honolulu (island of O'ahu), Hawai'i County (Hawai'i Island), Maui County (islands of Maui, Moloka'i, Lāna'i, and Kahoolawe), and Kaua'i County (islands of Kaua'i and Ni'ihau)
Entered the Union: August 21, 1959, as the 50th state
Population: 1,334,023
Life expectancy: Female 82, male 76
Literacy: 81%
Ethnic groups: Hawaiian/part Hawaiian 22.1%; Caucasian 20.5%; Japanese 18.3%; Filipino 12.3%; Chinese 4.1%
Religion: Roman Catholic 22%; Buddhist, Shinto, and other East Asian religions 15%; Mormon 10%; Church of Christ 8%; Assembly of God and Baptist 6% each; Episcopal, Jehovah's Witness, and Methodist 5% each
Language: English is the first language of the majority of residents; Hawaiian is the native language of the indigenous Hawaiian people and an official language of the state; other languages spoken include Samoan, Chinese, Japanese, Korean, Spanish, Portuguese, Filipino, and Vietnamese

The loveliest fleet of islands that lies anchored in any ocean.

—Mark Twain

GEOGRAPHY & ENVIRONMENT

Land area: An archipelago of 137 islands encompassing a land area of 6,422.6 square mi in the north-central Pacific Ocean (about 2,400 mi from the West Coast of the continental United States)
Coastline: 750 mi
Terrain: Volcanic mountains, tropical rain forests, verdant valleys, sea cliffs, canyons, deserts, coral reefs, sand dunes, sandy beaches
Natural resources: Dimension limestone, crushed stone, sand and gravel, gemstones
Natural hazards: Hurricanes, earthquakes, tsunamis
Flora: More than 2,500 species of native and introduced plants throughout the Islands.
Fauna: Native mammals include the hoary bat, Hawaiian monk seal, and Polynesian rat. The humpback whale migrates to Hawaiian waters every winter to mate and calve. More than 650 fish and 40 different species of shark live in Hawaiian waters. Freshwater streams are home to hundreds of native and alien species. The humuhumunukunukuāpua'a (Hawaiian triggerfish) is the unofficial state fish.
Environmental issues: Plant and animal species threatened and endangered due to hunting, overfishing, overgrazing by wild and introduced animals, and invasive alien plants

Hawai'i is not a state of mind, but a state of grace.

—Paul Theroux

ECONOMY

Tourism and federal defense spending continue to drive the state's economy. Efforts to diversify in the areas of science and technology, film and television production, sports, ocean research and development, health and education, agriculture, and floral and specialty food products are ongoing.

GSP: $40.1 billion
Per-capita income: $30,000
Inflation: 1%
Unemployment: 4.3%
Workforce: 595,450
Debt: $7.3 billion
Major industries: Tourism, federal government (defense and other agencies)
Agricultural products: Sugar, pineapple, papayas, guavas, flower and nursery products, asparagus, alfalfa hay, macadamia nuts, coffee, milk, cattle, eggs, shellfish, algae
Exports: $616 million
Major export products: Aircraft and parts, naphthas, medical equipment and supplies, fruit, steel scrap, electronic components, unleaded gasoline, artwork, cocoa, coffee, flowers, macadamia nuts
Imports: $2.6 billion
Major import products: Crude oil, electronic and digital equipment, coal, passenger motor vehicles

In what other land save this one is the commonest form of greeting not "Good day," or "How d'ye do," but "Love?" That greeting is "Aloha"— love, I love, my love to you ... It is a positive affirmation of the warmth of one's own heart, giving.

—Jack London

Debate has waxed and waned for more than a century over how and when to return to native Hawaiians more than 1 million acres of land and other assets seized when American business interests overthrew the island monarchy in 1893. Certain native factions still advocate a return to independent nationhood. Sovereignty gained new momentum in the 1990s with the passage of a federal law formally apologizing for the overthrow and urging reconciliation. Momentum has since fizzled. Hawai'i's current governor has renewed efforts to have Congress recognize Hawaiians as an indigenous people, much like Native Americans and Alaskans. The governor also has pledged to support continued funding of health care, language, and other cultural programs, and to achieve state and federal obligations to distribute homestead lands to qualified Hawaiians.

DID YOU KNOW?

■ Hawai'i is home to the world's most active volcano: Kīlauea, on the Big Island.

■ 'Iolani Palace had electricity and telephones installed several years before the White House, and is the only palace on U.S. soil.

■ Hawai'i has about 12% of all endangered plants and animals in the United States; 75% of the country's extinct plants and birds were Hawaiian.

■ The Royal Hawaiian Band is the only intact organization from the time of Hawaiian monarchy that is fully functional and still preserves Hawai'i's musical history.

THE ALOHA SHIRT: A COLORFUL SWATCH OF ISLAND HISTORY

Elvis Presley had an entire wardrobe of them in the 1960s films *Blue Hawai'i* and *Paradise, Hawaiian Style*. During the 1950s, entertainer Arthur Godfrey and bandleader Harry Owens often sported them on television shows. John Wayne loved to lounge around in them. Mick Jagger felt compelled to buy one on a visit to Hawai'i in the 1970s. Dustin Hoffman, Steven Spielberg, and Bill Cosby avidly collect them.

The roots of the aloha shirt go back to the early 1930s, when Hawai'i's garment industry was just beginning to develop its own unique style. Although locally made clothes did exist, they were almost exclusively for plantation workers and were constructed of durable palaka or plain cotton material.

Out of this came the first stirrings of fashion: beachboys and schoolchildren started having sport shirts made from colorful Japanese kimono fabric. The favored type of cloth was the kind used for children's kimonos—bright pink and orange floral prints for girls; masculine motifs in browns and blues for boys. In Japan, such flamboyant patterns were considered unsuitable for adult clothing, but in the Islands such rules didn't apply, and it seemed the flashier the shirt, the better—for either sex. Thus, the aloha shirt was born.

It was easy and inexpensive in those days to have garments tailored to order; the next step was moving to mass production and marketing. In June 1935 Honolulu's best-known tailoring establishment, Musa-Shiya, advertised the availability of "Aloha shirts—well tailored, beautiful designs and radiant colors. Ready-made or made to order ... 95¢ and up." This is the first known printed use of the term that would soon refer to an entire industry. By the following year, several local manufacturers had begun full-scale production of "aloha wear." One of them,

Ellery Chun of King-Smith, registered as local trademarks the terms "Aloha Sportswear" and "Aloha Shirt" in 1936 and 1937, respectively.

These early entrepreneurs were the first to create uniquely Hawaiian designs for fabric as well—splashy patterns that would forever symbolize the Islands. A 1939 *Honolulu Advertiser* story described them as a "delightful confusion [of] tropical fish and palm trees, Diamond Head and the Aloha Tower, surfboards and leis, 'ukuleles and Waikīkī beach scenes."

The aloha wear of the late 1930s was intended for—and mostly worn by—tourists, and interestingly, a great deal of it was exported to the mainland and even Europe and Australia. By the end of the decade, for example, only 5% of the output of one local firm, the Kamehameha Garment Company, was sold in Hawai'i.

World War II brought this trend to a halt, and during the postwar period aloha wear really came into its own in Hawai'i itself. A strong push to support local industry gradually nudged island garb into the workplace, and kama'āina began to wear the clothing that previously had been seen as attire for visitors.

In 1947, for example, male employees of the City and County of Honolulu were first allowed to wear aloha shirts "in plain shades" during the summer months. Later that year, the first observance of Aloha Week started the tradition of "bankers and bellhops ... mix[ing] colorfully in multihued and tapa-designed Aloha shirts every day," as a local newspaper's Sunday magazine supplement noted in 1948. By the 1960s, "Aloha Friday," set aside specifically for the wearing of aloha attire, had become a tradition. In the following decade the suit and tie practically disappeared as work attire in Hawai'i, even for executives.

Most of the Hawaiian-theme fabric used in manufacturing aloha wear was designed in the Islands, then printed on the mainland or in Japan. The glowingly vibrant rayons of the late '40s and early '50s (a period now seen as aloha wear's heyday) were at first printed on the East Coast, but manufacturers there usually required such large orders that local firms eventually found it impossible to continue using them. By 1964, 90% of Hawaiian fabric was being manufactured in Japan—a situation that still exists today.

Fashion trends usually move in cycles, and aloha wear is no exception. By the 1960s the "chop suey print" with its "tired clichés of Diamond Head, Aloha Tower, outrigger canoes [and] stereotyped leis" was seen as corny and garish, according to an article published in the *Honolulu Star-Bulletin*. But it was just that outdated aspect that began to appeal to the younger crowd, who began searching out old-fashioned aloha shirts at the Salvation Army and Goodwill thrift stores. These shirts were dubbed "silkies," a name by which they're still known, even though most of them were actually made of rayon.

Before long, what had been 50¢ shirts began escalating in price, and a customer who had balked at paying $5 for a shirt that someone had already worn soon found the same item selling for $10— and more. By the late 1970s, aloha-wear designers were copying the prints of yesteryear for their new creations.

The days of bargain silkies are now gone. The few choice aloha shirts from decades past that still remain are offered today by specialized dealers for hundreds of dollars apiece, causing many to look back to the time when such treasures were foolishly worn to the beach until they fell apart. The best examples of vintage aloha shirts are now rightly seen as art objects, worthy of preservation for the lovely depictions they offer of Hawai'i's colorful and unique scene.

—DeSoto Brown

"The Aloha Shirt: A Colorful Swatch of Island History" first appeared in *ALOHA Magazine*. Reprinted with permission of Davick Publications.

HAWAIIAN VOCABULARY

Although an understanding of Hawaiian is by no means required on a trip to the Aloha State, a *malihini*, or newcomer, will find plenty of opportunities to pick up a few of the local words and phrases. Traditional names and expressions are widely used in the Islands. You're likely to read or hear at least a few words each day of your stay.

With a basic understanding and some uninhibited practice, anyone can have enough command of the local tongue to ask for directions and to order from a restaurant menu. One visitor announced she would not leave until she could pronounce the name of the state fish, the *humuhumunukunukuāpua'a*.

Simplifying the learning process is the fact that the Hawaiian language contains only eight consonants—H, K, L, M, N, P, W, and the silent *'okina*, or glottal stop, written '—plus one or more of the five vowels. All syllables, and therefore all words, end in a vowel. Each vowel, with the exception of a few diphthongized double vowels such as *au* (pronounced "ow") or *ai* (pronounced "eye"), is pronounced separately. Thus *'Iolani* is four syllables (ee-oh-la-nee), not three (yo-la-nee). Although some Hawaiian words have only vowels, most also contain some consonants, but consonants are never doubled.

Pronunciation is simple. Pronounce *A* "ah" as father; *E* "ay" as in weigh; *I* "ee" as in marine; *O* "oh" as in no; *U* "oo" as in true.

Consonants mirror their English equivalents, with the exception of W. When the letter begins any syllable other than the first one in a word, it is usually pronounced as a V. *'Awa*, the Polynesian drink, is pronounced "ava," *'ewa* is pronounced "eva."

Almost all long Hawaiian words are combinations of shorter words; they are not difficult to pronounce if you segment them. *Kalaniana'ole*, the highway running east from Honolulu, is easily understood as *Kalani ana 'ole*. Apply the standard pronunciation rules—the stress falls on the next-to-last syllable of most two- or three-syllable Hawaiian words—and Kalaniana'ole Highway is as easy to say as Main Street.

Now about that fish. Try *humu-humu nuku-nuku āpu a'a.*

The other unusual element in Hawaiian language is the *kahakō*, or macron, written as a short line ([m]) placed over a vowel. Like the accent ([ac]) in Spanish, the kahakō puts emphasis on a syllable that would normally not be stressed. The most familiar example is probably *Waikīkī*. With no macrons, the stress would fall on the middle syllable; with only one macron, on the last syllable, the stress would fall on the first and last syllables. Some words become plural with the addition of a macron, often on a syllable that would have been stressed anyway. No Hawaiian word becomes plural with the addition of an *S*, since that letter does not exist in the language.

What follows is a glossary of some of the most commonly used Hawaiian words. Hawaiian residents appreciate visitors who at least try to pick up the local language.

'a'ā: rough, crumbling lava, contrasting with *pāhoehoe*, which is smooth.
'ae: yes.
aikane: friend.
āina: land.
akamai: smart, clever, possessing savoir faire.
akua: god.
ala: a road, path, or trail.
ali'i: a Hawaiian chief, a member of the chiefly class.
aloha: love, affection, kindness; also a salutation meaning both greetings and farewell.

'ānuenue: rainbow.

'a'ole: no.

'apōpō: tomorrow.

'auwai: a ditch.

auwē: alas, woe is me!

'ehu: a red-haired Hawaiian.

'ewa: in the direction of 'Ewa plantation, west of Honolulu.

hala: the pandanus tree, whose leaves (*lau hala*) are used to make baskets and plaited mats.

hālau: school.

hale: a house.

hale pule: church, house of worship.

ha mea iki or **ha mea 'ole:** you're welcome.

hana: to work.

haole: ghost. Since the first foreigners were Caucasian, *haole* now means a Caucasian person.

hapa: a part, sometimes a half; often used as a short form of *hapa haole*, to mean a person who is part-Caucasian.

hau'oli: to rejoice. *Hau'oli Makahiki Hou* means Happy New Year. *Hau'oli lā hānau* means Happy Birthday.

heiau: an outdoor stone platform; an ancient Hawaiian place of worship.

holo: to run.

holoholo: to go for a walk, ride, or sail.

holokū: a long Hawaiian dress, somewhat fitted, with a yoke and a train. Influenced by European fashion, it was worn at court, and at least one local translates the word as "expensive mu'umu'u."

holomū: a post–World War II cross between a *holokū* and a mu'umu'u, less fitted than the former but less voluminous than the latter, and having no train.

honi: to kiss; a kiss. A phrase that some tourists may find useful, quoted from a popular hula, is *Honi Ka'ua Wikiwiki:* Kiss me quick!

honu: turtle.

ho'omalimali: flattery, a deceptive "line," bunk, baloney, hooey.

huhū: angry.

hui: a group, club, or assembly. A church may refer to its congregation as a *hui* and a social club may be called a *hui*.

hukilau: a seine; a communal fishing party in which everyone helps to drive the fish into a huge net, pull it in, and divide the catch.

hula: the dance of Hawai'i.

iki: little.

ipo: sweetheart.

ka: the. This is the definite article for most singular words; for plural nouns, the definite article is usually *nā*. Since there is no *S* in Hawaiian, the article may be your only clue that a noun is plural.

kahuna: a priest, doctor, or other trained person of old Hawai'i, endowed with special professional skills that often included prophecy or other supernatural powers; the plural form is *kāhuna*.

kai: the sea, saltwater.

kalo: the taro plant from whose root *poi* (paste) is made.

kamā'aina: literally, a child of the soil; it refers to people who were born in the Islands or have lived there for a long time.

kanaka: originally a man or humanity, it is now used to denote a male Hawaiian or part-Hawaiian, but is occasionally taken as a slur when used by non-Hawaiians. *Kanaka maoli*, originally a full-blooded Hawaiian person, is used by some native Hawaiian rights activists to embrace part-Hawaiians as well.

kāne: a man, a husband. If you see this word on a door, it's the men's room. If you see *kane* on a door, it's probably a misspelling; that is the Hawaiian name for the skin fungus tinea.

kapa: also called by its Tahitian name, *tapa*, a cloth made of beaten bark and usually dyed and stamped with a repeat design.

kapakahi: crooked, cockeyed, uneven. You've got your hat on *kapakahi*.

kapu: keep out, prohibited. This is the Hawaiian version of the more widely known Tongan word *tabu* (taboo).

kapuna: grandparent; elder.

kēia lā: today.

keiki: a child; *keikikāne* is a boy, *keiki-wahine* a girl.

kona: the leeward side of the Islands, the direction (south) from which the *kona* wind and *kona* rain come.

kula: upland.

kuleana: a homestead or small plot of ground on which a family has been installed for some generations without necessarily owning it. By extension, *kuleana* is used to denote any area or department in which one has a special interest or prerogative. You'll hear it used this way: If you want to hire a surfboard, see Moki; that's his *kuleana.*

lā: sun.

lamalama: to fish with a torch.

lānai: a porch, a balcony, an outdoor living room. Almost every house in Hawai'i has one. Don't confuse this two-syllable word with the three-syllable name of the island, Lāna'i.

lani: heaven, the sky.

lau hala: the leaf of the *hala,* or pandanus tree, widely used in handicrafts.

lei: a garland of flowers.

limu: sun.

lolo: stupid.

luna: a plantation overseer or foreman.

mahalo: thank you.

makai: toward the ocean.

malihini: a newcomer to the Islands.

mana: the spiritual power that the Hawaiian believed inhabited all things and creatures.

manō: shark.

manuwahi: free, gratis.

mauka: toward the mountains.

mauna: mountain.

mele: a Hawaiian song or chant, often of epic proportions.

Mele Kalikimaka: Merry Christmas (a transliteration from the English phrase).

Menehune: a Hawaiian pixie. The *Menehune* were a legendary race of little people who accomplished prodigious work, such as building fishponds and temples in the course of a single night.

moana: the ocean.

mu'umu'u: the voluminous dress in which the missionaries enveloped Hawaiian women. Now made in bright printed cottons and silks, it is an indispensable garment. Culturally sensitive locals have embraced the Hawaiian spelling but often shorten the spoken word to "mu'u." Most English dictionaries include the spelling "muumuu."

nani: beautiful.

nui: big.

ohana: family.

'ono: delicious.

pāhoehoe: smooth, unbroken, satiny lava.

Pākē: Chinese. This *Pākē* carver makes beautiful things.

palapala: document, printed matter.

pali: a cliff, precipice.

pānini: prickly pear cactus.

paniolo: a Hawaiian cowboy, a rough transliteration of *español,* the language of the Islands' earliest cowboys.

pau: finished, done.

pilikia: trouble. The Hawaiian word is much more widely used here than its English equivalent.

puka: a hole.

pupule: crazy, like the celebrated Princess Pupule. This word has replaced its English equivalent in local usage.

pu'u: volcanic cinder cone.

waha: mouth.

wahine: a female, a woman, a wife, and a sign on the ladies' room door; the plural form is *wāhine.*

wai: freshwater, as opposed to saltwater, which is *kai.*

wailele: waterfall.

wikiwiki: to hurry, hurry up (since this is a reduplication of *wiki,* quick, neither W is pronounced as a V).

Note: Pidgin is the unofficial language of Hawai'i. It is a Creole language, with its own grammar, evolved from the mixture of English, Hawaiian, Japanese, Portuguese, and other languages spoken in 19th-century Hawai'i, and it is heard everywhere.

Maui Essentials

PLANNING TOOLS, EXPERT INSIGHT,
GREAT CONTACTS

There are planners and there are those who, excuse the pun, fly by the seat of their pants. We happily place ourselves among the planners. Our writers and editors try to anticipate all the issues you may face before and during any journey, and then they do their research. This section is the product of their efforts. Use it to get excited about your trip to Maui, to inform your travel planning, or to guide you on the road should the seat of your pants start to feel threadbare.

GETTING STARTED

We're really proud of our Web site: Fodors.com is a great place to begin any journey. Scan Travel Wire for suggested itineraries, travel deals, restaurant and hotel openings, and other up-to-the-minute info. Check out Booking to research prices and book plane tickets, hotel rooms, rental cars, and vacation packages. Head to Talk for on-the-ground pointers from travelers who frequent our message boards. You can also link to loads of other travel-related resources.

▮ RESOURCES

ONLINE TRAVEL TOOLS

ALL ABOUT MAUI

For more information on Maui, Moloka'i, and Lāna'i, check out ⊕*www.visitmaui.com* (Maui Visitors Bureau), ⊕*www.molokai-hawaii.com* (Moloka'i Visitors Association), ⊕*www.visitlanai.net* (Lāna'i Visitors Bureau), and ⊕*www.gohawaii.com* (official Web site of the Hawai'i Visitors & Convention Bureau). The Kā'anapali Beach Resort Association, ⊕*www.kaanapaliresort.com*, provides detailed information about the resorts, condominiums, attractions, activities, and special events at this 1,200-acre resort on the island's west shore. The Web site ⊕*www.mauimenusonline.com* has a database that lets you search for restaurants by location, cuisine, and price, and also has reviews and menus from several of the island's eateries. Sponsored by the Hawai'i Tourism Authority, ⊕*www.travelsmarthawaii.com* offers tips on everything from packing to flying.

Also visit ⊕*www.hshawaii.com* for the Hawai'i State Vacation Planner and ⊕*www.hawaii.gov*, the state's official Web site, for all information on the destination, including camping.

Safety Transportation Security Administration (TSA;) ⊕www.tsa.gov).

Time Zones Timeanddate.com (⊕www.timeanddate.com/worldclock)can help you figure out the correct time anywhere.

Weather Accuweather.com (⊕www.accuweather.com)is an independent weather-forecasting service with good coverage of hurricanes. **Weather.com** (⊕www.weather.com)is the Web site for the Weather Channel.

Other Resources CIA World Factbook (⊕www.odci.gov/cia/publications/factbook/index.html)has profiles of every country in the world. It's a good source if you need some quick facts and figures.

WORD OF MOUTH

After your trip, be sure to rate the places you visited and share your experiences and travel tips with us and other Fodorites in Travel Ratings and Talk on www.fodors.com.

VISITOR INFORMATION

Before you go, contact the Hawai'i Visitors & Convention Bureau (HVCB) for general information on Maui, Lāna'i, or Moloka'i, and to request a free official vacation planner with information on accommodations, transportation, sports and activities, dining, arts and entertainment, and culture. Take a virtual visit to the Islands on the Web, which can be most helpful in planning many aspects of your vacation. The HVCB site has a calendar section that allows you to see what local events are taking place during the time of your stay.

Contacts Hawai'i Visitors & Convention Bureau (✉2270 Kalakaua Ave., Suite 801, Honolulu 96815 ☎808/923–1811, 800/464–2924 for brochures ⊕www.gohawaii.com). In the U.K. contact the **Hawai'i Visitors & Convention Bureau** (✉36 Southwark Bridge Rd., London SE1 9EU ☎020/7202–6384 🖷020/7928–0722 ⊕www.gohawaii.com).

▮ THINGS TO CONSIDER

GEAR

Probably the most important thing to tuck into your suitcase is sunscreen. This is the tropics, and the ultraviolet rays are powerful, even on overcast days. Don't forget to reapply sunscreen periodically during the day, since perspiration can wash it away. Consider using sunscreens with a sun-protection factor (SPF) of 15 or higher. There are many tanning oils on the market in Hawai'i, including coconut and *kukui* (the nut from a local tree) oils, but they can cause severe burns. Hats and sunglasses offer important sun protection, too. All major hotels in Hawai'i provide beach towels.

As for clothing, Hawai'i is casual: sandals, bathing suits, and comfortable, informal clothing are the norm. In summer, synthetic slacks and shirts, although easy to care for, can be uncomfortably warm. Only a few upscale restaurants require a jacket for dinner. The aloha shirt is accepted dress in Hawai'i for business and most social occasions. Shorts are acceptable daytime attire, along with a T-shirt or polo shirt. There's no need to buy expensive sandals on the mainland—here you can get flip-flops for a couple of dollars and off-brand sandals for $20. Golfers should remember that many courses have dress codes requiring a collared shirt; call courses you're interested in for details. If you're visiting in winter or planning to visit a high-altitude area, bring a sweater or light- to medium-weight jacket. A polar-fleece pullover is ideal.

If your vacation plans include an exploration of Maui's northeastern coast, including Hāna and Upcountry Maui, you'll want to pack a light raincoat. And if you'll be hiking Haleakalā National Park, make sure you pack appropriately as weather at the summit can be very cold and windy. Good boots are recommended if you'll be hiking.

SHIPPING LUGGAGE AHEAD

Shipping your luggage in advance via an air-freight service is a great way to cut down on backaches, hassles, and stress—especially if your packing list includes strollers, car seats, etc. There are some things to be aware of, though.

First, research carry-on restrictions; if you absolutely need something that isn't practical to ship and isn't allowed in carry-ons, this strategy isn't for you. Second, plan to send your bags several days in advance to U.S. destinations and as much as two weeks in advance to some international destinations. Third, plan to spend some money: it will cost at least $100 to send a small piece of luggage, a golf bag, or a pair of skis to a domestic destination, much more to places overseas.

Some people use Federal Express to ship their bags, but this can cost even more than air-freight services. All these services insure your bag (for most, the limit is $1,000, but you should verify that amount); you can, however, purchase additional insurance for about $1 per $100 of value.

Contacts Luggage Concierge (☎800/288–9818 ⊕www.luggageconcierge.com). **Luggage Express** (☎866/744–7224 ⊕www.usxpluggageexpress.com). **Luggage Free** (☎800/361–6871 ⊕www.luggagefree.com). **Sports Express** (☎800/357–4174 ⊕www.sportsexpress.com)specializes in shipping golf clubs and other sports equipment. **Virtual Bellhop** (☎877/235–5467 ⊕www.virtualbellhop.com).

TRIP INSURANCE

We believe that comprehensive trip insurance is especially valuable if you're booking a very expensive or complicated trip (particularly to an isolated region) or if you're booking far in advance.

Comprehensive travel policies typically cover trip-cancellation and interruption, letting you cancel or cut your trip short because of a personal emergency, illness, or, in some cases, acts of terrorism in

Trip Insurance Resources

INSURANCE COMPARISON SITES		
Insure My Trip.com		www.insuremytrip.com
Square Mouth.com		www.quotetravelinsurance.com
COMPREHENSIVE TRAVEL INSURERS		
Access America	866/807–3982	www.accessamerica.com
CSA Travel Protection	800/873–9855	www.csatravelprotection.com
HTH Worldwide	610/254–8700 or 888/243–2358	www.hthworldwide.com
Travelex Insurance	888/457–4602	www.travelex-insurance.com
Travel Guard International	715/345–0505 or 800/826–4919	www.travelguard.com
Travel Insured International	800/243–3174	www.travelinsured.com
MEDICAL-ONLY INSURERS		
International Medical Group	800/628–4664	www.imglobal.com
International SOS	215/942–8000 or 713/521–7611	www.internationalsos.com
Wallach & Company	800/237–6615 or 504/687–3166	www.wallach.com

your destination. Such policies also cover evacuation and medical care. Some also cover you for trip delays because of bad weather or mechanical problems as well as for lost or delayed baggage. Another type of coverage to look for is financial default—that is, when your trip is disrupted because a tour operator, airline, or cruise line goes out of business. Generally you must buy this when you book your trip or shortly thereafter, and it's only available to you if your operator isn't on a list of excluded companies.

Neither Medicare nor some private insurers cover medical expenses anywhere outside of the United States besides Mexico and Canada (including time aboard a cruise ship, even if it leaves from a U.S. port). Medical-only policies typically reimburse you for medical care (excluding that related to pre-existing conditions) and hospitalization abroad, and provide for evacuation. You still have to pay the bills and await reimbursement.

Expect comprehensive travel-insurance policies to cost about 4% to 7% of the total price of your trip (it's more like 12% if you're over age 70). A medical-only policy may or may not be cheaper than a comprehensive policy. Always read the fine print of your policy to make sure that you are covered for the risks that are of most concern to you.

■ TIP➜OK. You know you can save a bundle on trips to warm-weather destinations by traveling in rainy season. But there's also a chance that a severe storm will disrupt your plans. The solution? Look for hotels and resorts that offer storm/hurricane guarantees. Most guarantees do let you rebook later if a storm strikes.

BOOKING YOUR TRIP

Online Booking Resources

AGGREGATORS

Kayak	www.kayak.com;	also looks at cruises and vacation packages.
Mobissimo	www.mobissimo.com	
Qixo	www.qixo.com	also compares cruises, vacation packages, and even travel insurance.
Sidestep	www.sidestep.com	also compares vacation packages and lists travel deals.
Travelgrove	www.travelgrove.com	also compares cruises and packages.

BOOKING ENGINES

Cheap Tickets	www.cheaptickets.com	a discounter.
Expedia	www.expedia.com	a large online agency that charges a booking fee for airline tickets.
Hotwire	www.hotwire.com	a discounter.
lastminute.com	www.lastminute.com	specializes in last-minute travel the main site is for the U.K., but it has a link to a U.S. site.
Luxury Link	www.luxurylink.com	has auctions (surprisingly good deals) as well as offers on the high-end side of travel.
Onetravel.com	www.onetravel.com	a discounter for hotels, car rentals, airfares, and packages.
Orbitz	www.orbitz.com	charges a booking fee for airline tickets, but gives a clear breakdown of fees and taxes before you book.
Priceline.com	www.priceline.com	a discounter that also allows bidding.
Travel.com	www.travel.com	allows you to compare its rates with those of other booking engines.
Travelocity	www.travelocity.com	charges a booking fee for airline tickets, but promises good problem resolution.

ONLINE ACCOMMODATIONS

Hotelbook.com	www.hotelbook.com	focuses on independent hotels worldwide.
Hotel Club	www.hotelclub.net	good for major cities worldwide.
Hotels.com	www.hotels.com	a big Expedia-owned wholesaler that offers rooms in hotels all over the world.
Quikbook	www.quikbook.com	offers "pay when you stay" reservations that let you settle your bill at check out, not when you book.

OTHER RESOURCES

Bidding For Travel	www.biddingfortravel.com	a good place to figure out what you can get and for how much before you start bidding on, say, Priceline.

Unless your cousin is a travel agent, you're probably among the millions of people who make most of their travel arrangements online.

But have you ever wondered just what the differences are between an online travel agent (a Web site through which you make reservations instead of going directly to the airline, hotel, or car-rental company), a discounter (a firm that does a high volume of business with a hotel chain or airline and accordingly gets good prices), a wholesaler (one that makes cheap reservations in bulk and then re-sells them to people like you), and an aggregator (one that compares all the offerings so you don't have to)?

Is it truly better to book directly on an airline or hotel Web site? And when does a real live travel agent come in handy?

▌ ONLINE

You really have to shop around. A travel wholesaler such as Hotels.com or Hotel-Club.net can be a source of good rates, as can discounters such as Hotwire or Priceline, particularly if you can bid for your hotel room or airfare. Indeed, such sites sometimes have deals that are unavailable elsewhere. They do, however, tend to work only with hotel chains (which makes them just plain useless for getting hotel reservations outside of major cities) or big airlines (so that often leaves out upstarts like jetBlue and some foreign carriers like Air India).

Also, with discounters and wholesalers you must generally prepay, and everything is nonrefundable. And before you fork over the dough, be sure to check the terms and conditions, so you know what a given company will do for you if there's a problem and what you'll have to deal with on your own.

▌TIP➔To be absolutely sure everything was processed correctly, confirm reservations made through online travel agents, discounters, and wholesalers directly with your hotel before leaving home.

Booking engines like Expedia, Travelocity, and Orbitz are actually travel agents, albeit high-volume, online ones. And airline-travel packagers like American Airlines Vacations and Virgin Vacations—well, they're travel agents, too. But they may still not work with all the world's hotels.

An aggregator site will search many sites and pull the best prices for airfares, hotels, and rental cars from them. Most aggregators compare the major travel-booking sites such as Expedia, Travelocity, and Orbitz; some also look at airline Web sites, though rarely the sites of smaller budget airlines. Some aggregators compare other travel products, including complex packages—a good thing, as you can sometimes get the best deal by booking an air-and-hotel package.

▌ WITH A TRAVEL AGENT

If you use an agent—brick-and-mortar or virtual—you'll pay a fee for the service. And know that the service you get from some online agents isn't comprehensive. For example Expedia and Travelocity don't search for prices on budget airlines like Southwest, or small foreign carriers. That said, some agents (online or not) *do* have access to fares that are difficult to find otherwise, and the savings can more than make up for any surcharge.

A knowledgeable brick-and-mortar travel agent can be a godsend if you're booking a cruise, a package trip that's not available to you directly, an air pass, or a complicated itinerary including several overseas flights. What's more, travel agents that specialize in a destination may have exclusive access to certain deals and insider information on things such as charter flights. Agents who specialize in types of travelers (senior citizens, gays and lesbians, naturists) or types of trips (cruises, luxury travel, safaris) can also be invaluable.

TIP→ Remember that Expedia, Travelocity, and Orbitz are travel agents, not just booking engines. To resolve any problems with a reservation made through these companies, contact them first.

A top-notch agent planning your trip may get you a room upgrade or a resort food and beverage credit; the one booking your cruise may arrange to have a bottle of champagne chilling in your cabin when you embark. And complain about the surcharges all you like, but when things don't work out the way you'd hoped, it's nice to have an agent to put things right.

If this is your first visit to Maui, Lāna'i, or Moloka'i, a travel agent or vacation packager specializing in Hawai'i can be extremely helpful in planning a memorable vacation. Not only do they have the knowledge of the destination, but they can save you money by packaging the costs of airfare, hotel, activities, and car rental. In addition, many Hawai'i-specialist travel agents may offer added values or special deals (i.e., resort food and beverage credit, a free night's stay, etc.) when you book a package with them. The Hawai'i Visitors & Convention Bureau provides a list of member travel agencies and tour operators.

Agent Resources American Society of Travel Agents (☎703/739–2782 ⊕www.travelsense.org).

Maui Travel Agents AA Vacations (☎800/321–2121 ⊕www.aavacations.com). **AAA Travel** (☎800/436–4222 ⊕www.aaa.com). **All About Hawai'i** (☎800/274–8687 ⊕www.allabouthawaii.com). **Aloha Destinations Vacations** (☎800/256–4280 ⊕www.mccoyvacations.com). **Blue Hawai'i Vacation** (☎800/315–1812 ⊕www.blue-hawaii.com). **Delta Vacations** (☎800/654–6559 ⊕www.deltavacations.com). **Funjet Vacations** (☎888/558–6654 ⊕www.funjet.com). **Travel-Hawaii.com** (☎800/373–2422 ⊕www.travel-hawaii.com). **United**

Vacations (☎800/699–6122 ⊕www.unitedvacations.com).

❚ AIRLINE TICKETS

Most domestic airline tickets are electronic; international tickets may be either electronic or paper. With an e-ticket the only thing you receive is an e-mailed receipt citing your itinerary and reservation and ticket numbers.

The greatest advantage of an e-ticket is that if you lose your receipt, you can simply print out another copy or ask the airline to do it for you at check-in. You usually pay a surcharge (up to $50) to get a paper ticket, if you can get one at all.

The sole advantage of a paper ticket is that it may be easier to endorse over to another airline if your flight is canceled and the airline with which you booked can't accommodate you on another flight.

TIP→ Discount air passes that let you travel economically in a country or region must often be purchased before you leave home. In some cases you can only get them through a travel agent.

Aloha Airlines, go! Airlines, Hawaiian Airlines, IslandAir, and PWExpress offer regular service between the Islands. In addition to offering very competitive rates and online specials, all have frequent-flyer programs that will entitle you to rewards and upgrades the more you fly. Be sure to compare prices offered by all of the interisland carriers. If you are somewhat flexible with your dates and times for island-hopping, you should have no problem getting a very affordable round-trip ticket.

Interisland Carriers Aloha Airlines (☎800/367–5250 ⊕www.alohaairlines.com). **go! Airlines** (☎888/435–9462 ⊕www.iflygo.com). **Hawaiian Airlines** (☎800/367–5320 ⊕www.hawaiianair.com). **IslandAir** (☎800/323–3345 ⊕www.islandair.com).

PWExpress (☎888/866–5022 ⊕www.pacific-wings.com).

CHARTER FLIGHTS

In addition to its regular service between Honolulu, Lānaʻi, Maui, and Molokaʻi, Pacific Wings offers a variety of charter options including premiere (same-day departures on short notice), premium (24-hour notice), priority (48-hour notice), group, and cargo/courier. The company also has a frequent-flyer program.

Paragon Air offers 24-hour private charter service from any airport in Hawaiʻi. In addition, the company provides regular service to any Maui County airport, excluding Kalaupapa on Molokaʻi. In business since 1981, the company prides itself on its perfect safety record and has served a number of celebrities including Bill Gates, Michael Douglas, and Kevin Costner, among others. Charter prices start at $375. Should you want to explore Kaluapapa or other sites on Molokaʻi and Maui from the air and ground, you can book tours through Paragon that depart from either the Kahului or Kapalua-West Maui airports.

Charter Companies Pacific Wings (☎888/575–4546 ⊕www.pacificwings.com). **Paragon Air** (☎800/428–1231 ⊕www.paragon-air.com).

▮ RENTAL CARS

Should you plan to do any sightseeing on Maui, it is best to rent a car. Even if all you want to do is relax at your resort, you may want to hop in the car to check out one of the island's popular restaurants. On Lānaʻi and Molokaʻi, four-wheel-drive vehicles are recommended for exploring off the beaten path. Of the major agencies, Dollar is the only company with locations on all of the major Hawaiian Islands.

While on Maui, you can rent anything from an econobox to a Ferrari. Rates are usually better if you reserve though a rental agency's Web site. It's wise to make reservations far in advance and make sure that a confirmed reservation guarantees you a car, especially if visiting during peak seasons or for major conventions or sporting events. It's not uncommon to find several car categories sold out during major events on the island.

Rates begin at about $25 to $35 a day for an economy car with air-conditioning, automatic transmission, and unlimited mileage, depending on your pickup location. This does not include the airport concession fee, general excise tax, rental-vehicle surcharge, or vehicle license fee. When you reserve a car, ask about cancellation penalties and drop-off charges should you plan to pick up the car in one location and return it to another. Many rental companies in Hawaiʻi offer coupons for discounts at attractions that could save you money later in your trip.

Want to see the island in your own VW camper? Imua Camper Company rents older VW Westfalia Campers for $99 per day that accommodate up to four adults.

In Hawaiʻi you must be 21 years of age to rent a car and you must have a valid driver's license and a major credit card. Those under 25 will pay a daily surcharge of $15 to $25. Request car seats and extras such as a GPS when you book. Hawaiʻi's Child Restraint Law requires that all children three years and younger be in an approved child-safety seat in the backseat of a vehicle. Children ages 4 to 7 must be seated in a rear booster seat or child restraint such as a lap and shoulder belt. Car seats and boosters range from $5 to $8 per day.

In Hawaiʻi, your unexpired mainland driver's license is valid for rental for up to 90 days.

Since many of Maui's roads are mostly two lanes, be sure to allow plenty of time to return your vehicle so that you can make your flight. Traffic can be bad during morning and afternoon rush hour.

Car Rental Resources

AUTOMOBILE ASSOCIATIONS		
U.S.: American Automobile Association (AAA)	315/797–5000	www.aaa.com; most contact with the organization is through state and regional members.
National Automobile Club	650/294–7000	www.thenac.com; membership is open to California residents only.
LOCAL AGENCIES		
AA Aloha Cars-R-Us	800/655–7989	www.hawaiicarrental.com
Adventure Lānaʻi Eco-Centre (Lānaʻi)	808/565–7373	www.adventurelanai.com
Aloha Rent A Car (Maui)	877/452–5642	www.aloharentacar.com
Discount Hawaii Car Rentals	888/292–3307	www.discounthawaiicarrental.com
Hawaiian Discount Car Rentals	800/882–9007	www.hawaiidrive-o.com
Imua Camper Company (Maui)		www.imua-tour.com
Island Kine Auto Rental (Molokaʻi)	866/527–7368	www.molokai-car-rental.com
MAJOR AGENCIES		
Alamo	800/462–5266	www.alamo.com
Avis	800/230–4898	www.avis.com
Budget	800/527–0700	www.budget.com
Dollar	800/800–4000	www.dollar.com
Enterprise	800/261–7331	www.enterprise.com
Hertz	800/654–3131	www.hertz.com
National Car Rental	800/227–7368	www.nationalcar.com
Thrifty	800/847–4389	www.dollar.com

Give yourself about 3½ hours before departure time to return your vehicle.

CAR-RENTAL INSURANCE

Everyone who rents a car wonders whether the insurance that the rental companies offer is worth the expense. No one—including us—has a simple answer. It all depends on how much regular insurance you have, how comfortable you are with risk, and whether or not money is an issue.

If you own a car and carry comprehensive car insurance for both collision and liability, your personal auto insurance will probably cover a rental, but read your policy's fine print to be sure. If you don't have auto insurance, then you should probably buy the collision- or loss-damage waiver (CDW or LDW) from the rental company. This eliminates your liability for damage to the car.

Some credit cards offer CDW coverage, but it's usually supplemental to your own insurance and rarely covers SUVs, minivans, luxury models, and the like. If your coverage is secondary, you may still be liable for loss-of-use costs from the car-rental company (again, read the fine print). But no credit-card insurance is valid unless you use that card for *all* transactions, from reserving to paying the final bill.

■ TIP → Diners Club offers primary CDW coverage on all rentals reserved and paid for with the card. This means that Diners Club's company—not your own car insurance—pays in case of an accident. It *doesn't* mean that your car-insurance company won't raise your rates once it discovers you had an accident.

You may also be offered supplemental liability coverage; the car-rental company is required to carry a minimal level of liability coverage insuring all renters, but it's rarely enough to cover claims in a really serious accident if you're at fault. Your own auto-insurance policy will protect you if you own a car; if you don't, you have to decide whether you are willing to take the risk.

U.S. rental companies sell CDWs and LDWs for about $15 to $25 a day; supplemental liability is usually more than $10 a day. The car-rental company may offer you all sorts of other policies, but they're rarely worth the cost. Personal accident insurance, which is basic hospitalization coverage, is an especially egregious rip-off if you already have health insurance.

■ TIP → You can decline the insurance from the rental company and purchase it through a third-party provider such as Travel Guard (www.travelguard.com)—$9 per day for $35,000 of coverage. That's sometimes just under half the price of the CDW offered by some car-rental companies.

■ VACATION PACKAGES

Packages *are not* guided excursions. Packages combine airfare, accommodations, and perhaps a rental car or other extras (theater tickets, guided excursions, boat trips, reserved entry to popular museums, transit passes), but they let you do your own thing. During busy periods packages may be your only option, as flights and rooms may be sold out otherwise.

Packages will definitely save you time. They can also save you money, particularly in peak seasons, but—and this is a really big "but"—you should price each part of the package separately to be sure. Be aware that prices advertised on Web sites and in newspapers rarely include service charges or taxes, which can up your costs by hundreds of dollars.

■ TIP → Some packages and cruises are sold only through travel agents. Don't always assume that you can get the best deal by booking everything yourself.

Each year consumers are stranded or lose their money when packagers—even large ones with excellent reputations—go out of business. How can you protect yourself?

First, always pay with a credit card; if you have a problem, your credit-card company may help you resolve it. Second, buy trip insurance that covers default. Third, choose a company that belongs to the United States Tour Operators Association, whose members must set aside funds to cover defaults. Finally, choose a company that also participates in the Tour Operator Program of the American Society of Travel Agents (ASTA), which will act as mediator in any disputes.

You can also check on the tour operator's reputation among travelers by posting an inquiry on one of the Fodors.com forums.

About half of the visitors to Maui, Lāna'i, and Moloka'i travel on package tours. All of the wholesalers specializing in Hawai'i offer a range of packages from the low to the high end. Because of the volume of business they do, wholesalers typically have great deals. Combine that with their knowledge of the destination and wholesale packages make a lot of sense. However, shop around and compare before you book to make sure you are getting a good deal.

Organizations American Society of Travel Agents ((ASTA) ☎703/739–2782 or 800/965–2782 ⊕www.astanet.com). **United States Tour Operators Association** ((USTOA) ☎212/599–6599 ⊕www.ustoa.com).

Hawai'i Tour Operators American Express Vacations (☎800/528–4800 ⊕www.americanexpressvacations.com). **Apple Vacations** (⊕www.applevacations.com). **Classic Vacations** (☎866/230–2540 ⊕www.classicvacations.com). **Creative Leisure** (☎800/413–1000 ⊕www.creativeleisure.com). **Pleasant Holidays** (☎800/742–9244 ⊕www.pleasantholidays.com).

▨ TIP➔Local tourism boards can provide information about lesser-known and small-niche operators that sell packages to only a few destinations.

▮ GUIDED TOURS

Guided tours are a good option when you don't want to do it all yourself. You travel along with a group (sometimes large, sometimes small), stay in prebooked hotels, eat with your fellow travelers (the cost of meals sometimes included in the price of your tour, sometimes not), and follow a schedule.

But not all guided tours are an if-it's-Tuesday-this-must-be-Belgium experience. A knowledgeable guide can take you places that you might never discover on your own, and you may be pushed to see more than you would have otherwise. Tours aren't for everyone, but they can be just the thing for first-time travelers to Maui or those who enjoy the group-traveling experience. None of the companies

offering guided tours in the Hawaiian Islands include Moloka'i or Lāna'i.

Whenever you book a guided tour, find out what's included and what isn't. A "land-only"tour includes all your travel (by bus, in most cases) in the destination, but not necessarily your flights to and from or even within it. Also, in most cases prices in tour brochures don't include fees and taxes. And remember that you'll be expected to tip your guide (in cash) at the end of the tour.

Globus has six Hawai'i itineraries that include Maui, one of which is an escorted cruise on Norwegian Cruise Line's *Pride of America* that includes two days on the island. Tauck Travel and Trafalgar offer several land-based Hawai'i itineraries that include three nights on Maui. Both companies offer similar itineraries with plenty of free time to explore the island. Tauck offers 7- and 11-night multi-island tours, including a "Magical Hawai'i" trip for families. Trafalgar has 7-, 9-, 10-, and 12-night multi-island tours. With the Tauck tours, participants will discover the majesty of Mt. Haleakalā, while the Trafalgar tours all include visits to verdant 'Iao Valley.

EscortedHawaiiTours.com, owned and operated by Atlas Cruises & Tours, sells more than a dozen Hawai'i trips ranging from 7 to 12 nights operated by various guided tour companies including Globus, Tauck, and Trafalgar.

Recommended Companies Atlas Cruises & Tours (☎800/942–3301 ⊕www.EscortedHawaiiTours.com). **Globus** (☎866/755–8581 ⊕www.globusjourneys.com). **Tauck Travel** (☎800/788–7885 ⊕www.tauck.com). **Trafalgar** (☎866/544–4434 ⊕www.trafalgar.com).

SPECIAL-INTEREST TOURS

CULTURE
Elderhostel offers several guided Hawai'i tours for older adults that provide fascinating in-depth looks into the culture, history, and beauty of the Islands. The

non-profit educational travel organization has been leading all-inclusive learning adventures around the world for more than 20 years. For all Elderhostel programs, travelers must purchase their own airfare if coming from outside of Hawai'i. Below are a few typical trips; the Web site shows more options.

Presented in association with Volcano Arts Center, Moloka'i Museum & Cultural Center and Hawai'i Pacific University, *Islands of Life in the Pacific* is a 15-night, 5-island, Elderhostel tour that includes 3 nights each on Maui and Moloka'i. Prices for the tour start at around $3,420 per person and include accommodations, meals, ground transportation, interisland air and ferry transportation between the islands and all activities.

A *Tall Ship Sail Training: Sailing the Hawaiian Islands* is an incredible six-night sailing adventure through the Hawaiian Islands aboard the SSV *Makani Olu,* a Coast Guard–certified, 96-foot, three-masted schooner. Prices for this tour start at about $1,080 per person and include accommodations and meals on board the schooner.

The Entire Island Is a Classroom is a six-night tour to Moloka'i that examines the island's historical and cultural significance to Hawai'i. Offered in conjunction with the Moloka'i Museum & Cultural Center, travelers will learn traditional Hawaiian fishing practices, dances, songs, and crafts. A highlight of the tour is a day trip to Kalaupapa National Historic Park. Prices start at about $800 per person and include accommodations, meals, activities, and ground transportation.

Contacts **Elderhostel** (☎800/454–5768 ⊕www.elderhostel.org).

ECOTOURS

Hawai'i's Humpback Whales and Marine Environment is a six-night tour that provides visitors with an in-depth study of these gentle giants that migrate to Hawaiian waters every year. You'll participate in whale-watch cruises and snorkel trips with research and conservation groups. Prices start at around $1,070 per person and include accommodations, meals, ground transportation, and activities.

Contacts **Elderhostel** (☎800/454–5768 ⊕www.elderhostel.org).

HIKING

Hawai'i Three Island Hiker is a seven-night hiking tour to Maui, the Big Island, and Kaua'i. Included in the per-person price of about $3,100 are accommodations, meals, interisland air between the three islands, shuttle transportation, support vehicle, professional guides, a T-shirt, and water bottle. Hikers will spend two nights on Maui exploring Hāna's Wai'ānapanapa State Park, Kīpahulu Valley, and Hāmoa Beach; plus the 7-mi Sliding Sand Trail within Haleakalā Crater. The trip is rated moderately easy to moderate. The World Outdoors has been organizing and leading adventure trips around the world for nearly 20 years.

Contacts **The World Outdoors** (☎800/488–8483 ⊕www.theworldoutdoors.com).

▌CRUISES

For information about cruises, *see* chapter 1, Experience Maui.

TRANSPORTATION

Getting around Maui is relatively easy as there are really only a few major roads leading to and from the major towns and must-see sights. Honoapiʻilani Highway will get you from the central Maui towns of Wailuku and Kahului to the leeward coast and the towns and resorts of Lahaina, Kāʻanapali, Kahana, and Kapalua. Depending on traffic, it should take about 30 to 45 minutes to travel this route. Those gorgeous mountains that hug Honoapiʻilani Highway are the West Maui Mountains. North and South Kīhei Road will take you to the town of Kīhei and the resort area of Wailea. The drive from Kahului to Wailea should take about 30 minutes, and the drive from Kāʻanapali to Wailea will take about 45 to 60 minutes. Your vacation to Maui must include a visit to Haleakalā National Park and you should plan on 2 to 2½ hours driving time from Kāʻanapali or Wailea. Hoʻokipa and Baldwin beaches are on the Island's North Shore, just a stone's throw from Kahului and could easily be combined with a day in Upcountry Maui. The drive from Kāʻanapali or Wailea to the charming towns of Makawao and Kula will take about 45 to 60 minutes. And you must not miss the Road to Hāna, a 55-mi stretch with one-lane bridges, hairpin turns, and some of the most breathtaking views you will ever see.

■ BY AIR

Flying time is about 10 hours from New York, 8 hours from Chicago, and 5 hours from Los Angeles.

Hawaiʻi is a major destination link for flights traveling to and from the U.S. mainland, Asia, Australia, New Zealand, and the South Pacific. Some of the major airline carriers serving Hawaiʻi fly direct to Maui, allowing you to bypass connecting flights out of Honolulu. For the more spontaneous traveler, island-hopping is easy, with flights departing every 20 to 30 minutes daily until mid-evening. International travelers also have options: Oʻahu and the Big Island are gateways to the United States.

Although Maui's airports are smaller and more casual than Honolulu International, during peak times they can also be quite busy. Allow extra travel time to either airport during morning and afternoon rush-hour traffic periods. Plan to arrive at the airport 60 to 90 minutes before departure for interisland flights.

Plants and plant products are subject to regulation by the Department of Agriculture, both on entering and leaving Hawaiʻi. Upon leaving the Islands, you're required to have your bags X-rayed and tagged at one of the airport's agricultural-inspection stations before you proceed to check-in. Pineapples and coconuts with the packer's agricultural-inspection stamp pass freely; papayas must be treated, inspected, and stamped. All other fruits are banned for export to the U.S. mainland. Flowers pass except for gardenia, rose leaves, jade vine, and mauna loa. Also banned are insects, snails, soil, cotton, cacti, sugarcane, and all berry plants.

You'll have to leave dogs and other pets at home. A 120-day quarantine is imposed to keep out rabies, which is nonexistent in Hawaiʻi. If specific pre- and post-arrival requirements are met, animals may qualify for a 30-day or 5-day-or-less quarantine.

■ TIP→ If you travel frequently, look into the TSA's Registered Traveler program (w www. tsa.gov). The program, which is still being tested in several U.S. airports, is designed to cut down on gridlock at security checkpoints by allowing prescreened travelers to pass quickly through kiosks that scan an iris and/or a fingerprint.

Airlines & Airports **Airline and Airport Links.com** (⊕www.airlineandairportlinks. com)has links to many of the world's airlines and airports.

Airline-Security Issues **Transportation Security Administration** (⊕www.tsa.gov)has answers for almost every question that might come up.

Air-Travel Resources in Maui **State of Hawaii Airports Division Offices** (☎808/836–6417 ⊕www.hawaii.gov/dot/airports).

AIRPORTS

All of Hawai'i's major islands have their own airports, but Honolulu's International Airport is the main stopover for most U.S.–mainland and international flights. From Honolulu, there are departing flights to Maui leaving almost every hour from early morning until evening. In addition, some carriers now offer nonstop service directly from the U.S. mainland to Maui on a limited basis. Flights from Honolulu into Lāna'i and Moloka'i are offered several times a day.

HONOLULU/O'AHU AIRPORT

Hawai'i's major airport is Honolulu International, on O'ahu, 20 minutes (9 mi) west of Waikīkī. To travel interisland from Honolulu, you can depart from either the interisland terminal or the commuter-airline terminal, located in two separate structures adjacent to the main overseas terminal building. A free bus service, the Wiki Wiki Shuttle, operates between terminals.

Information **Honolulu International Airport (HNL)** (☎808/836–6413 ⊕www.hawaii.gov/dot/airports).

MAUI AIRPORTS

Maui has two major airports. Kahului Airport handles major airlines and interisland flights; it's the only airport on Maui that has direct service from the mainland. Kapalua–West Maui Airport is served by Aloha Airlines, Hawaiian Air, and Pacific Wings. If you're staying in West Maui and you're flying in from

another island, you can avoid the hour drive from the Kahului Airport by flying into Kapalua–West Maui Airport.

Information **Kahului Airport (OGG)** (☎808/872–3893). **Kapalua–West Maui Airport (JHM)** (☎808/669–0623). **Hāna Airport (HNM)** (☎808/248–8208).

MOLOKA'I & LĀNA'I

Moloka'i's Ho'olehua Airport is small and centrally located, as is Lāna'i Airport. Both rural airports handle a limited number of flights per day. Visitors coming from the U.S. mainland to these islands must first stop in O'ahu or Maui and change to an interisland flight.

Information Lāna'i: **Lāna'i Airport (LNY)** (☎808/565–6757). Moloka'i: **Ho'olehua Airport (MKK)** (☎808/567–6361).

GROUND TRANSPORTATION

If you're not renting a car, you'll need to take a taxi. Maui Airport Taxi serves the Kahului Airport and charges $3.50, plus $3 for every mile, with a $.30 surcharge per bag. Cab fares to locations around the Island are estimated as follows: Kā'anapali $87, Kahului town $13 to $18, Kapalua $105, Kīhei town $33 to $53, Lahaina $74 to $79, Mākena $65, Wailea $57, and Wailuku $20 to $27.

SpeediShuttle offers transportation between the Kahului Airport and hotels, resorts, and condominium complexes throughout the island. There is an online reservation and fare-quote system for information and bookings.

Information **SpeediShuttle Hawai'i** (☎877/242–5777 ⊕www.speedishuttle.com).

FLIGHTS

ATA flies into Maui from Los Angeles, Oakland, and Phoenix; and also serves O'ahu and the Big Island. America West flies into Maui and Honolulu from Las Vegas and Phoenix. Delta and Northwest serve Maui and O'ahu. American has daily nonstop flights into Maui from Los Angeles, Chicago, and Dallas-Fort

Worth; and also serves Oʻahu, Kauaʻi, and the Big Island. United flies from Chicago, Los Angeles, and San Francisco to Maui; and also serves Oʻahu and the Big Island. Continental flies into Honolulu.

Aloha Airlines flies from California—Oakland, Sacramento, San Diego, and Orange County—to Maui, Honolulu, and the Big Island. Aloha also flies from Las Vegas and Reno, Nevada. Hawaiian Airlines serves Maui and Honolulu from Las Vegas, Los Angeles, Phoenix, Portland, Sacramento, San Diego, San Francisco, San Jose, and Seattle.

Aloha, Hawaiian, and Island Air offer regular interisland service to Mauiʻs Kahului and Kapalua airports, as well as the Molokaʻi and Lānaʻi airports. go! Airlines provides interisland service between Kahului Airport and Oʻahu, Kauaʻi, and the Big Island. Pacific Wings has service between Honolulu and Maui (all three airports), Molokaʻi, and Lānaʻi. Paragon Airlines offers private charter service to all the Islands.

Airline Contacts America West/US Airways (☎800/428–4322 ⊕ www.usairways.com). **American Airlines** (☎800/433–7300 ⊕ www.aa.com). **ATA** (☎800/435–9282 or 317/282–8308 ⊕ www.ata.com). **Continental Airlines** (☎800/523–3273 for U.S. and Mexico reservations, 800/231–0856 for international reservations ⊕ www.continental.com). **Delta Airlines** (☎800/221–1212 for U.S. reservations, 800/241–4141 for international reservations ⊕ www.delta.com). **Northwest Airlines** (☎800/225–2525 ⊕ www.nwa.com). **Southwest Airlines** (☎800/435–9792 ⊕ www.southwest.com). **United Airlines** (☎800/864–8331 for U.S. reservations, 800/538–2929 for international reservations ⊕ www.united.com).

Interisland Flights Aloha Airlines (☎800/367–5250 ⊕ www.alohaairlines.com). **go! Airlines** (☎888/434–5946 ⊕ www.iflygo.com). **Hawaiian Airlines** (☎800/367–5320 ⊕ www.hawaiianair.com). **Island Air** (☎800/323–3345 ⊕ www.islandair.com). **Pacific Wings** (☎888/575–4546 ⊕ www.paci-ficwings.com). **Paragon Airlines** (☎800/428–1231 ⊕ www.paragon-air.com).

∎ BY BOAT

There is daily ferry service between Lahaina, Maui, and Mānele Bay, Lānaʻi, with Expeditions Lānaʻi Ferry. The 9-mi crossing costs $50 cash (or $52 if you pay with a credit card) round-trip, per person and takes about 45 minutes or so, depending on ocean conditions (which can make this trip a rough one). Molokaʻi Ferry offers twice-daily ferry service between Lahaina, Maui, and Kaunakakai, Molokaʻi. Travel time is about 90 minutes each way and the one-way fare is $42.40 per person (including taxes and fees); a book of six one-way tickets costs $196.10 (including taxes and fees). Reservations are recommended.

At this writing, a high-speed interisland ferry service, Hawaiʻi Superferry, that will run between Oʻahu, Maui, and Kauaʻi is scheduled to begin in July 2007. The ferry will depart Honolulu daily at 6:30 AM and arrive into Kahului at 9:30 AM. The Kahului to Honolulu ferry will depart at 10:30 AM. One-way, advance purchase Web fares will be $42 Tuesday through Thursday and $52 Friday through Monday. One-way base passenger fares will be $50 Tuesday through Thursday and $60 Friday through Monday. Children under the age of two will be $15 each way.

Information Expeditions Lānaʻi Ferry (☎800/695–2624 ⊕ www.go-lanai.com). **Hawaiʻi Superferry** (⊕ www.hawaiisuperferry.com). **Molokaʻi Ferry** (☎866/307–6524 ⊕ www.molokaiferry.com).

∎ BY BUS

Maui Bus, operated by Roberts Hawaiʻi, offers eight routes in and between various Central, South, and West Maui communities, seven days a week, including all holidays. Passengers can travel in and around Wailuku, Kahului, Lahaina,

Kā'anapali, Kapalua, Kīhei, Wailea, Mā'alaea, and Upcountry (including Pukalani, Hāli'imaile, Ha'ikū and Pā'ia). The Upcountry Islander route includes a stop at Kahului Airport. The Kahului and Wailuku loops are free; others are $1.

Bus Information **Roberts Hawai'i** (☎808/871–4838 ⊕www.co.maui.hi.us/bus).

▌ BY CAR

Asking for directions will almost always produce a helpful explanation from the locals, but you should be prepared for an island term or two. Hawai'i residents refer to places as being either *mauka* (toward the mountains) or *makai* (toward the ocean) from one another.

Hawai'i has a strict seat-belt law. Those riding in the front seat must wear a seat belt and children under the age of 17 in the backseats must be belted. The fine for not wearing a seat belt is $92. Jaywalking is also very common so please pay careful attention to the roads.

Traffic on Maui can be very bad branching out from Kahului to and from Pā'ia, Kīhei, and Lahaina. Parking along many streets is curtailed during rush hours, and towing is strictly practiced. Read curbside parking signs before leaving your vehicle.

Lāna'i and Moloka'i are the islands where renting a 4X4 makes the most sense. Both islands boast neither traffic, nor traffic lights, and only a handful of paved roads. Make sure you've got a good map.

GASOLINE
You can pretty much count on having to pay more for gasoline on Maui than on the U.S. mainland.

PARKING
With a population of more than 140,000 and nearly 30,000 visitors on any given day, there are parking challenges on Maui. Lots sprinkled throughout West Maui charge by the hour. There are about 700 parking spaces in the Lahaina Center; shoppers can get validated parking. *This Week Maui* often has coupons for free parking at this lot, as well as at Whaler's Village.

ROAD CONDITIONS
It's difficult to get lost throughout most of Maui as there are really only four major roads. The Hawai'i Visitors and Convention Bureau's red-caped King Kamehameha signs mark major attractions and scenic spots. Ask for a map at the car-rental counter. Free publications containing good-quality road maps can be found at airports, hotels, and shops.

Maui has its share of impenetrable areas, although four-wheel-drive vehicles rarely run into problems. Moloka'i and Lāna'i have fewer roadways, but car rental worthwhile. On these smaller islands, opt for a four-wheel-drive vehicle if dirt-road exploration holds any appeal.

In rural areas, it's not unusual for gas stations to close early. In Hawai'i, turning right on a red light is legal, except where noted. Use caution during heavy downpours, especially if you see signs warning of falling rocks. If you're enjoying views from the road or need to study a map, pull over to the side. Remember the aloha spirit; allow other cars to merge, don't honk (it's considered rude); use your headlights and turn signals.

ROADSIDE EMERGENCIES
If you find yourself in an emergency or accident, pull over if you can. If you have a cell phone with you, call the roadside assistance number on your rental-car contract or AAA Help. If you find that your car has been broken into or stolen, report it immediately to your rental-car company and they can assist you. If it's an emergency and someone is hurt, call 911 immediately.

Emergency Services **AAA Help** (☎800/222–4357).

ON THE GROUND

■ COMMUNICATIONS

INTERNET

If you've brought your laptop with you to Maui, you should have no problem checking e-mail or connecting to the Internet. Most of the major hotels and resorts offer high-speed access in rooms and/or lobbies. You should check with your hotel in advance to confirm that access is wireless; if not, ask whether in-room cables are provided. In some cases there will be an hourly charge posted to your room that averages about $15 per hour. If you're staying at a small inn or B&B without Internet access, ask the proprietor for the nearest café or coffee shop with wireless access.

Contacts **Cybercafes** (⊕ www.cybercafes. com)lists over 4,000 Internet cafés worldwide.

■ HEALTH

Hawai'i is known as the Health State. The life expectancy here is 79 years, one of the longest in the nation. Balmy weather makes it easy to remain active year-round, and the low-stress aloha attitude certainly contributes to general well-being. When visiting the Islands, however, there are a few health issues to keep in mind.

The Hawai'i State Department of Health recommends that you drink 16 ounces of water per hour to avoid dehydration when hiking or spending time in the sun. Use sunblock, wear UV-reflective sunglasses, and protect your head with a visor or hat for shade. If you're not acclimated to warm, humid weather you should allow plenty of time for rest stops and refreshments. When visiting freshwater streams, be aware of the tropical disease leptospirosis, which is spread by animal urine and carried into streams and mud. Symptoms include fever, headache, nausea, and red eyes. If left untreated it can cause liver and kidney damage, respiratory failure, internal bleeding, and even death. To avoid this, don't swim or wade in freshwater streams or ponds if you have open sores and don't drink from any freshwater streams or ponds.

On the Islands, fog is a rare occurrence, but there can often be "vog," an airborne haze of gases released from volcanic vents on the Big Island. During certain weather conditions such as "Kona Winds," the vog can settle over the Islands and wreak havoc with respiratory and other health conditions, especially asthma or emphysema. If susceptible, stay indoors and get emergency assistance if needed.

The Islands have their share of bugs and insects that enjoy the tropical climate as much as visitors do. Most are harmless but annoying. When planning to spend time outdoors in hiking areas, wear long-sleeved clothing and pants and use mosquito repellent containing deet. In very damp places you may encounter the dreaded local centipede. On the Islands they usually come in two colors, brown and blue, and they range from the size of a worm to an 8-inch cigar. Their sting is very painful, and the reaction is similar to bee- and wasp-sting reactions. When camping, shake out your sleeping bag before climbing in, and check your shoes in the morning, as the centipedes like cozy places. If planning on hiking or traveling in remote areas, always carry a first-aid kit and appropriate medications for sting reactions.

For information on travel insurance and medical-assistance companies see Trip Insurance under Things to Consider in Getting Started, above.

▌ HOURS OF OPERATION

Even people in paradise have to work. Generally local business hours are weekdays 8 to 5. Banks are usually open Monday through Thursday 8:30 to 3 and until 6 on Friday. Some banks have Saturday-morning hours.

Many self-serve gas stations stay open around-the-clock, with full-service stations usually open from around 7 AM until 9 PM. U.S. post offices are generally open weekdays 8:30 AM to 4:30 PM and Saturday 8:30 to noon.

Most museums generally open their doors between 9 AM and 10 AM and stay open until 5 PM, Tuesday through Saturday. Many museums operate with afternoon hours only on Sunday and close on Monday. Visitor-attraction hours vary throughout the state, but most sights are open daily with the exception of major holidays such as Christmas. Check local newspapers or visitor publications upon arrival for attraction hours and schedules if visiting over holiday periods. The local dailies carry a listing of "What's Open/What's Not" for those time periods.

Stores in resort areas sometimes open as early as 8, with shopping-center opening hours varying from 9:30 to 10 on weekdays and Saturday, a bit later on Sunday. Bigger malls stay open until 9 weekdays and Saturday and close at 5 on Sunday. Boutiques in resort areas may stay open as late as 11.

▌ MONEY

Prices throughout this guide are given for adults. Substantially reduced fees are almost always available for children, students, and senior citizens.

CREDIT CARDS

Throughout this guide, the following abbreviations are used: **AE**, American Express; **D**, Discover; **DC**, Diners Club; **MC**, MasterCard; and **V**, Visa.

It's a good idea to inform your credit-card company before you travel, especially if you're going abroad and don't travel internationally very often. Otherwise, the credit-card company might put a hold on your card owing to unusual activity—not a good thing halfway through your trip. Record all your credit-card numbers—as well as the phone numbers to call if your cards are lost or stolen—in a safe place, so you're prepared should something go wrong. Both MasterCard and Visa have general numbers you can call (collect if you're abroad) if your card is lost, but you're better off calling the number of your issuing bank, since MasterCard and Visa usually just transfer you to your bank; your bank's number is usually printed on your card.

Reporting Lost Cards American Express (☎800/992–3404 in the U.S. or 336/393–1111 collect from abroad ⊕ www.americanexpress.com). **Diners Club** (☎800/234–6377 in the U.S. or 303/799–1504 collect from abroad ⊕ www.dinersclub.com). **Discover** (☎800/347–2683 in the U.S. or 801/902–3100 collect from abroad ⊕ www.discovercard.com). **MasterCard** (☎800/622–7747 in the U.S. or 636/722–7111 collect from abroad ⊕ www.mastercard.com). **Visa** (☎800/847–2911 in the U.S. or 410/581–9994 collect from abroad ⊕ www.visa.com).

TRAVELER'S CHECKS & CARDS

Some consider this the currency of the cave man, and it's true that fewer establishments accept traveler's checks these days. Nevertheless, they're a cheap and secure way to carry extra money, particularly on trips to urban areas. Both Citibank (under the Visa brand) and American Express issue traveler's checks in the United States, but Amex is better known and more widely accepted; you can also avoid hefty surcharges by cashing Amex checks at Amex offices. Whatever you do, keep track of all the serial numbers in case the checks are lost or stolen.

LOCAL DO'S AND TABOOS

Hawai'i was admitted to the Union in 1959, so residents can be pretty sensitive when visitors refer to their own hometowns as "back in the States." Remember, when in Hawai'i, refer to the contiguous 48 states as "the Mainland" and not as the United States. When you do, you won't appear to be such a *malahini* (newcomer).

GREETINGS

Hawai'i is a very friendly place and this is reflected in the day-to-day encounters with friends, family, and even business associates. Women will often hug and kiss one another on the cheek and men will shake hands and sometimes combine that with a friendly hug. When a man and woman are greeting each other and are good friends, it is not unusual for them to hug and kiss on the cheek. Children are taught to call any elders "auntie" or "uncle," even if they aren't related. It's a way to show respect; it's also reflective of the strong sense of family.

When you walk off a long flight, nothing quite compares with a Hawaiian lei greeting. The casual ceremony ranks as one of the fastest ways to make the transition from the worries of home to the joys of your vacation. Though the tradition has created an expectation that everyone receives this floral garland when they step off the plane, the state of Hawai'i cannot greet each of its nearly seven million annual visitors.

If you've booked a vacation with a wholesaler or tour company, a lei greeting might be included in your package. If not, it's easy to arrange a lei greeting before you arrive into Kahului International Airport. Kama'āina Leis, Flowers & Greeters lei greetings. To be really wowed, request a lei of plumeria, some of the most divine-smelling blossoms on the planet. A plumeria or dendrobium orchid lei are considered standard and cost about $18 per person.

Information Kama'āina Leis, Flowers & Greeters (☎808/836–3246 or 800/367– 5183 ☎808/836–1814 ⊕www.alohaleigreetings.com).

LANGUAGE

English is the primary language on the Islands. Making the effort to learn some Hawaiian words can be rewarding, however. Hawaiian words you are most likely to encounter during your visit to the Islands are *aloha* (hello), *mahalo* (thank you), *keiki* (child), *haole* (Caucasian or foreigner), *mauka* (toward the mountains), *makai* (toward the ocean), and *pau* (finished, all done).

Hawaiian history includes waves of immigrants, each bringing their own language. To communicate with each other, they developed a language known as pidgin. If you listen closely, you will know what is being said by the inflections and by the body language. For an informative and somewhat-hilarious view of things Hawaiian, check out Jerry Hopkins's books titled *Pidgin to the Max* and *Fax to the Max,* available at most local bookstores in the Hawaiiana sections.

VISITING & ALOHA

If you've been invited to the home of friends living in Hawai'i (an ultimate compliment), bring a small gift and don't forget to take off your shoes when you enter their house. Try to take part in a cultural festival during your stay in the Islands; there is no better way to get a glimpse of Hawai'i's colorful ethnic mosiac.

And finally, remember that "aloha" is not only the word for hello, good-bye, and love, but it also stands for the spirit that is all around the Islands. Take your time (after all you're on vacation and "Hawaiian time"). Respect the *aina* (land) that is not only a precious commodity in this small island state but also stands at the core of the Polynesian belief system. "Living aloha" will transform your vacation, fill you with a warmth unique to Hawai'i, and have you planning your return before your tan fades.

American Express now offers a stored-value card called a Travelers Cheque Card, which you can use wherever American Express credit cards are accepted, including ATMs. The card can carry a minimum of $300 and a maximum of $2,700, and it's a very safe way to carry your funds. Although you can get replacement funds in 24 hours if your card is lost or stolen, it doesn't really strike us as a very good deal. In addition to a high initial cost ($14.95 to set up the card, plus $5 each time you "reload"), you still have to pay a 2% fee for each purchase in a foreign currency (similar to that of any credit card). Further, each time you use the card in an ATM you pay a transaction fee of $2.50 on top of the 2% transaction fee for the conversion—add it all up and it can be considerably more than you would pay when simply using your own ATM card. Regular traveler's checks are just as secure and cost less.

Contacts American Express (☎888/412–6945 in the U.S., 801/945–9450 collect outside of the U.S. to add value or speak to customer service ⊕www.americanexpress.com).

▌ SAFETY

Hawai'i is generally a safe tourist destination, but it's still wise to follow the same common sense safety precautions you would normally follow in your own hometown. Rental cars are magnets for break-ins, so don't leave any valuables in the car, not even in a locked trunk. Avoid poorly lighted areas, beach parks, and isolated areas after dark as a precaution. When hiking, stay on marked trails, no matter how alluring the temptation might be to stray. Weather conditions can cause landscapes to become muddy, slippery, and tenuous, so staying on marked trails will lessen the possibility of a fall or getting lost.

Ocean safety is of the utmost importance when visiting an island destination. Don't swim alone and follow the inter-

> ## WORST-CASE SCENARIO
>
> All your money and credit cards have just been stolen. In these days of real-time transactions, this isn't a predicament that should destroy your vacation. First, report the theft of the credit cards. Then get any traveler's checks you were carrying replaced. This can usually be done almost immediately, provided that you kept a record of the serial numbers separate from the checks themselves. If you bank at a large international bank like Citibank or HSBC, go to the closest branch; if you know your account number, chances are you can get a new ATM card and withdraw money right away. **Western Union** (☎ 800/325–6000 ⊕ www. westernunion.com) sends money almost anywhere. Have someone back home order a transfer online, over the phone, or at one of the company's offices, which is the cheapest option.

national signage posted at beaches that alerts swimmers to strong currents, man-of-war jellyfish, sharp coral, high surf, sharks, and dangerous shore breaks. At coastal lookouts along cliff tops, heed the signs indicating that waves can climb over the ledges. Check with lifeguards at each beach for current conditions and if the red flags are up, indicating swimming and surfing are not allowed, don't go in. Waters that look calm on the surface can harbor strong currents and undertows, and many people who were just wading have been dragged out to sea.

Women traveling alone are generally safe on the Islands, but always follow the safety precautions you would use in any major destination. When booking hotels, request rooms closest to the elevator and always keep your hotel-room door and balcony doors locked. Stay away from isolated areas after dark; camping and hiking solo are not advised. If you stay out late visiting nightclubs and bars, use caution when exiting night spots and returning to your lodging.

■TIP➔**Distribute your cash, credit cards, I.D.s, and other valuables between a deep front pocket, an inside jacket or vest pocket, and a hidden money pouch. Don't reach for the money pouch once you're in public.**

TIPPING GUIDELINES FOR MAUI	
Bartender	$1 to $5 per round of drinks, depending on the number of drinks
Bellhop	$1 to $5 per bag, depending on the level of the hotel and whether you have bulky items like golf clubs, surfboards, etc.
Hotel Concierge	$5 or more, depending on the service
Hotel Doorman	$1 to $5 if he helps you get a cab or helps with bags, golf clubs, etc.
Hotel Maid	$1 to $3 a day (either daily or at the end of your stay, in cash)
Hotel Room-Service Waiter	$1 to $2 per delivery, even if a service charge has been added
Porter at Airport	$1 per bag
Skycap at Airport	$1 to $3 per bag checked
Taxi Driver	15% to 20%, but round up the fare to the next dollar amount
Tour Guide	10% of the cost of the tour
Valet-Parking Attendant	$2 to $5, each time your car is brought to you
Waiter	15% to 20%, with 20% being the norm at high-end restaurants; nothing additional if a service charge is added to the bill
Spa Personnel	15% to 20% of the cost of your service

■ TAXES

There's a 4.16% state sales tax on all purchases, including food. A hotel room tax of 7.25%, combined with the sales tax of

4%, equals an 11.41% rate added onto your hotel bill. A $3-per-day road tax is also assessed on each rental vehicle.

■ TIME

Hawai'i is on Hawaiian standard time, 5 hours behind New York, 2 hours behind Los Angeles, and 10 hours behind London.

When the U.S. mainland is on daylight saving time, Hawai'i is not, so add an extra hour of time difference between the Islands and U.S. mainland destinations. You may find that things generally move more slowly here. That has nothing to do with your watch—it's just the laid-back way called Hawaiian time.

■ TIPPING

As this is a major vacation destination and many of the people who work at the hotels and resorts rely on tips to supplement their wages, tipping is not only common but expected.

FOR INTERNATIONAL TRAVELERS

CURRENCY

The dollar is the basic unit of U.S. currency. It has 100 cents. Coins are the penny (1¢); the nickel (5¢), dime (10¢), quarter (25¢), half-dollar (50¢), and the very rare golden $1 coin and even rarer silver $1. Bills are de-nominated $1, $5, $10, $20, $50, and $100, all mostly green and identical in size; designs and background tints vary. You may come across a $2 bill, but the chances are slim.

CUSTOMS

Information **U.S. Customs and Border Protection** (⊕ www.cbp.gov).

DRIVING

Driving in the United States is on the right. Speed limits are posted in miles per hour, between 25-55 mph on the island of Maui. Watch for lower limits near schools (usually 20 mph). Hawai'i has a strict seat-belt law. Passengers in the front seats must be belted. Children under the age of three must be in approved safety seats in the backseat and those ages 4 to 7 must be in a rear booster seat or child restraint such as a lap and shoulder belt. Morning (between 6:30 and 9:30 AM) and afternoon (between 3:30 and 6:30 PM) rush hour traffic around Kahului, Pā'ia, Kīhei, and Lahaina can be bad, so use caution. In rural areas, it's not unusual for gas stations to close early. If you see that your tank is getting low, don't take any chances; fill up when you see a station.

If your car breaks down, pull onto the shoulder and wait for help, or have your passengers wait while you walk to an emergency phone. If you have a cell phone with you, call the roadside assistance number on your rental car agreement.

ELECTRICITY

The U.S. standard is AC, 110 volts/60 cycles. Plugs have two flat pins set parallel to each other.

EMERGENCIES

For police, fire, or ambulance, dial 911 (0 in rural areas).

EMBASSIES

Contacts **Australia** (☎ 202/797–3000 ⊕ www.austemb.org). **Canada** (☎ 202/682–1740 ⊕ www.canadianembassy.org). **United Kingdom** (☎ 202/588–7800 ⊕ www.britainusa.com).

HOLIDAYS

New Year's Day (Jan. 1); Martin Luther King Day (3rd Mon. in Jan.); Presidents' Day (3rd Mon. in Feb.); Memorial Day (last Mon. in May); Independence Day (July 4); Labor Day (1st Mon. in Sept.); Columbus Day (2nd Mon. in Oct.); Thanksgiving Day (4th Thurs. in Nov.); Christmas Eve and Christmas Day (Dec. 24 and 25); and New Year's Eve (Dec. 31).

MAIL

You can buy stamps and aerograms and send letters and parcels in post offices. Stamp-dispensing machines can occasionally be found in airports, bus and train stations, office buildings, drugstores, and convenience stores. U.S. mail boxes are stout, dark-blue steel bins; pickup schedules are posted inside the bin (pull down the handle to see them). Parcels weighing more than a pound must be mailed at a post office or at a private mailing center.

Within the United States a first-class letter weighing 1 ounce or less costs 41¢; each additional ounce costs 17¢. Postcards cost 26¢. Postcards or 1-ounce airmail letters to most countries cost 90¢; postcards or 1-ounce letters to Canada or Mexico costs 69¢.

To receive mail on the road, have it sent c/o GENERAL DELIVERY at your destination's main post office (use the correct five-digit ZIP code). You must pick up mail in person within 30 days, with a driver's license or passport for identification.

Contacts **DHL** (☎ 800/225–5345 ⊕ www.dhl.com). **Federal Express** (☎ 800/463–

GETTING STARTED / BOOKING YOUR TRIP / TRANSPORTATION / ON THE GROUND

3339 ⊕ www.fedex.com). **Mail Boxes, Etc./ The UPS Store** (☎800/789–4623 ⊕ www. mbe.com). **United States Postal Service** (⊕ www.usps.com).

PASSPORTS & VISAS
Visitor visas aren't necessary for citizens of Australia, Canada, the United Kingdom, or most citizens of EU countries coming for tourism and staying for fewer than 90 days. If you require a visa, the cost is $100, and waiting time can be substantial, depending on where you live. Apply for a visa at the U.S. consulate in your place of residence; check the U.S. State Department's special Visa Web site for further information.

Visa Information **Destination USA** (⊕ www.unitedstatesvisas.gov).

PHONES
Numbers consist of a three-digit area code and a seven-digit local number. The area code for Hawai'i is 808. For local calls on Maui, you only need to dial the seven-digit number (not the 808 area code). If you are calling businesses on other neighboring islands while on Maui, you will need to use "1–808," followed by the number. Calls to numbers prefixed by "800," "888," "866," and "877" are toll free and require that you first dial a "1." For calls to numbers prefixed by "900" you must pay—usually dearly.

For international calls, dial "011" followed by the country code and the local number. For help, dial "0" and ask for an overseas operator. Most phone books list country codes and U.S. area codes. The country code for Australia is 61, for New Zealand 64, for the United Kingdom 44. Calling Canada is the same as calling within the United States, whose country code, by the way, is 1.

For operator assistance, dial "0." For directory assistance, call 555–1212 or occasionally 411 (free at many public phones). You can reverse long-distance charges by calling

"collect"; dial "0" instead of "1" before the 10-digit number.

Instructions are generally posted on pay phones. Usually you insert coins in a slot (usually 25¢ to 50¢ for local calls) and wait for a steady tone before dialing. On long-distance calls the operator tells you how much to insert; prepaid phone cards, widely available in various denominations, can be used from any phone. Follow the directions to activate the card (there's usually an access number, then an activation code), then dial your number.

CELL PHONES
The United States has several GSM (Global System for Mobile Communications) networks, so multiband mobiles from most countries (except for Japan) work here. Unfortunately, it's almost impossible to buy a pay-as-you-go mobile SIM card in the U.S.—which allows you to avoid roaming charges—without also buying a phone. That said, cell phones with pay-as-you-go plans are available for well under $100. The cheapest ones with decent national coverage are the GoPhone from Cingular and Virgin Mobile, which only offers pay-as-you-go service.

Contacts **Cingular** (☎888/333–6651 ⊕ www.cingular.com). **Virgin Mobile** (☎888/322–1122 ⊕ www.virginmobileusa. com).

INDEX

PHOTO CREDITS

Cover Photo (Adult Green Sea Turtle with snorkeler along West Coast of Maui): *Michael S. Nolan/age fotostock.* F5, *SUNNYphotography.com/Alamy.* **Chapter 1: Experience Maui:** 7, *David Fleetham/Alamy.* 8 (top), *S. Alden/PhotoLink/Photodisc.* 8 (bottom left), *Douglas Peebles/age fotostock.* 8 (bottom right), *Walter Bibikow/viestiphoto.com.* 9 (top), *Ron Dahlquist/Maui Visitors Bureau.* 9 (bottom left), *Walter Bibikow/viestiphoto.com.* 9 (lower right), *Chris Hammond/viestiphoto.com.* 11, *Maui Visitors Bureau.* 12 (left), *Danita Delimont/Alamy.* 12 (top center), *David Schrichre/Photo Resource Hawaii.* 12 (bottom center), *David Fleetham/Alamy.* 12 (right), *Andy Jackson/Alamy.* 13 (top left), *David Fleetham/Alamy.* 13 (bottom left), *Mitch Diamond/Alamy.* 11 SuperStock/age fotostock. 13 (bottom right), *Jim Cazel/Photo Resource Hawaii/Alamy.* 13 (right), *Starwood Hotels and Resorts.* 14 (top left), *Jim Cazel/Photo Resource Hawaii/Alamy.* 14 (bottom left), *Robert Holmes/Alamy.* 14 (right), *SuperStock/age fotostock.* 15 (left), *Jim Cazel/Photo Resource Hawaii/Alamy.* 15 (top right), *Andre Jenny/Alamy.* 15 (bottom left), *Douglas Peebles Photography/Alamy.* 15 (bottom right), *Douglas Peebles Photography/Alamy.* 18-19, *Dana Edmunds/Starwood Hotels and Resorts.* 20, *Douglas Peebles/age fotostock.* 21 (left), *Joe Solem/HVCB.* 21 (right), *Danita Delimont/Alamy.***Chapter 2: Exploring Maui:** 23, *Maui Visitors Bureau.* 43, *National Park Service.* 46, *Maui Visitors Bureau.* 47, *Karl Weatherly/Photodisc.* 48, *Maui Visitors Bureau.* 51, *Chris Hammond/viestiphoto.com.* 53, *Ron Dahlquist/Maui Visitors Bureau.* 54, *Chris Hammond/viestiphoto.com.* 57, *Richard Genova/viestiphoto.com.* 58, *SuperStock/age fotostock.* 59, *Chris Hammond/viestiphoto.com.* **Chapter 3: Beaches:** 61, *Brent Bergherm/age fotostock.* **Chapter 4: Water Activities & Tours:** 73, *Eric Sanford/age fotostock.* 90, *Ron Dahlquist/HVCB.* **Chapter 5: Golf, Hiking & Outdoor Activities:** 99, *Superstock/age fotostock.* 112, *Luca Tettoni/viestiphoto.com.* 113, *Jack Jeffrey.* **Chapter 6: Shops & Spas:** 121, *Douglas Peebles Photography/Alamy.* 126 (top), *Linda Ching/HVCB.* 126 (bottom), *Sri Maiava Rusden/HVCB.* 127 (top), *leisofhawaii.com.* 127 (2nd from top), *kellyalexanderphotography.com.* 127 (3rd, 4th, and 5th from top), *leisofhawaii.com.* 127 (bottom), *kellyalexanderphotography.com.* **Chapter 7: Entertainment & Nightlife:** 136, *Gaetano Images, Inc./Alamy.* 138, HVCB. 139, *Thinkstock LLC.* **Chapter 8: Where to Eat:** 147, *Douglas Peebles Photography/Alamy.* 153, *Polynesian Cultural Center.* 154 (top), *Douglas Peebles Photography.* 154 (top center), *Douglas Peebles Photography/Alamy.* 154 (center), *Dana Edmunds/Polynesian Cultural Center.* 154 (bottom center), *Douglas Peebles Photography/Alamy.* 154 (bottom), *Purcell Team/Alamy.* 155 (top, top center, and bottom center), *HTJ/HVCB.* 155 (bottom), *Oahu Visitors Bureau.* **Chapter 9: Where to Stay:** 173, *Renaissance Wailea Beach Resort.* **Chapter 10: Molokai:** 203, *Greg Vaughn/Alamy.* 204 (top), *Walter Bibikow/viestiphoto.com.* 204 (bottom left and right), *Molokai Visitors Association.* 205 (top), *Molokai Ranch.* 205 (center), *Walter Bibikow/viestiphoto.com.* 205 (bottom left), *Douglas Peebles/age fotostock.* 205 (bottom right), *Walter Bibikow/viestiphoto.com.* 213, *Walter Bibikow/viestiphoto.com.* 214, *IDEA.* 215–216, *Walter Bibikow/viestiphoto.com.* **Chapter 11: Lanai:** 239, *Walter Bibikow/viestiphoto.com.* 240 (top), *Walter Bibikow/viestiphoto.com.* 240 (bottom left), *Lanai Visitors Bureau.* 240 (bottom right), *Walter Bibikow/viestiphoto.com.* 241 (top), *Michael S. Nolan/age fotostock.* 241 (bottom left and right), *Lanai Image Library.* 242, *Lanai Image Library.* **Color Section:** Waterfall on the Road to Hana: *Superstock/age fotostock.* Windsurfer at Hookipa Beach: *Superstock/age fotostock.* Dancers at the Old Lahaina Luau: *Chad Ehlers/Stock Connection Distribution/Alamy.* Haleakala National Park: *Phil Degginger/Alamy.* Watching the sunrise at Haleakala: *Ken Ross/viestiphoto.com.* Green Sea Turtle: *SUNNYphotography.com/Alamy.* Makena Beach (popularly known as Big Beach): *Tomas Del Amo/Alamy.* Humpback whale calf breaching: *Michael S. Nolan/age fotostock.* Fire knife dancer: *David Olsen/Photo Resource Hawaii/Alamy.* Fruit stand: *Ron Dahlquist/Maui Visitors Bureau.* Kahakuloa, West Maui: *Walter Bibikow/age fotostock.* Horses on Maui's North Shore: *Superstock/Alamy.* Waianapanapa State Park on the Road to Hana: *Richard Genova/viestiphoto.com.*

ABOUT OUR WRITERS

Wanda A. Adams was born and raised on Maui and now makes her home on O'ahu. She has been a newspaper reporter for more than 25 years, specializing in food, dining, and travel. Wanda worked on the Where to Stay chapter of this guide.

Cathy Sharpe, our Essentials updater, was born and reared on O'ahu. For 13 years she worked at a Honolulu public-relations agency representing major travel-industry clients. Now living in Maryland, she is a marketing consultant. She returns home to visit family and friends, relax at her favorite beaches, and enjoy island cuisine.

Joana Varawa has lived on Lāna'i for 30 years and is editor of the *Lāna'i Times*. She writes for Hawaiian and Aloha airlines' magazines, has authored three books, and could lead you around "her" island blindfolded. For this edition, Joana sailed across the Pailolo Channel to update chapter 10, Moloka'i.

Amy Westervelt was lucky enough to spend summers growing up on the Big Island, and now divides her time between Kona and San Francisco. She writes about travel and all things wedding-related for publications including *Travel + Leisure, Modern Bride*, and the *San Francisco Chronicle.* Amy worked on Beaches; Water Sports & Tours; Golf, Hiking & Outdoor Activities; and Entertainment & Nightlife.

Shannon Wianecki was raised on Maui and loves divulging its secrets. With over a decade of experience in the travel industry, she splits her time between writing and conservation. She is the food editor for *Maui nō ka 'oi* magazine and the outreach coordinator for a high-school science curriculum based on the ecosystems of Haleakalā. Shannon updated Experience Maui, Exploring Maui, Shops & Spas, Where to Eat, and Lāna'i.